From Fort Laramie to Wounded Knee
In the West That Was

Charles W. Allen
Edited and with an introduction
by Richard E. Jensen

University of Nebraska Press
Lincoln and London

In association with the
Nebraska State Historical Society
Lincoln, Nebraska

♾

First Bison Books printing: 2001

Library of Congress Cataloging-in-Publication Data
Allen, Charles Wesley, 1851–1942.
From Fort Laramie to Wounded Knee : in the West that was / Charles W. Allen ;
edited with an introduction by Richard E. Jensen.
    p. cm.
Includes bibliographical references and index.
ISBN 0-8032-1045-0 (cl : alk. paper)
ISBN 0-8032-5936-0 (pa : alk. paper)
1. Frontier and pioneer life—West (U.S.)—Anecdotes. 2. West
(U.S.)—History—1860–1890—Anecdotes. 3. West (U.S.)—
History—1890–1945—Anecdotes. 4. Allen, Charles Wesley,
1851–1942—Anecdotes. 5. Dakota Indians—History—Anecdotes.
6. Wounded Knee Massacre, S.D., 1890—Anecdotes. 7. Ghost dance—
Anecdotes. I. Jensen, Richard E.   II. Title.
F596.A3795   1997
978—dc21
97-20276   CIP

Contents

List of Illustrations   vii

Foreword   viii

Introduction   ix

Acknowledgments   xxv

1   A Pioneer in Embryo   1

2   Mystery and Mules   8

3   Red Cloud Cuts the Flag-Pole (Part One)   14

4   Red Cloud Cuts the Flag-Pole (Part Two)   20

5   Freighting to the Black Hills   26

6   On to Deadwood   34

7   Old Fort Laramie   40

8   The Founding of Pine Ridge   49

9   Changing Conditions   58

10   Building for Schools   67

11   Trails and Trials of a Primitive People   73

12   The First White Men among the Indians   84

13   The Advent of the Railroad   96

14   Meeting Civilization   102

15   At Valentine   112

16   At Chadron   118

17   The Early Far West Weekly Newspapers   127

18   A "Good Neighbor" Act – A Burlesque Speech   131

19   The Celebration   140

20   Gathering War Clouds   149

21   The Ghost Dance at Pine Ridge   156

22 The Crush at Pine Ridge   167
23 Reporters at Pine Ridge   175
24 Big Foot's Arrival   182
25 The Last Fight of North American Indians   191
26 Back to the Agency   203
27 Concluding Incidents   211
    Notes   220
    Bibliography   267
    Index   276

Illustrations

Following page 126

Charles Wesley Allen in the 1800s
Charles Wesley Allen about 1916
Fort Laramie
Red Cloud Agency
Deadwood, Dakota Territory
Red Cloud's house
Pine Ridge Agency
Valentine, Nebraska, in 1885
Chadron, Nebraska, in 1888
Addison E. Sheldon
Remains of makeshift tents at Wounded Knee
Lt. S. A. Cloman, First Infantry
Louis Mousseau's store at Wounded Knee
Allen's Map of Wounded Knee

Map

The West of Charles Allen   page xxvi

Foreword

Charles W. Allen, writer of this story of the Great Plains frontier, has been my personal friend since 1888. He has had rare opportunities to know the western frontier: soldier, freighter, rancher, clerk, blacksmith, contractor, editor, war correspondent, Pine Ridge postmaster, philosopher, and poet. Married into the Oglala Sioux tribe, faithful husband, father of a fine family who represent the best blood of both white and Indian races.

Mr. Allen has a faculty for making friends. He is a keen observer—and a lover of truth and justice. He is one of the very few survivors of the Battle of Wounded Knee, last conflict between the Indians and the white men, fought December 29, 1890. He wrote the first account of that battle to reach the world public through the daily press.

I am glad to commend Mr. Allen's book to the great public eager to read first-hand truth of the frontier life on the Great Plains.

Addison E. Sheldon
[1938]

Introduction

In the opening lines of his reminiscence, Charles Allen tells his readers: "These sketches are only intended to record and describe some of the more interesting incidents of my personal experience. . . ." He goes on to relate incidents beginning in 1871 when he was a nineteen-year-old green-horn on a cattle drive from Kansas to a ranch near Fort Laramie and ending with his description of the Ghost Dance troubles and his eyewit-ness account of the massacre on Wounded Knee Creek in 1890. Within this twenty-year span Allen describes other adventures and events in east-ern Wyoming, western Nebraska, and South Dakota. He was at the Red Cloud Agency in 1874 when the Lakota came within a heartbeat of wip-ing out the little white enclave. Two years later he hauled freight to Dead-wood and described the town at the height of the Black Hills gold rush. Allen moved to Valentine, Nebraska, in 1883 when the town was only a year old and later settled in Chadron, Nebraska, whose genesis he de-scribes. Allen devoted two chapters to stories and legends told to him by his Lakota friends.

Allen devoted nearly one-third of *From Fort Laramie to Wounded Knee* to a description of the events surrounding the Wounded Knee massacre. At the time he was a part owner and editor of the *Chadron Democrat* and accompanied the Seventh Cavalry to report on the arrest of the Lakota Ghost Dancers under Chief Big Foot. On the morning of December 29, Allen was walking idly through the captured Indians' camp when the first shots were fired leading to the slaughter.

His description of that tragic event and the incidents surrounding it is arguably the best of all the eyewitness accounts. Allen was an experi-enced newspaper reporter with sufficient ability to be hired by the *New York Herald* to cover the Ghost Dance period from the field. Although he was not fluent in the Lakota language, what knowledge he had gave him an advantage over other reporters. Allen had been to Pine Ridge on numerous occasions and knew many people there. His wife was part Lakota and her relatives on the Pine Ridge Reservation were a useful source of information. Finally, his record is especially valuable because he was present when many of these events took place or was able to obtain accounts from eyewitnesses shortly afterwards. While familiarity does not assure accuracy, Allen's memoirs do not contain flagrant bias or notable misrepresentations. It is an attempt by an observant and intel-ligent man to record a turbulent and complex time.[1]

From Fort Laramie to Wounded Knee is a personal account, but it also chronicles the passing of an era. When Allen arrived in the West, the region was still the land of free-roaming Lakotas and Cheyennes. Within a few years the tribes were confined to reservations and a new lifestyle was forced upon them. By 1884 a railroad skirted the southern edge of these reservations and whites flooded into the country. The prairies were plowed and Valentine, Chadron, and other towns sprang up. It was a time of rapid and unprecedented change when "civilization" and "progress" were the watchwords of the new emigrants.

Charles Wesley Allen was born on September 10, 1851, in Noble County, northeastern Indiana, to William Maynard Allen and Saphronia Meeker Allen. In 1852 they moved to a farm in Jasper County, Iowa, and in 1866 they migrated to Wamego, Kansas. Although only in his mid-teens, Charles hauled lumber from Wamego to the new town of Wichita, Kansas, about 150 miles away. It was valuable experience and undoubtedly contributed to his decision to become a freighter after settling in Wyoming a few years later. In the fall of 1868 Charles enrolled in the Kansas State Agricultural College in Manhattan, but completed only the winter term.[2] In the spring he enlisted in the Kansas State Militia, Company B, Second Battalion. The military had been patrolling the western part of the state primarily to calm the fears of settlers, who felt they were in danger of being attacked by bands of Cheyenne and Lakota Indians. Throughout the summer and fall Allen was stationed at a remote outpost on the Solomon River near present day Cawker City, Kansas. After completing an uneventful six-months tour he was discharged on September 30, 1869, and returned to Wichita.[3] In late June 1871 Allen joined a cattle drive to a ranch near Cheyenne, Wyoming, and then found work on a ranch south of Fort Laramie.[4] In January 1872 he went to work for the Cuny and Ecoffey Freighting and Contracting Company near Fort Laramie. The company hauled freight, usually for the army, in addition to operating a cattle ranch and a road ranche for travelers. In his autobiography Allen did not feel it was necessary to mention the brothel at the ranch headquarters.[5]

It was at this time that Allen met Cuny's young niece, Emma Hawkins. She was the daughter of Susan Lunan, a mixed-blood Lakota woman, and Henry Hawkins, a Fort Laramie trader. Charles and Emma were wed on August 23, 1873, and took up residence in a two-room cabin seven miles above Fort Laramie. Allen devoted part of a chapter of *From Fort Laramie to Wounded Knee* to the defense of such unions and especially of the character of white men who married Indian women. From the tone of this chapter it is apparent Charles carried a lingering resentment for having been called a "squaw man" or some similar epithet. The couple were married for over fifty years and had twelve children.[6]

Shortly before his marriage, Allen bought a small freight wagon and four horses and went into business for himself. He hauled hay and wood in the vicinity of Fort Laramie and Fort Fetterman and also received contracts to bring supplies from the railroad in Cheyenne. Although he does not explain his reasons for leaving Cuny and Ecoffey, there was probably a monetary incentive. Ranch hands and herders at the time earned about $30 and board per month. As the owner of a team and wagon he would have been able to earn much more, but there was also a substantial capital investment. A four-horse team cost between $200 and $500 and a four-horse wagon between $125 and $150. Perhaps Allen had saved enough to pay for the team and wagon, but if not, he would have had to borrow money at the nearly prohibitive interest rate of two percent per month.[7]

When rumors of gold in the Black Hills were finally confirmed, Allen was in a position to be one of the first to reach the new El Dorado, but he did not catch gold fever. Although he was not afraid to take some risks, he must have realized the odds of finding a paying claim were minuscule. Instead of joining the gold seekers Allen stayed in the freighting business and in 1876 made his first trip to Deadwood with a load of onions. Allen provided a vibrant picture of the town, but pointed out that he did not participate in the coarse entertainments available at that time. Freighting even such mundane cargo was profitable, but as the number of freighters grew, the competition for contracts also increased. They underbid each other until it was difficult to earn a living.

It was during this time that Allen took up a potentially lucrative sideline, but one that was also illegal. In early 1874 his activities were brought to the attention of Col. John E. Smith, Fort Laramie post commander, when a party of Cheyennes came to the fort to complain that some white men had stolen thirty-eight horses from them. Colonel Smith asked the Indians how they knew it was white men, the Cheyennes said the Lakotas told them. At first Smith doubted the story because he suspected the Lakotas were the thieves and were trying to cast suspicion on others. A short time later, however, Smith uncovered evidence convincing him the horse thieves were indeed three whites, James "Jack Nasty Jim" Wright, "Curly" Jim Conners, and Charles W. Allen. It was also apparent to the colonel that in addition to stealing Cheyenne horses, the three men were carrying on a regular whiskey trade with the Lakotas. When Smith's informants discovered the location of the accused men's camp, a detachment of troops was sent to apprehend the trio, but the soldiers found only Curly Jim. He was arrested and turned over to the civil authorities in Laramie City. In spite of a mandated prohibition against selling liquor to Indians, Colonel Smith felt a white jury would probably not convict another white of this offence. It was perhaps this attitude that precluded any further search for Allen and Jack Nasty Jim. Apparently the close call convinced Charles to give up his sideline for there is no other evidence to suggest he ever again operated outside the law. It is unfortunate, although perhaps not surprising, that Allen omitted this escapade from his memoirs.[8]

In February 1879 the Allens sold their home on the Laramie River and moved to Pine Ridge.[9] A new agency for the Oglala Lakota was under construction, and there were better job opportunities than his declining freighting business. Allen helped build schoolhouses on the reservation, operated a lime kiln, and also did some freighting. By coincidence, one of the schools was on Wounded Knee Creek less than two miles above the site of the massacre he would witness a decade later. Allen provides a vivid picture of the new agency and of some of its inhabitants. He also uses this opportunity to attack some of the stereotypical views about Indians held by whites at that time.

After about four years at Pine Ridge the Allens moved to Valentine, Nebraska, which was then a frontier community of about 400 people. In his reminiscence Allen described the town, the sad plight of a cheated homesteader, and a gun fight he witnessed.

Allen was employed as a clerk in the government warehouse where Indian annuities were stored. Freight arrived on the Fremont, Elkhorn, and Missouri Valley Railroad, which had just been built to the town. The cargo was unloaded at the warehouse and then transferred to freight wagons and sent on its way to the Brulés at the Rosebud Agency and the Oglalas at Pine Ridge. In March 1884 Allen resigned his government job and bought an interest in a blacksmith shop in Valentine. It must have seemed like a sound financial move, because it was the only shop in the town, but Allen must have recognized the risks for he had no training in blacksmithing. He admitted he was only the "chief tinkerer."

While at the blacksmith shop, Allen became friends with Burley C. Hill, editor of the local newspaper, the *Valentine Reporter*. In 1885 Hill decided to move his publishing business to the new town of Chadron, then little more than some surveyor's stakes beside the recently completed tracks of the Fremont, Elkhorn, and Missouri Valley Railroad.[10] Hill offered Allen a partnership in the venture, and, although the offer came as a complete surprise, Allen accepted. It was certainly a welcome opportunity, for Allen's tinkering at the blacksmith shop probably provided only meager financial rewards and the move would also bring them closer to Emma's relatives on the Pine Ridge Reservation. While the move offered certain advantages, Allen was not confident that the publishing business could support him and his family. On July 9, 1885, a month before leaving Valentine, Allen applied for a homestead on 160 acres located just two miles north of Chadron. The family's first home was a dugout, but it was not long before a three-room frame house was built. After occupying the farm for only two years Charles was able to convert the homestead to a $200 cash purchase.[11]

In the summer of 1885 Hill, Allen, and a third partner, Robert Lucas, met in Chadron and organized the Democrat Publishing Company and began printing the *Chadron Democrat*. Their first shop was a small, dirt-floored shack, but construction in Chadron was moving rapidly and soon they were able to move into suitable quarters on Main Street. The first issue of their weekly newspaper was published on August 27, 1885. The eight-page paper was typical of most small town publications at this time.[12] The *Democrat* could boast one distinctive feature. It was printed on yellow paper. The Valentine *Democratic Blade* noted that the Chadron paper was "exclusive as to color" but "No, we don't like it either." Hill ran the press and stayed with the *Chadron Democrat* for many years. Robert Lucas was the editor until September 1886, when he went to Gordon to publish another paper, the *Gordon Advocate*.[13] After only a year's apprenticeship Allen became the editor of the *Democrat* and continued in the position until he sold his interest in the business in 1891.

During his six years with the *Democrat*, Allen faced formidable competition for subscribers from two other weeklies. The *Dawes County Journal* under the editorship of Ed E. Egan, was the first paper in Chadron and began publication on November 6, 1884.[14] Unfortunately, only a few issues prior to 1892 have survived, but it seems similar to Allen's paper and probably offered the most serious competition. The *Northwestern Temperance Advocate* began publication in November 1887, and in his reminiscence Allen characterized it as "a commendable Sunday-school tract."[15] The description was certainly apt, at least for the first year of publication. Addison E. Sheldon became the publisher in October 1888 and in August 1889 the name was changed to the *Chadron Advocate*.[16] Under Sheldon's editorship the paper broadened its coverage of local events, although it continued to report church news in detail and offered articles on spiritual and moral guidance. Every issue contained articles advocating a prohibition on the consumption of alcohol.

While Allen rarely mentioned Egan and the *Journal*, it seems he never missed an opportunity to ridicule Sheldon and the *Advocate*. Allen's remarks were usually more humorous than slanderous, but had Sheldon possessed an excessive degree of pride or deep feelings of insecurity, the little barbs might have led to fistfights, lawsuits, or even worse as sometimes happened in the newspaper business of a century ago. Certainly there were ideological differences between the two men that could have led to enmity. Allen was a steadfast Democrat, while Sheldon was an ex-Republican who had become an ardent supporter of the Prohibition Party. Allen was not opposed to the moderate consumption of alcohol, a position Sheldon occasionally mentioned with mild scorn.[17] Sheldon's avocation as a lay preacher provided his rival with the opportunity for some good-natured ridicule. On one occasion Sheldon delivered a sermon to the inmates of the county jail. Allen reported on the event and noted that Sheldon "told us confidentially . . . that he had never addressed a more appreciative audience. 'Just think of it' he said, 'I spoke for three quarters of an hour and not one of them left the building.'"[18] Sheldon also enjoyed writing poetry and published the verses in his paper. Allen rarely missed an opportunity to scoff at the offerings. One instance occurred shortly after the U.S. Army occupied the Pine Ridge Reservation during the Ghost Dance. The two men had gone to the agency to investigate the "uprising" for their papers. Allen reported that "Sheldon is expected to quell the disturbance by reading his latest poetical effusion, translated into the Sioux tongue expressly for this occasion, and if this doesn't have the desired effect, he will read the same thing over again."[19] Despite their differences and their attacks and counterattacks in the press Allen and Sheldon maintained a cordial relationship throughout their lives.

While he was at Chadron, Allen was briefly involved in show business. A friend, Henry C. Clifford, had made some money by charging people fifty cents to see his collection of fossils at the Gold Bar Opera House.[20] Allen had a collection of Native American clothing, weapons, and other artifacts and the two men decided to combine the collections and display them in Chicago. Apparently the venture was not a financial success. After about two months the *Chadron Advocate* reported that the "curio" was "about ready to take its flight to a better world."[21]

Although Allen avoids a discussion of politics in *From Fort Laramie to Wounded Knee*, it was an important subject during his years at Chadron. He was a staunch Democrat and when elections neared, his editorials in the *Democrat* alternated between extolling the virtues of his party and denigrating the opposition. In the fall of 1885 Allen campaigned for the office of county judge. Although he claimed to have "had experience on the bench," there is no evidence to corroborate the assertion. Evidently the voters were not impressed by his qualifications for he lost the election to F. H. Fall by a vote of 433 to 538.[22] In 1890 Allen ran for state senator from the Fifty-third District, consisting of Dawes, Sheridan, Sioux, and Box Butte counties. The Democrats had been gaining strength and the prospects for a victory looked good. The race was against E. L. Heath, and Allen's popularity at home was revealed by a two-to-one plurality in Chadron. Heath carried the rest of the district and the final vote was 720 for Heath and 602 for Allen.[23]

Allen's editorials were usually about local matters. He exhibited a marked degree of civic pride and was quick to attack anyone who made even mildly derogatory comments about Chadron. On occasion the editorials provide a glimpse of Allen's personality. One especially insightful column was written after a campaign was in full swing to close houses of prostitution in Chadron. When Allen discussed this issue, he expressed his compassion for others while at the same time severely scolding those who were less sympathetic:

> Chadron, like all other live towns, has always had a quota of sporting men and women. In fact no town that has pretensions beyond a post office, blacksmith shop and one store, was ever or can ever hope to live without social evil, and it is manifestly the duty of both city and county officials to control the element that constitutes the evil, but it is not within the province of their office to undertake to drive them out root and branch and when ever they or any of them arrogate to themselves such power, the question arises, have these people a right to live? We believe they have, our county attorney to the contrary notwithstanding. Admitting the fact that they may breathe, they have as much right to live in one town as in another, so long as they comply with the spirit of the law by paying the stipulated statutory fines for the transgression of the law. It is the duty of every municipality to keep under subjection and control the disreputable elements of society, but no town has a right, whether legally or morally, to dispose of bad characters by imposing them on some other town. Of course these sporting women are and by right ought to be, condemned in the interests of society and for example, but those who practice what they preach will always temper the condemnation with pity.[24]

Allen's liberal outlook was also expressed in his discussions of the problems facing his Indian neighbors. In an age when condescension and outright bigotry by whites towards Native Americans was almost universally accepted, Allen expressed an uncommon degree of sensitivity and understanding. When rumors of the Ghost Dance religion reached Chadron, Allen did some investigating and wrote a surprisingly accurate description of the new religion. Although he undoubtedly felt the goals of the new sect would not be realized, his writing was without contempt or criticism. Forty years later, when he was writing the final draft of *From Fort Laramie to Wounded Knee*, his empathy for others was still evident.

This is not to suggest Allen was a color-blind saint. In 1890 he published an article in the *Democrat* titled "Short Bull—Brigand of the Badlands." It was a fatuous story composed by the reporters stationed at Pine Ridge during the Ghost Dance troubles. Allen explained that the reporters composed the story only as a means to relieve the monotony during those quiet days before the disaster at Wounded Knee. While it was meant to be humorous, the story was also blatantly racist. He included it in the first draft of his manuscript, but then realized its derogatory tone and deleted it. His final draft is not entirely free of condescension when writing about certain individuals, some white, some Native American, and some African American. He was, after all, a man of his own time and was not free from prejudice. Had he lived in the age of political correctness *From Fort Laramie to Wounded Knee* would have undoubtedly been somewhat different.[25]

Chadron's newspaper editors benefited from the troubles descending upon the Lakota in 1890. Rumors of an "outbreak" by the Indians, the Ghost Dance, and the military occupation were stories guaranteed to boost circulation. Allen received an additional bonus. After the army occupied the reservations, correspondents from many big eastern papers rushed to Pine Ridge to cover the story. Allen was hired as a special correspondent for the *New York Herald*. His colleagues probably considered him to be something of an expert on the subject of the Ghost Dance. He had published his first article about the religion in early May, shortly after it was introduced on the reservation. A week later he had assembled enough information to present a remarkably astute editorial concerning the revivalistic sect.[26]

The Ghost Dance offered hope to the reservation Indians that they might return to their old way of life unincumbered by the dictates of the whites. The way to freedom was revealed in a vision to Wovoka, a Paiute Indian. It was a pacifistic doctrine in which Christ would return to earth bringing with him all of the Indians who had died in the past. There would also be a return of huge herds of buffalo and other wild game. Wovoka told his listeners they should not show any aggression towards the whites for when Christ returned the whites would disappear and the

Indians would be able to go back to their former nomadic life. To hasten the advent of the revitalized Indian world Wovoka urged his listeners to perform a ceremony based upon a Paiute round dance.

The new religion spread rapidly westward into the Plains and south into Indian Territory during the summer and fall of 1890. Some tribes or factions of tribes quickly rejected Wovoka's teachings, but many embraced the new creed. Of those who adopted the Ghost Dance, the Lakota were the only ones who were persecuted by whites to any appreciable degree. The situation on the South Dakota reservations differed noticeably due to a combination of factors. The Pine Ridge Reservation was a hotbed of Ghost Dance activity, and the newly appointed agent, Daniel F. Royer, was terrified of the believers. Rather than allowing the ceremonies to be held and letting the revival run its course as he had been advised to do by more knowledgeable associates, Royer was convinced the Indians were about to take up arms and kill him and the other government employees as well as the settlers in the area. Royer began sending telegrams to Washington, first hinting, then demanding that the army be sent to protect the white population. About this same time Allen was telling his readers it was worth traveling many miles to see a Ghost Dance. While the dancers were aware some white officials opposed the ceremonies, they did not mind if a few visitors came by just to watch.

Royer's demand for protection was echoed by many whites living near the reservations. Some undoubtedly recognized the great economic boost an army occupation would bring. They may even have hoped that military intervention would result in the removal of the Lakota and the opening of the reservations to white settlers. At the same time there were other whites who were genuinely frightened, because they likened the Ghost Dance to a war dance and acted accordingly. Either they did not know, or chose to ignore, the basic tenet of the religion. The Ghost Dancers were not going to war. First, they were devoting too much of their effort to bringing Christ to earth and, second, they had no need to fight the whites since God was going to dispose of them.

The pleas by Royer and the settlers were finally heard in Washington, and the order was given to send in the army. On November 20 soldiers began the occupation of the Lakota reservations. Six weeks later Allen rode out of the Pine Ridge Agency with the Seventh Cavalry to witness the surrender of Big Foot's band of Miniconjou Lakotas. The next morning, in a camp on Wounded Knee Creek, the soldiers began to disarm the Indians who were considered "hostiles" because of their refusal to discontinue the Ghost Dance and for leaving their reservation without permission. Allen was walking idly among their tents when a friend yelled,

"Look out Charley." An instant later a shot rang out heralding the start of the Wounded Knee massacre in which more than 300 people may have died.[27]

In March of 1891, after more than five years in the business, Allen sold the *Chadron Democrat*. He claimed he sold the paper simply because he found buyers willing to meet his asking price. While this may be true, there is also the likelihood that the paper was not as profitable as it once was. The drought of 1890 and declining prices for farm products were causing a terrible financial strain on rural communities throughout the West and especially in western Nebraska. During these hard times it is likely many of the nearly destitute farmers and ranchers canceled their subscriptions. While there is no evidence of a catastrophic drop in circulation, the new owners of the paper were forced to reduce the yearly subscription rate from $2 to $1.50.[28] If Allen anticipated increasingly hard times, he did not admit it in his farewell editorial published on March 12:

> To our friends and patrons everywhere, greetings. With this issue *The Chadron Democrat* ceases to be. . . . The *Democrat* has been a successful enterprise to its founders and proprietors and we wish the new management all the financial success possible, and all the political failures imaginable.[29]

The new managers, Burley C. Hill and W. L. Bailey, assured their readers that they would "always be found working for what it believes to be the best interests of the Republican party and the people in general." Although they switched its political allegiance and retitled the paper *The Chadron Citizen*, they promised it would be "printed on yellow, not by reason of our partiality for that color but because our patrons have become used to seeing the 'yellow paper' and might perhaps feel lost without it."[30]

After the sale of the *Chadron Democrat*, Allen bought cattle and started a ranch on the reservation near the mouth of Porcupine Creek. He and his neighbors founded the Oglala Stock Association to assign cattle brands, deter theft, and generally protect their ranching interests. Charles was elected the first secretary of the organization.[31]

Allen may have maintained his interest in the ranch, but in the spring of 1893, he was named postmaster for Pine Ridge and shortly thereafter the family moved to the agency.[32] Allen recognized the financial rewards he might reap by combining a store with his post office and entered into a partnership with William McGaa to buy a store at the agency. McGaa reached an agreement to purchase one owned by Henry A. Dawson, but for some unknown reason Allen was not included.[33] Allen then purchased a small stock of goods and opened his own store in conjunction with the post office. The combination might have assured a modestly prosperous business, however, fierce competition from four other traders forced him to abandon the agency and resign from the postal service.[34]

Before giving up the store Allen had some idle time that he spent compiling data on the life of the Oglala chief, Red Cloud. He planned on a three-hundred-page, profusely illustrated book, but when portions were published in a monthly magazine it was a much more modest offering.[35]

In August 1895 the Allens moved to Pass Creek, but this move also proved to be a mistake. For some reason people began abandoning this corner of the reservation and Allen was forced to sell his store there in the early fall of 1896.[36]

Shortly after the sale the family moved again and settled near a little community at the upper reaches of Bear In The Lodge Creek. This would become Allen, South Dakota, named in Charles's honor. A post office, day school, and an issue station was established in the neighborhood. During this time he also had a ranch located about twelve miles up Eagle Nest Creek.[37]

In 1902 Charles and Emma moved once again to a ranch on the south side of the Little White River about six miles southwest of present Martin, South Dakota. As a registered member of the tribe Emma and her children received this land in severalty when allotments began in August 1904.[38] Despite the acquisition of this substantial parcel of land, financial problems continued to plague the Allens. In 1908 Charles went to Lincoln, Nebraska, to look for employment. While there he visited his friend and former newspaper competitor Addison E. Sheldon, who confided in his diary that Allen was "broke—sad case."[39]

In 1909 Warren K. Moorehead, an Indian rights activist whom Allen had met during the Wounded Knee troubles, offered him a job. Moorehead was investigating conditions on the Pine Ridge Reservation for the Bureau of Indian Affairs and asked Allen to be his interpreter. Despite Allen's strained financial situation he had to refuse, admitting "I do not speak the [Lakota] language but very imperfectly."[40]

Allen made one last attempt in the newspaper business shortly after Bennett County was carved out of the reservation and opened to white settlement on June 29, 1911. Allen founded the weekly *Martin Messenger* and stayed with the paper for about four years.[41]

In 1913 he applied for a position as an inspector with the Bureau of Indian Affairs and turned to Sheldon for a letter of recommendation. His old friend wrote to the assistant commissioner of Indian affairs saying, "I have known Mr. Allen as only rival editors come to know each other, and know him to be a square man in all the relations of life. He has 'roughed it' on the frontier since boyhood and lacks some of the polish that we put on in the colleges, but is a man of real ability and something of a poet and writer as well." In spite of the generally favorable recommendation, Allen was unsuccessful in getting the position.[42]

Ranching continued to be Allen's principal occupation although for a time he dabbled in some failed but expensive experiments in improving steam engines. Then tragedy struck when Emma contracted influenza and died on March 14, 1925. Charles continued to live on the ranch for a time, but soon retired and moved to Martin. In 1929 he entered the State Soldier's Home in Hot Springs, South Dakota, although he continued to spend much of his time at Martin.[43]

It is not known when Allen began writing *From Fort Laramie to Wounded Knee*, but it was probably in the early 1930s when he was over eighty years old. It may not have been his first attempt since he submitted a manuscript titled *Once in Nebraska* to the Torch Publishing Company in Cedar Rapids in April 1910. Although it was rejected and this manuscript has since been lost, there is some evidence that it dealt with frontier life in northwestern Nebraska and was perhaps an initial version of *From Fort Laramie to Wounded Knee*.[44]

In 1936 Allen's manuscript was nearing completion and he turned again to Addison Sheldon for assistance. As superintendent of the Nebraska State Historical Society, Sheldon was in a position to offer support to anyone writing about early Nebraska history. Allen gave him part of the manuscript to review, but apparently forgot it contained a section that could have offended Sheldon. Allen had written a sarcastic parody of a speech Sheldon gave inviting the Lakotas from the Pine Ridge Reservation to participate in Chadron's Fourth of July celebration. Allen's spoof was humorous, but it made Sheldon look like a pompous fool.[45] A short time later Allen realized the potential for offending his associate and sent a letter in which he apologized profusely for the speech. Allen wrote: "I felt that I had unwittingly given you just cause for offense, and had foolishly lost a valued friend. So I destroyed the imaginary bombastic agency speech, and hence-forth confined myself to matters pertaining to the actual affairs of Indians." Sheldon was magnanimous in his reply. "I have no objections whatever to the purported speech made by myself . . . It serves to enliven the literary landscape if nothing more."[46] The speech was retained in the surviving manuscript.

While Sheldon reviewed the first chapters of *From Fort Laramie to Wounded Knee*, Allen was writing the concluding sections. He hoped to have the task completed by March of the following year but failed to make the deadline.[47] There was no further mention of the work until February 1938 when Allen called on Sheldon at his office in Lincoln and left the manuscript with him. The society director read it and noted in his diary, "It is greatly improved from [the] old draft but still lacks." By now Allen was eager to have the manuscript ready for publication so he paid Sheldon $35 to "read and criticize" it and to "have it revised" within thirty days. In view of the modest payment, the work was probably limited to copy editing. Sheldon called upon Mari Sandoz, an employee of the Historical Society and later a successful Western author, to read the manuscript and to advise Allen on obtaining a publisher. After the review was completed, a copy of the manuscript was submitted to the *Atlantic Monthly*. In late April a rejection letter came back saying the magazine would not publish the manuscript without some rewriting. The manuscript was given to another Historical Society employee to "copy and correct" and it was returned to Allen in July. During the summer he sent the manuscript to two more publishers, but both rejected it.[48]

Allen seems to have given up all hope of publishing his work, but in 1940 Sheldon agreed to publish the third and fourth chapters. In these Allen described a confrontation he witnessed between Oglala warriors and U.S. soldiers in October 1874 at the Red Cloud Agency near present Crawford, Nebraska. The chapters appeared in *Nebraska History*, the Historical Society's quarterly magazine, under the title "Red Cloud and the U.S. Flag."[49]

A year after the chapters appeared in print, Elmo Scott Watson tried to rekindle Allen's interest in the manuscript. Watson was the editor of *Publishers' Auxiliary*, a trade journal for newspaper publishers. He was researching early western reporters and began corresponding with Allen. Watson encouraged him to submit his work to Houghton Mifflin because of the firm's demonstrated interest in western history and biography. Allen replied with a polite thank-you note pointing out that the company had turned him down once and he did not wish to go through a second rejection, although he thought the manuscript had "been much improved since its first submittal."[50]

Allen did make at least one major change in the manuscript. He recognized the distinct racial overtones in the chapter entitled "Short Bull–Brigand of the Badlands," and in an attempt to soften its impact he prefaced the chapter with an assurance that it was not intended to offend anyone. Later, he realized that in addition to the racial slurs, the chapter had definite literary and historical shortcomings. In the end Allen replaced it with "Trails and Trials of a Primitive People," a tale of murder and revenge in a Lakota camp told to Allen by an elderly white trader.[51]

By early spring of 1941 Allen was desperate for a publisher and wrote to Watson with a final alternative: "If I could obtain a reasonable amount I would sell my M.S. and the purchaser could use it . . . and make changes or deletions as he chose."[52] Allen had given a copy of the manuscript to Watson, but a year and a half passed, and no offers were forthcoming. In the late summer of 1942 Watson paid a visit to Allen at Hot Springs. Although Allen was ninety years old, Watson described him "as alert mentally and active physically as many a man half his age."[53] His health deteriorated rapidly, however, and on November 16, 1942, Charles Wesley Allen died at the State Soldier's Home.[54] Two weeks later Watson published a condensed version of Allen's chapter dealing with the Wounded Knee massacre in the *Publishers' Auxiliary*.[55]

Three copies of Allen's manuscript are in the Nebraska State Historical Society's Charles W. Allen Collection. The earliest draft is a typescript containing the Short Bull chapter. There are also numerous small errors, some of which were corrected and initialed by Addison E. Sheldon. This early draft tells the same story as the other two, but the writing style is cumbersome and details found in the later drafts are lacking. The second draft is a typed carbon copy dated 1938 and was donated after Sheldon and his staff completed their review. A third copy was presented to the Society in 1981 by Peter Allen, Charles's grandson. When Peter Allen asked about the possibility of publishing the manuscript, Society editor and historian Leigh G. DeLay pointed out that the Society was not then publishing books. After reviewing the copy, however, DeLay described it as a "Cadillac among reminiscences."[56]

The 1981 manuscript is a photocopy of the 1938 typescript, but it contains a number of changes made in Charles Allen's unsteady and unmistakable handwriting. Most of Allen's changes are minor, such as adding a word dropped from the typescript or changing the tense of a verb. Major changes occurred on three pages and these had been retyped. It seemed unnecessary to mention Allen's minor changes, but the retyped pages are noted in the endnotes. Allen apparently intended this to be the final version and it was the draft used for this book.

In editing the manuscript for publication, scattered typographical errors were corrected, but Allen's punctuation and often unique word division were retained. The only major editorial change was the relocation of two chapters dealing with early Lakota origins and legends that fell in the middle of Allen's account of the Wounded Knee disaster. Originally "The First White Men among the Indians" was found between "Gathering War Clouds" and "The Ghost Dance," while "Trails and Trials of a

Introduction

Primitive People" fell between "Reporters at Pine Ridge" and "Big Foot's Arrival." By moving these chapters to their present location the Wounded Knee story is presented without interruption. When Allen transcribed the legend he called "The Lost Children," he inserted it at the end of Chapter 17 in the midst of a discussion about the development of Chadron, Nebraska. It seemed more logical to include it in Chapter 11, which deals with other Lakota stories he had been told.

Richard E. Jensen

Acknowledgments

Although only one name appears as the editor of this book, it is, in reality, the result of contributions by a number of people. I would like to thank Randy and Sheila Reese of Cornelius, Oregon, who provided a great deal of useful information on Charles Allen that otherwise would have been unavailable. Mr. Reese is Allen's great-great-grandson. Roseana L. Blount of Cedar Hill, Texas, is another family member who also gave valuable data. Professional colleagues who were especially helpful include LaVera Rose, archivist, South Dakota State Historical Society; Ann Nelson, senior historian, Wyoming State Museum; and Mark Wolfe, historic preservation officer, Deadwood, South Dakota. James E. Potter, R. Eli Paul, and Thomas Buecker of the Nebraska State Historical Society staff provided countless suggestions and leads. I owe a debt of gratitude to former Historical Society director James A. Hanson and present director Lawrence J. Sommer for allowing the research to be completed. Finally, I wish to thank my wife Bess for her continued support and encouragement.

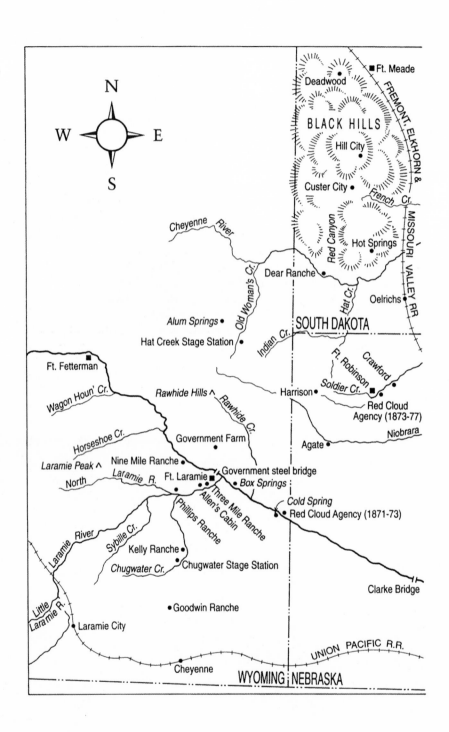

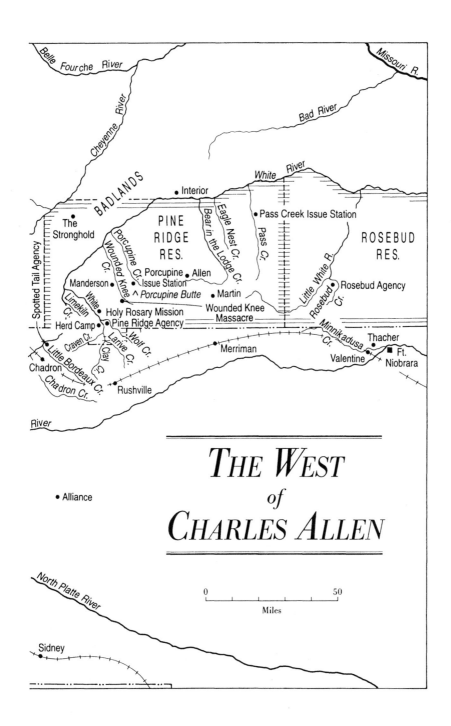

THE WEST

of

CHARLES ALLEN

0   50

Miles

CHAPTER 1

A Pioneer in Embryo

These sketches are only intended to record and describe some of the more interesting incidents of my personal experience during fifty years passed on the extreme frontier in what was Indian country for the most part.[1] Naturally, a summary of events that brought me into this country of the Sioux Indians and of the occupations I was engaged in for a time thereafter will make the narrative more or less biographical.

However, I trust the readers (if such there be) may not feel imposed upon by too many trivial happenings or self-exaltations. I have no desire to emulate the super-hero nor to imitate the hair-breath escapes portrayed in much western narrative. Barring the exuberance of youth, prompted by extreme romantic propensities, the tenor of my life has been that of the average normal man.

In the summer of 1871, at Wichita, Kansas, together with several young friends I hired out to a trail boss, Mr. O. P. Goodwin, who was in charge of a herd of one thousand head of Texas cattle which had been brought up the Chisholm Trail. His crew of herders desired to quit at this point and accompany any other herds that were short-handed to Abilene, Kansas, on the Union Pacific Railroad, which at that time was the shipping-point of all the southern herds destined for market, and the terminal of the Old Chisholm Trail that had its starting-point in southern Texas.[2]

However, the stock herds that were destined for the northwest ranges usually left the famous old trail at Wichita and followed up the Arkansas River to some point nearest their home ranch. In our case this was a large sheep and cattle ranch at the foothills of an east spur of the Rocky Mountains. It was owned by E. W. Whitcomb and located along Boxelder Creek in Wyoming—a tributary of the Cache La Poudre River in Colorado.[3] Arriving at this place in the latter part of August, we helped brand the cattle and place them on the range, then we boys scattered in search of work.

Mr. Whitcomb had already secured me a job of herding with a ranchman by the name of Hiram Kelley, at Point of Rocks near Chugwater Station, Wyoming, on the Cheyenne and Fort Laramie mail road.[4] On September 10, 1871, while riding the range for this man through the hills and valleys of the above named stream and its tributaries, I celebrated my twentieth birthday.

I had been furnished with a good Winchester repeating rifle and ammunition, as everyone carried a gun at this time. Also I was instructed to be on guard against roving Indian parties that were continually stealing away from the Indian Agency and committing depredations on the whites whenever found in isolated and unprotected places.[5] I did not see any hostile Indians while riding this range, but an incident occurred just before I left this place that proved that I just happened to be fortunate.

It was in the latter part of September. I had finished my rounds through the hills and was riding out into the Chugwater Valley when I saw a long string of cattle being driven by a regular trail outfit coming down the broad freight road. I came up with the herd and engaged in conversation with the owner, one Mr. Powell. He told me he had brought the herd from Texas and was going to locate somewhere on the Little Laramie River near where it emptied into the Big Laramie. When our ways parted, he cordially invited me to call on him if at any time I should ride that way.[6]

As I recall the time, it was about six weeks later that Mr. Kelley received an order from the quartermaster at Fort Fetterman to furnish forty head of beef cattle for the post.[7] After the cattle were rounded up and forty head cut out, James Payton and I were delegated to deliver them to the fort. Payton was one of the men about the ranch and knew the country, and was somewhat older than myself.

We were provided with a pack-horse to carry our bedding, provisions, and cooking utensils. Starting from the round-up camp at once, we stopped that night a little above the mouth of the Chugwater. Mr. Kelley accompanied us that far, remained over night, and took his turn at night herding. As we were handling beef cattle we trailed slowly. After crossing the Big Laramie, the road continued up the lesser stream until we came opposite the Powell ranch in the evening. His invitation was too tempting to be resisted. We detoured and went in.

Mr. Powell received us with the usual frontier welcome. He urged us to corral our cattle, put our horses in the stable, and stack our camp outfit away "and forget it" until the next morning. All this we gladly did, and were pleased to compliment the gentleman and his helpers on the number of substantial log improvements they had been able to erect in the short time they had been located. We spent a pleasant and restful night with Mr. Powell and his half-dozen helpers. The next morning he expressed his intention of accompanying us for a short time, as he wished to look for a bunch of his stock that had, he thought, strayed down one of the creeks leading to the Platte.

Soon all three of us were out on the road with the cattle, visiting as we rode along. We passed through a few miles of rough, rolling hills studded with stunted pines and came out on an expansive plateau, fringed with more or less timber on the northern edge, through which ran a fair-sized creek.

When we were about half-way across the plateau Mr. Powell bade us good-by and started off in a northeasterly direction which, if continued, would have brought him to the creek about five miles below where we would cross it on the road ahead. A very ordinary occurrence, yes, and we did not then give it another thought; but it proved to be the last time this unfortunate rancher was ever seen alive by white men.

After our friend left us, we traveled by easy stages in order to conserve the weight and beef-quality of our cattle. Our way lay mostly along the base of the mountainous foothills, but frequently we were in sight of the broad Platte at varying distances eastward. At night we left the regular road and sought more sheltered camping-places in the nook of some quiet little stream that meandered down from the mountains.

Nothing out of the ordinary occurred during the rest of our journey. A soft snow fell intermittently during each day and night, but never developed into a storm. On the afternoon of what we knew would be our last night on the trail we refrained from smoking when we discovered that there was but one match left between us. It grew dark as we went down a long declivity to a little stream known as the Wagon Houn' because of its frequently recurring bends of that shape. We found the bed of the stream about eight feet broad and perfectly dry, but it had recently been covered with a few inches of light snow. This we brushed away with our feet and unpacked on the dry gravel, having turned our cattle down through the timber and little valleys to rest. The banks of the stream were about four feet high on either side, thickly covered with dead vines that drooped to the gravel bed. As we wanted to get a cozy, sheltered place, the snow from these was also brushed away.

Having fixed our camping-place for the night, we began hustling through the timber for sticks, chunks and limbs until we had a goodly pile of nice dry wood. After searching through our mess kit it dawned upon us that all our paper and been used in starting previous fires. I had two perfectly dry dollar bills, and we decided to hold one of them in readiness while I touched a match to the other. We were about to execute this plan when a better one occurred to my partner. Calling a halt, he took off a tattered old coat he was wearing and began stripping the cotton batting from the lining and spreading it out in a thin layer under and over the dry vines with which we had enclosed a pyramid of small sticks. This done, the one lighted match was applied and the fire started.

None of our provisions had been cooked except the bread, and we were very anxious for a hot meal. We filled our coffee pot and a large can with snow and soon had hot water for all purposes. In a short time we had bacon parboiled and fried, potatoes sliced and cooked, and soon were partaking of a meal that was delicious to us—especially as we knew that a good smoke was in the offing for desert.

We were on our way by daylight the next morning, reached the post in the evening and delivered our cattle in good shape. The butcher at the post showed us his house, barn and corral at the outer edge of the fort, telling us to put up our horses, put our pack in the bunk-house and make ourselves at home for a few days until rested for our return trip.

We laid over there the next day and went around and through the post buildings, including mess house, barracks, barns and warehouses. We also visited the large trading-store that furnished the soldiers, citizen employees, and quite a number of Indians camped near by, with supplies. The post was situated at the confluence of the North Platte River and Nonparle Creek, a well timbered mountain stream of goodly size. During our stay we walked up this creek to where the Indians had their camp, and spent the afternoon watching them perform in native games and at their usual occupations.

That evening we informed our host of our intention to depart, and early next morning started back to the home ranch. While it took us five days to make the trip to the post, we were only two days going back.

On the afternoon of the second day, while we were traversing the road through the Powell range, we met one of the herders who surprised us by asking if we had seen anything of Mr. Powell. He said that Powell had not returned to the ranch since that morning when he had left with us; that they found where he had left our trail and gone off across the flat, but could not follow the tracks far on account of the heavy grass that had straightened since his passage. He further added that they had searched for him, but figured that he might have run across some hunters or trappers and gone on with them to Fort Laramie, where he had been desirous of going. After a few words of regret at his disappearance and best wishes for his early discovery, we continued on our way and arrived at home that evening.

It was fortunate for us that our trip was completed, as the snow began falling and drifting continuously until the ground was covered to such depth that a contemplated search for Mr. Powell, who by now had been given up for dead, had to be abandoned until warm weather should bare the ground. I remained with Mr. Kelley until the holidays, when I took a ten-day rest—riding about, making acquaintances, and observing things generally. Then I began working for the Cuny & Ecoffey Freight and

Contracting Company, the largest operators in that section at that time, with three bases from which their various industries were carried on.[8] Their headquarters were two large buildings that stood at right angles, one being used for general merchandise, store-room, and living quarters for the clerks; the other being a billiard hall and bar, with eating-house and large corral in the rear. All of these buildings stood within a few hundred yards of the Laramie River, three miles above old Fort Laramie, Wyoming, and the place was known throughout the country as "Three Mile Ranch."[9] Thirty miles below the fort on the north side of the Platte River, at the site which was formerly the old Red Cloud Indian Agency, was located a large Indian trading store.

The stock ranch was situated about forty miles west of Three Mile Ranch, on the west side of a broad valley that was separated from a range of mountains by a fair-sized creek called the Sibylle, which ran into the Laramie River some twelve miles to the north.[10] None of the range of mountains was noticeably lofty except Laramie Peak, which could be seen from a great distance on every side. They were, however, exceedingly picturesque, as they were green with tall pines interspersed with towering piles of steel grey granite that rose from mammoth granite walls, broken here and there into narrow, deep, irregular canyons whose rivulets were hidden under the dense and variegated foliage of trees of softer woods.

About six miles southeast of the ranch one could come upon the storied pass through which the famous old scout and guide, Jim Bridger, conducted General Halleck and his army in their early-day march to the extreme west to establish Fort Halleck at the foot of Elk Mountain in Wyoming in 1862.[11] The pass was about eight miles wide, its perpendicular walls of stone rising to two hundred feet in some places. Sometimes these walls were so close together that there was just enough room for wagons to pass; in other places one would find a nice little valley broad enough to accommodate a large camp.

This great gorge through the granite hills was supplied with a fine stream of water whose flow was constant, and was known to early settlers as Halleck's Canyon. The road through its length made a continuous, gradual ascent until it emerged at the edge of a great plateau, and at this point the scenery was most impressive. Behind and below stretched a broad forest of pine-clad hills and rocky gorges, while ahead and at each side rolled a vast expanse of grass-carpeted valleys and low hills that formed the Laramie Plains.

Far across these plains the eye could catch a vast, irregular, sky-piercing wall of pyramids; a blue, snow-capped, pine-girdled range—the Rocky Mountains, "rock-ribbed and ancient as the sun." Often this view was enhanced by a high rolling column of smoke rising from a large Union Pacific engine as it guided its train along the track either to or from Laramie City at the southeastern extremity of the plain. More often than not the picture would disclose bands of wild game–deer, elk or antelope, scudding away from the strange and fearsome monster.[12]

The entire country was full of game of all kinds, therefore the work-crew at the ranch was always abundantly supplied with fresh meat by the ranch hunter, John Russell, known as "Buckskin Jack."[13]

My job at the ranch was that of helper wherever help was required. The foreman seemed to use me as utility man for extra work as it arose. Thus it chanced that late in February [1872] I was sent with a four-mule team down to the Three-Mile Ranch for supplies. The road was mostly new to me, as I had been over only a portion of it on horseback, but after rising from the valley into a broad plateau it was only a matter of keeping straight ahead. The road ran across this plain to the east for a distance of twenty miles over ground whose fertility was evidenced by the luxuriant grasses of various kinds; a fertility since proved by vast agricultural developments. The thriving little city of Wheatland, Wyoming, is now the center of this plain.

Leaving the upland, the road dropped into the Chugwater Valley just above its confluence with the Laramie River. At this point F. M. Phillips, the beef contractor for the post, had a large cluster of ranch buildings that accommodated his crew and cattle herd.[14] The river valley from there down to the ranch was a succession of bends, some of them meadow-land, others sagebrush and cottonwood groves, with here and there a house and corral. These were usually unoccupied, as the owners were off engaged in freighting.

On my arrival at the ranch that evening I learned that the body of the unfortunate Mr. Powell, whom they had searched for diligently ever since the snow had begun to disappear, had been found about twenty-five miles up the Platte River and a detail had gone out from the post that morning to bring it in. The following afternoon this detail, in passing, stopped at the ranch for a few minutes and a number of us viewed the body, which, having been found under a large snowdrift, was well preserved. There were two bullet holes through the head, either of which would have caused instant death. The hat, the coat and boots were gone; otherwise it seemed not to have been disturbed. The body was taken to the post and given a Christian burial under the auspices of the post chaplain.[15]

In a day or two I started back to the stock ranch with supplies, also instructions to hook another span of mules that belonged to the team, bring it back, and join the freight train that was composed of eight wagons, with six mules to the wagon. This I did, and was thus inducted into the Ancient Order of Mule Skinners—which, being interpreted, means simply mule drivers.

CHAPTER 2

Mystery and Mules

Teaming was brisk. In fact, for years it remained the chief industry of the country, whether as to wood, logs, hay or freight. Sometimes our trips would be to Fort Fetterman, sometimes to the old Red Cloud Agency, sometimes to Fort Laramie; but always, except in the case of wood, logs or hay, we loaded at Cheyenne, Wyoming.

The train had come in from one of these trips, and after we had rested for several days, repairing and putting our several outfits in order, we were sent to old Red Cloud Agency to transfer beef hides from there to the railroad.

On our arrival we found that the river had been rising for several days and that the ford was impassable, so we dropped around the bend to the south of the agency and pitched our camp near the river bank. We were visited the next morning by the manager of the company store who had crossed the river in a small boat. He and the wagon boss soon concluded arrangements by which we were to get our cargo. High water of a week or two in late May and early June was not an uncommon occurrence, therefore the agency was fairly well supplied with small boats and a group of larger flat-bottomed scows. All of these were soon assembled a considerable distance above our camp on the agency side, and local teams began hauling dry hides to that point.

The late spring weather was mild and warm, and the next morning a boat came across and took a number of us hands over to a point much below our freight. We would tow the boats from this point up the bank to the hides, load them to their fullest capacity, bind them with ropes, and then, with two men on each side launch them into the swift, rolling waves. We crossed over by using one hand to guide the boat and the other as a paddle. A number of the Indian helpers seemed to get a lot of fun out of the operation. After a few trips we were able to make a landing quite near our wagons, and the hands whom we left ashore loaded the hides. In about three days the whole job was completed and we were out on the road to Cheyenne, where we arrived in due time, delivered our freight, and reloaded with merchandise for Fort Laramie and home.

We had camped at the ranch about a week when another driver and myself were accosted by the wagon boss and told to get our teams ready to start that evening for an all-night drive to the agency for a couple loads of freight which had to be moved immediately. We were at a loss to figure out what it was all about. There had been recent rumors of an Indian outbreak, but at that time such rumors were frequent and to be expected in an Indian country. They were heeded to the extent of being prepared, but never allowed to interfere with the business at hand.[1]

We attributed this latter war talk to the fact that the Indians were getting ready to move north for their annual hunt of the late summer and early fall. Further, much was being said to the effect that their agency was to be moved farther north and located somewhere on the Big White River in Nebraska, and many of them objected to such a movement. However, it was not for us to reason why [we] were started off so unceremoniously. Our business was to go.

We left the ranch about three o'clock that afternoon, and before dusk were out on our way below Fort Laramie on what was one of the broadest and best-worn roads in Wyoming at that time. It was known far and near as the Old Oregon or Mormon Trail, but the Mormons were not the only ones who traversed it. All the migration from the central west and east followed this road up the North Platte beyond Green River, into and through the Rocky Mountain passes, to their various points of destination.

The night was very dark. The driver of the lead team kept his mules urged to a fast walk continuously, and I followed him closely. We were perhaps twenty miles down the Platte when I distinguished a slight noise on the road behind. Slipping quietly from my perch on the saddle of the near wheeler, I ran cautiously ahead and told my partner of the sound in the rear.[2] He stopped his team and took his gun from its usual place on the front of the wagon box. I secured mine also, and, going to the rear of my wagon, we stooped low to the ground and listened. We could soon tell that it was the hoof-beat of a single horse. At a proper distance we hailed the newcomer, who stopped immediately and answered.

It proved to be our wagon boss, who, as he rode along with us, berated us slightly for not having made better time, for by his calculations we would not be able to reach the agency, load up and get out before daylight. I assured him that the teams had been kept at the fastest walk they were capable of, and that we probably should have started from the ranch at the time we were told to get ready, instead of later. He thought so too, but claimed he had notified us as soon as he learned of the trip. Then, as we rode along in the darkness, he became quite affable and vouchsafed the true reason for our night ride.

All the western military posts, when supplied with improved firearms, sold their old muzzle-loading Springfield rifles and their cap and ball ammunition. A large quantity of these paper, powder and ball cartridges had been sold by the Government to various traders throughout the country.

They were easily disposed of to the Indians, trappers and hunters for their powder and lead, which they could remold and shape to fit their rifles of various calibers. It seems that our employers had about two wagon loads of boxes containing this kind of goods and had received a tip that there was a plot hatching among the Indians to seize this lead and powder when the village went to hunt, for at that time they were poorly supplied with modern guns.

The mystery of the night trip now solved, we were more at ease. We were expected to slip into the agency under cover of darkness and get this tempting commodity out of their reach without their knowing it until it was safely away.

Grey dawn was appearing as we came to the river ford just above the large Indian village that lay between it and the agency. In crossing the various sand-bars and rushing rivulets that formed the Platte at this place during low water, we could tell that the rise had started by the shifting sands and the bubbling of the water. After crossing we turned to the right and ascended a slight eminence, then meandered on the road that wound through the village to the trading store.

The smoke was rising from all of the lodges, and those Indians who were astir about them stood gazing at us in wonderment. Anyone who thinks an Indian village can be surprised at or near daylight may guess again, for long experience seems to have taught all of the tribes that, in their warfare with other tribes, daybreak is the danger hour when enemies can charge through their villages with less danger to themselves than at any other time.

We soon had our wagons parked at the company warehouse, and while we ate breakfast the force about the store began loading into our wagons the small lead-colored boxes, about eighteen inches by twelve by ten, all branded "U.S.I.C." and provided with slotted handholds.[3] When we had finished and came out, we were surprised to note that a large group of Indians had been watching the whole proceeding.

We set out immediately on our way to the crossing, which we entered, and kept our teams moving as fast as possible, as there were various streaks of quicksand to be traversed and our loads were heavy and a dead weight.

We had gone about two-thirds of the way across when the front team became stalled. We were out in the water at once, unhitching the rear team and doubling it onto the front one while the wagon was slowly settling in the sand. We strung the twelve animals taut and gave them the word to go. They tried to move the load, but failed. After a few more such failures we were joined by the wagon boss, the store manager, and one or two other men on horseback. This gave pause to our work, and in looking about we saw that we had been putting on quite a show. The whole river-bank, on the side we had just left, was literally covered with Indians of all sizes, sex and age. They had been watching our nearly disastrous maneuvers with astonished amusement. The wagon boss gave us orders to unhitch our teams, take them to the opposite shore, and turn them loose to graze.

It was while complying with this order that I first took note of a cluster of lodges and tents that were supplied with a buggy, a light wagon, and several large freight wagons, a short distance below us. My partner told me that this was the camp of a well-to-do old Frenchman by the name of Nicholas Janis, who had an Indian family, a few cattle, and two or three six-yoke ox freight teams.[4] Some of the teams must have been near at hand, for we had but finished turning our animals out when we saw our two bosses coming along with a driver and six yoke of cattle. These were soon attached to the front wagon. The driver's whip cracked and the oxen started forward, but they failed to move the load.

From our position on the shore we could see a short consultation. Then an interpreter began to harangue the Indians on the river bank, and as they began to shed their robes and blankets, turn them over to their womenfolk and start into the stream, we saw the covers come off the wagons and a couple of men mount each load and begin handing down boxes to the first warriors that arrived. They carried them to the bank on which we were standing and our wagon boss showed them where to pile the heavy boxes so that loading could be effected easily.

The carriers were so numerous that a continuous string of boxes was being landed. In a short time the wagons were empty and the front team coming across with one that had been stopped beside the stack of boxes. Some of the Indians were loading this while the others brought up the second wagon, and soon our loads were ready for the trail again. The Indians left immediately for the trading store, where they had been promised provisions for a feast.

My partner and I were sitting on the grass, chatting about the wonderful secrecy of our trip, when our wagon boss come out of the camp below and called us to him, saying that we were to have dinner there. We were directed to a small tent where we found washing utensils. On our way we passed a large lodge, the skirts of which were raised about three feet, and inside we saw an elderly man reclining on a couch of buffalo robes. Near him a much younger man was reading aloud.

Then we were called into a commodious tent dining room, where dinner was set on a large canvas spread on a clean ground floor. The dishes were tin with exception of the platters and bowls that contained victuals, which in this case consisted of dried boiled beef and wild-turnip soup, and black coffee.[5] As was the usual custom among these people, only men ate at the first table. If there was not room for all of them at the first sitting, the rest ate with the women, who always followed the men. The viands were replenished from time to time by two young girls of mixed blood, daughters of Mr. Janis, who sat at head of the table in tailor fashion, as we all did.

After dinner, in conversing with the reader whom I had seen in the lodge, I learned that his name was George Colhoff and that he was a store clerk, but, being temporarily out of work, Mr. Janis employed him for no other duty but to read to him—fiction always preferred.[6]

It was about three o'clock when the boss told us that we had better hitch up and pull to Cold Springs three or four miles up stream, where there was better grass for our teams. He said that he would overtake us and we would have a better start in the morning. This we did, and he came up to us just as we reached the crest of the last hill, where the road branched off and led down to the Cold Springs camp. From the hilltop we could see that a large Indian village had been located there since we last passed that way.

There was plenty of room for all, however, and we meandered down and went into camp. We soon found that this was a camp of Cheyennes and as they kept coming on horseback by twos and threes and turning their horses loose, we had no doubt that they had been among the Sioux carriers at the ford and knew as much about the contents of our wagons as we did.

We had plenty to eat but were short on sleep. We retired early and slept soundly until daylight; then, while the wagon boss was driving in the mules, we got breakfast and soon were on our way home.

We figured that we had made a perfectly good trip—barring the secrecy of the program. Arriving home at about five o'clock that evening, we were pleased to find the rest of the train out on a trip. This meant that we would be sure of rest for an indefinite number of days until the train should return.

For some time I continued to work with this train, but meanwhile had acquired two horses. They were broke to work, but also were saddle horses. One of them, a dark flea-bitten bay with black markings, was an exceptionally fine saddler and an all-around Texas cow horse.

A short time later one of the small freighters, Andrew Tabor by name but known all over the territory as French Andy, whose outfit consisted of one six-horse and one four-horse team, offered to put two work animals with mine and give me $65 a month to drive.[7] This gave him three teams. I accepted his offer. This work continued until late winter weather made it impracticable, when he laid me off until spring.

In the interim I secured a wagon and two more horses, and started the summer work with a four-horse outfit of my own. I had also traded for a two-room cabin situated in one of the meadow bends of the Laramie River, about seven miles above the post. This gave me a permanent camp where, on occasion, I could turn my animals out to rest and be at home with the other freighters along the river, above and below me, as neighbors.[8]

Old Red Cloud Agency had been moved in the meantime (August 1– 10, 1873) and located on a picturesque site on Big White River, about two miles west of the present city of Crawford, Nebraska.[9] The military post, which was about the same distance west of the Agency, had been established May 8, 1874, and given the name of Fort Robinson in honor of Lieutenant Robinson, who a few months earlier had lost his life in the rugged hills north of the Platte and about twenty miles above Fort Laramie, while leading a detachment of his company in pursuit of a band of marauding Indians.[10]

Here I indulge in a slight digression to state that teaming remained the principal industry of the country for a number of years. This was my employment continuously, notwithstanding the fact that on August 23, 1873, I was married to Miss Emma Hawkins, aged eighteen years. She was the niece of Adolph Cuny, the senior partner of the firm that had formerly employed me. Our matrimonial alliance continued intact for fifty-two years and we were the parents of twelve children, nine of whom are alive and living with their families in states all the way from North and South Dakota to Washington, Montana and California. All are self-sustaining, respected citizens.

My wife, afflicted with pneumonia, passed away on the 24th day of March, 1924, at the home ranch seven miles southwest of Martin, South Dakota. She left not only a mourning family but a host of saddened friends, comprising all who knew her. She was a quiet, unpretentious, faithful wife and a loving, careful mother. To my mind these are the chief attributes of a Noble woman.

CHAPTER 3

Red Cloud Cuts the Flag-Pole

Part One

My wife and I lived on our little homestead, where I cut hay and gardened between freighting trips. I was so engaged when, one balmy autumn morning, October 25, 1874, being at the Post after mail, I met an old friend known as "Big Bat." This was Baptiste Pourier, post guide and interpreter, who importuned me to accompany him to Fort Robinson and the Red Cloud Agency, as he had been ordered to deliver dispatches there by ten o'clock the next day.[1]

Not being specially busy at the time, and never having been over that section of the country, I acceded to his wish. It was arranged that he would be at my place about three o'clock that afternoon and we would start from there, as he had planned to make the trip mostly after dark. I made my arrangements for a few days' absence and had a lunch prepared, with a surplus in the saddle bags for an emergency, when he came.

After eating a bite we started out in a northeasterly direction through the low rolling hills that lie between the Platte and Laramie rivers. Leaving the fort to the southeast, we crossed the river on an old Indian trail and continued to the northeast until we intercepted the government road that runs between Forts Laramie and Robinson, a distance of about ninety miles.

Conserving the fettle of our mounts, we kept a fast single-foot walk on this road that leads along the eastern base of the Rawhide Buttes, from which flows a creek of that name. Rawhide Creek is a stream of rapid, clear-flowing waters. For many miles it runs eastward as though seeking union with the Running Water. Then, with a sharp turn, it flows south to join the waters of the North Platte about twenty miles east of Fort Laramie.

When we came to the Rawhide night was coming on, so, after watering and grazing our horses, we rested until it was quite dark. The road between this point and White River was considered the most dangerous to travel, for the reason that roving war parties were frequently crossing and recrossing it, either in sneaking out of or back to the Agency.

We now had a fairly level road of approximately thirty miles between the two streams named above. Keeping our horses down to a fast walk until they were well warmed up, then giving them the rein, we got off to a swift gallop. This we continued for two or three miles, then slowed down to a fast walk for about half that distance, then raced again. This

14

alternating gait we kept until we reached Running Water, where we rested. The long stretch of road bearing east of north between there and the breaks of the White River is hilly and rough, but we made very good time by racing up and trotting down all of the longer grades we came to.

When we reached the point where the road begins to descend into White River Canyon we left it, and, seeking the shelter of a dense plum thicket, we turned our horses out to graze and took our saddles and effects into the thicket. There we built a fire, for the early morning was chilly. We could enjoy the heat and at the same time obscure the blaze by sitting on either side of the fire and hovering over it with our saddle blankets drawn over our shoulders as we slowly chewed our lunch, smoked, chatted, and possibly dozed a little during the short time we had before daybreak.

The affection that a rider usually shows to his mount is almost always reciprocated. The animal that is kindly treated likes to be near its master, especially in desolate places, as it seems to break the loneliness and give a sense of security. So when we were ready to start we found our horses near the camp, as expected, and were on our way.

We soon reached the last hill overlooking the spring that is the extreme western source of White River, and were surprised to see encamped there some government teams with an escort of United States regulars who were accompanying them as advance and rear guards. Big Bat recognized Lieutenant Vroom, the officer in charge, and after a short conversation with him we moved on down to the last stretch of our journey over a road that ran through a closely linked chain of box elder groves. It seemed that we crossed the stream every quarter of a mile. Only once, at a place where the road had not been worked through the trees, did we detour a couple of miles from the creek up to the side of the cliffs to the south.[2]

About the center of this detour the road narrowed around a point of pine-studded bluff, where but a few weeks before the man who drove the mail wagon between Fort Laramie and Fort Robinson was shot from ambush and scalped. The peace-preserving person would ask, "What was done about it?" Nothing was done, beyond a Christian burial and some formal investigation for record. In nearly all such cases it was found impossible to fix proof of guilt upon those who committed crimes against the whites at that time. The most authoritative chiefs could not have done so, even had they been inclined to attempt prosecution; and such inclination was entirely wanting on their part, as the next chapter will disclose.

Another man was put on the route with his team, and the mail went on regularly. But this man, traveling on a cut-off road that ran nearly south from the Running Water crossing after leaving the Rawhide Butte road to the west and approaching Fort Laramie from the east, was jumped by a war party in the hills near Box Springs six miles east of the post. Engaging the Indians in a spirited fight, he succeeded in holding them off with a new repeating rifle that he handled so effectively that they finally withdrew altogether, and he was able to make his way to the post hospital with nine bullet wounds on his person and a badly wounded team. Fortunately, he finally recovered.

A record of this incident has been inserted here to show that anything was liable to happen during an ordinary day in that period on the extreme frontier of our middle west. So much bombastic trash has been written that those lacking knowledge of the facts are justly inclined to think it all faked adventure.[3]

Returning to the point where the unfortunate mail man met his death, we followed the return bends of the detour and soon were again among the trees where the embryo river, in the form of a rippling brook, wound its serpentine course through the falling leaves that were stirred from their branches by the cool October breeze.

Within a mile or two of the mouth of this picturesque canyon where the little valleys begin to broaden, we came upon a bevy of Indian boys with bows and arrows out hunting birds, rabbits, or any small wild life they chanced to find. They ranged from eight to fourteen years of age, and seemed to be having a great deal of fun until they paused to stare at us. Among the group of youngsters I discovered what to me was a startling freak of nature, and I began staring myself. These boys all wore the long black hair hanging down over their shoulders and backs, Indian style, except two who kept to the style but not the color. Their hair was grey, the grey of a white person fifty or sixty years old.

I learned from Big Bat that all except these two were boys that belonged to a camp of the Arapaho that we were approaching, and that the youngsters whose extraordinary locks attracted my attention were brothers and belonged to a Cheyenne family whose children nearly always were grey at birth. Hence the name of the family was Grey Hairs.[4]

The road left the little stream with its numerous springs that gradually broadened and deepened into the White River, and rose to the top of a hill at the edge of an extended valley surrounded by irregular pine ridges. Immediately in front of us on either side of the road an extended Arapaho village met our gaze. A little farther on, near the mouth of Soldier Creek, Fort Robinson was situated; and up this branch still farther to the north, but near by, was a large Cheyenne village. To the east, in plain view, was a cluster of buildings, and from the front of one rose a crude miniature tower with portico attachments which, through the haze of morning, were suggestive of some ancient feudal castle.

This was the Red Cloud Agency, and about it, up the small rivulets that came out of the hills, camps of family groups of lodges were scattered in every direction. However, Red Cloud's main camp of thousands a little farther east was obscured by a low chain of grass-covered hills.

All this interesting panorama lay before me as we dismounted and I stood holding our horses while Big Bat delivered his despatches to the commander of the post.[5] When he rejoined me I learned that he was given the remainder of the day, October 26th, and the next to rest before returning to Fort Laramie. So we cantered merrily down toward the agency.

Just before reaching the promontory on which the agency stood, we came to a spring creek on which stood a cluster of tall trim lodges that we visited, as their owner, Rocky Bear, was one of the head men of the Oglala and a relative of Big Bat's Indian family. Nearby were three neatly built double log houses that were occupied by white men with Indian families, and with whom we had become acquainted on the Laramie River. They were David Cottier, a Frenchman; John Davidson, an American; and Manuel Romero, a Mexican.[6] During our visit these residents of the village insisted that we be their guests while we remained at the agency. It was then agreed that I would stop with them and Big Bat would visit his interpreter friends at the agency proper.

Accordingly my horse was placed in their bunch, and after visiting for a while I sauntered up to the agency and amused myself by looking it over. I met a number of old acquaintances, among whom was a young mixed-blood interpreter then known as Billy Hunter, but whose real name was William Garnett.[7] With this young man whom I had known on the Laramie I had dinner, then, having already looked over the structural arrangement of the agency, I stayed and learned much of its daily topics of interest. I found that uppermost in the minds of its residents was the controversy between Dr. Saville, the Indian Agent, and Chief Red Cloud over the erection of a flag-staff.[8]

It seems that the Indians at this time, being entirely ignorant of the general significance of this simple patriotic ceremony of raising the flag over all public institutions, felt that the flag was only an emblem of their natural enemy—not of the soldiers themselves, but of the army in action; and that in some way the placing of the flag over the agency would make soldiers of them.

Red Cloud and many (but not all) of his head men joined in the opposition to the raising of the flag. It is said that Red Cloud in emphatic tones told the agent that it should not be done; that the soldiers already had the flag floating over their fort, and they should be satisfied with that.

The agent, being right and knowing it, told Red Cloud with equal emphasis that the flag would be raised. It was reported that the chief and the agent had several quarrels over the matter, when one day the agent's teams pulled into the yard with a fine, tall pole and deposited it in the court under the angry glances of many eyes; but no actual opposition arose, and the men went on about their business.

Whether these controversies over the flag-raising were conducted in a calm prudent, and conciliatory manner on the part of the agent is not now known, but current rumor had it that both he and the chief were hot-headed. One thing is certain, if the agent permitted temper to usurp the place of cool reasoning, he and many others soon had ample cause to regret it.

The last Oglala agency to be named for Chief Red Cloud was situated in a picturesque bend of the White River a mile or two above the present site of the city of Crawford, Nebraska. It stood on fairly level ground and was built in form of a square, with its principal face to the south, but it also faced the east and the west, with the inner space at the rear of the buildings forming a sort of court. To the north were located the wood and hay yards, with the barn and large barnyards on the crest of the hill that leads down to the river. All of the long ricks of dry pitch-pine cordwood, the long, tall stacks of hay—in fact, everything save the three entrances of the main building, were surrounded by a tall fence of native pine lumber furnished by the sawmill on the river bank below the hill.

On each side of the main buildings, across the space of an average town square but not at very regular angles, were numerous log residences and the traders' stores. These were three stores conducted by their respective owners, namely, J. W. Dear, Frank Yates and Walters Brothers.[9]

A word about Fort Robinson, which I had previously visited and observed with some care. It comprised all the buildings considered necessary to the customary military post of the frontier, but larger than were required for the few companies of cavalry then occupying it. These buildings, like those of the agency, were of rough lumber sawed from the nearby pines, with here and there one of sawed or peeled logs. Near all the living quarters, mess houses and the bakery were ricks of fine, dry pine wood. Hundreds of cords of the same fuel were ricked at right angles on the east and north fronts of the main buildings, serving as temporary fence and windbreak. In the yards near the spacious barn were long, tall ricks containing hundreds of tons of hay.

I had noticed these details naturally, without any particular motive, as one is apt to do on entering an interesting place for the first time; but this picture in a different setting came vividly to my mind less than twenty-four hours later.

Having spent the afternoon and evening in visiting and looking over the agency, I returned to the cabins for the night. Here I found another man added to the party—George Armstrong, an itinerant laborer and professional wood-chopper—who had drifted in from his camp in the hills for supplies and a short visit. Thus it was that five men went to sleep in the several cabins that night and awakened the next morning to a day of strange entertainment.

CHAPTER 4

Red Cloud Cuts the Flag-Pole

Part Two

There seemed nothing unusual about the early morning of October 27, 1874.[1] The same clear sunshine tempered the soft, balmy breezes that characterized the late fall weather in this latitude. Yet everyone seemed to feel that strange events were pending. Rumors? Yes. The air was full of them. It seemed that everyone eagerly sought or more eagerly gave of them. On the western front the denizens of those vast spaces listened to and liked them. To them, rumor was the spice in the lonely monotony of their lives, as radio is to the lonely lives today. They knew, of course, that rumor was always accompanied by the aggravating static of unreliability; but they also knew it to be self-analyzing, and that sooner or later its component parts, its truth—if any—would stand revealed.

As visitors, mostly women, were continually coming and going to and from the Rocky Bear lodge, rumors of the flag dispute grew thicker and darker. We remarked also that riders were beginning to scatter hither and yon in rather systematic order. Most of them were in warrior regalia, their steeds painted in varied colors and manes and tails decked with feathers of gaudy hues. We soon discovered that each hill and prominent knoll was occupied by several warriors, sitting on their mounts silently in the capacity of lookout sentinels.

Our view from the depression incident to the spring branch was not extensive to the east and south, but to the north the short distance to the box elder trees that skirted the river and the high stone hills beyond was unobstructed. It was also clear up the river to the post and the Cheyenne and Arapaho villages, and the whole pine-encircled amphitheater in which they nestled. To the south and west, as far as the base of the timbered hills, only the outlines of a galaxy of small prairie hills were visible. We could see the lodges farthest south of the agency and the open spaces near them, and about each of these we saw bunches of ponies, all hobbled.

At the time I was not sufficiently versed in the customs of the Indians to realize the significance of the arrangement; and my companions, thinking perhaps that I knew as well as they, said nothing of the fact that these ponies were being held in readiness to be packed or hitched to travois containing all the camp equipment of their owners, should occasion arise.

It was about nine o'clock when first a low, rumbling sound from the east reached our ears. As its source approached it grew louder and clearer and was easily recognized as the thundering of horses' hoofs, and we realized that the threat of opposing the flag-raising was being carried out. We could also distinguish the sounds incident to the hurrying and scurrying of the people at the agency and adjacent lodges.

Presently Rocky Bear came slowly down the hill road, turned to the bend in which his ponies were feeding, and dismounted as he took off the hobbles. He then remounted and drove them past us up to a small corral that the cabin owners had improvised for the purpose of handling their work-horses conveniently. He let down the bars and drove the ponies in, then replaced them, mounted, and rode up to the old woman who had remained to watch the lodge. Then, after exchanging a few words with her in low tones, he rode past us again in stoical silence on his return trip to the agency.

The speed of the charge had slackened as the riders neared the lodges east of the agency buildings. The wild, rhythmic sound that for some time had mingled with the clatter of hammering hoofs now swelled into the ancient war song of the Sioux, and was pierced continually with their shuddering yells of defiance.

Thus far we had judged the momentous proceedings by the sounds arising therefrom, but our understanding was afterward fully verified by the many recitals of those within the stockade—that inviting but dangerous trap that appeared to be the only shelter from the terror confronting them. It soon contained not only the agent and all of his employees, but every civilized person in the vicinity except ourselves and one or two others who were caught on the east side of the agency.

We were on the west side, which was no ill luck, however, for had the riot gotten from under control (which at all times it seemed on the point of doing) there was but one fate awaiting all—death, either swift or lingering, with the additional horror of cremation for those who would have faced their slayers inside the stockade or at the military post.

I learned from John Farnham (who was employed at the agency at that time) and from Big Bat and others, that Louis Richards and Joseph Bissonette, Jr., were then the official interpreters of the agency. They were intelligent mixed-bloods of the Sioux, of middle age and of standing and influence among their people. Others of the same class were equally efficient as interpreters, among them Louis Shangreau and William Garnett, who, with the two first mentioned, were of the Oglala—Red Cloud's band of Sioux.[2]

There were other interpreters who chanced to be present from the Spotted Tail and Missouri River bands, Louis Bordeau, John Bruguier and Louis Robideaux. Bordeau was official interpreter at the Spotted Tail Agency, and was noted for his fluent command of both the English and the Sioux Indian language.[3] There were several others whose names I failed to learn, but all were of mixed blood. No white interpreter was used on that occasion. It required men of the tribe who were loyal to both sides to be effective, and only through the untiring efforts of these men was catastrophe averted.

Under the direction of the agent and the guidance of the experienced men about him in a room just behind the portico platform from which they spoke, these men, in relays of two, were kept busy constantly haranguing their excited and misguided brethren in the interest of peace.

All those on the agency hill could see the approaching mass of men, estimated to have been about fifteen hundred mounted warriors, increasing their speed gradually but methodically until within half a mile from the agency, where they began their charge. They showed down as they came to the outer edge of the village, through which they scattered and reassembled on the open spaces about the buildings. There they came to a halt while Red Cloud, accompanied by several of his sub-chiefs, opened and passed through the double gates, then marched out to the center of the court where lay the pole that was to have served as flagstaff. Here, with axes that had been hidden under their blankets, they cut the pole into short lengths and then returned, to disappear among their waiting comrades. Immediately John Farnham was despatched to the gate, to take the part of "Horatio at the Bridge."

During all of this time there was a roar of argument voicing conflicting sentiments among the Indians assembled in front, and earnest pleadings for peace from the interpreters on the balcony.

The advocates for and against the execution of a sentence of death and destruction continued hour after hour. Often they came to blows with whips or bows (wild Indians did not use their fists) on the heads and shoulders of their opponents, accompanied by assorted epithets. "Get back, you coward!" "Begone to the lodge with the other women; you are only brave in a crowd." "Would you kill your own relations? Many in there are our sons and nephews." "Think of your women and children being driven with hunger through winter storms by the soldiers that will follow us."

Admonitions of this tenor were continuous among the shrieks and yells of the opposing forces, in unison with the fervid preaching of the interpreters from the balcony. And the never-ceasing stream of pacific oratory rolling out over the heads of the avengers was steadily producing the desired effect as the hours passed.

The women of the nearby lodges and camps, practically all of whom were for peace, contributed their share to the cause by following the usual Indian custom of preparing feasts for all, friend and stranger alike. These not busy with the food mingled with the seething throng, collecting them in parties of three to five by coaxing them to "Come and eat," and taking care that a goodly number of the most rabid agitators were in each party. Always the invitation was accepted, and, stalking sullenly or riding, they went in to the feast. Though they ate rapidly and returned at once to the strife, it was with temper more pliable and demeanor more sane, try as they would to conceal it.

This was true also of the massed cordon of those on foot completely surrounding the stockade, who had enlarged knotholes and cut other openings through the high board fence with their butcher-knives, giving them a clear view of everything within. They carried tufts of dry grass under their blankets, and were ready at the signal to hurl firebrands onto the ricks of wood and stacks of hay in the yard.

After feasting, however, their number had dwindled and they seemed much less intent upon trouble. These details were hidden from us by the elevated ground, but were noted carefully by those in the stockade who let no incident escape them. Our view up the river was clear, and we could see not only the post but the Cheyenne and Arapaho villages and their surroundings.

It was nearly eleven o'clock and we were moving about our restricted space in the cabin yards when there came riding coolly and quietly down the road from the agency a young man who was recognized at once as Michael Dunn, the boss of the beef herd a few miles south.[4] It seems that he was at the agent's office and was caught with the others. He was acting in the capacity of courier to the post, to which service he had volunteered. We divined the purpose of the trip and admired his unconcerned attitude and even gait—his surest warrant of safety. The Indian outlooks on the many hills paid little or no attention to his movements.

It was not long after he entered the post until we saw a file of cavalrymen move out and take the road toward us. As the detail passed we counted some twenty-five or thirty men, with Mike Dunn riding in front beside an officer whom my companions recognized as Lieutenant Crawford.[5]

This passing of soldiers toward the stockade was the most ominous incident we had yet observed. My companions, who understood Indians, felt positive that their appearance would be like a lighted match to the magazine, and that their smaller number was an invitation. For a short time it seemed that their prophecy was to be fulfilled, for when the detail first appeared on the scene we could hear pandemonium break loose in wild yells and the resumption of noisy strife. Then there was a rush for the soldiers which the peace party frustrated, and this led to another and more personal mix-up in which the usual taunting language was heard, together with vigorous whipping over the head with quirts and switches. Occasionally a few braves broke through, but were forced back before they reached the soldiers. It was said that one of the warriors laid hold of Lieutenant Crawford's bridle rein, but the Lieutenant reached down and caught him by the shoulder, whirling him from the path as he kept steadily on to the gates, that were quickly opened by John Farnham and as quickly closed after the detail had filed through.[6]

It was natural and fitting that when the little city of Crawford sprang up at this historic point, it should be named for the man who so heroically executed his orders that day in the face of a picture that could not have portrayed certain death more vividly. It was for this and other meritorious conduct during the years that followed that this gallant officer received the promotions rapidly accorded him.[7]

The friends of Red Cloud claimed that he had overplayed his hand and lost control of the situation, as his only object was to prevent the raising of the flag. It was said that he and his advisors had remained inactive in a nearby lodge during the whole disturbance. Be that as it may, another staff was soon secured and the flag went up without opposition.[8]

I have never learned of a reasonable excuse for sending for those soldiers. Under the circumstances they could not have rendered any saving service. They were a dangerous aggravation to the Indians at first, but a different idea soon prevailed among them. They did not even try to follow the soldiers through the gate. Why should they? If the threatened storm had broken, they would have been just so many more mice in the trap. The troop was well equipped with arms—yes; but so were we all. Arms, when outnumbered a hundred to one, might just as well have been toothpicks.

However, so far as the question of safety was concerned, the little detail might as well be there as at their home post, of which we had a complete view. The verdure between us, which for years had been ravaged by fire and by the later onslaught of camps and herds, was not dense, and from the earliest agitation at the agency to the close of the disturbance we could see that all of the prairie ground lying between the post and the base of the pine-covered hills to the west and north was black with Cheyenne and Arapaho warriors. Sitting silently on their mounts, they virtually surrounded the post on all sides save the east which faced the agency. The significance of this arrangement was plain, as they were waiting for the first puff of smoke to go up over the stockade as a signal for the onslaught, and they would have duplicated at the post whatever occurred at the agency. This means that within ten minutes from the receipt of such a signal, the weakly garrisoned post would have been a seething inferno, with Death stalking on every side over its parade grounds and through all of its byways. The tinder of its pine structures and other inflammable material would have furnished a flaming sepulcher for those who remained in the post, and those who fled would have met death at the hands of the cordon of Indians who awaited their appearance.

As the afternoon wore away the portents of peace became more apparent. The watchers on the hills were constantly but quietly retiring from their positions, and the babble of voices was subsiding to more frequent lulls. About half past two o'clock the troop of cavalry marched back to the post; groups of Indian riders could be seen frequently, moving toward the east; and the women were returning to their several homes. Then Rocky Bear came riding past, and, seeing a more serene face as he lowered the bars and turned his ponies out to graze, we knew that the nightmare of uncertainty was ended.

From that moment until bedtime we were in constant conversation with those who had witnessed the whole proceeding. It was then we learned that before the boss herder, Michael Dunn, had volunteered to take a despatch to the post, the agent had sent a loyal Indian, named Speeder, on the same mission, but his own people had intercepted him and beat him so badly that he lived only a short time.

The following morning Big Bat and I started on our return trip, leisurely. About midnight we camped in the hills twenty-five miles north of Fort Laramie and rested in our saddle-blankets until the grey dawn, then proceeded to the post and home.

CHAPTER 5

Freighting to the Black Hills

In the early summer of 1876, after laying aside a nice, flourishing garden that I had planted on one of the fertile bends of the river and had carefully cultivated the previous year, I joined with a couple of my freighting friends, Amos Battelyoun, who had an eight-mule team, and Austin W. Means with a six-horse-and-mule team, and started for Cheyenne to get a load of freight for Deadwood.[1]

The price paid for freight to that point, starting at the alluring figure of fifteen cents a pound, had been gradually falling as the roads became more passable and teams from surrounding states were flocking in to share in the hauling. This we had heard from the outside, and we found it to be a fact as we traveled down the long hill to the plateau north of Cheyenne, upon which that city is beautifully situated.

Most of the many large board corrals were then located at the northeast edge of the city and were literally teeming with young shave-tail mules, and the green grass openings near them were covered with stacked parts of new red wagons that men were busy assembling. Others were as busily engaged in leading out mules over the plain in practice driving—furnishing the passing spectators with a real Wild West wagon rodeo.

The newly established business men of the Black Hills had made arrangements with the older mercantile houses of Cheyenne to receive and ship their goods. The I. C. Whipple firm and the Nagle General Merchandise Company did most of their business at that time.[2]

Charles Miller of the Nagle Company, who managed most of the shipping, was always very considerate of the small freighters with only two or three wagons, and when possible he favored them with the most desirable freight.[3]

Mr. Miller informed us that he had on hand only a rough, miscellaneous assortment of freight, but if we would wait a day or two a trainload would arrive from which he could fit us out nicely. We took his advice and waited. We were staying (as did most of the individual wagoners) at the commodious barns, corrals and dwellings, each provided with iron cots and conveniences for cooking, in the northwest part of town and owned by a man named Tracy.[4]

We were not strangers in the city by any means, as our many previous visits had made us familiar with the location of the bright lights where "joy was unconfined"—as well as the pitfalls inseparable from such places.

The vaudeville and variety shows were many, and all were running at full capacity from three in the afternoon until about the same hour next morning, with always a host of hilarious patrons. Of all these attractions, the old McDaniels Theater ranked highest.[5]

All kinds of business were represented here, forming a part of the magical panorama of this throbbing, thrilling, thriving city of the plains. The chief lines were barber shops, saloons and hotels, also an assortment of eating places. Of barbers, though numerous, there seemed none too many; for, aside from the local trade, there were arriving at all times from all points north a string of freighters, ranch hands and travelers, the sight of whose matted locks and dust-laden whiskers would stampede a modern community. The first thought of these men was to get a shave or trim, haircut and bath. The barbers of that day were not lacking in high-pressure trade talk, but their new-fangled accessories and tonsorial fads were not so numerous then as now. They relied upon the shampoo for big money.

There was a certain story to the effect that several of the old "barber boys" kept out of sight a convenient tin which they used as a corral for a choice assortment of greybacks produced by prior customers, who had long been roughing it in the wilds and had plenty of them to spare. The use of these nimble and aggressive little creatures was never resorted to unless the customer proved deaf to the tonsorial arguments in favor of a shampoo. But when this was the case and the artist saw that his linguistic batteries were without effect, there would be an adroit movement and lo! the barber held between thumb and finger a live and struggling louse which he displayed to the astonished customer—and the shampoo was on.

Cheyenne at that time was an "all-night town," and at no time were all of the places of amusement and drinking closed. Some were always open to the night hawks who delighted in prowling and howling through the "wee sma' hours" when right- minded people were asleep; but, all in all, Cheyenne was a fine little city. Only for a short time did it serve to portray in shadow that which shortly after became a real picturesque panorama of the wild life at Deadwood, South Dakota. All of this was changed when transportation became available and the fantastic high life of the old wild frontier moved north to the gold fields.

We soon received loads of very desirable freight which, from a freighter's point of view, is freight that is not dead weight but will yield and spring when subjected to the continual jar of the road, and which can be most easily loaded and unloaded if the wagon should become stuck and need to be unloaded to extricate it—which often occurred.

We were soon out on our way and in a few days were back in Fort

Laramie, where we were stopped by military orders and made to wait until our number should increase to a point where we were considered able to take care of ourselves against the hostile Indians. It was the latter part of June 1876, and as we had heard of the Custer Massacre on our departure from Cheyenne, we were not surprised to learn of orders to wait until our party should be strengthened by added numbers.[6] In fact, at the fort we first heard of the killing of the Metz family in Red Canyon and of other attacks, hence were glad to wait for the strong escort which was not long in arriving.[7] On about the fifth day of our lay-over we numbered thirty-six teams and were permitted to depart, with instructions to organize and to be constantly on the lookout for an attack.

So we left Fort Laramie. Crossing the North Platte on the new government steel bridge, we followed what was once an old road but at this time was being used again. It led up a small stream flowing from the north side of Rawhide Hills, thence to a small valley up in the hills known as the Government Farm, for the soldiers at the fort had farmed it for a couple seasons before a great Chinese Wheel had been placed in the swift current of the Laramie, above the post, for irrigation. In this little valley, with its evidences of former habitation, we made an early camp and supper.[8]

Then we proceeded to organize. As head of the expedition we chose Jerome Parrot. He had two good six-mule teams and two drivers whom he, well mounted, supervised. It was soon apparent that we had made a good choice, for as manager and wagon boss he proved very efficient. He chose two assistants from the extra men who were interested in some of the wagons; and from other extras who were working their way to the hills he selected several night herders and mounted them on extra saddle horses, with which the train was well supplied. Our organization was then complete and functioned efficiently.

The next morning our teams were all in the corral formed by our wagons, and after feeding them and ourselves we got an early start on a comparatively new but clearly marked road. That night we camped on the Running Water, which runs east and helps to form the Niobrara River in Nebraska. At this camp we laid over one day to give everyone—especially the women of the several families—a chance to rest and wash up, to repair the wagons and rearrange the loads.

We made camp the next night on Hat Creek at the stage station ranch kept by Jack Bowman. Here a company of infantry under command of Lieutenant Taylor was also located.[9] The following morning we traveled about six miles east through a fairly level meadow of waving grasses and wild flowers, over a road that led to the top of a hilly ridge and turned northward. From this point we could see Hat Creek and the tops of the trees on Indian Creek. It was here that the Indians, a short time before, had attacked a wagon train which, to their surprise, happened to have small military escort from the Fifth United States Cavalry and with which was the famous Buffalo Bill. The Indians were soon repulsed with the loss of their leader, who was said to have been shot by the noted scout himself.[10] Here too the stage coach, on its trip to Cheyenne, sustained an attack on this road of rough hills and ravines all the way to where it turned north to the Cheyenne River. With their six horses on a dead run and the guards firing on the war party from the top of the stage, they made their escape with no loss of life. But one man, known as "Stuttering Brown," was seriously wounded while riding with the driver.[11]

We camped at noon that day on the ridge above Alum Springs; and for the night on the Cheyenne River a few miles west of where the road crossed it. Just before reaching the crossing next morning our road led into a grove of young cottonwood trees through which the Cheyenne Stage Company had cut the way, using the felled trees to corduroy the boggy swales that they encountered. But we found these in quite bad condition and soon had to begin doubling teams—a great time-consumer to an outfit of any size. Finally our manager crossed to the ranch on the opposite side and came back with its proprietor, named Madden. With them they brought a four-mule team, chains, lead bars, and all the necessary tackle. Then they began doubling the stalled teams over the marshy ground and onto the plateau near the ranch, where they waited for the rest of the train.[12]

It was nearly three o'clock before we were assembled again. Without making camp for dinner we moved on to the mouth of Red Canyon, where we encamped for the night on a picturesque little flat through which ran a rivulet of pure water from the mountainous country north of us.

Early next morning we were winding our way up through the narrow passes and dark defiles of Red Canyon. The continuous crossing of the little creek that runs through it made our progress very slow, so when we came to a fair-sized plateau in one of its bends we camped for the noon hour. A rock wall of considerable height rose near the trail to the west, while a short distance east of us the bank of the creek was skirted with tall cottonwoods and box elder trees, with shrubbery covering the ground.

It was at this spot beneath the inviting shade that the Metz family—a man and wife with several children and a colored cook—were massacred shortly before. They had come from Laramie City, Wyoming, en route to Deadwood, and of course were unaware of the vast number of Sioux, Cheyenne and Arapaho Indians who were returning from the Custer carnage and scattering through the country, like ants, from Canada to Nebraska. Peacefully enjoying a rest in the shady camping spot, they were the first to become prey of one of those savage bands as the Indians started forth on their devil's holiday. We saw the graves in which they had first been placed, and from which they were taken back to Laramie City.

About the middle of that afternoon our train emerged from the canyon and came out into an expanse of rolling prairie of considerable extent, but surrounded by timbered hills on all sides. On the northern edge of this stretch of open country, near some springs, we stopped for the night.

The next morning our road led to the northwest and up a well-grassed valley that grew narrower as it neared the mountainous country ahead of us. As we left this valley our road turned to the right over pine-covered foothills on either side of the little stream that our road seemed to follow; then it started up through a pass of smaller hills and out into small occasional prairies surrounded by pines. We traveled through this variegated scenery, then descended into the valley of French Creek and made early camp a few miles above Custer City. Later a number of us strolled down the valley to the town, enjoying the various sights and making a few purchases. On our way we passed several mining camps, constructed partly of logs and partly of native lumber.[13]

Custer, at that time, consisted of several well-furnished general stores and the usual quota of hardware stores, barber shops, restaurants and candy shops, saloons, dance halls, and the accompanying hilarity. It was a typical mining town. When we returned to camp we learned that the train was to lie over the next day for a rest and clean-up, also to give the animals a rest and chance to graze.

This news was pleasing to us, as it does not take long for people traveling slowly and camping frequently to become uncomfortably grimy and out of sorts. A change of clothing was also indicated, and our supply was low. During the time that we had camped on questionable grounds at Fort Laramie we had become infected with vermin, and campers along well beaten trails know that greybacks are prolific.

Thus it was that when the sun had risen over the tips of the mountains on the east, the many cool clear, eddying pools in the numerous bends of French Creek became temporary bath-houses with laundry attachments. Beginning early in the evening and continuing through the following morning, the ant-hills that abounded there were covered with parcels of soiled clothes so that the ants might have the first chance of cleaning the garments of vermin. This custom of using ants as shock troops to annihilate the lice was often resorted to by travelers even though the stop was but an hour or two, as it assured the annoyed one of temporary relief at least.

Most of the men remained at camp during the afternoon, while others went scouting over the mountains and brought back specimens of rock that were strange to us. The most attractive were the many lustrous rubies found along the banks of French Creek. They ranged in size from a bead to a large garden pea and were very pretty but none was perfect, as each had a flaw of some sort.[14]

The receding sun had just begun to withdraw its light from the fast-forming shadows on the western slopes of the mountains. Various topics were being disposed of by more or less heated discussions. The ant and its wonderful power in proportion to size had been dwelt upon, when to the surprise of all a tall and gawky individual came forward with the positive assertion that a greyback could whip an ant. Of course he was disputed instantly, whereupon he offered to back his assertion with a plug of tobacco. He was called by many, with the result that both chewing and smoking tobacco, boxes of matches, penknives and other trinkets were soon placed in the hands of stake-holders. Those betting accepted the one condition made by the challenger, that he be permitted to select and arrange the arena for the combat. Then began a search for husky specimens of the little animals that were to decide the affair, while the gawky individual shuffled away to his wagon. Soon all returned. The fight promoter then cleared off a small place on the ground and, slipping a new and perfectly clean tin plate from under his sweater, set it level on the cleared spot, then placed the combatants in the center of the plate and the bugs went into their battle.

The ant, a fine specimen, attempted at once to charge the louse, that perhaps it deemed easy prey to be hoisted with its foremost tentacles. Instead, it slipped and fell, but regained its feet with some effort, and made the second advance.

The greyback, in perfect imitation of an angry boar brought to bay by a hound, rose to brace itself on its haunches and receive the impact with its snout thrust forward, disclosing the little incisors—its only weapon.

The ant again failed to reach its opponent, for as it crouched to charge it slipped back further than before. When the wiry little creature regained equilibrium it tried strategy by an approach at the side or back of the other bug, but the porky little louse, without leaving the original position on the smooth, glossy center of the plate, slowly turned to meet the ant from any angle it chose to approach.

The ant's backers had long since bid good-by to their little bets and were enjoying the fun with the rest of us when, just as the ant had withdrawn to the rim of the plate which it tried in vain to scale, the herd was driven into camp and all of us scattered to catch and feed our teams and attend to the evening's chores. The winner, after disposing of the warriors, took his cheaply won prizes and went back to his mess kit.

Then and Now

This digression is the result of a suggestion made by a friend (Joe Johnson of Hot Springs, South Dakota), to the effect that it would interest him much to travel over the stretch of country just described by automobile instead of a loaded freight wagon, and to mark the changes time had wrought during the lapse of fifty-six years. The fact that he had been ranching in that particular section for a long time and was thoroughly familiar with it, besides knowing all of the people who lived along the route, prompted me to take advantage of the opportunity he offered.

Accordingly, early in April of 1932 we started for the city of Edgemont, South Dakota. As its name implies, it is located in the southern edge of the Black Hills, on the Cheyenne River.

As we approached the river a short distance below the town, I recognized the pine bluffs that range along its southern banks, the cottonwood grove that lies between them, and the river where we had such difficulty in getting through the swamps and swales. The bank where the old road came up out of the river and meandered off to the mouth of Red Canyon in the northwest was also recognizable. After visiting friends in Edgemont and refueling the car, we followed the road that led to our first camp grounds at the mouth of the canyon.

This old camping ground appeared strangely changed, yet it grew more familiar as I walked over it endeavoring to form a mental picture that would bridge the gulf of years. Following the highway that hugs the base of the hills, first on one side of the creek and then on the other, every now and then we passed an old, deserted log house and several neat little houses nestled in the small open space formed at the junction with a lesser canyon. Soon we came out on the edge of open country, where we stopped at a ranch, well stocked and improved, belonging to Ralph Fay, whose estimable wife served us a fine dinner. During the enjoyment of this meal the conversation centered on the exact spot where the Metz massacre occurred, as it had become a subject of controversy among the later settlers.

After dinner, in company with Mr. Fay, we retraced our steps down the canyon and explored the ground thoroughly. Every indication of the topography fitted my recollections. I walked over the plateau and the sod-covered yet still distinguishable old trail and found that the hills on each side were familiar, but the creek and its banks on the east side of the little valley had been so torn up by flood-erosion through the years that it became a puzzle. Where I had stood by the shallow, gaping graves that had held those bodies for a time, the floods had torn the soil asunder and the roots of the huge trees were washed to the sun. Moreover, the underbrush of a younger grove had so completely changed the landscape that the best I could do was to say, "I believe this to be the place."

As we followed the highway out across the rolling prairie previously mentioned, the changes that had taken place were quite impressive. Then, nothing but a vast stillness seemed to prevail, broken only by the sudden scampering of wild game and the flurry of birds as they fluttered away at our approach. Now, the hills are interspersed with farms provided with substantial buildings, half hidden by the foliage of orchards and artificial groves, and with men plowing and sowing the cultivated fields.

This variegated panorama of changes continued until we left the old trail of '76 at Custer. Nothing along its winding way had seemed complete and wholly familiar save the "Eternal Hills," their sides clothed in perennial green and their towering tops crowned with the gorgeous glints of shimmering sunshine on varicolored rocks.

CHAPTER 6

On to Deadwood

Both men and animals were refreshed by our short rest, and in the early morning we were on our way. Entering the town from the west on a road that is now a smooth highway, soon we were traveling through the Custer of 1876. After passing over a street leading east, which then was the main thoroughfare, we turned north and entered the mountains on the last leg of our journey. Our train seemed continually to be climbing hills that were farther up than down, till at last we traveled along the very crest of the range that spreads its kaleidoscopic scenery over the sixty miles that separate Custer and Deadwood.

The traveling was rough and our progress slow, and not until mid-afternoon did the terrain begin to slope rapidly downward until from our wagons (which were near the center) we could see the front of the train move out and across a small valley where a cluster of houses nestled on the east side of the road. Just as our wagons were almost opposite, the train came to a stop due to some trouble up in front. There were perhaps half a dozen log houses, well built of new logs and covered with dirt. Some of them showed two or more good-sized rooms and looked like pleasant home places, but all were empty and seemed to have been so for a long time. These few buildings comprised all there was of what is now Hill City, another live and thriving town.[1]

Several of the teamsters left their wagons and went to inspect the vacant houses and to gather the berries that grew near by, but when they heard the front wagons rumble into motion they hastily sought their own wagons as we passed on. The rumor was noised along the train that the owners of the empty houses had heard the call of some newly pro-claimed Eldorado and, with bag and baggage, had joined the stampede for that place. We saw no person during our passing to explain the mystery of this deserted village, but subsequent developments proved that no second Goldsmith was needed to sing its death knell.

We forded many small streams, and occasionally one that would have been difficult to ford was provided with a strong, safe bridge of logs over which the toll was twenty-five cents per team—a fee that we were glad to pay. The shacks of these toll collectors were sometimes built where a new better grade had been whittled out of a protruding bank and the road worked to permit the freighter to make a cut-off or avoid some long, steep hill over a road primarily blazed by the Indians, hunters and early prospectors. This was the work of the Western Stage Company and others with but one idea, to provide passage along its narrow, stony surface over which the wagon wheels played a constant tattoo among the shifting rocks that furnished a succession of jolts and jars to the traveler.[2]

But not all of the trail required such tedious floundering. We might next find ourselves winding around the side of some heavily timbered mountain whose towering trees extended both above and below the road until lost in the depths of a canyon. Again, we might find complete relaxation in moving easily through the stretches of a smooth green valley that lay between lofty peaks, each one of which, as it sloped down to the valley, was fringed with little groves of cedar and fir.

After enjoying such scenes for a time, our train might come to broken foot-hills with stony stretches of road, or move over an extensive plateau of rich black soil covered with a forest of tall pines. Some of these trees measured three to four feet in diameter and their first branches were set high upon the trunk. They were commercial timber. Often two of these trees stood so close together, cutting off the only possible road, that broad, deep notches had been chopped between each near side of them to allow passage for the wagons. This was "the forest primeval."

We made our camps night by night on the clear, cool streams abounding in that section, but to us most of them were nameless and it would be almost impossible for me to designate them now.

No incident of import occurred on this, the last stage of our journey. When our attention could be spared from guiding our teams over the rough places, it was intently fixed on the wild, romantic beauty of the ever-changing scenery. But finally we experienced the thrill of winding down the long, dangerous grade of the high hill under which the railroad tunnel now passes, at the foot of which lay Deadwood, South Dakota.[3]

Naturally, our movement as a train ended with our arrival. We scattered at once, each seeking the owner of the freight he had brought. I soon found the one to whom my load of sacked onions was consigned—a grocer named Berry whose store stood on the south side of the main street at the extreme west end.[4] Upon stopping at the rear of his store and reporting my arrival, his help was at once put to work carrying in the sacks. I told him I had eaten some of the onions on the trip. "That's all right!" he remarked absently. After passing a few sacks over the scales and glancing at the condition of the rest, he told the boys to stack them up without weighing, returned to his desk, and began to weigh the gold-dust for payment. I asked for and received sufficient currency for expenses. While the yellow dust was being weighed and poured into a chamois poke at one end of the counter, the onions I had brought were being weighed and sold at twenty-five cents a pound to a crowd of anxiously waiting customers at the other end of the counter.

Our mess consisted of three besides myself, and we had decided on a large barn in the eastern part of town, with a high board corral which extended to the creek in the rear, as our rendezvous. The street had been crowded with heavy freight wagons drawn by long strings of oxen, mules or horses, but as all the drivers observed the rule of the road for right-handed passing, we got along very nicely with the "traffic cop" and I soon joined the others at the big corral.

With our weary animals turned loose where they could run at will to a long rick filled with hay, and with plenty of grain and water, we decided to remain a day or two and let them roll or rest as they chose. Our empty covered wagons formed our bunks, an there was a room equipped with conveniences for cooking; but, being anxious for a respite from camp fare, we browsed among the many restaurants.

After an early, enjoyable supper we set forth to be properly tonsured. Some had their whiskers put on paper; others retained them to adorn their shirt-fronts and incidentally obviate the need of a necktie—never popular among the rough and ready men of the time. Then we donned our best togs, which would not mean much to an easterner, but we thought we looked real pretty as we helped occupy the many chairs and benches ranged outside the office and front of the barn. There we exchanged experiences with our corral neighbors and smoked until an early bedtime, for we were very tired and knew that the sights of Deadwood would remain for twenty-four hours at least.

As I lay on my well-aired blankets that were on the floor of a spacious wagon-box, with the wagon cover fastened up on each side to permit the cool mountain breezes to fan over me, the sounds floating down the long street from the town were not exactly soothing lullabies to induce sleep. Too often they were punctuated by shrill yells and the crack of a forty-five. However, such whoopee was not particularly disturbing, as I was too well aware of what a large percentage of healthy, husky pioneers considered a good time to let their racket annoy me. Finally the various noises blended with the gurgling water of the creek and the sighing wind through the pines, and I slept to awaken to a miniature world in coma.

We were up early, as was the custom of men in the open, but there was nothing to break the stillness except the "chonk-chonk" of feeding animals and the movements of the men who cared for them, with now and then the twitter and call of birds as they flitted from pine to pine. Light was being broadcast from the firmament, but the sun had not yet smiled over the peaks of the mountains into the amphitheater which was Deadwood.

When the town began to show signs of normal activity I began to ramble about, with two others of our mess, to look things over. We meandered slowly along the board sidewalks, noting everything attentively as we passed, and when we finally arrived at the west end of the main street we were satisfied that all the necessary lines of business were well represented, with saloons, restaurants and barber shops predominating in the order named—as was usually the case in the "hurry-up" towns of the west.

Most of the frame buildings were constructed of native lumber from the nearest mills, but there were a few well-built log structures also. Here and there some frames were stoutly joined with boards running up and down on the outer sides, leaving the houses to be finished later. Only a few buildings were finished with commercial siding even at the front. The most conspicuous of these was one with a freshly painted front of pea green which came alive in the early evening as the then noted and still historic "Old Green Front."[5]

Having visited this city several times since those days, I am reminded that the primitive forests of evergreen growth interspersed with towering rocks, which then landscaped the surrounding mountainsides, have gradually yielded to the suburban growth of neat modern homes with smoothly terraced lawns and driveways.

We were well rested as darkness fell on the second night of our sojourn in the Mecca of the mountains, so a few kindred spirits—devotees of sobriety and morality, of whom I was one—decided to make a pilgrimage through its lanes of bright light and mystery in the bloom of its golden era. As the Green Front dance hall was the nearest to our camp, we entered at the time when hilarity was nearing the apex—which had nothing in common with a funeral hush. Its bar room was ten or twelve feet wide, extending the full width of the building, and along its front wall an attractive bar behind which were several busy attendants. In a partition, some ten feet in front of the bar, was a broad archway connecting with a spacious hall. This was the play-room and the main attraction for weary, lonesome, wayfaring strangers. While the back of this hall was reserved for dancing, the space between that and the bar was furnished for the entertainment of visitors, among whom were always potential customers. The space each side of the corridor leading from the dance floor through the archway was provided with tables and chairs where one could rest while listening to the music and be served with refreshments if desired. And there were many who sat quietly watching the dance. Across the room opposite the tables were all manner of gambling devices and always surrounded by an interested group.

The orchestra had just ceased its rhythmic beats as we, mingling with the crowd, were greeted with the clarion call "Waltz your partners to the bar!" Then frenzied men and wild women pushed their way through the arch, lined themselves against the bar, and ordered their favorite refreshments. We edged among the throng until we found a vacant table and seated ourselves for more leisurely observation. As we were not on a mooching party but were willing to pay for our part of the show, as soon as we could catch the eye of one of the busy barmaids we ordered beer and cigars and soon were contributing our share to the pungency of the atmosphere. Happily all the windows were open. By this time the orchestra was off again in high, three sets were whirling in the giddy dance, and some of the dancers were "tripping the nimble foot" most fantastically.

This human phantasmagoria, including the gymnastic contortions and rollicking excursions to and from the bar, the busy attendants, the click of ivory and the clink of coin, the haggard but always smiling gamblers, and the motley crowd of players and potential victims proved to be a fascinating time-consumer, as our watches disclosed.

Exchanging this scene for the hubbub of the street, we frequently met a group of revelers whose penchant for whoopee and gun-music indicated that they thought it "the glorious Fourth." We walked the full length of the street, up one side and down the other, dropping in for the once-over of every place that showed the bright lights of revelry, but we found them "all of a sameness." Some had small rooms at the rear for the more exclusive customers, some had vaudeville attractions, but one general description covered all.[6]

Three noted characters—Jack Crawford, the poet-scout, Calamity Jane and Wild Bill Hickok—were in Deadwood at the time, but we did not meet any of them on our nocturnal tour.[7]

While wending our way back to our wagon abodes, some of our little party became exuberant over the fact that we had seen Deadwood by daylight, starlight and lamplight; but others of us felt that we had seen but the froth and foam of an agitated rivulet, the source of a mighty river of development. We were satisfied that even then, in newly built homes in the suburbs and in the diminutive valleys fringing the surrounding hills, were families planning for the erection of churches, schools, and the organization of other groups that would give their community the hall-mark of a higher order of society. This was in the early days of 1876.

The next day was one of comparative rest. We had only to put our harness, wagons and mess kits in order for the start to be made early next morning. We had our empty wagons, fresh teams and long days and made good time on our return trip, which was without incident. We reached Fort Laramie in the afternoon of the sixth day from Deadwood, having been gone from home about thirty days on this trip.

During the next few years, owing to the influx of large ox and mule freight outfits from all over the country, the smaller outfits found hauling reduced to furnishing hay, wood, and various short-haul supplies for the post. A number of my neighbors had gone to the new Pine Ridge Agency, then under construction, and as they reported that the freighting was good between that point and the Missouri River, from whence the material and supplies were being shipped, I decided to make the move.

Accordingly I disposed of my little place on the Laramie River and completed all necessary arrangements, and early in February 1881, I bade adieu to the storied old post and its picturesque surroundings with a strange feeling of regret.[8]

CHAPTER 7
Old Fort Laramie

In the year 1820 Jacques LaRamie, a French trapper, pitched his tent on the bank of a beautiful stream that came swiftly flowing down through the mountains to the west and emptied its clear waters into the North Platte about two miles below the spot he had chosen for his camp. Subsequent events proved that he had chosen wisely in electing a field for plying the ancient and honorable occupation of fur-gathering. Unfortunately he was drowned in the stream that was to bear his name and, still later, to share that name with one of the most noted military posts in the West.[1]

This central and easily accessible spot in a country full of fur-bearing animals (among them beaver, otter and mink) soon attracted the attention of other trappers and a trading post was established there by Campbell and Sublette which was later purchased by the American Fur Company and called Fort William until subsequently the name was changed to Fort John. It was situated but a short distance from the bank of the Laramie River, and it prospered as a commercial station—chiefly because of the constantly increasing travel over the Oregon Trail (then new) that wound through its irregular streets.[2]

In 1849 the post was purchased by the United States Government and enlarged, fortified and garrisoned by the troops for protection of travel over the Oregon Trail.[3] Then it was rechristened Fort Laramie, and soon became known far and wide as the vedette of a new western world. Under the strong arm of the government, it quickly became the pioneer Mecca of men of all races for hundreds of miles around. It was a haven of rest for the weary travelers on the winding, dust-covered trains; a refuge for hard-pressed scouts and messengers; a home for worn wanderers in a surrounding wilderness of mountains, emerald swards and shaded waters adorning the bosom of rugged hills jewelled with pine and cedar.

There, under the rippling folds of Old Glory flying from the center of its spacious parade grounds, the air resounded with the echo of bugle calls and the tramp of armed regiments of its tented thousands through the rolling years of "The West That Was."

If a detailed record of the various events that occurred in this old oasis of the dim past could be unrolled, what reams of romance, tragedies and near-tragedies it would reveal! There was the lingering death of Ah-ho-appa, the daughter of Spotted Tail, dramatically told by Robert

David in his historic Wyoming sketch, "Malcolm Campbell, Sheriff in 1892–94."[4]

There was also a time of near-tragedy when all the companies at the post happened to be out on scout or escort duty. The old veteran, Sergeant Schnyder, whose coat-sleeves were adorned with reenlistment stripes from shoulder to wrist, was thus left with about twenty men to guard the post with its women and children—about a dozen officers' wives and their maids, and perhaps the wives of a few more enlisted men and employees and a number of children.[5]

The excitement at the fort can be imagined when suddenly a party of sixty or more Indians, in full war paraphernalia, appeared on a ridge about a mile to the north and indicated their hostility by riding in a circle and flashing mirrors toward the opposite hills as signals to expected reinforcements—or so it seemed to the people at the post.

At once the sergeant instructed his men to whirl their few cannon to a position facing the Indians. Meanwhile he sent the women and children by a circuitous route to seek shelter in the commissary department. Here the children were made as comfortable as possible and the women donned soldiers' uniforms and arms. When all was ready it was agreed that, should the worst happen, they would reassemble in the magazine department, where kegs of powder were stored, and die in a vast explosion rather than fall into the hands of the Indians.

Then this Amazonian troop marched proudly across the parade ground and joined the men at the front rank—a very noticeable reenforcement. Meanwhile the members of the little company were milling around the sergeant, then slipping away unseen, one or two at a time, to assemble on a plateau lower than the parade ground, near the river bank and behind the guardhouse. The nearby barracks stood on the brow of the higher (parade) plateau. When enough had gathered there for a sizable formation they were marched across the parade ground in full view of the Indians, to whom they seemed to be a new reenforcement of troops.

After this maneuver had been repeated at regular intervals for several hours, the Indians moved over the ridge toward the Platte and were seen no more. The people at the fort were not disturbed again that day, and when the troops began to return from field duty they were relieved of all anxiety.

The Laramie River, from its tributaries in the Rocky Mountains, flows east across the Laramie plains and through the Black Hills of Wyoming. At the eastern base of the plains, ravines begin that soon drop precipitously and from rock-walled canyons between pine-covered hills that, beginning near old Fort Fetterman, form a chain of small mountains that run south to the Colorado line. From among these low mountains (of which Laramie Peak is the highest and can be seen quite distinctly for a distance of fifty miles), the river rushes through a deep rock canyon cut through the undulating hills, valleys and wooded plateaus until it empties unto the North Platte two or three miles below the fort. Here the Platte turns sharply southward and flows for about twenty-five miles through a broad valley and low-rolling grassy hills.

About twenty miles down the valley, near its west edge and close to the Oregon Trail, was situated the first and most widely known trading store and road ranch to be established in this valley. It was owned by James Bordeaux, old-time fur trader, who handled all kinds of merchandise and, as was usual with the western road ranches at that time, an assortment of liquors. Furs, pelts and robes were transferred to the markets on the Missouri River.[6]

A few miles up the road the firm of "Cuny & Ecoffey, Freighters and Contractors," built a trading post and placed a manager in charge. For a time they did a thriving business, but one day two rival factions happened to meet there, an altercation arose, and in the inevitable shooting the Janis brothers, mixed-bloods, and a white man known as Cy Williams were killed and several others injured. Shortly afterward, friends of the men who were killed sacked the ranch and burned it to the ground.[7]

Some distance up the valley, on the plateau along which lay the Oregon Trail, stood another fair-sized trading store known as the "Nine-Mile Ranche," that being its distance from the fort. For about a mile above and below the fort, space was reserved for transient campers. Eastward, between this camp and the junction of the Laramie River with the Platte, stood the lodges of the mixed population—the white men with Indian families. These men were trappers, hunters, guides, despatch carriers, freighters, wood haulers, haymakers, and men-of-all-work, and their lodges were scattered through the river-bends in neighborly, congenial clusters. About their abodes could be seen hay racks, wood racks, wagons, ox yokes and harness, log chains, grindstones, axes, and all the equipment necessary to a crude frontier husbandry.

On the Oregon Trail there were almost constantly moving trains of long, strung-out ox and mule teams, emigrant teams with work-stock of mixed animals making the train and people on foot driving animals of various kinds. Many of these trains of emigrants were Mormons en route to Salt Lake, while others were bound for different points in the far west.

About twenty-five miles below the fort, where the Platte runs more directly to the east, the Indian villages began and were scattered at convenient distances around the trading posts and on up the valley between the river and the trail to a point above Nine Mile Ranch near where the trail turned to the west around a spur of hills a short distance below the fort. At this turn, between the trail and the junction of the two rivers, lay a small plot of land that was a favorite place for the noon rest or one-meal camping.

This vast concentration of lodges along the valley of the Platte contained many thousands of Indians, and it seemed that all the varied bands of the then large Sioux Nation, from east of the Missouri to the Rockies, had assembled here in one great encampment to await a new treaty delegation from Washington. They watched this initial panorama from a westward-moving civilization that was destined eventually to encompass them. A thrill was furnished to all by the daily scene of tall covered wagons of big freight outfits miles long and interspersed with lesser trains of emigrants, accompanied by bunches of stock driven mostly by women or the younger folks on foot. The scene was varied at times by the more rapid passing of lighter vehicles or the rush and roar of the big six-horse mail stage-coach.

Many of these trains or subdivisions thereof would go into a rest camp somewhere near the fort for several days, or possibly a week or two, knowing that when they and their animals were thoroughly refreshed they could join an oncoming train for another leg of their journey at almost any time. No matter for what duration these camps were pitched, they were always visited by the villagers near by, eager for any news from the outside world. Usually they were eager to give in return all information (mostly straight but sometimes woefully twisted) that the travelers desired of the West and its ways and the customs of the country through which they were passing.

Thus it was that campers who had traversed the long stretch from the Missouri to Fort Laramie were glad to arrive at this much talked-of and longed-for resting place on the Oregon Trail, which in that day was the main artery of the broad Central Northwest. They had endured the heavy rains and the bad roads caused thereby, along with the wind-storms, dust-storms, and all other trials incident to the long trail. They were naturally inclined to be convivial and enjoyed the exchange of experiences with other travelers in camp. Not all those experiences were hardships, for many interesting and often amusing incidents occurred along the overland trails both en route and in camp.

The occurrence here related was only amusing to a small group of white men who had sauntered from their nearby camps to where a long ox train had just halted at the noon camping-ground and the teams were being turned loose to graze in the surrounding hills. Soon a few Indians appeared, then others and still others, but all they did was to gaze up at the high wagon-boxes with their canvas covers, their huge wheels, and the couplings of the trail wagon at the rear. Presently, however, they began to climb up on the wheels and push back the canvas to peep at the freight. Doubtless these children of the wilds were thrilled by the unaccustomed sights, much as we are by a rodeo, but they were becoming quite a nuisance.

When overland trains stop for camping they separate into two parts. The front part moves out to one side of the camping ground and forms a half-circle, the front wheels of each wagon being near to the hind wheels of the wagon just ahead. The rear part of the train moves to the opposite side of the camp and forms likewise; thus the space between these wings affords room for camp operations and a corral for catching the work-stock.

Among the visiting white men was an old French trapper by the name of Chet Dubrey, who was well known over the surrounding country as a wag and a great practical joker.[8] He spoke fluently the French, English and Sioux Indian languages.

The boss of the wagon train had long been annoyed by the habitual curiosity of wandering Indians, and on this day it got on his nerves. Addressing the general question to the group with whom he was talking, he asked,

"Who is the chief of this tribe?"

"I am!" answered Dubrey.

"Well I'll give you a ten-dollar gold piece if you'll drive these Injuns out of camp until we get away from here," the boss replied.

"Done!" said Dubrey.

He mounted the lazy-board on the side of the nearest wagon and began to harangue the Indians for their attention, which he soon secured. Then, pointing toward the upper wagon of the train, he advised,

"Don't go near that wagon up there, nor those two at the end."

The Indians were watching him questioningly as he continued, indicating the opposite wing of the train.

"Stay away from those three wagons in the middle across there, for the front one contains two dead men and there are sick men in the other two. They are down with the same sickness that killed the other two—smallpox."

Most of the western tribes had been sadly scourged by this dread disease at one time or another, and a stampede toward their villages was on instantly. The trainmen were smiling in pleased wonder and Chet's chums were laughing at the success of his ruse.

"Well," remarked the boss, "you are chief, sure enough!"

"You bet I am," replied Chet, as he pocketed the gold piece.

Such knowledge as I possess of Fort Laramie and the events that occurred there were gleaned during a residence of ten years (1871–81) at
the fort and in its near vicinity, as it was my post office and trading place.
All the country around for at least fifty miles comprised the neighborhood, and as neighbors the residents were all known to one another
more or less intimately. The information gained from any of them I found
most reliable, and it is from their personal experience and my own that I
have gathered the material here set down.

Early and late, during the seasons of the year that permitted, trains
kept wending their way back and forth across this grand old highway.
One day a party of Mormon emigrants stopped at the Nine Mile Ranch
long enough to help a sore-footed cow into the grassy hills on the west
side of the trail, where it might recuperate until such time as they could
move it up to their camp near the fort. When two riders went back to
bring the animal to camp they found no cow, but there was unmistakable evidence that it had been butchered not far from where it had been
left. The matter was immediately reported to the post commander. What
moves, if any, were made toward investigation I am unable to record,
never having heard such action mentioned. These customary prelimi-
naries may have been followed and duly entered in the official report,
but certainly they were not discussed locally.[9]

As to these local residents, the reader is advised against the too prevalent but unjust assumption that such communities were composed of
renegades and derelicts. It is true that they were like the pioneer life
they led—rough in their ways and uncouth in appearance, but as a rule
they were prompted by the same honorable impulses and actuated by
the same motives as are other civilized men, and they naturally lived by
the codes of their early training. Some had Indian families and others
had not, but those who had seemed to consider it their own business—
they had weighed the consequences and were willing to abide by them.
There were toughs among them, certainly, but they were appraised as
such and treated accordingly. There were also men of large operations
and financial standing—contractors, owners of cattle herds, freight trains
and merchant establishments—men of affairs. And it was from such men
that the details of the tragedy here described were secured.

It is difficult to understand what action may have been taken before
the final order that sent a troop of twenty-eight cavalrymen into contest
with several thousand Indians over this issue of the Mormon cow. Certainly it will be seen that the situation was fraught with danger, especially as this unfortunate group was officered by a man of immature

judgement and without veteran experience on the frontier.

On the 29th day of August, 1854, a lieutenant, but recently graduated from West Point Military Academy, accompanied by a mixed-blood Sioux Indian interpreter, rode proudly out of the fort and down the Oregon Trail at the head of 28 men under orders to bring in the culprit or culprits dead or alive.[10] He was young, with a vigorous mind, imbued by rigid training with the necessity of implicit obedience. Yet, had this young officer had longer and more varied experience, he would have known that he could retain all of his enthusiasm for obeying orders and still use reasonable discretion in the execution of instructions—in fact, that it was incumbent upon him to do so.

When the troop arrived at Nine Mile Ranch it was formed in line and marched to the brow of the bench land near the ranch buildings and halted in front of the headquarters lodges that stood on lower ground at the edge of the valley, which was occupied by lodges extending back to the river bank. The interpreter was sent to the chief of the village with a message that parley was desired.[11] The chief of this particular band among the many comprising the large encampment was Conquering Bear, and he and a number of his followers soon made an appearance.

Lieutenant Grattan recounted the circumstance of the killing of the cow and his orders to arrest the one or more responsible and bring them to the post to answer for the crime. Then, to the surprise of the chief and other listeners, he demanded the delivery of the guilty party. These details we learned from several men from the trading store who were present, and later from Indians who were also present and who afterward established friendly relations with the government.

The chief explained that whoever had killed the cow doubtless thought it abandoned, as was frequently the case when an animal became too lame to travel; and that now since trouble had started it would be almost impossible to determine those who were responsible. However, he said he might collect enough to pay for the cow, and that he would be at the fort soon and settle with the commander.

During this parley the Indians were constantly leaving the circle for the village, and a little later there was a great commotion up and down the river as far as the lodges could be seen. Men were making for the hills, some on foot and some on ponies, and all quite evidently headed for their individual herds.

The lieutenant rejected the chief's offer and pronounced an ultimatum to the effect that he would give a certain time in which the culprits should be produced, otherwise he would fire on the village.

As soon as the chief's proposal was rejected, the one remaining white citizen hurried to the store with the news. Immediately the heavy board windows were closed with shutters, the doors shut and barred, and arms and ammunition placed in readiness for an attack that fortunately did not occur, as the Indians were engaged with matters far more important to them. Signals of flashing looking-glasses and waving blankets were soon on every side—warnings of approaching trouble. The chief and his head men turned their backs on the lieutenant, who as he had said was holding his watch on them, and walked slowly back to their lodges.

How fortunate it would have been if this impulsive young officer, seeing how matters stood, had then wheeled his men into marching order and returned to the fort! There is no doubt that he could have done so without molestation. On the contrary, as the specified time neared its limit he ordered his men to make ready. One wonders what thoughts were passing through their minds as they stood awaiting the fatal order. Unquestionably most of them fully realized the impending catastrophe; but, like the heroic Six Hundred, "theirs not to reason why—theirs but to do and die."

This is exactly what they did when the order came to fire and the chief was mortally wounded by the volley fired into his group of lodges. All who have lived much in the country know the result of a stone hurled into a hornet's nest. The comparison is perfect.[12]

No sooner had the volley been discharged than all the open spaces were filled with fighting Indians with flashing guns and flying arrows, and in less than the time of this telling the lieutenant and his brave men lay dead upon the ground where they had stood in formation. Their mounts were stampeded and soon joined the herds of ponies that were being driven in from the hills.

Meanwhile, lodges were falling rapidly and camp effects being packed with a speed rivalling that of the ancient Arab. Tents were folded, travois and ponies were loaded, and some families were already crossing the river. Soon Indians could be seen making their way through the low hills east of the Platte until far enough from the fort so that, unseen, they could detour to the north and so gain the shelter of timbered hills and rock-walled canyons. Between them and the Canadian line lay the Empire of the Wilderness that they regarded as their own, and over which they held sway for many years.

When the chief had retired from the parley the interpreter eased his horse back from his position beside the lieutenant. Moving unobserved at the rear of the troop, he gradually worked his way from the plateau down among the lodges and thence to the upper end of the village and on across the broad flat that lay between it and the rough hills along the

Laramie River, which obscured the fort from view. He was within a mile or two of this hilly refuge when he urged his mount to a swift run. This attracted the notice of the Indian guards, whose business it was to see that no communication was made with the fort. Immediately they raced after him. He would have gained shelter, however, and probably could have eluded them entirely had not an Indian hunter come rushing down from the hills. Having heard the soldiers' volley and the answering shots from camp, and seeing the pursued and his pursuers, he shot at the lone rider, breaking his horse's leg and so throwing both horse and rider to the ground. There the Indians quickly despatched him, then raced back to the site of their village and on where the rear guard of their fleeing tribesmen had just crossed the river.[13]

Of course the civilians at the two trading posts, who had been watching every move, notified the officers at the fort as soon as it was safe to do so. A tumult of excitement broke loose there and at the camps of peaceful Indians and mixed bloods near by, and a military cavalcade was soon on its way to the scene of destruction. The body of the lieutenant was taken to the fort; relatives of the interpreter took charge of him; and the twenty-eight soldiers were given burial on the west side of the broad trail, a short distance from where they had fallen. From the rock-strewn hills near by a large flagstone of lime or granite was secured to cover each grave.[14]

The two ranches on the trail continued to do business as long as the travel followed the Oregon Trail, but when the whistle of the locomotive was heard on the Union Pacific near Cheyenne the whole scene changed. The road ranches were abandoned and the buildings gradually faded away until nothing was left to mark where they had stood save the mounds of weed-covered dirt, scars of the excavations and rotting logs, and the noted old highway had reverted to a country road.

Seventeen years later I walked over these moldering ruins that once were busy marts, through which as a young mule driver I had wandered many times. As I walked among the stones marking the resting place of the unfortunate soldiers, I pondered their sad fate and my mind reverted to the famous couplet of the Bard of Avon: "There is a destiny that shapes our ends, Rough hew them as we may."

These bodies were later moved to a government cemetery, in accordance with military custom. The fort was abandoned and sold by the government in 1890 and since has been taken over by the state. It is to be preserved and beautified as a state park, and will be Wyoming's historic contribution to the ages.[15]

CHAPTER 8

The Founding of Pine Ridge

The trip from Fort Laramie was uneventful, being just ordinary traveling in nice warm weather. On reaching Fort Robinson we laid over for two nights and a day visiting with friends and resting. It was immediately after the Cheyenne uprising under Dull Knife. He and his followers had stolen away from the Southern Cheyenne to join the Northern Cheyenne branch, and were pursued by soldiers. They were imprisoned but made a break for liberty and later were released. I saw the guard house where the trouble began, and several spots where an Indian had been shot before they were subdued and held in camp until an agreement was reached whereby they were allowed to live near their friends the Sioux at Pine Ridge until moved to a reservation of their tribe in Montana.[1]

The Oglala and Brulé bands of Sioux had but recently moved from the Missouri River, where the government had again tried to locate these two bands that for years had roamed the plains surrounding the Black Hills and could not adjust themselves to the southern climate. In 1879 they were permitted to return to their native land. The Brulé on the head of Rosebud Creek (now Todd County, South Dakota), and the Oglala at the junction of Wolf and White Clay creeks (now Shannon County, South Dakota), found locations which were and are picturesque.[2] White Clay has a source of well-fed springs in the uplands of northwest Nebraska, and flows north through pine-timbered hills crossing the South Dakota line less than two miles south of the agency. Each of the little bends and valleys through which it flows is studded with various kinds of lowlands timber, among which splendid old elm trees are most numerous.

About six miles south of the agency this stream was joined on the west by Craven Creek, and almost directly opposite this Larive Creek came meandering down from the east, through hills rich in merchantable timber. In order that these trees might be available for government construction projects, and for the further purpose of barring road ranches and the sale of liquor, an area about ten miles square of this Nebraska terrain was withdrawn from public use for a time, and placed under jurisdiction of the United States Indian Service.

A little farther east Wolf Creek has its source in Nebraska, as do most of the streams for about one hundred and fifty miles eastward, which is topographical evidence of a comparative low plain along this portion of northern Nebraska, until it comes to an extensive valley in South Dakota.

Here Wolf Creek turns west and winds serpent-like until it empties into the White Clay, which holds its course northward through a broad, heavily timbered canyon between high, broken pine-covered ridges on each side, interspersed with bald "bad lands" as it enters the valley of the Big White River and joins this stream some twenty miles north of the agency.

From the junction of Wolf and White Clay Creeks, back for several miles, the base of a pine ridge, extends a broad, grass-covered plateau. In contrast with the pine ridge on the south and the rolling, grayish-yellow, pine topped hills of bad-land formation west of White Clay, and the high, scattered groves of pine on the ridges to the north of the lesser streams, the landscape presented a view of entrancing beauty as I saw it for the first time on the sixth day of my move from Fort Laramie in the afternoon of an early February day in 1881 [1879].

There are many spots of scenic beauty in this region that surpasses the one here described, but this was the location of Pine Ridge Agency, which for a time caught the eyes of the world—especially with the beginning of events which culminated in a tragedy prominent in the historic annals of the country.

I called on Dr. Irwin, affable, elderly Indian agent who was about to retire.[3] He told me that a strip of land extending along the White Clay for some distance and east of the Wolf Creek crossing had been reserved for government purposes, and that traffic was to follow certain specified lines designated to become streets. Otherwise people were camping wherever they chose. I chose a small plot of ground north of Wolf Creek, above the agency crossing, and set out at once to cut and haul logs from the nearby hills for a comfortable house that was soon ready for occupancy. All building was done with logs at that time except the two churches, Episcopal and Presbyterian. For these, lumber was freighted from Missouri River points, but logs were used for their parsonages.

The agency itself was built of native lumber furnished by the large government mill that had been set up in a bend of Wolf Creek immediately north of the agency. Colonel O'Beirne from Washington, D.C., was supervisor of construction.[4] Teams of horses, mules and oxen brought the logs from the pine hills along Larive Creek about eight miles south.

Just across the creek in front of my place stood a neat little cabin of sawed logs occupied by the chief clerk at the agency, known to everyone through the country as Colonel C. P. Jordan. This title was bestowed upon him by his friends because of the popularity of his brother, Major Jordan, who was commander at Fort Robinson. They were cousins of General Custer, and highly respected by all. "Colonel" Jordan's first employment was in the Quartermaster's Department at Fort Robinson, after which he was appointed chief clerk at Pine Ridge while Dr. Irwin was agent, and then transferred to Rosebud landing as shipping clerk for both agencies. He had an enviable record in the Indian Service, and after retiring conducted a large mercantile establishment at the Rosebud Agency as a licensed trader.[5]

The next house was on the west corner of the street that led east from the broad avenue running north and south across the Wolf Creek bridge continuing on down White Clay Creek. It was a large peeled log hotel with a large barn and corral in the rear and was owned and operated by L. B. Lessert and family.[6] The next block south was vacant save for one long low building at the northwest corner, facing south.

On the northwest corner of the next block south stood the first and largest of the mercantile establishments, owned by George F. Blanchard, and with a large pool hall near by as a part of his business.[7] The building first mentioned stood across the street and was used for temporary storage of a billiard table and other property belonging to Thomas Cowgill, a newly licensed trader who was putting up several large log buildings on the southeast corner of the same block.[8] These were on the present site of the Presbyterian Church, and were being finished and made ready for large consignments of goods en route from the Missouri River. Merchants in the far-away-places were compelled to supply their stores in the autumn with an immense stock of goods for the reason that the long haul of freighting was impracticable in winter because of deep snow.

Across the street from the Cowgill store, between the northeast corner and the Blanchard store and pool-hall, were several small log buildings, one being a blacksmith and wagon shop operated by David Cockrell.[9]

These buildings comprised the business section of Pine Ridge at that time, but the beef camp was about two and one-half miles eastward, where Wolf Creek comes in from the south. Here were good quarters for the herders, barn, scale, slaughter-house, and a large corral.

Beef contracts were filled by the delivery of from five hundred to two thousand head of cattle at a time. To accommodate this number with sufficient feed and keep it inaccessible to the thousands of Indian ponies, a herd camp was established at the mouth of White Clay on the Big White River. Here cattle had ample range, and from this range were driven to the beef camp in sufficient number to supply the issue that was made every two weeks. Indians had advanced to the wheeling stage of transportation at this time, so the representatives from the tribe (on horseback and with travois) would be on hand to kill, butcher and carry the meat to their homes. The issue was made by the chief clerk, assisted by agency employees, and usually began at nine a.m. after the cattle had rested over night in the corrals. The issuing of beef to the Indians was always attended by many interested spectators, but was fraught with the possibility of serious accidents at all times.

A whole beef was allowed to a certain number of persons. Combinations were made up from neighboring families, one of whom was selected to represent the group. One or more members of these groups, mounted on their fleetest horses and armed with rifle or bow and arrows, formed in two lines facing each other and making a funnel-shaped lane only the width of the gate at the corral, but widening as it approached the broad plateau.

Meanwhile, at a smaller cattle-pen behind the slaughter-house and near the bank of the creek, the agency butcher and his helpers issued portions to individual ticket-holders scattered here and there through the bands.

When all was ready the chief clerk, list in hand, stood just outside the corral gate, with three herders inside between the cattle and the gate. They would string out two or three animals at a time as he called out the name of an Indian, who (with his helpers, if any) rode out into the lane and followed the frightened animal as it trotted along, swinging its head to search first one line of horsemen and then the other but never finding a friendly face. When the hapless creature reached the open space the race was on, and soon the shooting began. Thus cattle were kept loping and jumping through this living lane to a losing race with death, and soon the plain was covered with running, whirling, dodging steers, each followed by an Indian, crossing and crisscrossing each others' path, with bullets flying and arrows whizzing everywhere. Parties of the group to whom the animal had been issued rushed in with their travois and began butchering as soon as they saw their own animal drop.

Notwithstanding the dangers involved in this unique semi-monthly western rodeo, and occasional threats of the authorities to change the system, it continued for several years. During this time the near Nebraska homesteads were being settled upon, and farmers brought their families for miles and travelers laid over to see the issue of beef and watch the Indians perform on this, their Roman holiday.

Several accidents and near-accidents had been reported from time to time when, in 1885 or 1886, Henry Janis, an Indian in swift pursuit of his steer, encountered a swifter rifle ball that passed through his body and hurled him to the ground, dead. Undoubtedly this was an accident; in any case it had to be designated as such. The method of issue was changed after this and the beeves were killed by employees under direction of the agency butcher inside the great corral and handled by the owners. The Indians were inclined to resent the change but soon took a common-sense view.[10] They had enjoyed the rugged action of the chase as a reminder of their buffalo days—but a reminder is all it was, for only in the initial charge was there any similarity. The buffalo hunters, on foot or horseback, always kept down wind as they stole up close to a grazing herd to make their charge. As the animals raced to a center and formed a wedge-shaped mass they followed their leader like sheep. The hunters on their fleetest horses, racing close beside them, made their kill as they went; and the slaughter-ground, instead of being one large flat, was a line as long as the chase itself.

Pine Ridge Agency was then (and I believe still is) credited with being the largest in the United States. It was said the official rolls recorded seventy-five hundred names, but the Indians strenuously objected to being enumerated and it was difficult to get an exact count. At any rate there were a host of them. The Oglala were recognized as one of the important bands of the Sioux Tribe with Red Cloud, strategist and general, as their chief and Red Dog his ranking sub-chief, friend, and ever-ready and impressive orator.[11]

As a matter of record (and perhaps of amusement to the curious) I will set forth the names of the lesser bands and of some of the head men.[12] Of course there were several in each band to claim that distinction, and all called themselves chiefs, but I give only the names of those officially recognized as such. These were generally the head men of the band, but occasionally some personal difference with the agent led to the recognition of a less influential man. In accordance with human nature the world over, these head men all considered themselves the leader, and constantly vied with one another for that distinction.

History reveals the fact that all primitive subdivisions of the human race took their names, both collectively and individually, from some occurrence or performance, and such was the Indian custom also. Following are the names of the small bands of the Oglala Sioux and their principal leaders at the time of which I write, together with a few legendary episodes that I remember having heard as the origin of these names. Very trivial incidents often caused both the giving and the changing of a name.

"Loafers" was the name given to a band that always camped nearest a fort or an agency when the tribe was called in from the wilds by the government on business, or when they came in on a visit.

"Legs on a Pot"—so called because they were the first to receive an assignment of iron kettles instead of the old regulation brass kettles.

The "Wa Za Za" were named for the Osage Indians who, together with other tribes grouped with the Dakota or Sioux because of linguistic relationship, included the Omaha, Oto, Kaw, Ponca, Quapaw, Biloxi and Catawaba—all in the great Sioux family.

"Broken Arrow"—once a strong band numerically, but uncontrollable because of disrespect to the councils and chiefs and continual violation of the established rules of the tribe. The members kept leaving and attaching themselves to other bands until it had become reduced to a few scattered lodges.

"Bad Faces"—This was a subdivision of the Oglala—at one time a very large band, the chief of which was Bull Bear. He had a son named Little Wound, who with Red Cloud and numerous other young men constituted the embryo warriors of the village. Red Cloud became chief of the Bad Face upon the death of Bull Bear.[13] He seems always to have enjoyed the confidence of his young companions, and was usually chosen as the leader of their exploiting forays when opportunity offered a chance to steal away.

Sioux Bands	Pronunciation	English Names	Head Men
Ite Sica	Eta Secha	Bad Face	Red Cloud
Kiy Ksa	Keyoksa	Cut Off	Little Wound
Iya Sica	Eya Secha	Bad Talkers	American Horse
O Yuk Pe	O yu Ghe Pe	Pulls Down	Big Road
Waglu He	Wa Ga Ku Ka	Loafers	Blue Horse
Wa Ja Ja	Wa Za Za	Osage	High Wolf, Fire Thunder
Cih Hu Ha Tum	Chee Hu Hu Tum	Legs on a Pot	They're Afraid of his Horse
Hogan Yute Sni	Wo Gha Yuta Sne	Don't Eat Fish	No Water
Wan Na We Ga	Wan Na We Ga	Broken Arrow	

During these early years their village was encamped on the Chugwater in the Wyoming Territory when two or three wagons of Mexican traders came there with Navajo blankets, dried corn, onions, red beans, and other Mexican eatables and gewgaws. They also had some whiskey, which they handled very judiciously until they had traded their other goods for robes, ponies, pelts, furs, beadwork, tanned deer hides and other Indian handiwork, then they disposed of it quickly and departed.

It is a mistake to assume that Indians can never handle liquor without having trouble. When liquor was available they had their jamborees in good fellowship without bad effects until the morning after. But fights are apt to occur among men of any and all races when liquor is being consumed, and when this happened among Indians it was likely to be serious, for they knew of but two ways to fight—with whips and clubs, and then with the more deadly weapons. So it resulted in the death of Chief Bull Bear, and this big band of Bad Face Sioux was torn asunder.

After the death of his father, Little Wound and the relatives and closest followers of the dead chief, comprising quite a sizeable minority, left the Bad Face band and set up their village on a stream farther south. It was at this point, while a number of old men were sitting in council discussing their affairs, that the question of choosing a name for the new band came up and engendered much controversy. One of the old men who had become impatient happened to see a little green snake wriggling past. He caught it up, bit it in two, and throwing the two parts to the center of the circle he proclaimed "This shall be our name— Ke-Yok-Sa."[14]

In surprise and some amusement the name was adopted, and the Cut Off Band chose Little Wolf as their chief. The band remained Oglala, however, and all the damages resulting from the fight were adjusted satisfactorily by the payment of horses to the aggrieved in accordance with Indian custom. Little Wound remained throughout life as one of Red Cloud's principal chiefs.[15]

A brief summary of the simple operation of tribal affairs of government is here set forth to show the reader how the difficulties and uprisings were regulated and order maintained. In domestic affairs the older women and the elder son usually have control, but in matters pertaining to the community the "Medicine Men" exert a powerful influence which, to greater or less degree, extends to the more important individual undertakings of men. There are two cults of these practitioners. One chooses some outstanding wild animal (such as a deer, buffalo, bear or elk) through which the individual medicine man believes the Great Spirit works wonderful cures for him. The specialty of this cult is to drive out evil spirits, and this they assume to do by the beating of the tom-tom, accompanied by a lot of silly pantomime and other grotesque foolishness.

The "Medicine Men" of the other cult are herb doctors who claim to have had the curative properties of certain herbs passed down to them as family secrets from father to son. When we recall the home and field remedies of our grandmothers, the frequent success of the herb practitioners is not astonishing. The medicine men as such have little to do with the governmental affairs of their people except as men of wisdom and experience who hold the confidence of the tribe, especially the chiefs and head men constituting the village council, the ranking members of which sit in the central tribal council.

All councils were an open forum where suggestions of possible merit entered and were given consideration, but the laws or rules required for their government were the result of discussion and adoption by a committee of ranking members. The enforcement of these regulations was accomplished through an institution as old as the earlier council that had established it, and it was very simple. After secretly passing on the courage, temperament, judgment and fitness of the candidates, the council selected a number of men who would be notified by some member. The notification was mandatory and might be given in various ways, such as a tap on the shoulder, a slap on the back or a daub of paint on the cheek—all of which depended upon the whim of the notifier; but the recipient always considered himself honored and accepted the accompanying crisp command "Go to the council!" with pleasure. There he received his instructions, the purport being to obey tribal orders or suffer a severe penalty commensurate with his failure. Then he went forth as an accredited member of the oddly named "Dog Soldiers," the police force of the wilds. In addition to keeping the peace they had many other duties, of which the following is typical.

Suppose a council decided it necessary or advantageous to move the village to another locality, but one or two lodges dissented and refused to move. If, during the preparatory movements of the village to get under way, these lodges were making no effort but on the contrary showed determination to remain where they were, they would be visited by a party of mounted Dog Soldiers and ordered to get busy. Any hesitation on their part would bring the quirts of the soldiers slashing and flaying over the heads and shoulders of the men folks and they could only pull their blankets over their faces and take it, as that was the only defense their custom would allow. Meanwhile the women concerned (who always seemed to have more sense than the men) would be packing up the family effects, and presently the lodge would be down and folded and the recalcitrants would join the move.

In the conduct of individual affairs, none but those directly interested had anything to say so long as the matter was adjusted peaceably, but in tribal matters a glance at their governmental structure will show that in the final analysis the leading chiefs were always the law.

In the early eighties, when above-discussed component parts of this large division of the Dakota known as the Oglala Sioux (of which Red Cloud was head chief) were all centered within a radius of twenty miles from Pine Ridge, South Dakota, with its pine-covered hills, its wooded streams and broad verdant plateau between, with a boundary of a hundred miles of open space on either side, presented not only a picturesque scene but also a miniature world of activity.

With streamers of various colors waving from the tops of the taller lodges and here and there a high pole decorated with detachable, gaudy medicine totems, while horsemen in flamboyant regalia were cavorting about the grounds of their villages (that were strung out up the White Clay south of the agency for several miles, and down the creek to the north toward White River), a picture was created that was very interesting to the observer. The outskirts of the agency were fringed on every side with scattered lodges, and upper Wolf Creek and its several spring-fed branches out of range of the slaughter-yard also were lined with scattered villages that completed the picture.

The people of these villages at that time were at the peak of carefree life. They were living, not on charity as many people supposed, but on goods bought and paid for by the government through contracts which were dignified as treaties. These furnished them with the staples of subsistence in exchange for lands surrendered and vacated. Possibly it is a debatable subject, but that is the way the Indians figured it.

However, with the country full of game they felt that all they had to do was to keep their hunting grounds from being encroached upon by opposing tribes and the only world they knew was theirs. So the men hunted, raced horses and played their various tribal games, while the women did the necessary camp drudgery. In the afternoon and evening until late at night they made merry together—visiting, joking, singing, and dancing to the weird music of improvised flutes and drums.

Meanwhile, out on some lonely hill in the darkness of night, a medicine man wrapped in his blanket sat motionless, gazing at the heavens while he cogitated over the mysteries of the world and the workings of the Great Spirit, which his crude imagination caused to conform to the claimed virtues of his own medicine. Thus the human brain, cultivated or uncultivated, is constantly seeking light and truth amid the wonders of the vast unknown.

CHAPTER 9

Changing Conditions

A short time after the arrival of the new agent (a young army physician bearing the name of Valentine Trant O'Connell McGillicuddy, and with a moustache that equalled the name), the Indians were encouraged to move their respective bands out to their choice of the many streams of the reservation, where they were furnished with everything necessary for farming, including garden and farm seeds and a wagon.[1] A farm instructor was to be sent out, and schools were to be established for the children. In the beginning only a few of the bands took advantage of this opportunity, but as spring approached the large and picturesque villages previously described began to fade away, and eventually the present system of farm districts was permanently established.

In the meantime the building of the new agency was being rushed to completion. Logging trains were arriving at the sawmill (that was running full time), and carpenters were converting rough native lumber into temporary but commodious quarters for employees and shelter for the government property. Also, on a broad meadow across the creek west of the agency, a frame building was being erected for Red Cloud.[2]

The freighters were busy getting their outfits (mostly four-horse teams) ready to take to the road as soon as the grass should become sufficiently grown for their animals to subsist on. I was one of the first party that received orders for freight, and we were soon off for Rosebud as soon as able to do so. We kept the agency continually furnished with much needed supplies.

Our next notice to take the trail instructed us to go to the mouth of Yellow Medicine Creek where stood some abandoned buildings that had been the beginning of an agency which the Oglala refused to accept.[3] We were told that thereafter the steamboats would land all the Pine Ridge freight at that point. We continued freighting from this landing during the summer, with the usual short stops at home for rest and repairs.

It was on an occasion of this kind, about the middle of June, that we were treated to the first free rodeo exhibition at Pine Ridge. A large ox train had pulled in and was unloading new wagons, boxes of harness, wagon bows and covers—in fact, all the appurtenances belonging to a complete four-horse outfit. The agency force was busy, and as fast as the assemblies were completed they were issued to Indians who, with their travois-broke ponies, waited to receive them. Several instructors were present, of course, but the Indians vied with one another in showing their speed and adaptability. As their aides were generally anxious relatives, they often got the collar or hames on the animal upside down; and when at last the wheel-horses were properly hitched to the wagon they would attach the lead-bars to the bottom of the collars instead of to the fifth chain that was placed below the wagon tongue for that purpose.

When the many errors were corrected and all was in readiness, the instructors mounted to the drivers' seats and showed how to hold and use the lines; then, with an Indian on foot on each side of each team and holding a rein, the instructors piloted them out of the agency toward their camp. After their safe departure the several teachers mounted their horses and returned to the yards, much amused at the way they had divided the lines, bridle reins and whips among themselves as they kept on toward their villages.

This procedure continued for several days with frequent reports of upsets and runaways, but no injuries were reported. It soon became evident that the Indians were mastering the simple—but to them, complicated—art of teaming, for some were soon seen coming into town with only five drivers to each team. One man held each of the four lines while one handled the whip; but finally the drivers were reduced to three—one man with the whip and the others holding two lines each.

As time passed, Indians could be seen driving into town alone on the driver's seat, but with plenty of ready helpers standing behind him in the wagon box, and as a matter of fun and encouragement they were hailed with waving and cheers as they proudly turned street corners in a very creditable manner. Of course others followed, and their driving soon ceased to be a novelty. A month or two later we were not surprised at meeting a long train of four-horse teams pulling bright red wagons, most of them driven by one or two Indians on their way to the Missouri River for freight.[4]

We learned from one of the accompanying white men that the train had been divided into four sections of twenty-five wagons each, and each in charge of a wagon boss and assistant. We also learned that they were supplied with a wagon load of accessories and tools for making repairs when required, as they expected to be on the road for some time.

The induction of this Indian train and of a similar train that was fitted out later did not interfere with the local transportation business at the time, as we were all needed to transport the vast amount of material required in the building of the institution of Pine Ridge Indian Agency and the private interests concerned. At that period there were only two business houses in the adjoining town, but they were large commercially and it was estimated that each kept a stock of forty thousand dollars, with six months' supply ahead.[5] Such an arrangement was necessary, for this great aggregation of Indians always seemed to have a little money aside from their furs and pelts. Many were employed as herders and policemen, while others earned money by freighting. The government issued only staple eatables and clothing, so they bought quantities of everything else that looked good to them.

Early that fall I decided to take a vacation from the freight line and investigate a matter that I had been thinking over for some time. On my first arrival at the log-cabin town that was then the residential part of Pine Ridge (just east of the space reserved by the government for its agency), I had noticed that all of the buildings were daubed with mud. I soon learned that what little lime had been freighted into the place had been for the purpose of plastering the two churches and laying the foundations for the heavier and more substantial buildings at the agency. Upon inquiry I was told that the reason no one burned a lime kiln was that there was no limestone in that section.

Now I had just come from a part of the country that abounded with fine hard limestone of both the blue and white variety. As one of my nearest neighbors burned lime kilns as a regular business, I felt fairly well posted on the subject and decided that as soon as convenient I would look into the matter, and so my vacation was taken for this purpose.[6]

For three days I rode horseback through the rocky highlands and ragged canyons of the ridges both north and south of the agency, examining rock, but all I found was gray sandstone. On the fourth day's ride I came to the head branch of a small creek four miles west of the agency. I followed this stream down through hills of clay, some red and some cream-colored, and along narrow, high-walled gulches showing alternate strata of this clay and burnt-out coal veins about one foot thick. This black substance still contained enough gas to burn very nicely when placed upon a bed of live coals, and I realized that I had found a small section entirely different in formation from that of the surrounding country.

Soon I came to some small timbered bends in the main creek that were bordered on the south by perpendicular walls about twenty feet high and composed of various layers of flat rocks of grayish yellow color and varied thickness, which proved to be a soft limestone of the magnesian variety.

So when I found the object of my search, where wood was plentiful and handy, I employed some help and we completed, filled and burned a fair-sized kiln of lime. Thereafter during the summer seasons I divided my time between freighting and furnishing lime, as the market required, from my supply at a point on the little stream eight miles from the Pine Ridge Agency, that has been known ever since as Limekiln Creek.

As a result of this side-line venture, a gradual but continuous change of the dull, drab buildings of this extreme frontier community to a lighter and more cheerful color was soon apparent. The authorities were building substantial houses of either peeled or hewn logs out on the newly designated school districts, and these provided work through the winter for a number of builders and a few teams. I secured work on these buildings, and the weather was fine during the erection of the first three on which I was engaged. The logs were cut and hauled from the nearby hills on Porcupine Creek to a plat near the site of the present district station, then peeled and fitted into a neat and spacious school house.

It was late in the afternoon of a cloudy, murky day in mid-October when our building crew, which comprised two wagons with four men to the wagon, a camping outfit and provisions and tools for all of us, stopped on a rising piece of level ground that had been marked for a school site on Wounded Knee Creek, a mile or two below a spot which later was to be the scene of the tragedy of the Seventh Cavalry and Big Foot's band of Sioux. The building spot that had been chosen lay to the west of the road extending up and down the creek for miles and was the thoroughfare that connected the many Indian camps along the stream. Across the road to the east of the building site, in a broad bend of the creek, was the largest camp of all. In fact, it was a fair-sized village, and for that reason had been chosen as a desirable location for a school. It was known as Two Lance Camp—named, as usual, for its head man.[7]

While a meal (a combination of dinner and supper) was being prepared by the cook, the others were busy putting up the tent and arranging for what we supposed would be our camp for a number of weeks at least. However, as we sat down to eat it began to snow, and by the time we had finished the wind had risen and was blowing with such velocity that it took our utmost united efforts to turn our tent about so that the entrance would be opposite the oncoming storm, which had suddenly grown to the proportions of a swirling, howling blizzard. The wind calmed down during the night, but the snow continued to fall and in the morning the ground was covered with a deep blanket of the beautiful but unwelcome snow.

We cleared a space of ground in front of the tent and started a fire for breakfast. When we had finished, our employer, David Cockrell, proprietor of the carpenter and blacksmith shop at the agency, left camp after remarking that he would see what he could do about our situation. Of course we had no idea of his plans but we knew that he was an efficient workman and thoroughly reliable, for Dr. McGillicuddy gave these building contracts only to local men who had experience, and it was their responsibility to turn the completed job over to him in acceptable condition.

We had tied our horses to the wagons and had fed them the grain they had been waiting for, and were wondering what to do next, when Mr. Cockrell returned with the information that he had rented a large tepee for our use where we could cook, eat and sleep inside, sheltered from storms. He had first tried to rent the log house, but the Indians were reluctant to let him have it. The house was filled (more or less) with the family effects of the closely related lodges at the rear and was used by each of the families on occasion, while the big tepee had not been occupied for some time except as a storehouse and they agreed to have it nicely cleaned up by the time we could get there.

At once we began loading our wagons and hitching up the teams and were soon on our way, backtracking down the road about one-half mile to the lower end of the creek bend, where we crossed a broad swale and then turned east across a small plateau to our new camp. We found the lodge nice and clean and a fire burning in the fireplace, so we arranged our bed rolls about the inner edge of the lodge, as the Indians do, placed our mess kit on one side of the flap door and our axes and tools on the other side, and felt that we were comfortably located.

The schoolhouse that we were to build was to be constructed of hewed logs. This required trees of larger growth than those used in building with peeled logs. Our boss had been fortunate in finding among the workmen at the agency a man by the name of Freeman who had been a lumber-jack in the north woods and who was expert with a broad-ax. After dinner Cockrell and Freeman started on foot up the ravine that came down from the pine hills to the east above our camp, in search of the most convenient and desirable timber for our purpose. They were surprisingly successful, finding and marking a number of suitable trees a short distance up the canyon, and still greater number just over the ridge in another canyon not far north of us.

The next morning all hands but the cook were out chopping and trimming logs. After dinner my man and I started, with a wagon apiece, to haul them back a proper distance from the official stake that marked the schoolhouse site. The weather now had moderated, and though the nights and mornings were rather cold, warm sunshine through the day had thawed most of the snow. The work was steady but not too strenuous, and handling the fresh-cut pines was a clean and healthy job that was accompanied by plenty of wholesome food which our appetites were ever ready to dispose of; so, with comfortable quarters in which to pass our hours off duty, we had an altogether enjoyable time.

It was comparatively quiet here, as our nearest neighbors were usually engaged in the nightly hilarity of the large village south of us at the upper end of the bend in the creek. The varied sounds of revelry—the jingle of small bells worn by the dancers with their other adornments, the singing, the high and low boom of the drums and the shrill notes of their native flutes, though continued far into the night, were not awakening. The sounds were wafted to us on a breeze in unison and in perfect time, and as they were always from the same direction they soon became conducive to sleep.

There were other sounds emanating from this village (as from all Indian villages on occasion, and sometimes quite frequently) that were awe-inspiring and woefully distressing. Indians are very intense in their mourning for the dead. They seemed able to strike with countless variations every key of shrill shuddering notes in the sound scale, and when death fell upon one of a large family circle, pandemonium prevailed. The chief mourners cut off their long hair a little below the ears and slash themselves with knives in the fleshy part of the arms and legs, then moan and weep alternately while calling upon the Great Spirit and talking to and of the one departed. This is continued until the relatives become exhausted, but always there are others who are less closely affected who step into the breach.

This utter abandonment to grief under the stress of crazed impulses gave rise to many queer customs. Often a warrior became so frenzied over the death of some dear one that he grabbed his bow and quiver, or his gun, and ran through the village crying, singing his sorrow to the scampering, scurrying populace as he went. From his blundering course he turned neither to the right nor left to harm anyone, but woe unto those who failed to keep out of his way, for custom called upon him to kill any living thing that obstructed his path. As a whole the Indians frowned upon this ancient custom, as it was fraught with much danger and great inconvenience; still, when it was resorted to they deferred to its rules and repaired to their lodges, giving the grieving one the right of way. The practice rarely had serious consequences other than the death of a horse or a dog or two, which generally were paid for later.[8]

There was another berserk performance more dangerous and more dreaded by far, but of less frequent occurrence because the villagers made every effort to break the custom and a close watch was kept on brewing conditions. It might be termed the running duel, and developed usually in about the same way.

For example, some unfortunate and disgruntled warrior, pursued by ill luck for so long a time that he felt he was losing his rightful standing among his fellows, would brood over his failures and misfortunes—whether on forays against the enemy, on the hunt, in family difficulties, or trouble with his neighbors. The cumulative effect of these caused him to worry and grouch until at last he went off balance mentally and credited some one whom he considered his arch enemy with being the author of all his woes and so decided to "get him" before he should suffer any more misfortune. So he would strip to the waist and even decorate himself with war paint, arm himself with his deadliest weapon, then leap from his lodge with a wild yell and run amuck through the village, singing an improvised song to the effect that he would die together with his enemy. The burden of the song runs about as follows. "I am going to die today, and shall take _____, who has caused all my trouble, with me." He keeps repeating this wailing song as he moves directly toward the lodge of the man named. Of course the whole village is electrified, and occupants of the space between the prospective duelists is cleared with a rush.

The rules governing such clashes were very simple. Either the alleged enemy had heard of the attack or was instantly notified, and it was incumbent upon him to get out in the open, armed and ready for defense. Each of the principals was permitted to whirl, duck, jump—in fact, practice all of the dodges peculiar to Indian fighting, but neither might recede. Either they must remain in a certain spot or approach one another while shooting until one was killed or incapacitated. However, such affairs seldom reached this climax, for almost always before the aggressor had proceeded far on his trail of vengeance he was surrounded, disarmed, taken back to his lodge and held prisoner until he became sufficiently normal to accept and act on the good advice given him.

The reader doubtless will remark that I have made a digression from chopping logs and building schoolhouses, but he will please remember that we were still on the job and also that we were living in the midst of a large Indian village, for the benefit of whose children the school was being built on a spot within gun-shot distance of the site that later became historic ground—for there occurred the last armed conflict between Indians and United States soldiers. Let the environment account for my flashing panorama of logs, houses, dogs and Indians, mad and otherwise.

We had but a few more logs to get out of the timber below the camp, then were to move to quarters in the upper part of the big village closer to our work which, barring an occasional delay on account of storms, had progressed nicely. The boys were all anxious to make this move, for about the time that we settled in the big lodge a young man living near by became seriously ill and now was expected to pass away at any time. The rather quiet and orderly moaning and weeping through the nights had begun to get on our nerves and we dreaded the final outburst at his demise. But the anticipated escape was not to be, for he died three or four days before we were prepared to move. However, the disturbance was not what we had expected, thanks to our landlord. To our surprise he had taken the precaution of minimizing the tumult usual to such occasions, and our rest was not seriously disturbed.

It was about one o'clock on the night that the death occurred when I was awakened by a low, moderate weeping in the lodge of his family. The other members of our crew seemed to be sleeping soundly. I figured that this silent weeping was caused by the invalid's low spells, then his sudden rally would account for the hush, and so was listening intently when my attention was attracted to a slight movement near our lodge door. Then the door flap was turned slowly back and an Indian entered stealthily. I was about to accost him when he whispered my name and I knew he was our landlord. Noiselessly he approached my bed and produced a fair-sized package in which I could hear the clink of metal, and began whispering to me.

I was not adept in the Sioux language, in fact, could converse only a little on ordinary subjects, but he soon made me understand that the young man was dying, and his fear that the family might injure themselves in their frenzy had caused him to hide all the guns in camp and collect all the knives, which he asked me to keep until he should call for them. I took the flour sack that he handed me and placed it between the wall of the lodge and my bed; then my nocturnal visitor stole away as silently as he had come. When he had gone one of the sleepers across the campfire casually asked me what it was all about. As quietly as possible I explained, but at that moment the cries of grief broke forth among the lodges and wakened all the boys. They were not startled, realizing at once what had happened.

At first many Indians were heard rushing from lodge to lodge and in and out of the log house, presumably in search of instruments of torture, but soon their wailing voices receded toward the hills and the tumult near our quarters was lessened.

While breakfast was being prepared we examined the package left with us and found it to contain several butcher knives, three or four sharpened case knives, one dirk and an old derringer—a nice little collection to give proper emphasis to the sorrow of distracted mourners.

The death watch was being kept by neighbors, who also were preparing for the funeral, for the members of the immediate family, worn to the point of exhaustion, had yielded to the requirements of nature and were fast asleep. In the evening our landlord called and took his bundle of knives with an air of humility and resignation mixed with a touch of cunning satisfaction at having outwitted the others.

A few days later we camped near our work and all hands were engaged in construction. In about two weeks we had the building ready for inspection by the agent. The Reverend Amos Ross, Episcopal missionary, was the first teacher at this school—Two Lance Camp.[9]

CHAPTER 10
Building for Schools

Two or three weeks later, just after the holidays, the cold December days of storm had left the country covered with deep, crusted snow—precisely the kind of weather to make warm and comfortable quarters most enjoyable. It was at this time that I received a call from H. C. Clifford, the contractor for whom I had worked while building the Porcupine schoolhouse. He wanted me to help him on another building that Dr. McGillicuddy wished to have erected at the agency at once. This was to be 36 by 16 feet and built of sawed logs, which were to be delivered at the mill and then, with the finishing lumber, shipped to the school site.[1]

Mr. Clifford wanted me as one of his choppers and then, when all was ready, to help finish the building as I had done at Porcupine. He had two four-horse teams of his own and would do his own hauling. He would pay two dollars a day with everything furnished. As the right kind of timber could be gotten close to the agency, instead of going to some distant camp, I accepted his proposal. He located all necessary logs among the pine-timbered hills about four miles northeast of the agency, near the spring-fed rivulet emptying into a small creek about a mile north of the Wolf Creek crossing near the sawmill. This little stream is known as Cheyenne Creek in memory of a part of the remnant of Dull Knife's band which came down from Fort Robinson and camped along its crooked course during their stay among the Oglala.

One morning we left the agency early. Our boss was on horseback leading his two wagons, which were loaded with our camping outfit and lumber. We went through a broad canyon to the last water on an old Indian trail where he and his two drivers and John Woodruff (the same colored cook who was on the job at Porcupine) began clearing away the crusted snow and preparing camp. Meanwhile the other chopper and I made for the tall trees and began cutting logs. We were delayed a bit by the storms at that season, and I think it was the latter part of the third week when we had all the material on the ground.

We then moved into the agency, and were fortunate in getting the use of a comfortable four-room house. The week-end was spent in resting and arranging our camp paraphernalia. On the following Monday morning and each week-day morning thereafter, barring stormy days, we were on the ground and knocking the frost from our tools at five a.m. With an hour off for the noon meal, we were on the job as long as we had light to work by. A good warm meal and a good-natured cook to serve it, with the luxury of a table and bright lamplight during the evening, always awaited us and we were satisfied. The nights were long, but our evenings were spent pleasantly in the customary manner—visiting, joking, telling stories. Hank Clifford, who had been in the early buffalo-hunting days on the Platte and a long-time camp associate of John Y. Nelson—who later traveled with Buffalo Bill's Wild West Show as "The Champion Liar of the World"—could entertain us with some pretty strong ones, but as he was our boss we did not demand positive proof.[2]

This pastime was interrupted, however, whenever we got hold of a newspaper, for we read and digested everything in its columns even though a week or two old, as it was all news to us. Those who wished to go home Saturday nights were free to do so, though at least one man remained on guard over the tools and other property in order to prevent any delay.

One Saturday evening when we came into camp we found that we had two colored men instead of one, as our cook was enjoying a visit from his friend Alex Baxter from the Porcupine station. During our previous stay there they had become acquainted, and as both were old bachelors and the only colored men on the reservation except for an occasional itinerant cook, they soon became great friends. Certainly they had plenty to talk about, for our John had followed the Oglala from the Missouri to their present location, and Alex had trailed into Fort Laramie in an early day as cook for Major Wham, and a year or so later followed the band through all its meanderings from the Platte to the old Red Cloud Agency in Nebraska, to the Missouri, and then back to Pine Ridge. During this time he learned to speak the Sioux like a native and was at home among them anywhere, but he was generally to be found in his little shack near the camp of Chief High Wolf on the Porcupine.[3] John could not speak the Sioux language, so he found work about the agency with the freighters, loggers, and similar groups.

Alex Baxter, known to everyone as Old Alex, was a quaint character, tall, angular, awkward, comically witty and good-natured. He was the personification of every word in any language describing personal appearance the opposite of handsome, graceful, or its equivalent. He professed to sell cord wood for a living, but was usually found with very little—if any—wood. Yet he had plenty of time to putter around with some Indian friend, helping him to build a cabin, a pole corral, or whatever was to be done that didn't interfere with their visiting, smoking and eating. Nature had provided him with a good pair of lungs and a very loud voice, and while he rode his old pony from one camp to another he took pride in making the hills and canyons resound with native songs—

some of his own creation. This pleased his Indian friends, and coffee was always ready for him at camp. He did not go to church regularly, but quite often would "spruce up" and attend services. Always he delighted in the singing, and of course took part in it.

A friend who was a catechist in one of the churches told me of an amusing incident that occurred on a Sunday when Alex was one of the worshippers. The minister had given out the number of the hymn, but it seemed that Old Alex, sitting on the front seat, could not find the place and so the minister found it for him. Then they began to sing "Nearer My God to Thee," with Old Alex following through with great gusto, but all who were near enough to distinguish words noticed that he was substituting the preposition "by" for the pronoun "my." Think how a strong voice could make that sound!

One Saturday night, when it was my turn to stay on guard in camp, I had provided myself with reading material and after supper, when the other hands had gone, I sat alone reading while the two darkies were doing up the work in the kitchen. The door between us was open so that the heat might radiate. Now and then my attention was arrested by that amusing, throaty chortle which is peculiar to the laugh of many colored people.

At nine o'clock, our regular bedtime, I turned in with no idea that before I slept I was to be entertained with a "comedy number" that would have done credit to any amateur black-face trouper on the stage. There seemed to be but little change in the conversation of the boys, and, judging by the frequent lulls, they seemed to have exhausted all the usual subjects in their range of thought. I concluded that they were about to retire when their voices became audible again in discussion of the merits of religion and the various church denominations and creeds. This led to heated debate wherein arguments were sometimes presented in such ludicrous manner that the temptation to laugh was irresistible. I knew that neither of them could read and their discussion impressed me as verbal luxury. They were soon hurling scriptural quotations at each other to support their contentions, in a manner so blustering that a stranger would have thought they were quarreling, but it was all in good nature and often punctuated by that guttural chuckle which is beyond my ability to describe.

Then the subject changed from religion to politics—more by accident than by design. I will limit my narrative to a few high points stressed at the close of their argument. Though they seemed quite at home on religious matters, it was soon evident that politically both were floundering in controversial waters too deep for them, yet each arrogantly assumed to speak with authority. Their style of expression was inimitable and most interesting, yet had it been taken down verbatim it could scarcely have been presented without being considered sacrilegious. These men were entirely sincere and had no idea their little talkfest was being absorbed as rare comedy by another.

Finally John gave up his pupil as hopeless and remarked,

"Alex, you don't know nuthin'. You argurs de Bible jes' like de white folks argurs pollyticks."

"Pollyticks? What's dem pollyticks is?" Alex replied.

"No suh! I knows what clock ticks is, I knows wat dog ticks an' bed ticks and wood ticks is, but I don't know nuthin' 'bout pollyticks."

John named the major political parties and asked,

"Didn't you ever hear of dem?"

"Yes, I hearn of em."

"Well, dem's pollyticks—dat's all dere be to it. I done tole yuh dat if yuh lived wid de Injuns so long yuh done forgot it. Let's go to bed!"

As the years passed John's mind began to fail; he was finally sent to an institution, where he died. Old Alex continued to live in his wood-yard shack in the shadow of the pines until he passed away in 1907 among his Indian friends, who gave him Christian burial under the auspices of the church of which they were members, the Episcopal minister officiating.

In a few weeks we had completed a very neat building of sawed logs across the street south of where the old office and council-house once stood. This old place has been used as a cottage for employees after several frame additions had been made to it and been finished with shingles, sheeting and paint. The Indian agent, Dr. McGillicuddy, had some difficulty in securing suitable teachers for the first schools established because, in such an out-of-the-way place as Pine Ridge, there were very few eligible who were not otherwise engaged. On the recommendation of the Reverend Bishop Hare (South Dakota Diocese of the Episcopal Church), one of his first selections was Miss Julia McCloskey, a young mixed-blood Sioux. She was placed in charge of an Episcopal Mission School in Wounded Knee Creek, in what was then known as Red Dog's Camp but is now Manderson, South Dakota.

This selection proved satisfactory in every way, but before the young lady had done more than accept the position she made a pilgrimage back to St. Mary's Young Ladies Academy, where she had served as assistant matron and where she seemed to have a prior engagement, for she returned with a fine, thrifty young farmer and the name of Mrs. Joseph Kocer. Her husband secured immediate employment at the Wounded Knee School as a gardener and handy man, and made a record for honor and integrity in his long life as farmer, merchant and stockman on the Pine Ridge.[4]

Mrs. Kocer was the daughter of James McCloskey, a refined and intelligent old man who had been an early Indian trader among the Sioux, but who had settled on the Blue River in what is now Marshall County, Kansas. He helped to organize this county and was elected as its first county clerk. The daughter was quite young when her mother passed away and her father took her to the home of an old friend, John Doty, a representative of Richardson County in the Nebraska Legislature.[5] Arrangements were made for her to remain in this family, and in their Falls City home she was mothered and schooled.

At the age of eighteen Julia McCloskey began teaching on the Iowa Indian Reservation at White Cloud, Kansas.[6] With experience in this particular line it was not long before she as teacher and her husband as industrial instructor had the Red Dog School filled to capacity. An assistant was required. The agent authorized her to make her own selection and she wrote at once to her foster-mother asking that she induce one of her nieces to take the position. This request was complied with and on November 20, 1882, Miss Luella E. Melvin of Butler, Missouri, alighted in a state of startled wonderment among the array of tall lodges of Red Dog's Camp and became Mrs. Kocer's assistant. This position she filled for a year, during which time she married the agency telegrapher, William Coffield.[7]

Such were the crude beginnings, the formative period, of what later developed into an extensive and orderly day-school system with many well-finished school buildings and with modern teachers' cottages nestling cozily in grassy yards adorned with shrubs and flowers and backed by well-kept gardens. At the risk of being verbose in the domain of the trivial, I feel justified in paying humble tribute to the pioneer teachers who laid the foundations of this fine, civilizing, institution. There were two or three other teachers temporarily located in rented cabins in out-of-the-way places. Of these I can recall only one—a man named Palmer who taught at a camp near the mouth of White Clay Creek.[8]

About the time the Oglala were being located on the White Clay, R. O. Pugh, a sprightly young Englishman, came down from the mining country were he had spent the previous winter at Jenney's Stockade near Custer City.[9] He brought a good four-horse outfit and a small bunch of stock animals, took a claim some twelve miles above the agency on White Clay Creek, and built his houses and corrals for a small horse ranch. While his property was in Nebraska, Pine Ridge was his post office and trading post. When not working on his ranch he freighted with us teamsters, hauling government supplies from the Missouri River. He formed the acquaintance of Dr. McGillicuddy, whose favorable impression of his abilities was aided, no doubt, by the fact that Mr. Pugh could shuffle his H's and place them correctly even though the lights went out.

When the Porcupine school building was completed Mr. Pugh was placed in charge, and for over a year he organized and taught the school to the satisfaction of its authorities and patrons. But when the temporary, two-story frame building for the boarding school at the agency was ready for use, he was transferred there as superintendent and filled the position with credit to himself and all concerned for a term of eighteen months, when he was again transferred to the agency as its property clerk. He served in this capacity for a considerable time before being given the double duty of issue clerk and chief of police, and finally ended his fourteen years of service in the Indian Department as chief clerk of Pine Ridge Agency.

When Mr. Pugh was transferred to the agency, Mrs. William Coffield was relieved of her position as assistant at the Red Dog School and appointed teacher at the Porcupine School. Her efficiency in her chosen line was fully demonstrated through a term of several years, during which time her school was rated as among the best.

CHAPTER 11

Trails and Trials
of a Primitive People

The roaming habits of the tribes in the vast unoccupied spaces of early days enabled them to claim and hold as much hunting ground between the strategic points surrounding these locations as they could protect from enemy encroachment. This they essayed to do by reasonably frequent occupation of their preferred sites, setting up a large village. They also received sanitary and other benefits by these frequent changes from garbage-littered camps to clean and wholesome ones.[1]

The isolation of these far distant camps gave them almost complete protection from the annoyance of traveling whiskey peddlers, from the military and trading posts throughout the country. Yet, during the customary semi-annual visit of an entire band to these trading posts, there were always some who had formed the habit of drinking and knew all the tricks of the trade, and these were usually dependable go-betweens for disposing of such wares. But the Sioux people as a whole were—and still are—very much opposed to the unrestricted distribution of hard liquors.

Tragedy Lurks in the Wild

The Cheyenne River, having its source in the broken, ragged hills to the southwest of the noted Black Hills of South Dakota, flows to the northeast, skirting their base on the south, draining the waters of the numerous streams of their southern slope. While the interior of this broad area of rich, picturesque mountainous cluster is watered by numerous streams of varied size, they flow in a general easterly direction, joining others on their way to the Missouri. One of these larger streams takes its course along the northern fringe of the Black Hills and carries waters from their northern slope, emptying into the Cheyenne River near their eastern base. It was first known as the North Fork of the Cheyenne. But the beauty of the landscape through which it flows had so impressed the early French arrivals that they habitually referred to the stream as Belle Fourche, and thus the settlers came to call it "Pretty Fork," in French.

It was along the lower stretches of this stream of clear, cold mountain water, shaded by groves that flourished along its banks, with broad valleys spreading alternately back to rock-bound hills on either side, that the distant past was depicted in all its unmarred splendor. It was a scene of Nature's most romantic beauty, and it framed a large village of the Sioux—the habitat of a people of native simplicity, schooled only in the maneuvers of hunting and of war.

And here one quiet afternoon, as village affairs were going on as usual, an incident occurred that was charged with elements of danger during every moment of its duration.

Occasionally—yet not frequently—a roving hunter or trapper on horseback, or in some small wheeled conveyance, was seen passing one of these far-away Indian villages, and sometimes he stopped awhile—always an object of curiosity to the many watching eyes.

The advent of the visitor who figures in this story was related to me in detail by a middle-aged French Canadian, favorably known throughout the region as Sam Deon.[2] He had learned the trading business, mastered the Sioux language, and held the confidence and respect of the Indians. His reliability was evidenced by his continual employment in the service of large trading companies as field man in charge of their far-flung winter camps.

His story, told in broken but cogent English, was in substance as follows:

He had finished a very successful winter trade for his company and was having the wagons and teams put in shape for the return trip (as soon as the remnants of snow had gone and bad storms were no longer probable) to the home station on the Missouri. There the robes, furs, pelts, and other Indian wares secured would be housed and shipped on the first available down-river boat to St. Louis.

He was thus engaged when a covered wagon drawn by a span of lean, worn-out horses came down the slope toward his camp, which was near the eastern edge of the village. As the wagon drew near it was seen that a white man and an Indian were occupying the driver's seat. Deon at once recognized the Indian as one belonging to a more or less dissolute bunch of reckless members of the band who occupied a cluster of ill-kept lodges a short distance below the trading outfit. The driver halted his team and alighted, accosting Deon in western fashion as he approached.

During their talk this man told a story planned for camp circulation and which could also serve as a fair alibi if required. He claimed to be on what was to have been an extended hunt and had employed the Indian as a guide. But he had loaded too heavily with provisions, had exhausted his team, and would be compelled to lay over at the camp of his guide until the horses had rested. During this time he wished to dispose of a few cases of canned goods, a sack or two of flour, and such other heavy articles as he could spare.

Deon told me that during this interview and as he watched the party pull down the slope and pitch their tent on a small plateau above the guide's camp, he was entertaining some ideas of his own. As these did not relate to his own affairs, however, he said nothing.

During the next few days life in the village moved in its usual channel. The stranger and his Indian guide were being feasted by the latter's relatives, as was their custom. Here and there older Indians could be seen passing through the village to their several homes, each carrying a small bag of flour and a still smaller container of sugar or coffee, with perhaps a tin or two of canned goods; but the "hunter" did not seem overanxious to dispose of his provisions too rapidly.

In a short time there were indications of whiskey in camp. Of course there was no legally constituted authority (save some distant military post) that could be invoked to handle such cases; moreover, they were of such infrequent occurrence in these far-away villages that slight attention was given them unless some especially aggravating or disastrous incident occurred. In such case the perpetrators of the offense were apt to meet swift and severe punishment, as is disclosed by the following incident.

The bogus hunter and his native "man Friday" cautiously continued their illicit traffic for some ten days, always giving out a new story to the effect that they were soon to move on, which they were. But they and the entire camp were blissfully ignorant of the cause, time, manner and precipitation of their move.

On a certain mid-afternoon, in the clear and balmy spring air, groups of the older Indians were sitting before their lodges chatting and smoking. No doubt some of them were feeling quite comfortable as the result of a sly drink or two, but none were boisterous or even hilarious. One looking upon the tranquil picture presented by the village that pleasant afternoon would find it difficult to believe that within a few minutes all would change to a scene of tumult, terror and tragedy.

Near the center of the village a young man was standing beside the entrance of a large lodge, wrapped in a blanket which covered his head in such a manner as to conceal most of his face. Sitting upon a small log near him was his mother, who was old. She was speaking to her son in plaintive expostulation and his answers were petulant, indicating to passers-by that both had been drinking. And what then occurred justified the conclusion.

Down one of the irregular thoroughfares such as wind through an Indian village, an old man was coming slowly along on his pony. As the mother sitting by the lodge saw him, she hid her face in her blanket and began to cry. This irritated her son, who gruffly demanded to know what she was crying about. The mother then disclosed her face and, pointing to the approaching horseman, said,

"My son, you see that man coming? He has made me cry all my life. Thirty summers ago he made you and your sister cry too, for he killed your father."

Without a word the young man quickly stepped through the lodge door and returned with his gun. Leveling it at the old man as he was passing, he fired and killed him instantly. As the body fell to the ground the horse reared and stampeded through the village. Panic ensued at once.

Screams of the astonished witnesses alarmed those farther away and also impelled the culprit to make a mad dash for escape. Leaping and dodging among the lodges to avoid the missiles being hurled at him, he ran for the hills. At the end of a ledge of rock that rose sharply some ten feet above the rim of the valley, he scrambled through brush and stunted trees until he gained the crest of the ledge, where the foliage of dwarfed cedars screened him from view.

It was evident to his pursuers that he was seriously wounded and would be easy to capture; so, when he had crawled through the shrubbery to the edge of the crest and began raising the dust at their feet with an occasional bullet, they made a scattering pause, slowing their advance. In the meantime some of his neighbors (among them a cousin and other relatives) had followed his trail up the hillside and then taken an opposite direction in order to approach him from the rear. When this party was near enough, his cousin, a warrior in good standing, called to him to surrender and take his just punishment. At this the wounded man crawled to the verge of the precipice and, turning his gun upon himself, fired a bullet through his head and fell to the flat below.

At the sound of the shot that had killed the old man and the furor that instantly followed, the supposed hunter (who happened to be alone) needed no interpreter other than his own guilty conscience to apprise him that the thing he had known from the first might happen had actually occurred. Seizing his gun and ammunition and a few scraps of food, he ran down the slope toward the brush on the banks of the stream. Passing a woman of his guide's family who was friendly to him, he waved her toward his tent and kept running. She watched him enter a patch of brush, leafless but of a density that hid him from view; then when she saw him skipping from tree to tree far down the stream, she began carrying provisions from his tent to her family lodge.

Under cover of timber that grew between bank and bluff some distance farther down, the fleeing culprit came to the opening of a narrow gulch that led back into the hills, terminating in groves of dense cedar thickets. These high-walled gulches with their stony bottoms made tracking most difficult and so were adapted to easy escape. This gulch, it was later decided, he must have followed.

The woman to whom he had waved, and who had evidently been left to watch the camp, had considerable time for her trips between tent and tepee to secure what, for that place and time, were classed as luxuries: sugar, coffee, tea, fats and flour; also a blanket or two from the top of the bed in the covered wagon. Meanwhile most of the villagers were grouped at the scene of the last tragedy, weeping, moaning or exhorting in the interest of peace between relatives of both the victim and the suicide. Finally an understanding was reached, settlement postponed for a later date, and the tumult ceased.

Then attention reverted to the "hunter" who had caused all the trouble, and a rush was made back through the village, the "Dog Soldiers" followed closely by the crowd determined to wreak vengeance upon the culprit who had deceived and misguided them. Finding his tent deserted, they began throwing its contents out among the onlookers, who quickly began a game of grab. Then the tent was fired, the cover torn from the wagon, and blankets and a shoddy mattress hurled through the air. Beneath the mattress they found a thin layer of hay, and poking through this many gallon kegs of whiskey were disclosed. These small kegs, with bails for easy handling that made them prized for carrying water, were a good seller at all frontier trading posts. Filled with cheap whiskey, they were worth from $2.50 to $3.00 normally. In a remote Indian camp, however, each one was good for the purchase price of a horse or mule— though not under such conditions as here described! That wagon and its contents were at once run over into the burning tent, where hay, whiskey, some provisions, and various personal belongings of its former occupant were consumed. The woman who had been on guard was questioned closely, but all the information she would vouchsafe was that she had seen the white man run from his tent with his gun and on down into the thick brush.

Some effort was made toward scouting the timbered flat along the stream and the intersecting gulches, but always from a safe distance. They were not anxious to approach an armed fugitive shielded by brush or rock. But after the fuss and flurry occasioned by this tragic episode had begun to calm down, it was decided that both the fake hunter and his guide had succeeded in making their escape. As to the latter, he was one of them and, as they viewed it, had done nothing other than work for pay. But the authoritative arm of the village—the Dog Soldiers—wished to capture him not only for a possible flogging with their quirts but for a rigid questioning about the whole affair. Especially did they wish to learn what, if anything, he knew as to the hiding-place of the white man. But this wily individual seemed to have made his way to freedom, and in so doing avoided a savage death.[3]

The Lost Children
A Dakota Legend

Often during the trading season, after the fall hunt was over and the Indians were mostly congregated in one large camp for the winter, three or four large trading outfits were located at various points therein. The managers of these concerns, with their helpers, were given to spending their evenings together in social parties at one of the most convenient, roomy lodges. Here story-telling was always one of their major pastimes, and in this the older Indians who had been more or less noted for past activity and good memory were often star performers.

On one such occasion a very aged Indian regaled the party by recounting the following tribal episode. The old man, after slowly lighting his pipe and taking a whiff or two, passed it on to his next neighbor, then began:[4]

"Many winters ago when I was a little boy, I often heard my grandfather (then a very old man) say that he had heard his father tell how the old men of the village talked much of the time long ago, when the Sioux lived far away towards the east and were all in one large village and under one chief. They had enemies to the south and southwest who gave them great annoyance, and it was necessary to keep detachments from their village posted on the outskirts of their territory in several directions to guard against invasion. From time to time these guardsmen and their families were relieved and returned to the village.

"Thus intruders were checked and gradually driven farther away, until the Sioux following them finally established themselves in the country they had taken, and the strength of the village increased until it was a powerful one under the leadership of a great war chief whose name was The Yellow Horse. On the west side of the village another strong tribe was located who called themselves The Cut Fingers, but who were known then and since as the Cheyenne Tribe.

"The relation between these people and our own had been that of a watchful, suspicious peace which finally ended in war. Our people put the Cheyennes to rout and followed them relentlessly. Every year they had a fight and forced them further west, until finally they were driven across the Missouri River.

"This was not a war of extermination. The tribes took prisoners back and forth, and seemed to fight each other only for the reason that there were no other enemies to fight. But when they crossed the Missouri they soon discovered that there were powerful tribes both to the north and west; then the Sioux, following the advice of their chief Yellow Horse, decided to quit fighting the Cheyenne and to make allies of them if possible.

"Accordingly messengers were sent to the Cheyenne village among whom were Cheyennes that the Sioux had long held as prisoners. After traveling five sleeps they came to the village; then, the Sioux remaining at a distance, the prisoners went into the village and made known the object of their visit. Their message was cordially received, and the Sioux were escorted in, feasted, and entertained in a hospitable manner until the following day, when a council was held. There the Sioux stated that they had been sent by their chief, The Yellow Horse, to ask the Cheyenne tribe to move their village to a point midway between the two villages, where they would find the Sioux encamped for the purpose of holding a great council of peace.

"The Cheyenne accepted the proposition, and sent an escort of Sioux prisoners back with the messengers as evidence of their good intentions. At the appointed time and place the tribes met and set up their villages close together. The great council lodge of the Sioux was chosen as the place of deliberation.

"The council began with the Sioux chief, The Yellow Horse, and Long Bow, the Cheyenne chief, as the leading spirits. The first half of the day was spent in making speeches, The Yellow Horse telling the Cheyenne that they had been fighting so long they had now become well acquainted; that they were neighbors; moreover, that during their wars each side had taken so many prisoners that they were not only neighbors but relatives; that they were in a new country where their rights were likely to be disputed by powerful tribes, and it would be better for them to remain near each other and fight together in the future.

"He was followed by Chief Long Bow and others, all of whom favored the idea, and it was soon decided that such arrangements should be effected.

"The sun was now in the middle of the sky and the council was adjourned for the feast. After they had feasted the council met again and began to arrange the terms of peace, deciding the boundaries of their respective territory and the signals by which they were to communicate in event that either village should be attacked in force by an enemy. During the discussion of these matters they were continually being annoyed by the boys and girls of the Sioux village, who in their wild and boisterous sports made such a din that the councilors were greatly disturbed. Several times The Yellow Horse sent a soldier to order them to a more distant part of the village to play, but they soon returned.

"Finally, becoming exasperated, The Yellow Horse called out the Indian soldiers and instructed them to take all the children between the ages of eight and fourteen, mount them on old ponies, and instruct their relatives to furnish enough old lodges to house them and old women to manage them, then to take them some distance over a high ridge to another small creek and keep them there until the great council should be ended. He then explained the matter to the Cheyenne and the council adjourned again until the evening.

"The chief's order as to the children was carried out. In the evening the lodge fires were lighted again, the councilors assembled and were engaged in discussion, when a yell of distress was heard at a little distance from the council lodge.

"Immediately the council broke up in a stampede, some rushing for the entrance, others drawing their knives and slashing their own exit through the lodge. It was dark, but someone was heard to bellow in the Cheyenne tongue, 'I am killed!' while another in the Sioux tongue loudly boasted, 'I killed him!'

"It was afterward found that a Cheyenne had stolen the wife of a Sioux, had been discovered by the injured husband and shot; but no investigation was made at the time, for panic seized the people of both villages. Like magic the lodges were torn down and packed and the tribes started at breakneck speed in opposite directions, running from each other. On they went in wild confusion, each band imagining that the other was in pursuit.

"When they had traveled about half the night the Sioux suddenly missed their children, and a halt was called. After a short consultation they decided that if the Cheyenne were pursuing them they would not be able to search for the children, and as the rear guard of the party was crowding upon them The Yellow Horse directed that they go on until daylight, when they would camp and send a strong party back after the children. So they kept on.

"Daylight came and still they did not stop, but kept traveling until about the middle of the afternoon when they halted from sheer exhaustion. Nothing but rest and food for themselves and their animals could be thought of under the circumstances, so they decided to start in search of the forgotten children the next morning.

"In the meantime the youngsters had grown weary of their banishment, having waited patiently during the greater part of the time consumed by the stampede to be called back or to have a visit from some of their relatives. But no one came. Finally some of the older boys went out on their ponies to the top of the ridge where they could get a view of the village, and were astounded to see that there was no trace of the hundreds of lodges that they had left there the day before.

"Hurrying back to their camp, the scouts reported this fact to the women, who constituted the highest authority in their small band. It was decided to pull up and return at once, as the women held the hope that the boys were mistaken in the exact location of the lodges and so had viewed the wrong territory. But, traveling back over the hills with their ponies and travois, they were soon undeceived. The sun was fast dropping out of sight when they came to the last long slope down which they had to travel to reach the place they had lately left. When they found that the village had actually vanished, there began a chorus of wonder and wailing.

"It was finally agreed to follow the trail; but as there were two leading in opposite directions, the question at once arose: Which trail? The fast-falling darkness compelled a choice, and they began their journey. All night they traveled, resting the next day. In the evening they started again and went on through the night, resting by daylight as before. On the third night they saw the fires of a village in the bend of a small creek some distance ahead. Fearing that it might belong to the Cheyenne (as they had concluded that the council must have broken up in a fight), they halted while three of the older boys crawled up near enough to learn from the language used that this was indeed a camp of the Cheyenne. Returning to their party, they began to retrace their steps. Their ponies were old, gentle and tired, and they knew that safety lay in the fact that the Cheyenne were ignorant of their presence.

"All that night they traveled back along the trail, then rested until noon of the next day, when they decided to keep their course toward their old village. There they hoped to find some of their people, or some hint of where they had gone. But when they arrived at this place they were disappointed, and soon, growing despondent, they gave up the search.

"A party had been sent out by The Yellow Horse the second day after their banishment from the village, but when the scouts came to the place where they had located the children they were nowhere to be found. Giving them up as having been captured by the Cheyenne, they returned to the village disheartened.

"The old women who had gone out with the boys acted as councilors of the new village. They encouraged the boys to learn the art of making arrows and urged them to their best efforts in killing game, for the flesh was a necessity for food and the skins were made into moccasins, clothing, and lodges. Thus they passed through the first few years of their isolation.

"The following year the children began marrying and establishing lodges and families of their own. Tribal organization was effected by electing the oldest boy as chief under the name of The Yellow Horse.

"Seventeen years passed away and this band of youthful warriors had grown strong and efficient. They had met the enemy in battle many times and came off with credit, but as yet had found no trace of the parent village.

"But it happened one summer that they had drifted a great deal farther north than ever before and encamped along a small stream in a country that was new to them. Some of their party, who were hunting, turned a sharp angle of a hill and came almost face to face with another party of Indians of about their own number. Each party quickly wheeled, but stopped when only a short distance apart. Presently the leader of one party accosted the other, and each was surprised to find that the other spoke the same language. The younger men asked the others who they were, and the others replied:

'We are Sioux and we are from a large village a short ride from here, and our chief's name is The Yellow Horse. Who are you?'

'We are Sioux and our chief's name is The Yellow Horse.'

"Then the group of older Indians asked: 'Are you not the lost children?' On learning that they were they consulted a little; then, being told where their village was located, they put the whips to their ponies and rode back to their own village where they told the story. The chief immediately sent out a large party to visit the children, as they were still called, and ask them to come back home.

"The answer sent back to the old village was that they would never return to it as long as The Yellow Horse was alive. That he had cast them away when they were children, and now they were men and able to take care of themselves.

"This angered the old chief, who immediately declared that he would make them move in and thereupon called for warriors. But as the band of the younger Yellow Horse were looked upon as their children, he could get no volunteers to help him except the members of his own family and their close relatives. However, as these were numerous and great warriors, he concluded to start out with them.

"When the old chief reached the village of the younger Yellow Horse he was surprised at its size, yet was still able to think of them only as children. Stopping his warriors upon an eminence near the village, he sent a messenger to command them to take down their lodges and move to his village. In a short time the messengers returned bringing a defiant refusal. This so enraged the old chief, who for years had been accustomed to use his word as law, that he charged upon the village. Young Yellow Horse and his warriors met the charge with a shower of arrows and repulsed it. As the attackers turned to withdraw, the older Yellow Horse was seen to reel in his saddle, then fall from his horse. Examination proved that he was dead, but no wound could be found upon the body.

"Such an event could only be looked upon as some mysterious act of great medicine. As a result a parley ensued, during which the lost children agreed to move to the village the next day. This they did, and for a long time there was great feasting and rejoicing over the reunion thus effected after so long a separation.

"But eventually the tribe began to discuss the election of another chief. Many were in favor of choosing the younger Yellow Horse as chief of all the tribe; in fact, the members of his own band would listen to no other proposition. But many were opposed to him, and great dissension arose among them until it became evident that no chief could be chosen. Then it was suggested that they separate and each large, neighborly group of families go into a camp by itself and elect its own chief.

"This they did, circumstances similar to this often occurred among them and thus it was that the great Western Sioux were divided into so many bands."

CHAPTER 12

The First White Men among the Indians

The early French trappers in the employ of The Hudson Bay and the American Fur companies predominated this section of the Northwest, with only here and there a man of different nationality. Naturally the French language prevailed among civilized men for a number of years, but the ever-increasing transcontinental travel soon changed this and English became the language generally spoken.

Practically all of these young, sturdy and vigorous men took Indian wives, in accord with the centuries-old custom of the tribe; and of course they raised families. As the fur business became less remunerative and the demand for logs, cord-wood, hay and supply transportation at the military and trading posts became the more attractive work, they began building cabins in congenial and protective clusters at convenient points, thus establishing more permanent homes and within neighborhood distances.

There were no educational facilities whatsoever, but the children were given good paternal care as to sustenance, and crudely taught such customs, principles and usages of civilization as the tutors were able to impart. The boys were instructed in the use of the machinery and tools at hand and whatever work in which their fathers were engaged. But it was difficult to get them to apply themselves steadily, in that wild environment, after reaching the age when other boys consider themselves "gallants." Yet they learned the significance of industry; and when required, could do the work at hand.

Each of these advance frontiersmen had acquired at least one four-horse or mule team and a wagon. Some of the more thrifty had small trains of horses, mules or oxen, as the case might be. Some of them built and successfully operated large mercantile ranches on the principal highways. Several of these sent their older sons off to school, where they had opportunity to mingle with white students of their own age. Many of the boys profited thereby, learning language, deportment, and at least the rudiments of an education before yielding to the call of their native wild and pine-environed homes. It was from this class, and from their fathers, and here and there a bright young full-blood trained by the Church, that the earlier missionaries selected their first catechists and helpers, the army its most reliable interpreters and guides, and the representatives of government officials their most efficient translators.

The French pioneers here referred to came from many parts of the world. From and by way of St. Louis came men who had sailed from France; others came from Switzerland; but most were from nearby Canada. Yet all brought with them their inherent partiality for good fare, as well as a knowledge of the culinary art, and in this the women of their families were soon made proficient. Not only did they learn to prepare the choice meats that Nature provided at their doors, but also all kinds of simple pastries, for the head of the house was able to and did furnish all kinds of necessary ingredients, no matter how far overland they might be fetched. The more advanced among them sent their daughters to seminaries conducted by the Catholic Sisters, but it would have been difficult to establish that as a prevailing custom, for the last thing an Indian mother wishes to do is to permit a separation between herself and her children—especially her girls.

Naturally the widely distributed musical talent inherent in the race was there also, manifesting in many families and predominant in some, as evidenced by the various musical instruments seen in the homes, with organs mostly but here and there a piano occupying the place of honor. And it was among the women of these families that the early missionaries found their most willing and effective helpers in furthering the cause of Christianity. Readily, and without regard to sect, they joined the various missionaries and catechists in organizing their churches, auxiliary cults and kindred organizations.

In attempting the portrayal of the earliest neighborhood settlements in the Indian country, which always were located in the vicinity of some military post, large road ranche or Indian agency, I do not describe any particular locality but only present the features common to all such settlements, from Fort Fetterman to Fort Laramie in Wyoming, and at points along the Missouri River and elsewhere in South Dakota. And the picture would be incomplete if the Mexican camps nestling in some bend of the stream or cove in the hills, always separated from but adjacent to these early pioneer settlements, were not included.

It seems that these men, American citizens of our southwestern territories, early discovered the trade possibilities that could be developed with the Indian tribes of the great northern plains. Trips to this section therefore became an annual occurrence, always looked forward to by the Indians, who gladly exchanged their robes, furs and ponies for these goods that furnished them a yearly treat, dried corn, pumpkins and garden peppers, red and white beans, onions, potatoes, as well as Navajo blankets and other native wares.

Some of these traders, seeing the opportunity for team work and liking their new-found friends, the Sioux, remained and married among them. Many spoke English indifferently, but some were fairly educated according to their standards. They were constant and industrious teamsters, affable and friendly to meet, but had a penchant for segregating their camps, where they could and did converse in their provincial Spanish exclusively.

As to the pioneering French trappers, it was some of them whom I encountered on my advent into the Fort Laramie neighborhood in 1871. Many of them were still sprightly old men, retired from their former activities, and enjoyed themselves most when grouped together in reminiscent mood. As a youngster I was first amazed and then amused at their exaggerations (improvised for tenderfoot ears) in telling their stories of strange adventures and hairbreadth escapes; or thrilled by their soberly recounted tales of their life while alone in isolated trapping camps during the long winter seasons, as was required by the fur companies that employed them.

Among these men in their earlier days there had been, undoubtedly, uncouth and criminal characters such as are found among masses of men everywhere, but the law of the survival of the fittest eliminates them in time. At any rate the old-timers of this story were a convivial, jolly set, and following are a few samples of the life stories they told of that they had to contend with in their frontier life.

Trappers (unless working independently, as very few were) when employed were as completely under the domination of their superior officers as soldiers in the army. Only out in the wild did they act on their own initiative. In those days, as everywhere and at all times and in all lines of activity, little men would often get into big places and have command over men more trusty and competent than they; and men in far-away places were perhaps even more subject to unscrupulous dealings than elsewhere.

And so it was, among the trappers of that section at least, that a suspicion had somehow started and refused to [go?] down to [the] effect that all was not well with one of the fur-trading stations on the Missouri. Trappers, notwithstanding the hazards of their calling, for the most part were industrious and frugal men, some of whom had sizeable amounts due from the company. It was rumored that too many of these would go out for another season's fur gathering and fail to return.[1] Their supposed fate was probably only over-nursed imagination, but here is what one lone trapper did about it according to the old-time stories.

A young, shrewd and husky French trapper by the name of Joseph Vlandry, who spoke the Sioux language like a native and was wise to all the crafty tricks of the wild, found on one of his spring returns to headquarters that he had sixteen hundred dollars due for furs. So he decided to go down the river to civilization and start life for himself.[2]

When this fact became known, he was approached and urged, as one of the company's most dependable trappers, to remain another season. During this urging he thought he could detect a vein of flattery. But, wishing to visit a few of his old acquaintances in the neighborhood, none residing more than a hundred miles distant, he agreed to the proposal and spent the summer accordingly.

At the proper time in the following fall he, with his horse and pack animal, were wending their way toward the mountains. The third night out he had pitched his pack near a cluster of willows on the branch of a larger stream that lay over the hills a mile or two to the south, and while out staking his animals he saw a good-sized Government mule train pull to camp over the hills, on the larger stream.

Just as dusk was falling and he was making his spread for supper, a young Sioux, well armed and mounted on a fine American horse, rode into his camp. He accosted the stranger with the usual salutation, "How, Cola!" and invited him to light and eat, which he did. During the meal, in answer to questions, the Indian imparted the information that he was on the trail of some friends in a hunting party, whom he felt sure were but a short distance ahead. This he gave as his reason for not wishing to unsaddle and hobble his mount for the night.

Vlandry seemed to take this story as a matter of course, but as the meal was finished he startled the young Indian by asking abruptly "Now, my friend, why do you want to kill me?"

The accusing question was jokingly denied, and Vlandry's suspicions were increased thereby. As the Indian hung his head the trapper continued.

"You are getting that fine horse and rigging for this ride, and when you get back to the river you will be given a fine costume of feathers and flannels, provisions enough to put on a feast for your friends, and that will be all. Now I can tell you of something better than that. When it gets good and dark, you go over that hill and watch that herd of mules. When the herder lets them scatter, as he will have to do to give them a chance to feed, you know how to slip in behind a bunch you think you can handle and keep urging them farther away. When out of sight of the unsuspecting night-herder, move them slowly on; then, when you think it is safe, stampede them for the river.

"When you arrive at the village, having done this all by yourself, you will be a big man among your people. You can sell some of the mules to freighters for money enough to buy a fine dance rig and food to feast your friends whenever you want to do so, and you will be a chief."

This was very bad advice, most certainly, but it will be remembered that Mr. Vlandry considered himself in a position where he might either have to kill the Indian or be killed himself. He did not wish either event to happen, so he cunningly passed the buck to Uncle Sam. It may have been a mere suspicion that he acted upon, but he was convinced he was right and felt he could take no chances.

After their chat and smoke was finished the Indian left, in apparent good humor, with the remark that he would think it over.

Next morning, as Vlandry was breaking camp, he was interviewed by a wagon boss and a soldier with the query as to whether or not he had seen stray mules grazing about. He told them of his lone Indian guest at supper, how long he stayed and where he said he was headed for, adding that in his opinion their mules were a long way on the trail to the Missouri River by that time. Then, continuing on to a permanent camp, he made a successful winter's catch and satisfactory settlement with the company in the spring, and took a steamboat down the river to his desired destination. Nothing more was heard of the Indian or the mules.

Not long after the first trading posts were established at old Fort Laramie, Wyoming, Frank Salway, an intelligent, brawny and trusted employee, was called into the office of his company and given papers of importance to be delivered to a trading post on the Missouri in the vicinity of old Fort Pierre.[3] Certainty of delivery and assured return of answers being the sole object of the trip, Salway was instructed to go on foot, keep out of sight of Indians and all others, and travel only at night unless sure of not being observed. Time was not the consideration, but security of accomplishment was.

Having, of course, his own rifle, butcher knife, well filled powder horn, lead and molds, the company supplied him with provisions for his trip. The supplies furnished to all messengers on such errands consisted only of one small pouch of salt. But on trips where both security and speed were expected, a fleet horse and sustenance that could be had without noise were provided.

Mr. Salway's trip was made safely and in reasonable time and was not considered unusual in those days, for none but men of physical endurance, skill and judgement were asked to perform such feats, and he was known throughout that vast section as a man of great strength. In fact, in later years Dr. Addison E. Sheldon, superintendent of the Nebraska State Historical Society, gave him conspicuous notice in one of several published sketches of the Sioux Reservation, under the title "The Strong Man."[4]

Many of the earlier Indian traders, like some trappers, operated independently. No license was required. Men who had capital sufficient to outfit themselves could arrange with the chief or head man of an Indian band to do a season's trading at their winter camp. They were always anxious to have such accommodations.

But even in those remote western communities there were always men equipped to handle the business properly, and who understood the Indians, their language and customs. Large mercantile companies employed such men and placed them in charge of their trading expeditions. Among these capables who preferred to manage extensive trading operations was James McCloskey, already mentioned in this narrative, who later helped to organize Marshall County, Kansas, and Marysville, its county seat, on the bank of the Blue River.

These pioneers of the wild spaces had many strange and thrilling experiences. The following is but one of the many interesting tales of adventure with which Mr. McCloskey used to entertain his friends.

It was customary with the Indian traders of the old west to contact the source of tribal authority in the field shortly before the fall hunt was finished. At this meeting it would be learned just where the several bands covering their hunting area had decided to locate their main winter camp and the side camps, if any. When this information was secured the trader would know at about what time to leave the supply post, and what quantities of staples and new lines of goods (if any) he should take for the trade.

All these details had been agreed upon between Red Cloud and McCloskey. At what he considered the proper time, he and the usual assistant were in his light rig preceding four heavily loaded four-mule teams in charge of a wagon-master, en route to the rendezvous. He and his helper were going ahead of the train for the purpose of selecting a suitable location for their trading. He desired to have all in readiness when the Indians arrived and let them pitch their tepees to conform.

Finally they found the designated place and, after looking over the valleys, flats and converging streams, selected a site on a small plateau above a meandering rivulet and staked their tent to await the arrival of the train and the Indians. But it was not long before they realized that the train was unduly slow or had missed the correct route. Each day they passed the time hunting in the vicinity of their tent, familiarizing themselves with the valleys, creeks and timbered bends of the extended terrain that was to be the site of the Indian village. At night, by candle or lantern light, they conned the reading matter they had brought. Though growing more and more uneasy, there was nothing they could do but wait.

It was the evening of the fourth day when the assistant complained of not feeling well. He ate but a morsel for supper and retired at once, declining all proffered help and assuring his partner he would be all right in the morning. But McCloskey was worried, and an hour or so later when the ailing man called for water and he had taken it to him, he saw that he had a very high temperature and administered the water accordingly.

Now he was worried indeed, for this was one of his old acquaintances and a close friend. Men who went into the far places did not choose their companions in haphazard fashion, but for their dependable qualities and knowledge of the business at hand. He got out his first-aid kit with medicines and crude appliances, administered quinine, swathed his friend's head with moist bandages, and attended him closely through the night. But the patient grew steadily worse and passed out before noon the next day.

This was a trying situation for a lone man in the wilderness, but there was no help and he did the only rational thing possible. Wrapping the body in a new blanket he laid it on its bunk, raising the corner flaps of the tent near it for air. He wished to keep it as long as the balmy weather would permit. He then sat down to wait and wonder, but found he could not sit still long. Every little while he ran outside to scan the horizon for the approach of the mule train or even a straggling Indian hunter who might have wandered ahead of his tribe. But he sighted no one.

About three o'clock of that warm afternoon he concluded it might not be safe to hold the body any longer, so dug a temporary shallow grave and placed it there. That night, sadly ruminating over his friend's death and the disturbing delay, he was startled by what he felt sure was a groan.

"My God!" he cried. "Did I bury poor Bill alive?"

Rushing out into the darkness he stood long, listening, beside the grave but there was no sound save the rustling of the leaves and the call of night birds flitting among the boughs.

Satisfied that he had been mistaken, McCloskey returned to his chair and had but resumed it when he heard the sound repeated. Again rushing out and listening at the grave, he heard the call more clearly, coming from a distance up the main stream. Immediately he fired a signal shot, heard a shot in answer, and presently was joyfully greeting his wagon-master. In a few days his friend and helper had received decent burial in a smoothly built casket made of lumber from large dry-goods boxes, and then the advance travois of the Indian village were sighted, coming over a distant ridge toward their winter quarters.

The subject of Indian agencies could not consistently be passed by without mention of the intermarriages of white men who comprised a small part of the various agency communities. Reference to this subject—considering the manner in which it has usually been thrust upon public notice—will doubtless be received with a frown, and the presence of such men among the Indians pronounced a grave error. Perhaps from a superficial viewpoint this is correct, and most certainly it is true as regards the material interest of the parties themselves. But, in a broader and unbiased view, the question of propriety in such marriages by white men whose lives were fixed among wild Indian tribes as vedettes of an advancing civilization remains to be answered by future years. These remarks are not submitted as apology but rather as explanation of the facts. Presumably they may apply to the various tribes of American Indians, but refer more particularly to the plains Sioux and to the Brulé and Oglala bands.

As government activities were shifting to the east from the military posts in Wyoming, the communities that had been built around those posts naturally broke up. The people who had comprised them, following the demand for employment, settled where new agencies were being constructed and where freighting and all manner of employment was available.

Thus it was that, much later, when Pine Ridge Agency presented the warlike aspect before referred to, these men helped swell the crowds that filled the streets. They had established homes for their families along the various streams far out on the reservation; and, while cultivating gardens and occasionally more pretentious fields, accumulating chickens and domestic animals, still kept their cash-producing freight outfits and used them as judgment dictated.

It was the men of these homes that, when trouble seemed imminent, followed the example of Nebraska settlers and moved their families to a more protected quarter; and it was but shortly afterward that the military authorities ordered them all to the agency. Most of these men were Americans. Natives of practically every state in the Union could be found among them—often a number from some particular state but a few came from foreign countries.

At this point I beg the reader's indulgence while I puncture a few bubbles of venomous rumor that designing persons floated back to the home folks. In the absence of any knowledge to the contrary, they were naturally given credence as facts.

These men were not derelicts, wearing red shirts and beaded moccasins, living on government rations, smoking cigarettes and idling away the time in sun or shade, as suited their whim. Excepting for their marital relations they were precisely like the average of other men in any ordinary community. They were motivated by the same impulses and held the same ideals. I speak, of course, of the preponderant majority. Doubtless there were some among them who would answer to the disparaging description given; also a sneak thief and drunken loafer could be found here and there but such men were rated at their true worth—or worthlessness—and treated accordingly.

The families of these men drew rations after the treaty of 1868 that guaranteed the Sioux subsistence supplies for a term of thirty years.[5] Later this treaty was extended for a term of years with a discretionary clause that allowed the government to issue only to the aged, infirm, and children attending school, if conditions warranted. The Indians looked upon the supplies thus received as theirs by right of contract in the ceding of certain large tracts of land. The food furnished under said contract was adequate to the Indian standard of living while supplemented by the game and wild fruits then obtainable. It was considered by the "Working-White-Men" (that is just what the Indians called them) as a mere pittance compared with that which the majority of them furnished their families from the traders stores. From such sources they could always provide for their families, with or without cash, for their credit was good and they did not fail to keep it so.

If the old books of the merchants at the various agencies could speak, they would disclose the fact that the accounts of hundreds of thousands of dollars that encumber their pages because of credits extended these patrons (both white and Indian) show a higher percentage of collections than those of merchants of the average towns throughout the country.

The facts also disclose another angle to this question of rations. At that time all activities, directly or indirectly, were based upon team work. Double or single teams were always in demand; the latter, with driver, commanding four or five dollars per day. Naturally the owners of teams had an eye to thrift. A trip to the agency to bring home the rations required from three to six days. And what were the rations? A little bacon and flour, sugar and coffee, a few beans, a twenty-five cent can of baking powder, worth, all told, from two to six dollars according to the number of wards in the family. Common sense required the team owner to pronounce the ration system a nuisance and a racket, so far as his family was concerned. But let him suggest to his wife the wisdom of abolishing it, and the retort positive would be:

"No sir! This stuff is mine. We traded land for this."

Any married man knows the outcome of the argument.

While all these men, engaged in different callings, had been for years separated from their home ties, paternal influence, and the social surroundings in which they had been reared—separated by many hundreds of miles—it would be manifestly unfair to imply that all succumbed to the alluring influence of this peculiar environment. But many of them did so, and they were not by any means the weakest of the group. They were strong, upstanding characters, as were those who remained single until they went back to civilization or waited for it to overtake them. Those who were familiar with the domestic life of these people through the contacts of years know that the wild exaggerations of their everyday village customs and their home lives were, for the most part, rank libels.

As to the early French, most of them had been, at first, hard workers; later they became active and prosperous men of affairs, such as road-ranch merchants, hay and wood contractors for military posts and camps, and owners of transportation systems for various government supplies. They had raised respectable families which, when grown, had their own social activities such as picnics, parties and celebrations; but neighborhood dances were their chief entertainment.

On national holidays a grand ball and banquet marked the occasion, and here all white employees, from teamsters to office force, participated. These banquets consisted of all manner of viands splendidly prepared, wherein the French tutoring of the neat and comely mixed-blood women became self-evident. In those days, before their schooling, full-blood Indians were rarely represented at the "White Man's dances," as they termed them. A few of the older men and women sometimes watched the strange spectacle. They were always welcome and never left the hall hungry, but as a rule these dances were no attraction to them. They seemed too complicated; besides, they felt that they had far more interesting dances of their own every night.

The first act on the program for those dances was to select from three to five steady, level-headed young men as policemen for the night, and order and a good time were the rule.

Now I think that the veil covering the environment of sojourners in an Indian neighborhood of the early West has been raised far enough to show why those pioneers (usually but not always of French antecedents) had acquired many white sons-in-law in addition to those of mixed blood. Not all these were from among the steady and industrious young men who were classed as hired hands; a number came from the ranks of managers, clerks, bookkeepers, and even owners of various local industries. It was a custom of the time and place, and these marriages had long been solemnized by church or civil authority.

The unjust and uncalled-for obloquy heaped upon these men as a class by some designing Indian agents and office workers was done deliberately in an effort to degrade them. But as a matter of fact, as soon as those who had married among the Sioux had opportunity to mix with men in the towns along the railroads, they readily established friendship and credit among the citizens. Many who were not already affiliated with the various fraternal orders of the day applied and were accepted into membership. This should go far toward convincing the uninformed that they were not considered an aggregation of scalawags by the whites who lived nearest them.

Indian agencies in those days, naturally, were located in places far removed from civilization and authority. Too often the chief offices—sometimes even the chair of the agent himself—were filled by the friends of politicians without regard to ability or character: men totally devoid of human sympathy or sense of responsibility, but who looked upon their positions as a grove of political plum trees growing wild; theirs by right of discovery, and up to them to shake while the fruit was ripe and the shaking was good. As a rule they had nothing to fear from their government inspector, since he was one of their kind and made the official rounds in that placid state of mind that follows the consumption of fried chicken and mellow wines.

But when an inspector proved immune to such seductive influences, as a number of them did, then the agency official (or officials) appealed to congenial souls in the Indian Department at Washington, and under one pretext or another said inspector was summarily called back to headquarters. In event of further agitation the politicians stepped in, and the case was soon relegated to the status of "Hush-hush—for the good of the Party!"—any party that happened to be in power at the time.

The officials composing such cliques were always apprehensive, knowing well that they were on the reservation only by sufferance of the citizens. They knew too that the intermarried white men were honorable and devoted in their family life and would protect their own. Consequently it behooved all participants in shady official transactions to fortify their own positions by advance vilification of those possessing knowledge of the facts by virtue of their Indian marriage, and who certainly would be called as witnesses in Federal Court if an issue arose. Shrewdly they reasoned that their best safeguard against any such exigency lay in consistent undermining of the character and reputation for veracity of the men they feared, so that as evidence their words would have no weight.

Therefore they conspired to attack, as a class, that host of innocent and defenseless men whose only sin lay in the fact of intermarriage and fidelity. By official reports to Washington, by personal letters and widely quoted publicity of various kinds, they systematically slandered those potential enemies whom their own chicanery would array against them in event of any disclosure precipitating a public scandal.

Both the fact and the motive of all this infamous broadcasting were clearly evident not only to the sagacious victims thereof but to keen disinterested observers—yet nothing could be done about it. And little did the beneficiaries of this system care for the reflection of their conduct upon faithful and efficient employees holding similar positions.

In the main, these men who intermarried were formed of the sturdy pioneer fiber that helped conquer the West, and many realized fully that in "going native" they had crossed the sacred confines established by society and burned their bridges behind them. Yet personal considerations impelled them to the step regardless of consequences, thus unconsciously placing themselves at the mercy of officials in the Indian Service who were determined to cover, at any cost to others, their own nefarious schemes for cheating both the Indians and the government - which they did, continuously and outrageously.

Trusting that the reader has not found this subject any more uninteresting, unpleasant and annoying than has the author, who writes in the interest of justice, I leave it as grist in "the mills of the gods," confident that however slow the grinding, some future year will disclose the facts, for sometime, somewhere, truth shall find her place in "the scheme of things entire."

CHAPTER 13

The Advent of the Railroad

The Fremont, Elkhorn and Missouri Valley Railroad had just reached a point on the south side of the Niobrara River, one or two miles southwest of the old Fort Niobrara, and about the same distance southeast of the new town of Valentine, Nebraska, which had been started by C. H. Cornell—for many years one of its leading merchants, an outstanding citizen and a banker.[1]

It was understood that the railroad would remain at this point for an indefinite length of time while an enormous cut through the river bluffs was being made and the river (which here was fordable for teams most of the time) was bridged. Station facilities for the accommodation of passengers and freight had been provided and a post office established, named in honor of Albert Thatcher, a trader at the post.[2]

The government had begun to route its freight to this point, and a telegraph line connecting Fort Robinson in Nebraska with Pine Ridge Agency had been extended to the Rosebud Agency, in South Dakota along the Missouri River freight road.[3] About twenty-five miles west of Rosebud a new route had been made leading down the Minnikadusa Creek to Valentine, and all travel and transportation from the Pine Ridge section began moving over this road at once.

In consequence of this fact the Indian agent summoned R. O. Pugh, R. C. Stirk, James (Scotty) Philip, Michael Dunn, James Abner and myself to his office and, providing us with freight orders, instructed us to go with our teams to the Yellow Medicine Landing on the Missouri and bring back all the goods and moveable property belonging to Pine Ridge which remained there.[4]

These trips usually took from eighteen to twenty-five days, depending upon the state of the weather and condition of the road. On our arrival at the steamboat landing after a pleasant trip we were informed by the lone shipping clerk that there were only about three loads of Pine Ridge freight left. Ten days previous to our arrival he had loaded a number of Indian teams for that place.

The Indian freighters, by the way, had become proficient in handling their teams, so that large trains of them with their instructors had been taken from the road and they were permitted to go on their own. They could secure freight orders from official farmers in their respective districts and two or more of them could pull out for freight whenever they chose. The reason we had not met them as we went down was attributed to their habit of leaving the main road when on their own reservation and taking some by-road to one of their camps.

The freight remaining at the landing was made up of odds and ends—remnants of everything that had been stored away, but the edible commodities were missing. We had plenty of sacked shelled corn, half a sack of flour, one can of baking powder, a little salt and not too much coffee. There was no sugar, lard or bacon, but there was a tall jar that had been sent to Dr. McGillicuddy by some of his friends, and it was full of butter.[5]

These storehouses had always held purchasable goods for the freighters and we were disappointed that they should be out at this time, but as most of our party had been prepared to go on to Pierre and the Black Hills freight line as soon as this trip was over, and provisions could be had en route, they decided to continue on to Pierre. This left the three loads of freight to Philip, Abner and myself, as we were not prepared for the Black Hills trip at that time.

To us the most interesting feature of our return trip was the meager fare we had to subsist on. The clerk was about to abandon the government buildings and we took whatever he could scrape up for us and were thankful. When we pulled out for Pine Ridge each of us, I think, ruminated on the possible quality of the contents of a tall, old-fashioned crockery churn that Dr. McGillicuddy's friends had used as a jar to ship his butter in. It did not take us long to determine that the quality was excellent, and though the doctor found his quantity somewhat reduced he took it like a sport. He was pleased that none of the wagons were returning empty. In those days of slow communications he had no way of knowing when any Indians left their camp for freight, as his district farmers sent in their reports only as opportunity offered.

In ruminating over the trivial but amusing incidents that occurred during my ten years' experience as a freighter, those of this particular trip recur to memory with an urge for recording. There are two reasons for this. First, unknown to myself, it was the last time that I was to pull lines over a freight team. Second, the utter dissimilarity of characteristics of my two traveling companions.

James Abner was a man of average proportions and about forty-five years of age. He had dark gray eyes, crudely kept hair and whiskers, and was confirmed bachelor—but not from choice, as I had reason to believe. James was always sober, good-natured and accommodating, wholly without pep and yet always plodding away at some job: he did not seem lazy in the least. Like many men of the early frontier—some of them shrewd and acquisitive men of large business operations—he could neither read or write. Now this was not considered a basis of sport by his companions, yet his penchant for floundering in linguistic waters that were too deep for him made it impossible to stifle our amusement at times. I shall record here one or two examples of his mirth-provoking oddities.

On this trip we reached a point where a heavy rain had fallen shortly before. As we came to a hill that seemed to have been damaged by a wash, Jim called a halt.

"Hold on, boys! That hill looks bad. Wait till I take a look—maybe we can *revoid* it."

I had made many trips with Jim before and was familiar with his particular ways, therefore most of my amusement came from Scotty's surprised face as the breaks became frequent and even startling. The first night we were out we sat smoking by the campfire when Jim suddenly dived into the pocket of his coat and brought out a piece of paper which he pored over with interest, all the while making a deep guttural noise.

"What's the matter, Jim?" asked Scotty.

"Oh, that darned clerk down there made a mistake in my bill of lading."

"What kind of a mistake?"

"Oh, nothing much. When I get to the agent's office I'll have them correctify it, you bet!"

He was all right. He was just Jim.

Perhaps the old-timers of South Dakota who may read this will think me presumptuous in attempting to present "Scotty" Philip to them. Yet I feel justified in devoting a few lines, even though they remain obscure, in commendation of a comrade who, a few years later, became one of South Dakota's leading citizens. He had acquired several ranches and was well known as the owner of large herds of cattle, as well as of a great buffalo ranch six miles up the river from Fort Pierre and which flourished for many years with numerous bands of these animals roaming its pastures. One of the state's thriving cities was named for "Scotty" Philip, who was regarded by his neighbors and associates as a square-shooting, level-headed go-getter, and they honored him with a term in the state senate shortly before his death. He was a man![6]

My own intimate friendship with Scotty was formed when he was a young fellow over six feet tall, with broad shoulders and a compact physical structure, dark eyes, hair and whiskers. This was at the time when he had just arrived from the terrain of old Ben Lomond and its adjacent highlands, and still retained the broad rolling brogue of his native heath.

The menu at our first camp was Dutch-oven-baked bread with butter and black coffee without sugar. The culinary committee went into session and it was decided that we three, being husky outdoor workers who were unaccustomed to a vegetarian diet, should have meat of some kind. We had two guns in camp—Scotty's little single-barrel scatter-gun and Jim's old Spencer carbine, which had been run over by one of the wagons and bent slightly. The shot-gun would secure grouse and the other edible birds, and the fifty-calibre, crooked cannon of Jim's could be reserved for "ba'ar."

Jim also suggested that if we could get no birds we should eat prairie dogs. He claimed that they lived on grass, weed seeds and roots instead of nuts. We knew that this was no joke, yet had no thought of doing it. However, as we were unable to get any kind of birds, we ate prairie dogs and found that if they were nicely butchered and washed in hot water as one would prepare squirrel, rabbit or other meat, they were not bad. In fact, when cooked in Dr. McGillicuddy's butter they were quite tasty.

Later I recounted my experience on this trip to an acquaintance, and he countered with the following story. He and five or six other newcomers—"tenderfeet" as they were called—outfitted with a team and two saddlehorses, were traveling through the country between Yankton and another point on the Missouri near the mouth of the Yellowstone. They were well supplied with all provisions except a small amount of bacon, because, as was customary with travelers in those days, they depended upon the wild game of the country for their supply of meat. This time they encountered very little game, and what little they did sight was extremely wild.

One mid-afternoon, after they had made camp early on the banks of a timbered creek, one of the men who had been out hunting brought a porcupine into camp. A discussion arose as to its being edible, and only two of the party took the affirmative. They based their contention on stories they had read of travelers, lost in the forest, whose lives had been saved by eating porcupine; and also on the fact that this one was plump and fat.

"We were still arguing the question," said my friend, "when an old French trapper came riding out of the timber and into our camp, saluted and said:

"How yuh do, gentlemens!"

He was pleasantly greeted and someone asked him,

"Say, mister, are porcupines good to eat?"

With a broad smile he replied instantly,

"Yuh betch'er life! Yes siree—good as a dawg."

The old man seemed to think that the hilarious laughter of the bunch to whom his well-intentioned recommendation was given, was meant as a personal affront and became peeved. He gave us an icy stare and said,

"Say, yuh boys better go home. Yuh get lost! Yuh got no house, yuh got no lounge, yuh got no carpet, yuh got no rock-chairs, yuh got no table to eat on. Yuh starve to death!" Then, kicking his pony in the sides, he rode hurriedly away from our camp, leaving the boys still laughing.

The two who had been for eating the porcupine grabbed it and soon had it butchered, cleaned, cut up, stowed away in a Dutch oven with plenty of salt and pepper and bacon grease, and cooking nicely. When it was being turned and the lid was off the aroma was enticing. When it was thoroughly done to a nice brown it was set a little to one side of the regular meal. The two men immediately took a good helping and were followed presently by the others who began tasting—with the result that the tasting and the porcupine ended simultaneously.

One pleasant afternoon when we were some fifty miles from Pine Ridge, just traveling along slowly and quietly with Scotty's wagon in the lead, Jim's next and mine in the rear on a road that was smooth and comparatively level, with the prairie gently undulating on either side, we saw to the north, on our right, a dry pond with bed of chalky white. There was nothing strange about that, for we were in a section of alkali country, so with but scant notice we idled on, dreaming our own day-dreams.

When directly opposite the pond we were startled to see a fine antelope that apparently had risen from some declivity where it had been basking. Our teams came to a standsill and Jim had slipped down from his wagon with his old carbine when the antelope turned to run, but as Jim knelt and began aiming it stopped and bent its head slightly as it stared at our outfit. Jim was still aiming and Scotty and I were holding our breath at the defiant action of the beautiful creature and the nerve of Jim with his crooked gun.

Then—bang went the old carbine, and a puff arose in an alkali-dust column about fifty feet short of where the antelope had been standing. "Had been," yes, for we had seen through a thin screen of dust that the animal fell, and it had no more than hit the ground than Scotty lit on a run and I was down at the mess-box after a butcher-knife. I turned and saw the antelope begin to struggle, and Scotty leaped and fell all over it. By the time I reached him it had developed into a sharply contested wrestling match, with Scotty on top but having a hard time staying there. I dropped the knife near the beast's head and relieved Scotty's hold on the horns, twisting its nose to the sky as I did so. Scotty grabbed the knife and cut its throat, and remarked as he got up panting, "Now, by gawd, I guess you'll lie still!"

Just then Jim, who had taken his time in extracting the shell from his gun before putting it in the wagon, came on the scene and boasted, "I *thought* I had a dead bead on him!"

Scotty whirled and looked as though he were going to razz him, then just smiled and winked at me. We knew, of course, that the shot had ricocheted, but it was Jim's lucky accident, not ours. We looked for the place where the bullet had hit and discovered a groove, about one-quarter of the diameter of the ball, just back of the horns which had stunned it momentarily.

After disemboweling the carcass we loaded it on the wagon in the shade of the raised sheet, then moved on a few miles to where we camped on the Little White River. There we dressed it properly and added fresh antelope meat, fried in butter, to our menu.

Our trip was a pleasant fine-weather journey. I always enjoyed riding along over a smooth, dry road, perched on a high seat, the wagon beneath me steadied by an adequate load, and chuckling in unison with the rhythmic movements of a well-conditioned team. I enjoyed each breath of a cooling breeze that came wafting over a broad expanse of uninhabited country or out from the soughing trees. Notwithstanding the other side of the shield which was painted with rain, hail and snowstorms, and often accompanied by devastating winds and high waters that made the roads impassable, besides all the delaying accidents with which freighters are familiar, I would, for many years after quitting the business, became obsessed with a longing, an overwhelming urge to resume the ribbons and the wheel trail as the waving green grass began to beckon in the springtime.

Few if any songs have been written setting forth the splendid work performed by the freighters in the settlement of this country, but the fact remains that much credit is due to the adventurous spirit, the mental and physical ruggedness, of the actual drivers of the freight teams. This basic though not entrancing calling, of which the men with the wagons constituted the vast majority of those employed in the industry, furnished the pioneers of this continent, from the Atlantic to the Pacific, with the necessary (and, in the main, otherwise unobtainable) subsistence during the first stages of their settlement; and it was largely through the faithful perseverance of these men in all kinds of weather, over all kinds of road and facing all kinds of danger, that such settlement was possible.

CHAPTER 14

Meeting Civilization

In the early months of 1883 the agent asked me to rig up an easy-running, light-covered conveyance and take four distinguished visitors to the Rosebud Agency, where they would be furnished transportation to the railroad. The party consisted of United States Senator Teller of Colorado and his secretary; Mr Butterfield, who was a United States Indian Inspector; and an old gentleman whom they addressed as Mr. Shannon and who was from Sioux Falls.[1]

After conveying these men to the office of the Indian agent I went to the home of my friend, C. P. Jordan, who was chief clerk of the agency at that time. There he introduced me to Stephen F. Estes, who had just been designated receiving clerk for all the goods delivered at the newly erected government warehouse at Valentine, Nebraska.[2] He offered me employment with him and I accepted. I returned home, disposed of my team, and after arranging for an absence of several months I settled into my new job early in April.

The government warehouse to which I was assigned was newly built, about thirty by eighty feet, on a substantial foundation of heavy timbered piles close to the railroad, and of a height to bring the floor of the building level with a box-car floor. On the south side was a solid platform level with the top of a standard wagon-box. All the government supplies for Rosebud (thirty miles to the north) and Pine Ridge (one hundred twenty-five miles west) were delivered here for several years.

Later in the summer I purchased a house and moved my family to Valentine, where I continued my services to the government until March 1884. In partnership with David Cockrell, blacksmith and wagon-maker at the agency and my one-time employer in building schoolhouses on the reservation, I purchased the blacksmith shop at Valentine. This was the only public shop west of Ainsworth, Nebraska, at that time, and it had a trade radius of a hundred miles in other directions. The shop contained two standard brick forges and a portable buffalo forge, but as I had not learned the trade I hired skilled mechanics for the two large forges and did the tinkering myself.[3]

Valentine was then a busy and beautiful little city covering a broad plateau between two of the swift-flowing streams of northwest Nebraska. Like most other frontier railroad and mining towns, it had to pass through a cycle of rough rowdyism. During such storms of conflicting human elements, about all that the staid and law-abiding citizens could do was to attend to their own particular affairs, keep the even tenor of their way, and continue to build their homes and business blocks, their schools, churches and civic societies as best they could. Their passive courage was strengthened by the knowledge that the threatening clouds of evil forces would be forced to dissipate and to them would be the victory. Therefore the recorded facts of reckless escapades and death-dealing controversies, with which the early pioneers of many communities had to contend, should not reflect in any way on their civic morals or general good citizenship.

There were many large cattle ranches at different points along the Niobrara River and its tributaries in the sandhills to the south, and each of these ranches employed many men. Quite naturally Valentine became their trading center and post office. Most of the employees on these ranches had come up the trail with the stock from Texas, and occasionally they would congregate in town for a social jamboree. The town was wide open for gambling, and that of course was the high card in their entertainment. Gradually a few who considered themselves the better sportsmen quit the cowboy life, joined the few drifting professionals, and became the resident gambling element of the town. They were mostly jolly, good-natured but misguided youths who had grown to manhood in some one of the many sadly disorganized and war-distracted communities of Texas, where their environment was unavoidably wild and unrestrained. While it would not have been advisable to provoke them to a degree of fighting anger, there was but one here and there who was cursed with the killer instinct. On the whole they made it a point to be courteous and fair in all of their dealings. Their idea of a good time seemed to be plenty of noise—yelling and shooting, but no harm done.[4]

Valentine, at that time, was almost wholly north of the Fremont, Elkhorn & Missouri Valley Railroad (since changed to the Chicago & Northwestern) that lay east and west through the town. The old depot was immediately west of the crossing on the north side of the track. East of this crossing stood the Indian supply warehouse; and, beginning at the north edge of the right of way, the business street extended north. On the southwest corner were two large general merchandise stores— one owned by Charles H. Cornell and the other by two brothers, Al and Ed Sparks. The proprietors operated their own establishments. Next was a larger shop, several small cafes, Dr. Lewis' Drug Store, Joe Hall's Saloon and Pool Hall; and then Fritz Warren's larger establishment which was divided into two parts—a saloon and billiard hall with a medium-sized gambling room in the rear.[5]

On the corner of Second Street, adjoining Warren's place, was a large well kept yard surrounding a neat, nicely painted little house that was owned and occupied by a middle-aged widow known, locally and popularly, as "The Sage Hen." Most of the houses on either side of this narrow street were separated by a space of one or more vacant lots, some of which may have held small business houses not now recalled.

On the southeast corner of this street a barber shop was operated by a colored man (Parry), and the two lots adjoining on the north were occupied by the Hotel Donaher, a commodious two-story frame building built and operated by Peter Donaher, one of the earliest residents and leading citizens of the town. With alternate vacant lots between them were a restaurant, law office, real estate office, printing office of the *Valentine Reporter*, and the post office under the same roof, with B. C. Hill as editor and postmaster.[6]

On the corner of the first cross-street were a couple of small structures, some occupied by families and some by small traders of various kinds. Next to these were McDonald's Hardware Store and Billy Carter's Saloon, which was opposite that of Warren's on the west side of the street. These two saloons were quite similar and the largest establishments of their kind in the town. The butcher shop of Henry and John Stetter was next to Tim Higgins' saloon.[7]

The remaining broad expanse between the town and the creek was practically barren except for a large building of two and one-half stories that the county had purchased elsewhere and moved in for a court house.[8]

In the rear of the business houses on either side of the street were scattered dwellings, shops of various sorts, barns, livery stables, corrals, and a short distance south of the Indian supply depot were a few residences, mostly occupied by railroad employees. Half a mile southwest of these were one or two dwellings of stockmen whose ranches were in the adjacent Niobrara Valley. To the west of these was a cluster of houses, one being owned by a retired government packer named David Y. Mears.[9] He was then an old bachelor and a part of his building was rented by a man whose wife was an excellent cook. She conducted an eating house and enjoyed as large a patronage as any of the places in the town.

Alone on the southeast side of the tracks stood a newly built little cottage that was the home of Valentine's lone minister.[10] Always quiet and affable, he was rather inclined to be reticent, but performed the duties of his calling in an earnest, simple manner.

A few hundred yards to the north, about half-way between the restaurant group and the railroad, and some little distance west of the road that connected these buildings with Main Street at the railroad crossing, was a group comprising a large hall with several additions and a number of small adjacent buildings. This group was notorious and known as the "Hog Ranch," which was western parlance for a bawdy house, saloon and dance hall combined.[11] Here was where the devotees of the dizzy, deadly butterfly life "tripped the light fantastic toe" during the starry moments of their mad career.

Almost every evening during the heyday of Valentine's infancy, music would be heard here and the wild sounds of pandemonium floated out over the village into the "wee sma' hours." Especially was this true during the shipping season, when husky cattle-handlers were continually dropping in with the big herds of fat beeves that had been driven from the sand-hills at the south and the scattered ranches of the rolling prairies to the north, with a few from the west as far as the Black Hills. These were being held near by to wait their turn for shipment. On such occasions jamboree and carousal constituted the order of procedure, but these hilarious parties were usually concluded without a serious climax. At times, however, there were fistic encounters that wound up in shooting frays, ending fatally for some and perhaps with serious wounds for others.

During my sojourn in Valentine there were at least three such fatalities, and one of the victims was a girl who was an inmate of the dance hall.[12] There were always a bunch of six or eight ex-range hands and professional gamblers, constituting the local gang which spent most of its time in the two larger saloons engaged in all kinds of gaming, from poker, billiards to chuck-a-luck. Usually they played quietly but sometimes broke loose on a wild orgy. Such parties generally occurred in the late afternoon or early evening, after which they paraded down the street headed for the Hog Ranch, to return at any time that suited their drunken whim. They marched to the tune of off key snatches of song or wild yells, which were always accompanied by shots fired at either the earth or the sky.

There were other times—quite frequently too—when these same carefree, daredevil boys, who nearly always were musicians and good singers, sat soberly on the saloon porch through the moon lit evenings and rendered number after number of old-time songs of the south or of their homeland, accompanied by tambourine and banjo. The harmonious blending of their vocal instrumental music then spread through the highways and byways of the little community, a treat for all.

In comparing this halcyon scene with others not so peaceful, the question of law and order naturally comes to mind. In those days there were courts, grand juries and the usual officers of law, and arrests were made when possible. In such case the offender was thrown into the wooden jail. If the offense was serious his friends would contrive his escape, and usually a killer was outfitted and made his get-away at once. The coroner's report would be duly filed and the grand jury, at its regular term, would solemnly bring an indictment against the transgressor, though knowing that he was safely hidden in the wilds of one of the border territories— Canada or Alaska; and that his detention and return was beyond their limited finances.

Sometimes the law was used as camouflage to give an act of doubtful color (if not a flagrant crime) the appearance of legitimate procedure. It so happened that I witnessed all but the final act of a tragedy that many observers considered of this class.

For some time there had been whispering about illegal cattle killing and peddling of beef, but the general public paid little if any attention to such rumors. One day, however, a short, stockily built man appeared and registered at the hotel under the name of Hammond, from Cheyenne. He stayed in town for several days, making the acquaintance of the merchants and many citizens; then purchased a saddle pony and began making short trips to the country, ostensibly looking for a ranch location. He was convivial and always busy and therefore attracted no particular attention, as there were many doing likewise.

One of the stockmen along the Niobrara was a slim, wiry Texan. He was a pleasant fellow to meet, but had the reputation of being a bad man with a gun. It soon became noised about that he and Mr. Hammond were brothers-in-law, but somewhere in the southwest country they had engaged in a quarrel so serious that they had remained mortal enemies ever since. We heard that they would meet on the street without the slightest recognition; and though neither seemed to fear the other, they eyed one another sharply while passing. We soon heard that Hammond was a stock detective—a "dick," in the jargon of the street. Immediately he was a marked man and extremely unpopular with the tough element.

A little later these two happened to board the same train at a point down the line between O'Neill and Valentine, and as the train sped forward in the darkness they clashed in the smoking car. It was said that while Hammond's head was resting against the back of the car seat, his brother-in-law approached with drawn dirk, obviously intending to cut his throat; but they were being watched by some who knew them. The story circulated around town next morning was to the effect that Hammond's attacker was stopped and disarmed.

The episode was the talk of the town next day and for several days thereafter. One afternoon, as I stepped from the warehouse office to a small platform on the west end of the building, I noticed that the men and boys near this street were climbing up the sides of the box-cars and seating themselves on the running boards. A train had been broken for traffic and these cars were standing on a side-track. I ran down to where they were and asked what was going on. They replied that a group of men, headed by the newly elected sheriff, were after Hammond. Then those on the cars began to exclaim, pointing toward the distant tracks.

Then I saw Hammond cross the railroad west of the depot and head south toward the Niobrara, urging his horse into a fast running walk out across the undulating flat that lay between the village and the river. Two riders crossed the track west of where Hammond had crossed it, while three more came from the east and angled around the rear of the warehouse. All horse riders had their mounts in a fast single-foot walk and were headed directly for their victim.

Hammond was looking back and when he saw this movement he quirted his horse into a run. The pursuers did likewise, and as he made the rise of a low ridge and went over the crest they began shooting. I could see the dust from the bullets striking about him as they split and deployed, passing over the ridge on either side of where he had crossed. They were in a low swale and all I could see was their hats bobbing up and down. But I knew they had circled him, for two were approaching from the south and all were racing toward a common center, shooting as they advanced.

Presently the firing ceased and they circled around some object. Judging from the disappearance and reappearance of the hats as they stooped or stood I concluded that they were dismounting and making ready to return. The sheriff and another appeared and went back to town over the road from which they came; the others rode off leisurely through the low, rolling hills toward the river.

There was a commotion in town after that, during the coroner's inquest; but the aggressors, who had been hauled into court, had claimed and established their right to legal protection by showing that they had been regularly deputized to help serve a warrant on the victim; that it had been duly issued on complaint of one; and that they had constituted a perfectly lawful sheriff's posse.

In a short time the incident was forgotten, as Smith had disposed of his Cherry County holdings and moved away. Word floated up from the south, a few years later, that one of his old enemies had traced and killed him at a lonely cabin in the wilds of the Texas woodlands.[13]

Such scenes were not at all uncommon. In the early days of the West there were many towns compared with which Valentine would have seemed a haven of rest, and in one of these I attended my last district school. This was Ellsworth, Kansas, which for some time was the terminal of the Union Pacific.

It is a pleasure now to turn to the wall the dark side of the picture that I am trying to paint, and undertake the agreeable task of portraying, as briefly as possible, the brighter side of this struggling little village and its sturdy citizens who were busily laying the foundation for happier days.

In April 1884 the sod of the surrounding country was being turned over by homesteaders. All business was brisk and our shop was going full steam ahead with a continuous string of all kinds of blacksmith and wagon work that pertain to farming, ranching and freighting. The passenger trains unloaded a large number of home-seekers from Iowa and other points east almost every morning. Some looked over the nearby country; others, in parties of four or five, would secure rigs and an improvised camp outfit and scour the country adjacent to the prospective railroad line as far west as Chadron Creek and other tributaries of the White River. During these hurly-burly days it seemed but natural that numerous raw but harmless and crudely comic incidents should occur, and I am going to record a few such examples.

One warm, quiet afternoon a few of the local sports had moved a poker table from the rear hall in Fritz Warren's saloon and placed it near two open windows in the cool northeast corner of the bar room, with space between it and the bar opposite the street entrance sufficient for any bunch of customers that might appear. There were five or six of them enjoying a quiet but rather stiff game of draw poker when the minister walked in on them. He proceeded, as was his custom, to saunter quietly through the room with his hands clasped behind him, pausing to observe the games of billiard and pool and giving pleasant greeting to those he chanced to meet face to face, but otherwise he said nothing.

The habitues were accustomed to his occasional visits of observation and thought nothing of his coming; in fact, they seemed to like him and his quiet ways. As he moved out toward the street exit he paused to watch the poker game. One of the players suggested that they make a jackpot for the parson, and the response was unanimous. He smiled, no doubt thinking that they were just having a little fun at his expense, and continued to watch the game which to him must have been a mysterious procedure. The money rolled liberally to the center of the board, and presently the winner handed the surprised parson forty dollars. He politely but positively declined to accept it, but the boys argued that they were sincere in making it a donation to the church and that he would make better use of it than they. Finally he was prevailed upon to accept the gift for charity, but was never seen around games of chance after that.

One day, near the close of a busy forenoon, I was served with notice to appear that afternoon as a petit juror at the office of the county judge in a trial of two litigants from up the river. Everyone knew that the office referred to was the gambling room at the rear of Fritz Warren's saloon and that Fritz was the county judge, but at the appointed hour I joined the others assembled there and helped the judge move the faro table to the back of the wall and get a large poker table out of the way. A quarter-circle stud poker table in the northwest corner of the room was not disturbed; neither were the players who sat around it engaged in a fast-moving game. A small chuck-a-luck table was substituted as the judicial desk, having been moved to the center of the room opposite a row of six chairs in which the jurors were seated. The judge opened court and the trial of the cause began.

The statement of the attorneys and the evidence of the witnesses disclosed a damage suit for the destruction of three large ricks of hay in the preceding fall. The defendant had made a shipment of cattle from the Valentine stockyards, and part of his crew were returning to his ranch some distance up the Niobrara River. They had camped for lunch in a bend of the river, and after preparing their meal, as it was very windy, they snuggled down close to the ground in what little protection they could find. But they had not taken the precaution to put out their fire before eating, and when a whirlwind swept by, it scattered the coals among the dead grass and shrubbery leading directly to a hay meadow. They fought the fire desperately, but were unable to extinguish it before the hay was burned.

The trial lasted for about an hour while the stud game went on, making a close second in the race for attention of all in the room. As the deal went around, every high hand was called in a loud voice, so that each player would know just what he was betting against.

At the close of the case, while the attorneys were having a few words with the judge, I took the opportunity to whisper to the jurors. As the judge was about to deliver his customary instructions, I arose and unburdened myself about as follows:

"If your honor please, the jurors wish to know whether or not they have a fairly correct conception of the general trend of all the evidence submitted in this case. As we understand it, the defendants were on their way home after having loaded some cattle–deal ended, king is high. It was a windy day–a pair of deuces in sight. They stopped, built a fire and were having dinner–a pair of queens; a strong wind blew some burning brands into a meadow–three Jacks on the board. The cowboys' efforts failed to stop the fire–pair of eights up–and three large ricks of hay were consumed."

A lot of giggling and wisecracks floated over from the stud table as I sat down, but an air of dignity overspread the poker face of the judge as he said:

"I wish to compliment the jurors on their attentiveness. Your understanding is correct. You will now repair to one of the unfinished rooms in the new courthouse and agree on a verdict. Court is adjourned."

Another day, during an evening session of the court, I sauntered into the room during trial of a case involving two partners who had been operating a small farm together. They had a misunderstanding that led to dissolution of partnership, and were making amicable division of their joint property until they came to a yoke of oxen to which both laid claim and finally invoked the law. As I stood in the doorway between the saloon and gambling room I saw that the gaming was arranged as usual to give room for court procedure, except[14] that five or six players were engaged in a high and fast game of draw poker.

The trial was proceeding and the evidence disclosed that the oxen were large, red in color, well broken and their value was agreed upon as one-hundred-twenty-five dollars ($125.00). At this point one of the players exploded

"Bill, what do you know about that? A pair of red oxen over in that game is worth one-hundred-twenty-five dollars and a pair of red aces in this game is only worth two and a half."

This sally did not interrupt the court proceedings, and both "games" moved on in their respective channels. Aces and oxen when brought before the presiding judge didn't seem to mix.

Such incidents were subjects of amused discussion for perhaps an hour and then forgotten, for business was rushing—legitimate and otherwise. The town was full of confidence men whose favorite hours were from eight to ten in the morning and two to four in the afternoon, but they had night lures for the sucker also. Improvised stands made of inverted boxes were placed in small openings between buildings or at one side of an alley-way, and here various sorts of skin games were operated: dice, prize-envelope drawings, and the shell game with its moving but mysteriously elusive little black pea.

A little farther on might be seen (often right in the middle of the road) a tripod upon which rested a neat little box containing small bars of soap and small squares of soft white paper. Behind it would be seen the artistic manipulator—the sure-thing soap man who, with a continuous line of trade talk, was wrapping his little bars of soap in the squares of paper, occasionally inserting a crisp new greenback in one of them. When a customer unwrapped his soap and exposed a bill—one, two or five dollars, but more often the latter—the voice of the artist was heard from one end of the street to the other, expounding this wonderful luck and urging the astonished suckers to try theirs.

These bunco-steerers did not remain long in any one place, as the law soon made it too difficult to operate and they had to move on to another field ready for the harvest. It was their life, however, and they were tolerated for a time on the theory that it takes all kinds of people to make a world.

CHAPTER 15

At Valentine

The gypping gypsy gamesters whom I have been discussing were not the only shady schemers the good people of Valentine had to contend with. The town was situated near the eastern edge of a vast territory but recently surveyed and opened for homesteading. As the homesteaders were continually increasing, a United States land office had been established there and this created the industry of land locating. It was a worthy and necessary occupation and called for men who were more or less familiar with the country where the locations were to be made.

This vocation was a great convenience to the new arrivals who were prospective citizens, as the locators furnished the precise information needed and expedited their settlement. Many men were engaged in the business and most of them were honest and efficient and did the best they could for their clients, but a few among them were out to get the money and nothing else.

The meanest trick of these conscienceless money-grabbers was to have a fine piece of land covered in such a manner as would permit them to hold it indefinitely. This they would show to an unsuspecting victim, who of course placed full confidence in his guide and paid for the guidance. They gave him papers to complete his filing at the land office, and after receiving their final fee would be off after another victim for this or other similar tracts which they held.

The claimant would present his papers to one of the officials at the land office, who, with a glance at the descriptive numbers, would bring forth a book and spread out a map of the designated township. The homesteader then completed his filing without noticing that the numbers had been changed on the description of the land. This scheme was worked quite often, and as the land shark selected substitute numbers for his victims at random, it often occurred that the homesteader got as good land as he had been shown, but not always.

As a rule men were hesitant about interfering with the business of strangers, but when ever opportunity offered the prospective homesteaders were warned of this trap and directed how to avoid it. Mr. B. C. Hill, editor and proprietor of the one local newspaper, the *Valentine Reporter*, fought this and all other fraudulent schemes aggressively. In one case his editorial pointed to the chief offender so unmistakably that it led to blows.

About two months prior to the incidents related above there arrived among the vast crowd of passengers a man with his wife and four children, ranging in age from twelve on downward. He said his name was Patrick Corney, but for the purposes of this record it will be Pat.[1] A short conversation with him confirmed the self-evident fact that he was Irish, and disclosed further facts to the effect that he was not long from the old sod and was the possessor of a raw brogue and smooth blarney that were both interesting and amusing. He had been a soldier in the British Army in India and had seen the world in various climes.

Pat was a hard worker, jovial and witty, and soon had built a small tar paper shack across the railroad track to the northeast, a short distance from the Indian Supply Depot, where I often visited him. As soon as he had his family settled he went in search of odd jobs, and as he made friends easily he soon had all the work he could do.

Light conveyances which were provided with several spring seats, provisions and camp kits were constantly leaving for parts farther west. The home seekers were accompanied by a land locator, who gave them transportation with board and a guarantee of at least two weeks' travel over the country unless they found sooner a location that suited them. Pat's whole object in coming west had been to secure a farm home. With his slender hoard of fifty dollars which he paid for above accommodations, he took such a trip.

In due time his party returned, and Pat was elated with the thought that he had secured one of Uncle Sam's fine farms for the above figure, plus the filing fees at the land office. He continued his work about town until he had accumulated enough money to provide for this family during an extended absence. Then he outfitted himself with a new wheelbarrow; and, buying a saw, ax, pick, shovel, and such minor tools as he might need, he stowed them away in the "Irish buggy," together with his grub, blankets and camp outfit. Grabbing the ready shafts, he started pushing it vigorously with a smile on his face. He was absent almost a month when one day he was seen unloading his wheelbarrow and traps at his shack, having caught a ride home with a returning freighter. He was a much disgruntled and disappointed man as he told his friends the following story.

Pat reached his claim by tramping the trails and byways, and had completed the excavation of a fair-sized dugout in the side of a small hill on the edge of a nice flat that was covered with luxuriant grass. The forked posts, ridge logs and roof-poles he had cut from a grove on a nearby creek, and wheeled then to his dugout and was placing them in position when a stranger rode up on horseback and asked him what he was doing.

Pat protested vigorously but the stranger kept cool, doubtless feeling that here was just another dupe who had been tricked by a switch of his numbers.

After some argument, during which the stranger remained very pleasant, he suggested that they compare the filing numbers on the surveyor's stakes that marked the claim; then the stranger pointed to the numbers on the plat belonging to Pat and showed him that his real claim was three or four miles away, and offered to go with him and point it out. This offer Pat accepted, only to find that he had secured an almost worthless piece of land, covered with sand dunes and wind blow-outs. It was a hard blow.

This episode created such a whirlwind of indignation that the men known to be responsible for the fraud quickly disappeared. Pat was given all the work he could attend to and a movement was started to have his homestead rights restored—which meant a slow but reasonably sure procedure.

In the meantime things were happening. New locations in the west were being settled and men pushed forward, as the railroad company had designated most of its stations as far as Harrison, Nebraska, near the west boundary of the state.

Chadron, which had first been located by an enterprising woman attorney, Mrs. Fannie O'Linn, on her homestead on the White River which was some distance from the railroad site now chosen, was being moved to its present location and seemed to be the most promising point of business concentration in the northwest section of the state.[2] The continuous arrivals had brought with them E. E. Egan and family, who unloaded at Valentine a complete printing outfit for a country newspaper along with his household goods. He managed to rent, for a short time, a couple rooms in one of the larger residences, and after locating his family and storing his outfit he went to the new settlement of Chadron, at the confluence of Chadron Creek and White River. There he arrived in time to secure a homestead nearby, and after building the necessary quarters he returned for his family and goods and settled in Chadron, where he published the first newspaper west of Valentine in that section of the state.

This publication was called the *Dawes County Journal* but later changed to the *Chadron Journal*. It was a lively, wide-awake newspaper and did much in the upbuilding of that section of the country as well as the city of Chadron, to which Mr. Egan moved as soon as the Railroad Townsite Company had designated it as one which they intended to develop. Mr. Egan was an honest, industrious man, a square shooter and a hard hitter in controversy—as later I had ample opportunity to learn.

In order to clarify the events that follow I will bring myself into the picture for a time. You may recall that when I had reached the birthday of my majority, it was my second in the vicinity of the old Fort Laramie, Wyoming, where for about ten years my associates were composed of all manner and classes of men. There were soldiers from both the Union and Confederate sides of our Civil War among us. For the most part all prejudices and antagonisms had been swept aside and the unrestricted camaraderie of the West prevailed.

All the elections in all of our territories the voters were confined to voting for local officials and an occasional delegate to Congress. The presidential elections were usually discussed with moderation and the results awaited with interest, but fanfare campaigns were not on the program. It was not long, however, before I found myself in the midst of political strife for the first time at the age of thirty-three years, at Valentine, Nebraska, in a vigorously contested national campaign. I had an open mind but was unfamiliar with the party issues and isms, and cared not a whit for the political impressions and prejudices absorbed during my boyhood. I carefully studied the platform of each of the major parties and chose the one that appealed to me as most promising for the greatest good of the greatest number, and after my decision I could be found following the flambeaux and furnishing my part of the noise in the Grover Cleveland parades. The campaign of 1884 was on.[3]

As these events were transpiring, large groups of homesteaders were returning from the West, most of whom were well satisfied but a few felt that they had been cheated in location numbers. It so happened that at the same time there were numerous home seekers in town from the East, and when the two groups met they all seemed to be charged with the spirit of inquiry. Those from the East were anxious to learn about the country and the land still open to filing, while those from the West were interested in the presidential campaign. When these subjects had been discussed, conversation drifted almost automatically to the all-absorbing topic of crooked land locators. Occasionally I had furnished our home paper with sketches of such incidents, especially the unfortunate experience of Pat. These papers found ready sale, and many copies were mailed to "the folks back home."[4]

In due time the campaign excitement died down and the citizens reverted to their customary status of common sense. At about the same time snow began to fall in frequent squalls—an omen of the severe winter that followed. The men at the shop were mostly engaged in shoeing horses and I was relieved of my job as chief tinkerer, so, to pass the time, I visited among my business friends. One of my favorite haunts was the printing office of B. C. Hill, and it was here (in February, 1885) that he surprised me with a proposition he had long been mulling over, and I soon learned that he had all of the angles figured out. His idea was to resign as postmaster and sell his newspaper at Valentine; then, with me as editor and himself as mechanical manager, we would start a Democrat newspaper at Chadron.

This was too sudden for me. After I resumed breathing I declined, calling his attention to the fact that although I had done some yowling for the cause during the campaign, I was a raw recruit and a rookie in political affairs, without any political standing whatsoever; also, that he was a Republican. I also quoted him Shakespeare's line—"Fools rush in where angels fear to tread;" and added that our mutual friend, Robert Lucas, had an old army printing press and other shop equipment stored at Chadron for some time, expecting to hook up with some printer and start a paper as soon as he could.

Mr. Hill replied that he knew all that. He explained that Mr. Lucas was to be with us, and that his old press and a handful of type had been taken there in the hope that it would help to hold the field until he could perfect some such plan as he was then offering me. He wanted me to share the tripod with Mr. Lucas while he ran the mechanical department. All this set me to thinking, and I assured him I would consider the matter.

Robert Lucas, our mutual friend, was a young attorney recently graduated from Iowa City Law School. He came from an old family of Democrats that had lived in Iowa City for years, and President Buchanan had appointed his paternal grandfather as territorial governor of Iowa during the years of its early settlement.[5]

In a talk with Mr. Lucas himself a little later he reminded me that Mr. Hill had never shown any disposition for political controversy, either oral or written. Being a Vermont Yankee, he just swung his party ticket to the masthead of his paper during the campaigns and voted for it at the elections. His entire ambition seemed centered in the mechanical part of the business, of all the details of which he was unquestionable master. He took great pride in putting a clean, legible sheet on the streets; and job work, whether plain or fancy, he did to perfection.

As I was convinced that at least one of us had the record and antecedents for a party background that would justify the experiment, we formed a partnership to be known as the "Democrat Publishing Company—Lucas, Allen & Hill," and ordered new printing equipment to be shipped to Chadron, Nebraska. Mr. Hill resigned as postmaster and found a buyer for his newspaper. Mr. Lucas, who had just proved up on a claim that was joined to the townsite and later became the west half of the thriving little city of Gordon, went to Chadron to nurse his embryo printing plant until later developments.

In the early part of the summer my partner, David Cockrell, disposed of his property at Pine Ridge and joined me at Valentine. He soon purchased my interest in our business; and when we received word that our printing outfit had been shipped, Mr. Hill joined Mr. Lucas at Chadron and I was left in charge of the postoffice until the new appointee took it over. I was relieved late in July and arrived in Chadron in time to help arrange the plant for publication of our first issue of *The Chadron Democrat*, which made its appearance August 27, 1885.

CHAPTER 16

At Chadron

The train moved slowly and carefully down the newly constructed track, past walled canyons and through the beautiful groves of Little Bordeaux Creek to its junction with the larger stream of the same name that comes down through the timbered hills that border the White River Valley on the south. I could see and recognize the various camping grounds with which I had been familiar through recent years, when the ride always signified a saddle-horse or line-controlled wheels.

This was in mid-August of 1885, and I was on my way to memorable years at Chadron. When our train came in view of the depot, the round-house and warehouse that marked the end of the track, we could see an array of tents extending half-way across the valley that lies between the depot and the high, white rock hills that rise in castellated formation and are crested with scattered sentinels of tall pine, all forming a very picturesque background to Chadron from the south. In passing through the tented streets of what became the fixed center of business in the town, we saw that the tents were mostly large and walled. They were filled with goods of various kinds, and while business was being carried on here the substantial buildings designed to house it were going up near by.[1]

I found my partners actively engaged in assembling material and preparing copy for the first issue of our paper, and they welcomed me profusely as a green but handy acquisition to the force. In these pages I make no attempt to write a history of Chadron, for during my six years of residence there I was but one of the many who united their efforts to advance the interests and development of that community and the territory surrounding. I take pleasure in the fact that I had the opportunity to do my mite in helping to advance the small, tented city of Chadron from grass roots to the solid foundation upon which it now stands. As my efforts were along the line of publicity, I assume that it will not be amiss to sketch a few incidents peculiar to the time and place.

We were operating in a small, floorless shack that had been moved in from the south of Chadron Creek. It was about twelve by fourteen feet and located in the southwest part of town where the greensward furnished the floor. As it was the only shelter available, we managed in it for several weeks by placing our press on the east side of the building, protected by an improvised awning and windbreak, which provided more hours of shade for our work. But we soon enjoyed more comfortable quarters in one of the newly constructed buildings in the center of town.

Our new shop was located two doors west of Main Street. At the east end of the block on the northeast corner of Second Street (all there was of Egan Street at that time) was a newly constructed two-story building, the lower floor of which was then occupied by the post office and the upper floor by the *Dawes County Journal*. Both building and *Journal* were owned by E. E. Egan, the editor, and for whom the street had been named in appreciation of his earlier and most effective efforts in behalf of the town. In the opinion of many of the residents of Chadron (in which I concur), that name should have stood. However, I believe the change was made without prejudice. At any rate it exemplifies the adage: "How soon we are forgotten when we're gone!"

By mutual agreement we had assigned to ourselves the following duties: Mr. Hill, of course, carried the mechanical end of the enterprise. Mr. Lucas was placed on the tripod of the "Sanctum Sanctorum," for which task he was especially fitted by his rotund physique and rheumatic tendencies as well as his legal, scholastic and genealogical qualifications; while I, being of slim and wiry build at the time, gathered news, solicited patrons, and made the monthly collections.

The railroad was being pushed west and north to the Black Hills. The stage line that was first established between Cheyenne and Deadwood in 1876 was later (after completion of the Clarke bridge across the North Platte) transferred to a line starting from Sidney, Nebraska.[2] When this line, too, was abandoned in favor of the nearer railroad terminal at Chadron, we saw "Concord Coaches," for a time, leaving for Deadwood daily. Long strings of freight teams loaded with lumber and household goods were constantly on the move to different parts of the country. Stock was being loaded at the yards for shipment; tents were vanishing and roomy buildings appearing in their stead as if by magic. All this composed the picture that confronted the observer daily. In fact, for a time it seemed that everyone was trying to do everything at once. Temporary shelters were being replaced by substantial buildings (both business and residence) so rapidly that, although we had increased the size of our paper, space was often lacking wherein to note the changes.

I will give here only an outline of such changes as are necessary to form a cursory sketch of the struggles, squabbles, shadow and sunshine of the earlier publications at Chadron, for it was in this field that I labored and therefore I am most familiar with the part it played in the initial development of the town.

Almost from the beginning there were three banks. The first, as I recall, was owned by the Chadron Banking Company, composed chiefly of local men, though the moving figure in the venture at first was a man from Sioux City named Higman. When he retired Mr. Putman became president and F. S. Carly was cashier. The firm of Richards Brothers and Brown (DeForest and Bartlett Richards and Walter C. Brown) located their bank on the northwest corner of Main and Second Streets; while across the street to the south on the corner of Main and Second was the bank of Lake & Halley of Rapid City, South Dakota.

The Chadron Banking Company was the first in the town to introduce brick as a building material, having shipped them in for a two-story building of brick veneer on the southeast corner of Second and Egan Streets, facing the *Journal* building on the opposite corner north. The spacious room on the second floor of this banking house was used by the county as a court house for some time. The principal officials of the temporary county organization had their offices in the rear of the bank below.[3]

The buildings housing the Chadron Banking Company and the *Dawes County Journal* were always a center of activity in community affairs. They stand today upon the same old foundations as landmarks of a proud past—perhaps not quite so imposing as most of their neighbors, but in no way detracting from the structural solidity of their surroundings.

A fire that swept away most of the structures on and near the southwest corner of Main and Second Streets was responsible for the erection of buildings more nearly fireproof. The two-story brick bank of Lake & Halley, the brick business house with a full stone-walled basement belonging to Ricker & Houghton, the stone theater of P. B. Nelson, and various other buildings were built.[4] Stone for the theater was shipped from the Black Hills quarries and bore natural markings in "calico colors," as they were called. The choicest of these stones were arranged artistically in the front wall of the theater, above and around the plate windows of the two large store rooms in the lower floor, and made a unique and attractive front.

Without regard for orderly continuity in this hurly-burly period of push, I will simply state that from this time brick began taking precedence over other building materials. The supply was furnished partly by shipments and partly by a large cluster of kilns in the brickyard at the east edge of town. The firms of Richards Brothers & Brown and the Loewenthal Brothers (Ben and Max), who were clothiers on the north side of Second and between Main and Egan streets, had each shed their unsubstantial shells, for pretentious brick edifices, and others soon followed the trend.[5]

A brick court house costing thirty thousand dollars was lifting its tur-rets skyward on a block in the south central part of town—then only a plat of wild grasses, but now a fine lawn of bluegrass jewelled with flow-ers of gorgeous hue and shaded by splendid trees. This is due to the foresight and untiring labors of Mary E. Smith-Hayward, notable pio-neer business woman and benefactor of countless struggling mortals. First a merchant in the original tent city, she moved with the town to its new site and set up the "M. E. Smith Ladies' Furnishing Establishment" on the southwest corner of Second and Egan streets—a modest frame building which was duly encased in brick. A fountain in her honor in the courthouse park, and now the renaming of the park itself, bear witness to Chadron's regard for this one of her foremost citizens.[6]

A four-story hotel was built by a local stock company on the northwest corner of Second and Bordeaux streets. All the doors and windows of this fine structure were silled and crowned with blocks of hard, white limestone which was quarried in the hills about four miles from town. Its first proprietor was a man by the name of Hoyt, who after a few months transferred it to Ed Satterlee, an attorney from Harrison, Ne-braska. He immediately made a great improvement in its furnishings, christened it "The Blaine" and operated it successfully for several years. Then through a legal transaction it became the property of William Donehue, the late genial proprietor, who directed a second moderniza-tion to conform with its importance.[7]

With regretted omissions, necessitated by reasonable regard for brev-ity, this hop-skip-and-jump portrayal of the constantly changing aspects incident to the birth of a city will have to suffice. It is in order to state that business kept pace with the material improvements. The United States Land Office had opened with General Milton Montgomery, a one-armed Civil War veteran and attorney from Lincoln, as registrar. The Honorable Albert W. Crites, an attorney from Plattsmouth, was receiver; and they had as clerks two bright young men, John W. Cutright and John G. Maher. These four were kept busy transferring a portion of Uncle Sam's domain to eager home-seekers. The Chadron Building and Loan Company, with Robert Hood as president and C. Lutz as secretary, was covering its field of action adequately.[8]

A spacious high school building had been erected and grade schools provided for each ward. Churches kept pace with the schools, and the Mission Department of the Congregational denomination had finished the first of the college buildings whose grove-shaded grounds and blue-grass lawns form one of the beauty spots of south Chadron, now known as the Nebraska State Teachers' College. Hundreds of students, many from adjoining states, receive yearly instruction in their chosen lines under the able guidance of President E. P. Wilson and an efficient staff.[9]

The developments here chronicled were not all conceived and achieved by men, by any means. The ladies with their well organized groups of church, school and welfare workers contributed a notable share to the general advancement, not only through their constant efforts in the field of moral uplift and civic and charitable endeavor, but in more material ways also. For example, they spurred business men to the organization of the Greenwood Cemetery Association, and the result of this laudable effort can be appreciated by a glance at the towering grove just west of the city, where shimmering gleams from the still white sentinels play through the ever green foliage of soughing pines that hedge the avenues of this somber "City of the Dead."

As these shifting scenes of bygone days flash across the screen of memory, it is necessary to touch lightly upon certain personal bickerings and factional antagonisms, apparently unavoidable where men congregate en masse.

The major fraternal orders had their local organizations functioning, and the legal field, too, was well covered with the Knights of the Blackstonian Circle. Quite a number of these attorneys were only located temporarily, however, while they waited for new fields that were being opened as the railroad tracks penetrated the northwest. Others specialized in the side lines incident to their callings and were engaged in land-office practice, loans, collections and insurance. Among a few who seemed to confine their efforts exclusively to trials before the several courts of municipal, county, district, state and federal jurisdiction were Alfred Bartow, T. F. Powers, Allen G. Fisher and Albert W. Crites—after his retirement as receiver. They were able and honorable gentlemen, and most of their dissension was but the natural result of seeking through separate channels to decide the old, old question of "Who's who?" among men. I mention these, not because they were the sole moving spirits in public affairs by any means, but simply as fair representatives of the many who were.[10]

Mr. Bartow officed with the Chadron Banking Company as the legal advisor to the firm and to the county officials who were in the building at that time, also the *Dawes County Journal* was always ably assisted by Attorney T. F. Powers, whose office was near by. Allen G. Fisher, an energetic young graduate from an Indiana law school and junior member of the firm of Spargur & Fisher, chose to operate as a free lance in politics and civic affairs. He was of the same political faith as the first two attorneys named and cooperated with them on national and state issues, but there the affiliation ended. In fact, there was a serious rift in the Republican county organization, and I observed that the Democrats were losing no sleep in an attempt to harmonize the erring brothers.

It was said that the rift was caused by the allegations of J. D. Pattison, a prosperous farmer living in the south part of the county.[11] He and his friends insisted that Mr. Pattison had been duly nominated as one of the commissioners at the first convention for selection of temporary county officers, and that his name had somehow been shuffled out of the list of nominees. Young Fisher was one of the many later arrivals who, having familiarized themselves with the details of the controversy, sided with the Pattison or anti-*Journal* faction.

The links of the chain of narrative are usually unimportant incidents and not always in chronological order with the occurrence. Hence I shall sketch, as briefly as possible, the mode of procedure and the moods that actuated the people and press in this average community of the early West during a strenuously contested election—especially where the community was in the formative period and opposing factions were exceptionally anxious for supremacy.

The stage had been set for the G.O.P. county convention about as follows: Attorneys Alfred Bartow and T. F. Powers, County Clerk F. B. Carly and all the other county officers with E. E. Egan and his *Journal* in the van, were arrayed on one side, while on the other side of an all-Republican fence that divided them into hostile camps were J. D. Pattison, Allen G. Fisher and all of their friends. The Democratic minority, opposed to both factions, was marshalling its scattered band through the untiring efforts of Robert Lucas, J. C. Dahlman, Peter Cooper, Von Harris, L. J. F. Iager and other party chieftains—supported of course by the *Chadron Democrat*, which directed its shots of political buncombe at the *Journal* and its crew. We were kept busy firing volley for volley, because the dissenters of the G.O.P. had no newspaper representation.[12]

These two warring western sheets were of about the same standing as to office force, as Editor Egan had his brother Lucien as foreman, with one or two assistants as needed. We had Charles Conger as our foreman, his assistants, and our ever-present manager, B. C. Hill, who was a mechanical host within himself. He took no part in politics, but on election day he put aside his apron, went to the polls and cast a Republican ballot without even shutting his eyes.

The ethics of the profession in those days, especially in the West among the city dailies as well as sage-brush handbills, was often symbolized by the black flag that has flown on the slightest provocation and refused to remain furled. Editors nicknamed their competitors and their sheets to suit their whims, but it was all in a day's fight. Our managing partner had conceived the idea of printing our own sheet on yellow from the very first issue, and modeled the paper after one then being issued from Yellowstone Park. This gave our opponents the satisfaction of referring to the *Democrat* with such endearing phrases as "Apple Butter Windbag" or "Chestnut Sorrel"—but most of the time as "The Chestnut."

Here I shall relate but a few typical incidents of my newspaper experience "out in the sticks."

Robert Lucas had decided to withdraw from our firm and devote his time to the practice of law and to his real estate interests at Chadron, Nebr. Consequently he stepped down from the editorial tripod and placed me upon that mythical pedestal. So, realizing that I was not accustomed to the handling of heavy verbal artillery, charged with dynamic logic, I chose popguns as my implements of war, with mild buffoonery, buncombe and burlesque as ammunition. In retaliation for the pet names above mentioned I used to belittle my competitor by calling him simply "Mister," or "The Corkscrew."

Mr. Egan had taken a great dislike to J. D. Pattison, and in showering his unprotected head with verbal coals, he ignored the Biblical advice and did not offer any prayers—just a few pointed shafts, dipped in gall and wormwood, in each issue of his paper. He didn't seem to care who struck Billy Pattison; he was after Jim, and I am going to insert one of his frequent personal notices of Jim's arrival in town.

"J. D. Pattison came in from his ranch yesterday, and as usual hurried to the office of the Chestnut Sorrel to greet that Democrat bunch and warm his shanks and spit tobacco juice over the floor."

The time came when, after the usual lurid fireworks incident to such occasions, J. D. Pattison emerged from the Republican convention a duly authorized candidate for commissioner from the southern district of the county, and that announcement set things to happening. There was a tumult of wailing and gnashing of teeth; there was frenzied tearing of hair. In the *Journal* office Mr. Egan vehemently vowed that Pattison should not be included in the support the *Journal* gave the ticket, and that he would not even remain in the county during the campaign—which he did not, finding it convenient to spend his time in the East until after election. Before his departure, the *Democrat* extended the following condolence:

A Tragic Feast

Scene: Journal Office. Cast: Sir Corkscrew, valiant Knight of the Quill; Boot Black, Knight of the Box and Brush; Lucian, The Trusty; and Two Lieutenants.

Sir Corkscrew: "Is this a crow I see before me?"

Boot Black: "No, Mister, that's a swan."

Sir Corkscrew: "And who is he, who dares to interrupt my cogitations in an hour like this?"

Boot Black: "Rats!"

Sir Corkscrew: "Is this crow I see before me as palpable in form as the one I ate last year?"

Boot Black: "Aw, w'at 'er ye tryin' to chuch down ye? That's a peacock, man!"

Sir Corkscrew: "Lucian, seize this imp of hell and lead him hence ere I be tempted to roast and eat him with this crow; and then to me again, for I have that of import to impart."

Lucian: "I come; Your orders have been obeyed, sir."

Sir Corkscrew:" 'Tis well, Lucian. I have before me here a crow, which I am adjured by all the powers to eat; and yet, I like it not. It is not seemly food for such as I, and even now its loathsome looks have my fastidious stomach in dire commotion set. Therefore, dear Lucian, take thou this crow and cook it long and well, season it with mirth; and, when the sable feast is spread, summon my two lieutenants from yon brick castle high and tell them—stay, Lucian, tell them nothing! They know 'tis crow, but say to them that I do pray they eat. Uncork the harmony and let it flow to soothe their nerves the while, for I have urgent business in the East; and ere the morning sun shall shine upon the lifeless form of this cold crow, I'll hie me hence and there remain until this fowl most foul is quite devoured. I'll not eat crow!"

This contest resulted in Pattison's election as county commissioner, and the minority party emerged from the conflict with three of its candidates in some of the best offices in the county—an advantage that not only was held but improved upon as time brought other contests.

We were fortunate in securing a notable acquisition to our ranks in the person of Hon. Albert W. Crites, who had retired from the receivership of the United States Land Office and opened a law office where he had built up a very good clientele. Through previous acquaintance we had learned that he possessed not only ability but that priceless quality that should be the chief capital of all men especially those in positions of trust—integrity. He mixed but little in local politics, but his opinions were based on a rich store of knowledge and nearly always correct, and were continually sought and freely given to a large host of friends. When a new judicial district was created in northwestern Nebraska and he was given the judgeship, the people generally were deeply pleased.

I should not wish anyone to infer that the people of Chadron were continually at war with one another. Their factional differences were similar to those of all sizable communities with possibly a notable exception. When the general interest of the little city was threatened its entire citizenry became a solid phalanx, standing shoulder to shoulder in its defense. All local differences were forgotten for the time and there was complete unity of action.

Also, regardless of our differences, we were like most communities in that we had the grace to treat each other courteously during the casual meetings of the day. Mr. Egan and I, in company or in passing, were but ordinary acquaintances to the casual observer. We served on committees or as jurors without unseemly dissension; in fact, the two of us, with others, were sent to Pine Ridge to solicit the attendance of Indians at one of our Fourth of July celebrations, and we had an agreeable and successful trip. We snarled and showed our teeth only through our office type, as is evidenced by this paragraph that we published immediately after the fire heretofore mentioned:

> We desire to thank all those who assisted in removing our printing material from the fire that threatened it Saturday morning, and especially Messrs. E. E. Egan, Hawks, Sadler and L. Egan of the *Journal* office and Mr. Ernest Bross. These gentlemen, understanding the art, were able to handle the office material and help move it to safety without damage or disarrangement.[13]

An undated photograph of Charles Wesley Allen, probably taken in the 1880s. Courtesy of Roseanna L. Renaud.

A formal portrait of Allen taken at Towles Studio in Washington, probably about 1916. Courtesy of the Nebraska State Historical Society (P853).

Fort Laramie shortly after Allen's first visit to the garrison. Courtesy of the Nebraska State Historical Society (L323-3).

The Red Cloud Agency about the time of the flagpole incident witnessed by Allen. Courtesy of the Nebraska State Historical Society (J82-80).

The main street of Deadwood, Dakota Territory, photographed about the time Allen was there. Courtesy of the Nebraska State Historical Society (S726:63).

Red Cloud's frame house. Allen discusses the Office of Indian Affairs' reasons for building it. Courtesy of the Nebraska State Historical Society (W938:119-90).

The Pine Ridge Agency, shortly after Allen built schoolhouses nearby. Courtesy of the Nebraska State Historical Society (1392:16-1).

A bird's-eye view of Valentine a year after Allen arrived. Courtesy of the Nebraska State Historical Society (978.226 M560).

Chadron in 1888, three years after Allen arrived. Courtesy of the Nebraska State Historical Society (P132-1).

Addison E. Sheldon, editor of
the *Chadron Journal*, and a
longtime friend of Allen's.
Courtesy of the Nebraska State
Historical Society (P853).

The remains of the makeshift tents at Wounded Knee mentioned by Allen.
Courtesy of the Nebraska State Historical Society (W938:13-3).

Lt. S. A. Cloman, First Infantry. Lt. Cloman went to Wounded Knee with the burial party. Allen tells the story of the killing of Isaac Miller on 2 January 1891; Cloman arrested the Indian accused of the murder. Courtesy of the Nebraska State Historical Society (W938:119-29).

The store operated by Louis Mousseau at Wounded Knee, where Allen wrote his first description of the massacre. Photograph by C. G. Morledge, courtesy of the Denver Public Library, Western History Collection (F8843).

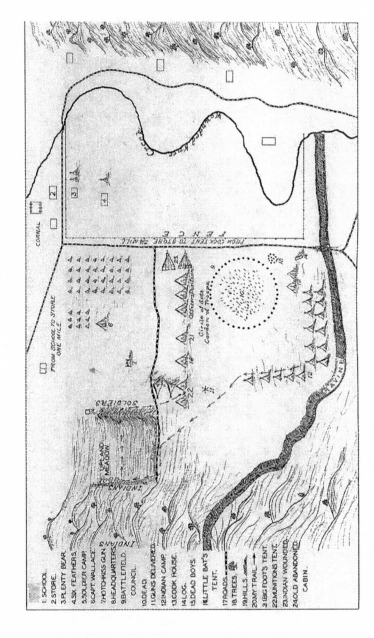

Allen's map of Wounded Knee. Courtesy of the Nebraska State Historical Society (M78357 1890 Al5n).

CHAPTER 17

The Early Far West
Weekly Newspapers

The early far West weekly newspapers often gave space to Indian life, sketches, lore and legends.

The old newspaper boys in what are now referred to as the early days of the Old West, while not among the noted personages of that time, in most cases were motivated by the same impulses as were pioneers of the days of Daniel Boone, Davy Crockett and Abraham Lincoln; the outstanding characters in their various locations. They were imbued with an urge to initiate. They had an ambition for personal achievement for the general good, and this was the spirit actuating the frontiersmen of this country from the Atlantic to the Pacific as a people whose borderland faced the setting sun and, in its time and turn, was always the Great West.

So the frontiersmen of the type and pencil who were in the newspaper field of which I wrote, between the years 1885 and 1891, were by force of circumstances made to seem a rough-and-ready lot who were apt to leave their softer sentiments outside the shop door and prepare for whatever issue was to be faced. Yet on the whole they were a jovial lot, and in their sunny hours they enlightened in shooting pithy and pungent paragraphs at each other in accord with the axiom: "A little folly, now and then, is relished by the wisest men."

At a much later period, while working on my ranch north of Merriman in Nebraska, just across the state line, a passer-by from town handed me a telegram asking me to come to Valentine to take charge of the *Democrat* during the campaign, as Editor Rice would be unavoidably absent for an indefinite period. As the message was signed jointly by Mr. Rice and the chairman of the county committee, I accepted and so managed the paper from the primaries until after the general election.[1]

This was my last whirl at the business until the organization of Bennett County, South Dakota. William Healy, a young newspaper man who was thinking of leaving Midland, South Dakota, was known to me and I induced him to bring his outfit to the surveyor's stakes that then represented Martin, South Dakota, and there we started the *Martin Messenger*. We had but a month to run before election for the first temporary organization, and stiff competition from the *Bennett County Booster* that was established a few months earlier by Miss Olive Hitchcock and her

127

brother; but we won, and Martin was chosen by a majority of the voters as the county seat of Bennett County, South Dakota.

As to many other papers, an accurate data is not at hand and cannot be had by reasonable effort. I knew intimately only one of the editors, Mr. Frank Broome, who had made Chadron his headquarters for several months while looking over the surrounding country in search of a suitable location for himself. He finally located at Alliance and became one of the earlier boosters, builder and prominent citizen of Box Butte County.[2]

While the sturdy and enterprising men of Northwest Nebraska were endeavoring to mold things to their hearts' desire in their respective communities, they were closely followed and sometimes outdistanced by active and far-seeing women and their vast following. The old-time organization of Good Templars was their rallying point, and the Band of Hope, composed of minors and their preceptors, with their blue-and-white colors and other temperance insignia flying in the breeze, could be seen marching in parade on frequent occasions. The question of National Prohibition was beginning to be seriously discussed, and the traveling evangelists confined their discourses almost wholly to that subject.

At Chadron on November 17, 1887, the various temperance groups of the city issued the first number of the *Northwestern Temperance Advocate*. The little sheet elicited but scant notice from the newspaper fraternity of that time and section. We gave it a line or two as a birth notice, of course, and it was regarded as a commendable Sunday-school tract. No one realized, until later, that it was one of the myriad fountainheads scattered over the land whose rivulets, converging at a common center, were destined to change the constitution of the United States for a number of years.

The little paper continued to proclaim the gospel of temperance (confounded with prohibition) until the spring of 1888 when Addison E. Sheldon, a young newspaperman from the eastern part of the state who was homesteading in Cherry County, and who on previous occasions had surveyed the Chadron field as related to his profession, purchased and enlarged it. Mr. Sheldon was well equipped in every way for the management and development of a successful newspaper. He had been a student in Doane College at Crete (his home town) and in the State University at Lincoln. He continued the temperance feature of the paper, but broadened its policy to include all progressive movements, moral or political. That policy later fitted in with the wave of Populism that for a time overspread Nebraska. His paper, shorn of its superfluous titles but not of its fervor for abstinence and appearing simply as the *Chadron*

Advocate, became the accredited voice of both the temperance and Populist movements. Mr. Egan of the *Journal*, a Republican, and I, a Democrat, but neither of us Prohibitionists, left open an inviting field of action which the *Advocate* utilized very effectively.

As a citizen and proprietor of one of its newspapers, the town of Chadron had readily accorded Mr. Sheldon full fellowship and acknowledged him as a desirable acquisition to its business circle. While he was strictly temperate and at all times practiced what he preached, he made no attempt to judge or to condemn those who chose another standard of conduct. On the contrary, jovial and friendly, he worked shoulder to shoulder with his neighbors in promoting all enterprises that tended to advance the interests and ideals of the community.

After serving the progressive cause (according to the Populist formula) through some of its warmest campaigns, in 1896 he was nominated the Populist candidate for state representative from that district and was elected. When his term of office expired he became successively assistant in the American History Department of the State University, founder of the Nebraska Legislative Reference Bureau, and Superintendent of the State Historical Society. This was congenial employment, being in the line of that historical research to which he has since devoted all of his time. He had, of course, disposed of the *Chadron Advocate*, which was merged with other newspapers. The field of political progress in this community was then covered by the *Chadron Chronicle* under the management of C. H. Pollard and his very efficient force.[3]

In chasing the news during the summer and fall of 1888 Mr. Sheldon and I became friends. As opportunity offered time for more extensive visits we discovered that while our experiences along the trails of life had differed widely, still there was an affinity in basic principles and ideals that established an intimacy enabling us to take and to give a joke without offense—and sometimes with great interest. In the matter of joking, both in and out of our papers, he had much the better of it. I was confined chiefly to gags based on his dry propensities, while he had the numerous political defeats of my friends and myself at which to aim his shafts.

Of course I reacted to his jibes through the paper, but concluded I could have still more fun by indulging in a little harmless personal annoyance. So, when my friend and I met along the street on our frequent rounds, I would nod knowingly toward one of the many saloons and say, "Won't you come in and have something?"

At first this only got me a quick, sharp glance and a caustic smile as he hurried on, but as the greeting was occasionally repeated I thought I could detect a milder, less stand-offish attitude. Finally one nice summer day, as we met in front of Jim Owen's two-story brick liquor emporium, I extended the invitation for the last time.[4] To my surprise he accepted and accompanied me through the door, past the office desk near a plate-glass window in the corner, and down an aisle between rows of kegs and barrels on one side and stacks of boxes on the other, to a bar at the rear where the talkative and eccentric proprietor stood with his eyes bulging as if they had stepped out to meet us. I called mine straight, feloniously, while my friend asked for lemonade. I partook leisurely and he sipped his cool, tall glass even more leisurely while answering rapid-fire questions from Mr. Owens. When I paused a moment on my way out to speak to a helper they passed me, deep in conversation, and I went about my business. Some time later, when I thought that Jim might be out of stationery, I called expecting my usual order, but was pleasantly informed that he had given Mr. Sheldon an order that would last for several months. I extended no more unwanted invitations.

CHAPTER 18

A "Good Neighbor" Act–
A Burlesque Speech

Close upon the events narrated in the preceding chapter were other and more important affairs that occupied the time and attention of everyone. The weather was propitious, fields were being planted, and all indications of another bumper crop were present. A feeling of prosperous security prevailed in our section and seemed to be general throughout the country.

Then, flashing over the wires, came the news of the Johnstown flood on May 31, 1889, and the world was shocked by the terrible suffering that had befallen that community. As this calamity was the main subject of discussion in our midst, I chanced to recall an incident that occurred in my home town of Wichita, Kansas, but a few years after I left there in 1871. I do not recall either the locality or the circumstances, but a misfortune had fallen, distress existed, and the good people of the then small town of Wichita responded with the donation of a trainload of corn to the sufferers.

Thinking of this, I wondered why Chadron could not do something of the sort. We had a surplus of potatoes that were slow to sell at ten cents a bushel, and corn was about the same price. No sooner was the thought conceived than I set out to submit the idea to some of my business friends. I had but mounted the stairs leading from the shop to the street when I met Mayor Cox, to whom I told the plan.[1] He grasped its significance at once and we decided to give it immediate test by interviewing all whom we met on the street while making also a systematic canvass of the town. When we compared notes at the finish we found that favorable sentiment was almost unanimous.

The mayor then went to the depot to interview C. C. Hughes, division superintendent, as to what might be expected in the way of transportation, and secured his unqualified endorsement of the undertaking and his promise to lay the matter before his superiors immediately, with every prospect for favorable consideration by the company.[2] We distributed hand-bills all over the town and in the adjoining country, calling for a mass meeting at a specified date.

A few days later we met at the court house to set forth our plan, and asked all present to help perfect the organization necessary to carry it out. Superintendent Hughes was present with the welcome information that the Fremont, Elkhorn & Missouri Valley and the Chicago & Northwestern railroads had guaranteed free transportation to Johnstown for all the produce we would be able to assemble on one train. All they required was that we send along a man to take charge, as they assumed no responsibility beyond delivery.

Committees were appointed; donations of corn, potatoes, and the use of several teams were accepted; and all who applied were hired to remove sprouts and sort the marketable potatoes on platforms erected for that purpose in front of the cars. All the potatoes that we received were worked over as fast as they arrived, and soon three cars of them and two cars of corn, each filled to capacity, were assembled. As time was the essence of the procedure, Major Cox was placed in charge, and the train pulled out for its destination amidst the simple ceremony of voluminous huzzas.

In the meantime the benevolent and enterprising citizens of our Sheridan County neighbor, Rushville, had assembled two or three carloads of like produce. These were picked up and attached to the train, before it rolled on to Johnstown, where, according to the following letter of thanks from the authorities there, it arrived at an opportune time and was duly appreciated.[3]

Commissary Department
STATE OF PENNSYLVANIA

Johnstown
June 20th, 1889

Mayor H. A. Cox
Chadron, Dawes County
Nebraska

Dear Sir:

Your consignment of five cars of corn and potatoes from Chadron has just been received this morning. Up to this time the question of providing feed for horses has been somewhat neglected on account of the great rush for provisions to sustain the people. Just as we were looking about to make provision for feed for many horses employed upon the streets here and owned by the survivors of this great disaster, your gift, contained in the five cars, came in sight of the Pennsylvania railway station. You can rest assured that this department was greatly relieved on receipt of your donation. The entire consignment was promptly distributed to the Valley district commissaries, and will be in possession of the proper parties by eleven o'clock today.

Thanking you and your people cordially for your consideration of this afflicted valley, I am

Respectfully yours,
J. L. SPANGLER
Ass't Com. Gen. of Pa.

While the details pertaining to this donation were being carried forward to completion, other affairs of import were taking place in our vicinity. We heard the usual annual rumors of the Indians preparing to break from the reservations, but for the most part the settlers did not pay much attention to them.[4] The Pine Ridge Indian Agency was then breaking into the headlines of the city dailies, and a government commission consisting of General Crook of the United States Army, Senator Warner of Missouri and ex-Governor Foster of Ohio had arrived at the agency to take the initial step in negotiating with all the bands of the Sioux Tribe, and were to hold their first council with the Oglala beginning Saturday, June 15, 1889.[5]

Many settlers along the Nebraska side of the state line and the citizens of the nearby towns, including Chadron, were there as spectators— I among them. A large pavilion had been erected on a grassy plot of ground just across the street south of the agent's office, and on an improvised platform sat the commissioners, surrounded by their secretaries and interpreters, and the Indian agent, Colonel Gallagher.[6] A short distance to one side the reporters were seated. The rest of the platform was occupied by Colonel Gallagher's wife and a party of visiting ladies, with Chief Red Cloud and his principal sub-chiefs and head men on the other side; while a host of tribesmen surrounded the pavilion. The two front rows of Indians were seated on the grass; the next few files were standing, and behind those was a solid mass of Indians on horseback. They were all eager to see and hear the men who had been sent to council with them, and whom they usually referred to as Big Cats from the Great White Father—which was their way of designating men whom we lionize. It was said that Spotted Tail, on some previous occasion, had told a similar set of commissioners that they were a lot of old bald-headed fools from Washington.

The agent, Colonel Gallagher, opened the meeting by tersely stating its object and telling them that the details would all be explained later, then he requested them to pay close attention to everything that was said during the meeting. Senator Warner was the first speaker. He began by addressing them as friends, and added that when he talked with friends he always liked to have them close enough so that he could look them in the face. He suggested that those at the rear should come around to the front of the platform, and as many as could find room complied with his request. The gist of his talk, as I now recall it, was about as follows:

First he called their attention to their environment and the great changes that had taken place: the total absence of buffalo and the increasing scarcity of other game, in the chase of which they had been assured of an independent living. Then shrewdly he fixed their minds on the vast area of unoccupied territory between the Missouri River and the eastern edge of the Black Hills, which they had already ceded for a cash consideration. He knew that he had their interested attention and proceeded to dwell forcibly on facts that he knew were apparent to them. In substance, this is the proposition he laid before them for consideration:

The government would take over land extending from the north line of the state of Nebraska to the Canadian line, exclusive of all tribal reservations allotted to and already in possession of the various Sioux bands. This land was to be thrown open to homesteaders at the regular price of $1.25 per acre, and the money would be placed to their credit in the Sioux Fund at Washington, less the costs of survey and administration. They would then be receiving an income, as the land was taken up by settlers, for that which at the time was utterly valueless to them.

Ex-Governor Charles Foster of Ohio then explained that plainly printed copies of the proposed treaty, with space for signatures, would be circulated among them by competent interpreters; that other copies would be in possession of the agent and the commissioners, and would always be available to those who wished to sign. He requested them to discuss and consider every angle, phase and detail of the proposition at their own councils and about camp as they found time, and at various intervals there would be an open forum at the pavilion where their chiefs (and any others who wished) might join the commissioners in a public discussion of all or any part of the subject. They were asked not to hurry, because the commissioners intended to remain until they had plenty of time to understand the matter thoroughly.

During these talks General George Crook, who had been ill the day before, attempted to withdraw to his quarters on the quiet, but succeeded only after running a gauntlet of hand-shaking Sioux who knew him and held him in high regard.

Senator Warner adjourned the meeting with a few pleasing remarks, and from then on for a week or ten days Pine Ridge, with its numerous surrounding villages, hummed with individual discussions and council oratory. As the Indians gradually came to understand the subject the signers kept increasing, and after a sojourn of about ten days the commissioners were able to leave with a vast majority of the adult males of the Oglala band favorably signed up. They then went on to Rosebud and other agencies on the Missouri to continue their work.

On my return from the agency I learned that the business men of Chadron had held a meeting and appointed a committee to perfect arrangements for our Fourth of July celebration, and had selected A. E. Sheldon and myself as delegates to Pine Ridge for the purpose of securing Red Cloud and his people as guests of Chadron in the entertainment planned for our three-day celebration.[7]

One day in late June we secured a team and buggy and started forth for Pine Ridge, where we arrived early in the afternoon. We found the place seething with excited Indians, and here and there a group of them were clustered about a commissioner who, with his secretary and interpreter, had been approached while on the way from one office to another. Reporters were everywhere present, as all were interested in the discussion of the pending treaty–the all-absorbing topic of the day. I had been introduced to some of the commissioners and other members of the staff on a previous trip, and Mr. Sheldon and I made it a point to meet them again on this occasion. We also sought out Little Wound, Blue Horse, No Water, Fire Thunder and other sub-chiefs and head men, to whom we explained our visit, and in each instance our invitation was gladly accepted and our suggestions agreed to.[8]

The next morning we visited Red Cloud at his home on the west side of White Clay Creek opposite the agency. We found him (as he usually was) surrounded by a number of his followers in the one large room of his frame house, over which floated the American flag and around which, from tall painted lodges, many bright streamers quivered in the breeze. Our interruption of their consultation was taken in a friendly manner. We stated our errand as briefly as possible and received a hearty response, with their promise to be in Chadron a day before the opening of the exercises.

On our return trip the thought occurred to me that I might create a little merriment among our friends at home by rendering a ridiculous account of our visit at Pine Ridge. After due consideration, and knowing that the home folks would get a clear and lucid account in the *Advocate* and would expect a similar write-up in the *Democrat*, I decided to and did publish the following giddy and wholly imaginary narrative:[9]

The Colonel at Pine Ridge

Last Saturday, in accord with instructions from the executive committee on Fourth of July arrangements, the Colonel and I started for Pine Ridge—a distance of about thirty-five miles—for the purpose of securing the attendance of Red Cloud and his people as guests and helpers with their dance and other tribal ceremonies at our approaching celebration. Now the Colonel, as everyone knows, is a prohibitionist not only in theory but in practice; yet after accompanying him on this trip we are able to state that he is quite companionable. He seemed to be continually bubbling over with merriment and ever ready to crack his little joke, and each time he did so the horses, that evidently had been accustomed to drawing a hearse, would slacken their speed, slowly straighten up in the harness, and step off in a sedate and dignified manner as if moving in unison with a funeral procession.

On these occasions I would direct the Colonel's attention to some special feature of the scenery on his side of the road and inadvertently drop the whip, and after continuing the proper distance would pleasantly ask him to go and get it. This he always did, and during his absence on such errands I would find time to examine the powder and see that it was still dry. I would also look at the camphor bottle to see that the thoughtful precaution against possible dire disaster had not been neglected; then accept his proffered whip with thanks and we would jog along on our journey.

We have stated that the Colonel was companionable, but if you will pardon the assertion we just about had to force him to be so. We have long held to the theory that all men have their weakness, no matter to what degree self-discipline has brought them toward purity of thought and action and high, noble aims, because somewhere in the deep recesses of each man's nature there lurks the germ of a vice that cultivation has not eliminated. Acting upon this hypothesis we were determined to find the weak spot in the Colonel's makeup, which we did.

First we suggested that somewhere in the dark depths of a valise (which we had borrowed) we might be able to find a phial of Cologne water, if in his judgment it would be an improvement on the fragrance of Nebraska's wild flowers. He firmly but very pleasantly refused to consider the suggestion, so we offered a cigar which he also declined with thanks.

Ignoring these rebuffs, we produced a small wrapped package

of linear shape and presented it to him. It was accepted at once. Ah, we had him! The Colonel did chew gum. His failing, in common with that of the rest of humanity, was made apparent and the old axiom proven again: "No man is without guile." For it is certainly a sad breach of propriety for a prohibition editor to chew gum. So depressed was I by this fall from grace that I relapsed into sullen mood during the remainder of the journey and let the editor of the *Advocate* chew his cud in silence, even forbearing the pleasure of dropping the whip.

However, as we neared the agency a tinge of romance seemed to revive the Colonel's spirits. The agency was the center of an imposing panorama—vast stretches of plateau across which were scattered irregular Indian villages and herds of grazing ponies; and all around the gray-yellow hills of the "bad lands" topped with pine and the more vivid coloring of the high pine-topped ridges. The agency itself teemed with Indians on foot and on horseback crowding the streets, presenting a picture never to be forgotten, and it became evident that the Colonel was getting pleasurably (even unduly) excited.

Half an hour later when we strolled forth from the hotel it appeared that he had calmed to normalcy, but a surprise was in the offing. We walked up to one of the larger trading stores operated by James Asay, who with others stood in front of the store, and as greetings and introductions were finished the Colonel, despite all previous warnings and protestations, unburdened himself of a wise-crack.[10]

At the words a venerable old gentleman with long billowy white beard and a distaff appeared from the shadows. Shading his eyes, he paused but a moment before embracing both the joke and the joker. These "ancient mariners" clasped in each other's arms and talking of their youth formed a scene of sadness, and although not given to tears we had to turn away, while Mr. Asay and the other gentlemen removed their hats.

Then tenderly we took the Colonel's arm and started back to the hotel, but on our way we met Chief Red Cloud. The Colonel grasped his hand and immediately proceeded to give him a shower-bath of words, regardless of breath, commas, or pauses of any kind. Once Red Cloud essayed to speak but the Colonel stopped him, saying,

"Never mind! Don't say a word! I know you'll come; and don't bother about your young men. If you can't get them to come I will get them for you, for I am going to speak to them tonight at the coliseum. Be 'round!"

We left the astonished chief wondering what it was all about and met an interpreter, with whom the Colonel soon had arrangements completed for a grand council that evening at which he was to be the speaker.

A good rest and a bountiful supper seemed to allay the editorial excitement but failed to bring him entirely back to earth. As the shades of night deepened the council formed about a blazing camp-fire and the Colonel marched magnificently to the center of a large circle of braves, his new-found interpreter at his side, and made the following speech.[11]

"My friends and fellow-warriors: Unlike Rienzi, the last of the Roman tribunes, I did come here to speak, and it is with a feeling of profound reverence that I greet you this evening. As I stand here in the mellow glow of this council fire, with the eye of the Great Spirit twinkling through the stars and the ears of the great warriors of a mighty nation straining to catch my every word, I am reminded of the fact that prohibition is a law that prevails on Indian reservations, and I am happy to be able to address an audience composed of temperance men who have never cast their vote for high license.

"Fellow Indians, it is not of this I came to speak. I have come from a city of the pale-face known as Chadron, and I was sent to request the noble Red Men of the Plains to hie themselves hence to our tepees and help us celebrate the glorious birthday of our great country and this you are to do by jumping and hollering as you keep time with the melancholy music of the tomtom.

"You may take me for a commissioner. So I am, but not such as come among you seeking your land. I am commissioned by the great council of a thriving city to bid you come and break bread with us, and we will furnish the bread and plenty of beef with all necessary condiments. The magnanimity of the people of our city is so great that they furnished me with a driver who knows the winding trails leading from the tepees of our city to this great village of nomadic braves.

"Most silent, sour and sullen Red Men, but a few short years ago where we now stand, the frontiersman roamed at large and the white hunter chased the elk and buffalo, flinched the fish from the streams and smoked his pipe of clay. Behold, now all is changed and magnificent! From the hilltops and the plains rise the homes of the children of the wild, and red streamers float from the tops of thousands of white-winged tepees.

A "Good Neighbor" Act–A Burlesque Speech

"My friends, it is this picturesque advancement on your part that causes your enterprising white neighbors to extend the hand of fellowship across the chasm of a dark and bloody past and bid you welcome to our city. We covet not your lands. Your goods and your pristine forests of grey-green sagebrush and growing groves of gorgeous greasewood constitute no temptation to the splendid city of Chadron that sits at the foot of her seven hills and from that throne of beauty puts a tax on dogs. I mention this tax, my friends, in the belief that your quick appreciation of intimated thoughts and your inherent tact for 'catching on' will cause you to leave all your dogs at home and bring away as many as you can.

"Now, my Red brethren, I have finished. I may have detained you too long, but I promised Red Cloud that I would use my influence to get you to accompany his party on this visit, and you have heard me speak."

Here it seemed to dawn on the Colonel that there had been no translation, either by sentence or by paragraph, so he boldly demanded that the interpreter come forward.

"This gentlemen will translate my remarks *verbatim at literatim*, neither adding to nor taking from. I have done! As the sun goes behind a cloud, so I leave you."

The interpreter moved to the front and said, in the Sioux language: "This man wants me to tell you what he has said. I know no more of what he has been talking about than you do. I tried to learn from the man he calls his driver, but all I could get from him, through a muffling handkerchief and mumbled sobs, was that the speaker had gone wrong in the head."

The Indians held a superstition that unbalanced mentality was caused by the possession of evil spirits, and they all vanished immediately.

The Colonel gazed on this strange procedure for a moment, then, calling them "unappreciative wretches," meandered on toward the hotel, pondering over the enigma of Lo as an audience.

CHAPTER 19
The Celebration

The Indian features of frontier celebrations are still interesting to many, and in that early day were a rare novelty. In our extensive advertising these had been especially stressed, with the result that most sections from Omaha to Casper (Wyoming) were represented at this, the largest celebration that had been put on in the western end of the state.

Early on the morning of the second, the Indians, who evidently had made camp late the previous evening on the lower stretches of Bordeaux Creek, were seen filing over the hill some two miles to the north. It seemed to be an endless string of wagons, skirted on either side by horseback riders whose warbonnets of eagle feathers trailed over their backs, and many crude banners floated above the various family groups in the wagon train which was still rising over the crest of the hill.

This sudden appearance of so many Indians in gaudy costume, with an occasional shot fired as a salute to the town, made an impressive scene. In fact, it was rather too impressive for the comfort of many women and children (and some others) whose sole knowledge of Indians had been gleaned from historic accounts of the conflicts between them and frontier settlements—which, as we all know, registered pictures that were dark indeed.[1]

All fears of the timid were soon allayed, however, when it was seen that the marshal of the day, F. M. Dorrington, with his mounted assistants—F. B. Carly, Tom Coffey, W. L. Cassady, John G. Maher and ex-Sheriff George Clark, accompanied by Sheriff J. C. Dahlman, were riding out to meet the approaching visitors.[2] Red Cloud and his cortege, in the van, were stopped only long enough for greetings, then the welcoming committee turned and with much pomp escorted their guests to the plateau just east of town that had been designated as their camping ground. Then a couple of beeves and other provisions were given to their own committee, to be issued to their family groups as they chose.

We had advertised three days' entertainment, and it was just that. The Indian cavalcade appeared on the morning of July second and their village vanished at dawn the fifth, while hundreds of erstwhile pleased and interested spectators had preceded their departure by many hours.

When the reception committee had met the oncoming visitors on the plain north of town, to conduct them to their camp, the primitive pageant began. Mounted and uniformed in impressive style, the escort on cavorting steeds led the procession through the principal streets that were lined with curious citizens. Many followed to the camp to watch with absorbed interest as the Indians freed and drove their ponies to pasture, unpacked their camp outfits and set up their lodges. In short, they witnessed what to them seemed miraculous rapidity in the creation of a large Indian village.

During the afternoon of July 2 there were continuous passing streams of visitors between the town and this village. The whites were eager to see everything possible pertaining to the home life of a wild roving people. The Indians, many of whom had never seen a white man's town, were equally curious about the strange activities of its inhabitants, engaged in their various chores. In the evening their village was alight with camp fires, and their usual festivities of song and dance were continued until a late hour, to the delight of many spectators.

The Third was observed by engaging in the various sports usual to such occasions. There were horse and foot races, a ball game on the diamond south of town, friendly visiting and other improvised forms of entertainment and pleasure. A small band of fantastically dressed Indian dancers paraded and performed through the streets, paying their respects to the business houses by pausing at the door until a small tribute had been offered in the form of goods or provisions.

On "the great and glorious Fourth" Marshal Dorrington with his mounted deputies and Sheriff Dahlman formed the procession on West Second Street, and the line of march traversed all the principal streets. First in the parade was the Chadron Silver Cornet Band; then, in the order named, came the carriage of the president of the day, T. H. Glover, and Mayor H. A. Cox; a carriage wherein Red Cloud rode in state beside J. F. Tucker; the Militant Rank I.O.O.F. in their picturesque regalia; the Uniform Rank of Damascus Lodge No. 64, Knights of Pythias; ladies on horseback; the Dorrington and railway hose teams; the Chadron trades display; citizens in carriages; and, bringing up the rear, a hundred mounted Indians.[3]

In due time this procession was dispersed on the court house grounds after music by the band and a song by a quartet—Mrs. A. C. Putnam, Mrs. C. P. Waller and the Misses Blanchard. The venerable and still venerated custom of reading the Declaration of Independence was properly performed by Professor J. S. Denton. Judge C. H. Bane closed the forenoon exercise with an able historical address.[4]

Relative to the Knights of Pythias marchers, let me remark: At the time mentioned I had been the senior officer of that company, but later moved to another state and became interested in ranching.[5] When President McKinley called a rally to the colors in 1898, I was much pleased to learn that a company had quickly volunteered at Chadron, and that A. G. Fisher and L. A. Dorrington, who had held the lieutenancies in the K. P. company, in the order named, were chosen as officers of the newly organized company of the United States Army. A. G. Fisher was captain, L. A. Dorrington, 1st Lieutenant, [and] Ed L. Godsell, railway conductor, who as a young man and the chief of special police and helped keep perfect order upon that gala day long past, was made second lieutenant.[6] Knowing these and many others of their comrades, it gave me particular pleasure to follow their creditable course at their post. At the conclusion of their service Mr. Fisher returned to the practice of law, Mr. Dorrington secured a commission as captain in the regular army and served in the Philippines, and Mr. Godsell resumed his work with the Chicago & Northwestern.

From a platform erected in the shade of heavily foliaged boughs across the green from the court house, the afternoon exercises were opened with music by the band; then came patriotic songs, speeches by visiting and local celebrities, and the address by Chief Red Cloud. As given to us by the interpreter, it was as follows:[7]

My Friends: I will say something today and shall ask you to listen to me. I was asked to come here to see you celebrate and show you our Indian ways and our great dance, but I have something to tell you besides that. I have told you many times before that all you people are my friends, and I hope that all your children and our children will treat each other like brothers—and also our children of the future—as if we were children of one family.

The Great Father has sent commissioners here to try to fool me like a child and take my land from me. They told me that if I did not give up the land it would be just like big fish in a pond with little fish—the big ones would eat the little ones all up. They said that the white people would take all the good land from me, and that I would have nothing but bad lands where I would starve to death. They said that if I had a high stone wall around me, the white people would get over it, and that if I did not sign the paper there would be no more Indians—they would be wiped out. But I am no child. They came to me like a child, so I did not sign the paper. The Great Father has bothered me so much about my land that I am getting tired of it. I have told him that I would never give up any more of my land, and I want you all to understand me.

The Great White Father has made many treaties with me and my people, but did not keep his word when the time came to pay the money to make his word good. I was always cheated, and so were my people. I don't like to make a fuss about this, for I want to be friends to you all. This land is mine. I want you to be my friends and we will live as friends in future.

I would say more, but do not feel well. Good-bye.

Red Cloud's short talk, I believe, evidences the fact that though the Sioux Tribe was noted for its many natural orators, he was not nor did he claim to be one of them. He left that detail to his lieutenants. He was their hard-headed, grim old general and chief planner. And so completely obsessed was he with the idea that he could keep "his world," the only world he had ever known, just as he had always known it, that it was next to impossible to convince him otherwise.

Reasoning from a fair but primitive code of justice, was Red Cloud to be blamed? If the limits of his untutored mind kept him from seeing the white man's viewpoint, naturally he could not understand the necessity of imposing barriers that it would be impossible for him and his people to surmount. I was but a young and disinterested observer at the time, but reflection has brought me to believe that this characteristic of Red Cloud, backed up by a few disgruntled white friends at and near the agency, was the root of all his difficulties with his agent, Dr. V. T. McGillicuddy. For it was incumbent on the doctor to give to him and his people their first instructions in civilized procedure.

The grand Omaha Dance that followed the speech of Red Cloud and continued until near sunset was the climax of the entertainment.[8] I shall touch upon only a few special features of this rendition of the Omaha dance—so called, it is said, because a Sioux war party once saw it being performed by the Omaha Indians while they were lying in wait to attack the village. The Sioux adopted and improved it to suit their own wild fancies, and its main features have been described and over-described many times in recent years.

That which most impressed and pleased me with the dance on this occasion was the fact that, although I had witnessed many such performances (and have since), this was the largest and most spectacular Indian dance I have ever seen. There were continuously, on the smoothed-off earthen floor, about one hundred Indians in constant action, keeping perfect time, while their fantastic regalia seemed to be an animated bundle of gaudy colored feathers and leggings adorned with jingling bells. Peculiar muscular actions and rapidly shifting movements, in rhythm with the strange wild strains of their weird music, added the touch that made this dance an unforgettable experience. I was pleased, for we had advertised it as the main feature of our entertainment, and I could readily see that the hundreds of visitors were simply enthralled.

These performances differed in only one respect from those sometimes given by returned Indian students, now more or less versed in civilized practices, who on occasion very properly enjoy themselves and furnish entertainment for their audiences by a perfectly accurate presentation of the old-time tribal dance and other customs of their ancestors. The vital difference is that these young men merely assume the role, like any legitimate actors; thus their own advancement is in no wise retarded.

Historic accounts of primitive races of men show clearly that, as more and more they come under the cultivating influence of civilization, their crude and often barbarous sources of amusement were automatically abandoned. And so it has been and will continue to be with the American Indian. The Sioux have already advanced beyond the spectacular cruelty of the Sun Dance.[9] The cruelty practiced in this dance, however, was not imposed by tribal or other edict. It was wholly self-imposed in a Spartan spirit of contest and physical endurance.

The Indian dancers who entertained the far-gathered audience at the frontier celebration at Chadron on July 4, 1889, were the ancestors of the Indian students here mentioned, and had been but very few years from the wilds of their native haunts—from the chase of the wild creatures of mountain, plain and stream that for generations had furnished them food, raiment and shelter.

The strenuous physical exertion required in a perfect execution of this dance, accompanied by a continuous chant by the dancers and punctuated by exultant whoops, necessitates frequent interludes for rest. At such times (indicated of course by a cessation of music), the braves seat themselves on the ground in a circle, at the outer edge of the arena, and for a time enjoy their turkey-wing fans and a few whiffs of kinakanic as the pipe is passed from one to another.

During this period of rest a band of women appear on the music side of the arena. Standing very straight, closely shoulder to shoulder, they chant in a sing-song rhythm to the beat of a tom-tom while they perform a sort of dance by jumping up and down, moving as a solid phalanx.

But this variation in procedure is soon ended, and its conclusion elicits a loud burst of applause from appreciative friends of the mixed audience. Then the rested dancers rush to the center of the arena and begin the repetition of their fantastic gyrations. Perhaps the next or several interludes will be filled by some brave who dashes to the center of the circle and orates on his personal achievements in the interest of his people.

If he is a noted hunter, his theme will be his extraordinary ability in finding and bringing in game in time of deep snows and near-famine. If a daring marauder—the great number of ponies and stock of the enemy he has brought home on numerous forays to replenish the herds of his band. Or, if a noted warrior, he discourses on the many fights in which he has been engaged and the "coos" he has counted—that is, striking the enemy while he is alive, which they consider the bravest feat. He tells of the battle charges he has made, his narrow escapes, the scalps he has taken, the wounds he has received and which he is likely to display.

The peculiar feature of these self-laudatory speeches, that have been heard time and again and never fail to hold the interest of the same listeners, lies in the original and ever-recurring oratorical variations of their presentation. Long established tribal custom permits their speakers to wander far afield in reproducing the event of which they speak, and to use all the bombastic braggadocio they are capable of creating, so long as they make no material false statement of the facts. This limitation was always carefully observed by a brave in recounting his deeds of valor. Well he knew that there were those in his audience who had been with him in every melee or adventure in which he had been engaged, and custom made it something of a duty (at least a privilege gladly appropriated) for them to rise and pronounce him a liar—to the echoing shouts of approval of his fellows. This custom enabled the tribe to keep an oral record of their feats of strategy, personal heroism and unusual events in their field of action, on a basis of comparative truthfulness.

As this performance was the last of the entertainment, a brief resume relative to incidents that occurred "off the record" may not be amiss.

As to accidents (that were always guarded against) there were none. Minor disturbances occurred frequently, but were always stopped in the beginning by the authorities.

Some of these disturbances culminated in laughable episodes, as in the case of an elderly colored cook, John Henry by name, who had constituted himself chief choreman of Chadron by right of discovery.[10] He was very black indeed and possessed of spontaneous wit, and often sarcastic tongue. He also possessed an appetite for strong drink, and on occasion got hopelessly drunk. At such times it was a routine custom of the marshal to take him to the jail, chuck him into a convenient cell and leave him there until he became sober enough to navigate and carry the burden resting on his rugged shoulders, then take him up to the kitchen of his old Texas friend the sheriff, J. C. Dahlman, whose wife would diet and nurse him back to normal strength.

During these two or three days of convalescence John voluntarily turned his hand to any chore that he saw should be done. As wood was the usual fuel, John generally took his reducing exercises over the sawbuck at Mrs. Dahlman's woodpile.

Now it so happened that in the early afternoon of the Fourth the town marshal had locked John Henry in the cell nearest the jail door for the purpose of letting him slumber back to normalcy. He had not thought of mentioning the matter to others of the force, thereby setting the stage for a bit of comedy.

Indians in those days did not seek the trail of the bootlegger as they learned to do later. In fact, during the three-day celebration I heard of none becoming intoxicated but the one that figures in this episode. Bootlegging had not then developed into a gainful occupation. There were occasional packhorse or wagon saloons that would spring up as near to a village or agency as thought safe and ply their trade until run out or captured by the authorities. But there were always those who could fund some reckless white "Cola" (chum) who would buy a bottle for them in friendly spirit, feeling perfectly safe as far as the law was concerned—for reasons to be stated.

It must have been by this route that Black Horse, a husky young Omaha dancer, developed such a state of inebriation in the heat and muscular action of the dance that the "Dog Soldiers" (tribal police) made him leave the arena.[11] Later he was found down town, making it unpleasant for some of his own people who were trading at the stores and quietly attending to their own affairs. This attracted the attention of Marshal Godsell. He called an assistant, who, understanding Indians and their language, remonstrated with Black Horse in a friendly way.[12] But the Indian, being drunk with pride and arrogance as well as liquor, struck an attitude of defiance.

Before he knew what was happening each arm was seized, a swinging scabbard was relieved of its long knife, and he was rushed along the street toward the jail. He essayed to lie down, but as hands were slipped under his armpits and he found himself being dragged, he decided to walk. Then, pulling back, he tried to wrench himself loose, but with no success.

The struggle that ensued was a spectacle in itself, for Black Horse was dressed in full war regalia plus the gaw-gaws of the dance costume. The tall white feathers of his war bonnet were scarcely more arresting than a bunch of smaller feathers, varicolored, suspended from a girdle. His body was hideously painted, and along the outer seams of his leggings small sleigh bells were sewn, running down to brightly beaded moccasins.

Naturally this scene drew a crowd, jeering and joking. The officers were so worn and aggravated by the continuous balking and struggling of their prisoner and by the heckling of the crowd that, when the jail was reached, they threw open the door of the first cell they came to and threw the warrior in with such force that he landed on his knees with a fierce "Wow-u-ugh" grunt almost over John Henry, unseen among the shadows of the cell. And John, startled from his drunken dream, let out one wild scream and scrambled up the wall like a monkey, stopping only as his head hit the ceiling.

The officers, guarding the open door, exploded with laughter. As John recognized them he slid to the floor, rolling his eyes. Black Horse, now sitting with his back to the wall, grinned drunkenly at the frustrated Negro who, when his breath returned, broke forth with vehemence.

"Say, Mistah Marshal, what yu-all throw that devil in heah on me fo'?"

"That isn't the devil, John. That's your friend come to visit."

"No friend o' mine, suh!"

"How'd you get in here, John?"

"Don't know, suh, lessen Missue Dahlman's outen stove wood agin."

"Do you want to go up town and behave yourself, or stay here with your new friend?"

"Oh, fo' de Lawd's sake, Mistah Ed, let me out!"

The marshal, seeing that his slumber and scare together had sobered John, released him. Instructing the interpreter to tell Black Horse that they would be back before supper to see how he was getting along, they locked the cell and left.

As before stated, among the "do-as-you-please" gentry of that time and territory there was a feeling of immunity from the law in regard to supplying an Indian friend with a pint of liquor on occasion. It was based upon the absolute reliability of the Indian thus served, for it was common knowledge that "all the king's horses" couldn't draw from an Indian any information as to who furnished him with whiskey. An incident that occurred a few years later at Pine Ridge fully illustrates this fact.

A large, slow-moving, droll-speaking young Indian, a returned student, who spoke English if given time to drag it out, was found by the police lying drunk with a quart bottle (two-thirds of its whiskey content gone) by his side. They took the young man to the guardhouse and turned the whiskey over to the agent. Next morning when brought into the office, the agent confronted him with the bottle and asked:

"Is this yours?"

"Y-e-s, sir."

"Where did you get it?"

"S-e-n-t f-o-r it."

"Where did you send?"

"Bos-t-o-n, N-e-w Y-o-r-k."

The agent controlled his risibilities, administered an effective lecture, and sent the boy home. I think he was never known to be in trouble again.

When boot-legging developed into a profitable enterprise, this dependability of Indian character was shattered, for state and federal officers began scattering paid Indian under-cover men here and there in order to secure proper evidence. This system enabled them to bring culprit and evidence into court together—a great deterrent, but not a cure.

CHAPTER 20

Gathering War Clouds

The fall and winter of 1889 passed on without any unusual trouble at Pine Ridge Agency, but as spring advanced there was excitement caused by the appearance of a new cult, the principal ceremonial of which was a rite called the Ghost Dance. Everything that could be learned in regard to this dance savored of the supernatural, but little attention was paid to it at the time. The crops had been fairly good the previous summer, fields were being prepared for the next planting, and business was being carried on as usual in the spring and early summer of 1890.

As the summer passed it was noted that the military forces at Fort Robinson were becoming unusually active. Small details of cavalry were making more frequent trips through Chadron on their way to the agency, either as scouting parties or messengers, and the settlers became restless as they were disturbed by an over-increasing anxiety concerning events that seemed continuously transpiring on an Indian reservation that lay practically at their doorstep. All these happenings, trivial or otherwise, lost nothing in being described by each passerby or neighbor returning from the Pine Ridge post office. The agent, Colonel Gallagher, a veteran Civil War officer of Greensborough, Indiana, who had succeeded Dr. McGillycuddy some three years before, was well liked and respected by the Indians. Above all, like his predecessor, he was not afraid of them.

The administration at Washington had changed, and President Harrison had not yet disclosed his Indian policy. But as Indian agents were appointed for a term of four years and Colonel Gallagher's tenure had about a year to run, he took the stand that public service was a heritage of the people and not of the party, and if his resignation were desired it should be called for officially; if not, he would continue at the post until his term expired.[1]

A number of politicians and Indian supply contractors were disappointed by this entirely unexpected attitude for an official of the opposite party to assume. It meant that the higher officials of the Indian Department—even the President himself—would have to be approached with complaints both reasonable and justifiable in order to accomplish his removal. Adequate cause for the removal of an Indian agent was hard to find when his only fault (which they called crankiness) was a rigid insistence that Indian supplies delivered at the agency should be up to contract specifications. Delicate manipulation, time, finesse in the proper building of frame-ups; misrepresentation and exaggeration of the more or less trivial incidents always occurring on the reservation—which at that time was in a chaotic state—all these were required, but the old boys in the political game worked very speedily.

It is not intended that these reminiscences should exalt one Indian agent above another, or picture the Pine Ridge Agency as a paragon of official rectitude. On the surface of affairs at any agency it was almost always evident that, no matter how good the agent's intentions or however commendable his effort, he was often obstructed by a cabal among the subordinates closest to him and in whom he should and did have implicit confidence. Taking advantage of that confidence, the petty officers were too often susceptible to outside influence and did many things of which their superior was ignorant. The office of Indian agent was a most difficult position to fill.

It was said by men who claimed to be (and certainly had opportunity to be) in the know, that while the Indians were hungrily awaiting receipt of a cargo of provisions, a shipment of mouldy flour, of spoiled, wormy bacon, and green coffee that looked as though it had been salvaged from a shipwreck, was received at the agency and Colonel Gallagher sent it back with an angry demand for edible food. The Indians took such supplies as could be given them and patiently waited for the replacements, but were disappointed time and again.

The explanation that follows is given only for the purpose of keeping the record straight. In all the accounts I have read relative to the trouble at Pine Ridge in 1890, the inference has been (no doubt inadvertently) that Colonel Gallagher was the agent who started the ball rolling. Such was not the case. On the contrary it was Colonel Gallagher, Chief Red Cloud and other influential Oglala leaders, Father Jutz of the Holy Rosary Mission, Charles S. Cook and Amos Ross, assistants in the Episcopal Mission, and Reverend Johnson of the Presbyterian Mission who worked continuously, individually and together to soften the effects of the Messiah craze.[2] Their efforts were as persuasive and conciliatory and earnest and did much to allay the excitement—but not enough.

Colonel Gallagher, during this period, could be seen any day in company with one or another of such men, driving his light two-seated rig to some "Ghost Dance" where they would appear, not officially or critically, but as observers who tried to study every phase of the performance so that they might understand it and thereby make their counsels more sympathetic and effective.

In the meantime exciting episodes and mounting uneasiness were becoming prevalent along the border of Nebraska, and neighbors were organizing scouting parties by day and watches by night. This was the situation when Dr. Royer, of Woonsocket, South Dakota (a protege of Congressman Pickler who represented his state in Congress at the time), arrived on the scene, the agent appointed to relieve Colonel Gallagher.[3]

The new agent appeared to be an able, kindly disposed gentleman, but of course wholly inexperienced in the duties of the position and the oddities of Indian characteristics. And, unfortunately, he arrived at a time when the "Ghost Dance" craze was seething to a boil. Shortly afterward the military took charge of affairs, and he was retired without an opportunity to show what his administration might have been.[4]

It is characteristic of the Indians on a reservation that when a new agent arrives there is always some strife between the lesser chiefs and the head men to see who can become acquainted with him first. In this they have a double object: they want to gain an advantage over the others, and to have the chance to size him up. Anyone who thinks that an Indian is not a first-class judge of a white man's nature (so far as their personal or tribal interests are concerned) is in error. Just a few interviews with a white man and the Indian has his measure and knows whether or not he can be used to his own advantage. If the decision is "suta" (signifying hard, firm or unyielding), he is looked up to, and if in addition his actions are kindly and fair he is respected and obeyed. But if the verdict is "suta sne," meaning the exact opposite, the treatment accorded the unfortunate object of this shrewd analysis is also the reverse. Query: Is this characteristic peculiar to the Indian alone? Be that as it may, and be the verdict just or unjust, "suta sne" was the estimate of Dr. Royer prevailing among the angry and excited Indians at Pine Ridge before he had been there three days; and naturally those who were belligerently inclined became steadily more impudent and defiant.[5]

The continuous furor at the agency caused homesteaders along the borders of the reservation to move their families into towns along the Chicago and Northwestern Railroad.[6] They became increasingly uneasy as the rumors increased in frequency and exaggeration, and they wanted more definite news of what was going on around them. These moves were generally a very distressing hardship, as they occurred at a season of the year when farm finances were at the lowest level.

At this time I was making weekly trips to the agency in compliance with the following telegram under a New York date line.

Please send Herald Short dispatches each day about Indians Stop
If any serious matter or engagement with troops want good graphic
story earliest possible moment Stop
                    J. G. Bennett[7]

On one of my trips I found it was being publicly alleged that during the still hours of the night or early morning the agent had moved his family to the nearby railroad town of Rushville.[8] This of course was his privilege and duty if he believed their safety to be jeopardized, but such action could and should have been performed boldly in the open light of day. While it created much adverse comment, the principal topic of discussion was the fact that he had called for troops while at Rushville. This, from the viewpoint of the Sioux, was an unpardonable sin. The news spread over the reservation with uncanny speed, and by the time the agent returned to his office, villages of excited Indians had hastily disbanded. Those who were under the influence of Short Bull and Kicking Bear moved farther north toward White River and the Badlands, while those inclined to the friendly attitude of Red Cloud remained where they were or moved in closer to the agency.[9]

The hubbub created on each side of the state line by this unexpected move presented the paradoxical scene of two (supposedly) enemy camps fleeing in opposite directions. Short of its tragic aspects of fear and suffering, this would have been ludicrous. Few if any agents for the Sioux had ever called for troops after the Indians had been peacefully settled on their reservations. They know the sentiment of the people under their charge regarding their experiences with our armed forces, and they had confidence in their own ability to handle any difficult situation because they respected that feeling of distrust among the Indians.

When details of this situation were flashed over the country the reaction was fast and furious. Immediately United States troops were en route from many points of the compass to Pine Ridge Agency. Gen. L. W. Colby posted his Nebraska state militia at the nearby county seats: Valentine, Rushville and Chadron.[10] Numerous volunteer home guards patrolled the breaks and hills of the border, among which lay the sources of numerous small creeks and streams that meandered northward into the reservation; and the regular troops from nearby military posts that had been despatched earlier were pitching their tents at the agency—designated as headquarters for field action.

I received a telegraphic order to meet Mr. Burkholder of Chamberlain, South Dakota, at Pine Ridge, he was to have instructions for our joint operations in the interest of the *New York Herald*. Mr. Jones of the *Olerich Advocate* had received similar instructions, and the three of us met at the appointed time and place. Mr. Jones told us that his stay would be uncertain, as he was needed very much at home. If memory serves me he remained with us for only about two weeks. He was very effective in his work, an agreeable companion, and we regretted his departure; but Mr. Burkholder and I teamed up and carried on together during the remainder of the trouble.[11]

At the agency itself events were moving rapidly. The arrival of additional soldiers seemed to have a pacifying effect on the friendly Indians, who were now being concentrated in one large camp on the flat just south of the agency under the supervision of Red Cloud and his subchiefs. The deficit in their food supply was being filled temporarily by the army quartermaster. The many riders who were continually on the go between the agency and what was then being designated as "the hostile camp," looked upon this military panorama with scowling disgust.

General Corbin was the ranking officer in command for a time, and had his headquarters in a part of the agent's house. He was succeeded by General Brooke, who maintained these official quarters until immediately after the climax, when General Miles had decided to change his divisional headquarters from Rapid City (South Dakota) to Pine Ridge.[12] The agency affairs were taken from the civil authorities, under Dr. Royer's supervision, and transferred to military supervision under Capt. Pierce, who preceded several other army captains who served in the capacity of acting agent at Pine Ridge. This changing detail of agents continued until peace was established; then Major Bell took charge until he was relieved by Capt. Charles Penny, who served a short term and was relieved by Capt. LeRoy Brown for a period of several years—whereupon Captain Penny was reinstated, served for some time and was again relieved, this time by Captain Clapp. During the latter incumbency the agency's affairs were turned back to civil authorities, and Maj. John R. Brennan of Rapid City was placed in charge.[13]

When the military occupancy (before the Wounded Knee affair) was completed, it was the current opinion of people about the agency that the military force assembled there consisted of about five thousand men.[14] All the units were represented in proportion to their possible requirement, and infantry and cavalry predominating, with auxiliaries of artillery and the medical and supplies departments. The infantry, including a small detachment of artillery, filled the vacant space lying across the street west of the Dawson store.[15] The west camp occupied the entire flat lying between the street on which the agency office fronted and an old wooden bridge that spanned White Clay Creek at that point, and on down to the site of the new bridge crossing the stream on the road to the cluster of school buildings. Across the old bridge, opposite the infantry camp to the south, the cavalry companies were camped along the stream in scattered formation for about a mile to the south. The rolling hills to the west furnished ample pasturage for their mounts.

If you will visualize this impressive military array, in conjunction with a large Indian village on a somewhat higher plateau just across the creek to the east of the cavalry camp, you will have a bird's-eye view of the usual scene during the period of watchful waiting in the fall of 1890 and winter of 1891 at the Pine Ridge Agency in South Dakota. Here in the village about two thousand Indians were camped in many tall, gaudily painted lodges skirting the road from Rushville, Nebraska—a road now filled with both loaded and emptied wagons in the business of hauling goods for the stores, the agency commissary and the army quartermaster. In the town itself numerous light vehicles were constantly passing on streets that teemed with citizens, soldiers and Indians, many of whom were on horseback. It was a memorable scene.

Soon after the reinstatement of the civilian Indian agent, the cattle industry, that had been fostered and encouraged by Capt. LeRoy Brown during his long term at the agency, was on the way out. The Indians had reacted to his plan with enthusiasm, rapidly becoming individual owners of herds of cattle that were well cared for. Indians took naturally to running, roping, and all the requirements of herd handling, and were a valuable acquisition to the round-ups.

But this splendid broad range was coveted, and under careful manipulation by their more civilized and crafty white neighbors the new and most promising enterprize was deliberately disintegrated. A tax of one dollar per animal over each one hundred owned by any individual was assessed and collected. In consequence, the full-bloods who owned more than that number began to sell and eat their taxable surplus. The Pass Creek District of the Pine Ridge Reservation, under the regime of Captains Brown and Penny, had often branded as many as two thousand calves, but as a result of the tax this number fell to a few hundred head—according to the statement of J. J. Boesle,[16] the industrial farmer who branded the annual calf crop until the general reservation round-up was entirely abandoned.

Those who observed the events of that period did not attribute the break-down of this system to the fact that civil agents were in charge instead of military men. It was Dr. V. T. McGillicuddy who issued the nucleus that formed the small herds owned by individual Indians at that time; and Maj. John R. Brennan, civilian agent at the time of the industry's demise, took a great deal of interest in the industry and under his direction it was progressing successfully. This deplorable change, like many other changes that militated against the Indians, was effected by outside pressure on officials at Washington through the misrepresentation of a few special Indian Department inspectors.

Once the green plains of May and the brown plains of September, in the various industrial districts of the Pine Ridge reservation, were dotted with roundup scenes—hundreds of horses ridden by Indians who were handling many thousands of cattle from their camps of many wagons. These were not only the local or official outfits, but outfits from neighboring ranches to the north and west that were accorded the privilege of active participation. These ranchmen were always represented by their wagons and crews, as were the reservation cattle men at the round-ups held adjacent to the reservation. All was going well until, at some point between these far pastoral scenes and Washington, avaricious plotters decided that the range was far too good for savages, and the industry was officially bled to death.

The Indians were again required to set their hand to the plow (which they detested) in lieu of the rope and saddle. Fields that had produced fairly well from the first turning of the virgin soil were allowed to languish for want of cultivation. Consequently in the following years, when cultivation was required, they reverted to the indigenous grasses of the plains growing up through the "crops" of waving weeds. All the Indians have to show for their agricultural experience are fairly good gardens along the little bands of the streams near which they build their homes. Although they have shared in the drought discouragement of the past few years, they have been able to secure some meager sustenance from their efforts.

CHAPTER 21

The Ghost Dance at Pine Ridge

In the far recesses of the Rocky Mountains, near Pyramid Lake in Nevada, a young Indian named Wovoka lay sick of a fever.[1] In his illness he dreamed dreams and saw visions that harmonized not only with his own pagan belief but with the religious training received from the family of whites who had partially educated him. These dreams recurred and developed until he became completely obsessed with the conviction that he was the chosen instrument of the Great Spirit to herald the second coming of the Messiah.

Guided by this hallucination, Wovoka proclaimed that it had been revealed to him that the purpose of the Messiah's coming was to restore to the Indian people, regardless of tribal divisions, the haunts and hunting grounds comprising their ancient possessions, with all the game and wild life that formerly existed therein. All their lost inheritance was to be returned to them, so that they might revel in their former unfettered freedom and enjoy the glories of their native splendor, as they lived before being hurled from their high (if crude) estate to the strata of the submerged.

No clearer or more precise account of the origin of the Messiah craze and its well meaning but mistaken originator can be found than in the following quotation from Doane Robinson's book, *The History of the Sioux* (page 459).[2]

> A Paiute Indian named Wovoka, but better known as Jack Wilson by reason of the fact that he had grown up in the family of Mr. David Wilson near Pyramid Lake, Nevada, was suffering from a fever at the time of the total eclipse of the sun on January 1, 1889. The Paiutes were naturally sun worshippers, and the eclipse always caused great excitement and consternation among them. Jack was a mild, kindly dispositioned fellow who was very industrious and trustworthy and held in high esteem by both Indians and whites. He spoke English fairly well and possessed the rudiments of English education.
>
> At this time of the eclipse he claimed to have fallen asleep in the daytime and to have been taken up to heaven, where he saw God and all the people who had died long ago engaged in their old-time sports; all happy and forever young. It was a pleasant land and full of game. After showing him all, God told him he must go back to earth and

156

tell his people they must be good and love one another, have no quarreling and live in peace with the whites. They must work hard and not lie and steal. That they must put away all the old practices that savored of war. That if thy faithfully obeyed his instructions they would at last be reunited with their friends in the other world, where there would be no more death or sickness or old age.

He was then instructed in the dance which he was commanded to bring back to his people. By performing this dance at intervals, for five consecutive days each time, they would secure this happiness to themselves and hasten the event.

Finally God gave him control over the elements so that he could make it rain or snow or be dry at his will, and appointed him his deputy to take charge of affairs in the west while the governor (meaning President Harrison) would attend to matters in the east and God Himself would look after affairs in the world above.

Jack then returned to earth and began to preach as he was directed, convincing the people by exercising the wonderful powers that had been given him. It will be seen at once that Jack's revelation embraced the old pagan superstitions in which he had been reared, together with the tenets of the Christian religion in which he had been instructed during the later years of his residence with Mr. Wilson, who with his family were religious people. Jack at this time was about thirty-five years of age.

It is apparent that this young man, in launching his propaganda of hallucinations, held nothing but the best intentions for his own people and intended no violent ill for other people. He seems to have ignored the existence of other races entirely, save to caution the Indians to have no quarrel with the whites. This fact is set forth in the Robinson history, in Wilson's written instructions to each delegation that visited him. It seems that Jack was engrossed in the simple faith of his new spiritual discovery, and he knew nothing of the words of Byron: "Ambition–'tis a glorious cheat; it enters the chamber of the gifted boy." Or the tepee of the wily Sioux!

This seems to have occurred in at least two other cases. Short Bull and Kicking Bear were medicine men, each of whom was ambitious to be the Messiah of his own people, with the privilege of deleting or magnifying the minor points of their instruction without hindrance. Many of the ceremonials and teachings that they caused to be introduced in the dances did, from a white man's point of view, savor of war whether so intended or not.[3]

The *Chadron Democrat* of May 8, 1890, carried a short, tentative article about a messiah appearing to Indians in Montana. It seems to have aroused Allen's curiosity and one week later he published the following description of the Ghost Dance religion based upon information supplied by informants from Pine Ridge. It is possibly the first reasonably accurate account of the religion to appear in print.

The Saviour and the Sioux.

A considerable number of the Indians, at Pine Ridge agency, are very much agitated over the wonderful prophetic revelations of some of the medicine men who have assumed the role of priests. For a long time there has been strange rumors among them concerning the coming of Christ, and these rumors have finally crystallized in a form of religion that is to save the Indians alone and restore them to their former independence and natural proprietorship of this continent, all of which is to be a vast, happy, hunting ground. The theory of their belief is that Jesus Christ came once to save the white man, and that the white men, by much wickedness, and especially in their treatment of the Indians by taking their land, pretending to pay them for it in provisions, and then starving them, have forfeited the right of salvation, and that Christ is now coming to save the Indians and kill off all the whites. They claim that the Saviour is now in the Wind River mountains, and several of the apostles of this new Indian faith claim to have made pilgrimages to this holy shrine, where the Lord appeared unto them, surrounded by departed Indians, who were in possession of all their ponies. They also claim that these departed Indians are surrounded by buffalo, deer, elk, and all kinds of game, and that Jesus told them that he was coming to Pine Ridge agency, when the cherries are black, and the exact period of his coming would be marked by four days of rain, and that he would be preceded by vast herds of wild game of all descriptions, and that as he progressed, all the whites would die with famine, and these pilgrims further preach that, while the Lord was telling them this, they saw white men come to him with their hats filled with gold, offering it as a price of salvation, and that Christ spurned them, saying: "Go away. I came once to save you and you nailed me to the cross. I come now to save the Indians. They will not treat me so. The gold you have is your God. I will not take it from you. You must perish." Then they say that Jesus told them to go back and tell their people that he was coming, and that when he had come they would live again on wild meat and soup, and that they would never again know hunger for the white man's food that they didn't get. He told them to start for home, and travel one day, and then camp at dark, and smoke, and after they had finished smoking, to point the pipe to the north, then to the south, and then to the east, and then to the west, and for all of them to pray, and go to bed. All of which they did, and on awaking the next morning, they found themselves camped near home with all their horses picketed in the same position that they were when they had gone to bed near the Wind River mountains. One of these three or four, who claim they have visited the great Indian mecca in the mountains, also claim to have in their possession, a letter written by Jesus Christ, substantiating the whole story of the advent. And this, they claim, was given them as credentials, and that on their way home, they allowed two white men to read the letter and they both died immediately. These new revelators have quite a following, and there is considerable controversy among them over the subject. Yet a number, perhaps the greater number of them, don't believe it. Many of them don't see how the creeks would all dry up if it rained four days, while others cannot conceive of a situation from which a white man could not extricate himself with a hat full of gold. It must be confessed that their theology is a little weak in places, and it has no time to strengthen, for the rays of the August sun will obliterate it entirely. Therefore these Indian medicine men should go out of the theology business, and confine themselves to romance. In bold and daring schemes and elegantly rounded lies, they could put Jules Verne to the blush, and if H. Rider Haggard is ever out done on wild, minutely detailed fiction, it will be by some future Indian novelist.

The emaciated condition of the dancers and the physical weakness of all the Pine Ridge Sioux for want of proper nourishment at the time was well known by the settlers of the surrounding country.[4] This fact made war seem more probable to them and justified every move they made toward self-protection. There were others nearer to the scene of action who were in position to know the rites of these medicine men. At stated times they would repair to their separate hills and ensconce themselves upon a consecrated spot, secluded by rocks and pines and not far from that part of the village occupied by their personal bands. Here, with streamers of red flannel floating to the breeze from the tall bushes, and with their personal and very private totems placed about them, they communed with the spirits as to what had best be done next. Devoted wives and mothers collected such luxuries as could still be found in the land, and bevies of maidens carried such sweetmeats to the Wakan shrine.[5] Thus the great medicine man was better able to propitiate the guardian spirits of the tribe by offering the only delicacies obtainable. The gifts were supposed to be offered to the first spirit appearing visibly, and as a looking-glass was an indispensable adjunct to the totem, no doubt the belief was covertly exemplified.

The medicine men grew fat and waxed bold in their sway over their people, but they do not stand alone in this. History records such practices through all ages of time and among all peoples. If these men and their followers had been more advanced and had attained a degree of civilization equal to that of our own modern prophets, they might have established a Zion City or other paradise on earth regardless of whether the world was flat or round.

The Ghost Dance had Kicking Bear and Short Bull as the grand masters of all its activities, but they were ably assisted by helpers from the various bands scattered over the reservation. This dance was looked upon by a constantly increasing number of adherents as a sacred religious ceremony, the strict performance of which would deliver them from want to plenty and from unaccustomed restrictions to their former tribal and individual freedom. Not all of the Sioux accepted this new creed, but it was spreading among them rapidly.[6] Had it not been for the unexpected climax of all the difficulty at Wounded Knee Creek on the morning of December 29, 1890, there is no doubt that all of them would soon have been converted to belief in their Messiah's fantastic but alluring prophecy—for the revelation of their visions told by these awakened dreamers entertained many awe-inspired tribesmen after each seance.

The old-time Indians, in many of their rites and customs, seemed to follow closely the principle of the Mosaic Law: "An eye for an eye, a tooth for a tooth." When an Indian lost a relative or very close friend at the hands of one of an enemy tribe, retaliation through the death of any member of that tribe was deemed adequate satisfaction. But not so if the perpetrator were one of his own people, for in that case revenge must be had upon the one who was guilty.

In all important "medicine" ceremonies, it was their custom first to undergo a purifying bath of steam. This was secured by pouring water over hot stones confined in a small tepee. Thus, when the Indians congregated for their "Ghost Dance," these improvised bath-houses were quite numerous. Blinds and shades were also constructed of boughs and old canvas, where the view of dancers who had fallen through utter physical exhaustion could be enjoyed with a reasonable degree of seclusion.

As the incantations of the master of ceremonies were completed, those who wished to participate formed a circle, each clasping hands with his neighbor to right and left.[7] The ring began action in a slow and solemn manner and soon was a revolving circle, conforming to the course of the earth. Jumping up and down, jerking one another's arms, the dance grew more strenuous as the speed of the circle increased and their chanted prayers rose in intensity and earnestness.

This is the prayer which, with minor variations, was repeated continuously during the dance: "I see our dead coming back seeking their mother" (the earth). "They are strong and happy. Our Father said this! Our Father said this!"

This performance continued, increasing in frenzy, until the weaker ones who had been eased to the ground outside the circle became so numerous that those still weaving upon their feet could withdraw with honor. So they went staggering to a place of rest and the ceremony concluded.

As each votary had recovered sufficiently to come out of the trance, he recited his experience to eager listeners, telling what he had seen and heard during his supposed absence from earth. And these descriptions lost none of their ghostly, weird mystery and picturesqueness while passing from mouth to mouth through the camps and villages.

In the earlier stages of this peculiar craze the dancers were held at points near the agency that were accessible to spectators from nearby towns and settlements across the line in Nebraska.[8] Others from a distance also availed themselves of the opportunity to study the strange procedure. All kinds of conveyances could be seen moving to and from the camps where the ceremony was being performed. The terms "hostiles" and "friendlies" had become common for the purpose of distinction between Indians who were angry, sullen and discontented, and those who were loyal to the new rule and peaceably inclined; but there were no hostilities other than minor stock thefts from neighboring ranches. The element opposing the dance was the most influential in the tribe. The principal chiefs overshadowed the medicine men, and the latter, well aware of this fact, used much caution in their warlike interpolations in the newly acquired creed. As an interesting piece of evidence of this fact, our dispatch of December 4, 1890, is reproduced.

> Another council was held today at the agent's office between Little Wound (leader, for a short time, of the hostiles) and the authorities. There were present at the council with Chief Little Wound, Agent Royer, Special Agent Cooper, and the local representatives of the *Herald*. Bad Yellow Hair, boss of the Wounded Knee Ghost Dancers, Yellow Bear, Broken Arm and Wounded Bear of Little Wound's camp were the prominent chiefs present. Little Wound reiterated his former statement in regard to his people's feeling toward the government. He also stated that he believed the Ghost Dance may have been organized by some, in order that they might get a greater control over the more ignorant Indians and thus prevent them from adhering to their present chiefs.[9]

It is apparent from such incidents that the influential men of the tribes, long looked up to as chiefs, were beginning to frown on the new religion as an encroachment and an undermining influence dangerous to their long-established prerogatives. Sitting Bull, one of the most potent medicine men, whose camp was on the Grand River with Standing Rock as his agency, fanatically espoused the tribal adoption of the new creed. He had established a fine reputation for warlike valor and campaign strategy during the trouble of 1876, and although he lost his life at the hands of his own people and in his own village in 1890, he had attained the loftiest ambition of an Indian: to be a medicine man and also acknowledged as principal chief of the northern Sioux.[10]

On the extreme southern edge of the Sioux country, about three miles north of Pine Ridge Agency on White Clay Creek, lay the Holy Rosary Mission. It consisted of two or three large brick buildings, with accompanying barns, sheds and outbuildings.[11] At this point, the valley through which the creek meandered narrowed to a succession of small grassy bends for eight or ten miles, then opened out to form a part of the valley of the Big White River—so called to distinguish it from a lesser stream of like name that was farther to the south. White Clay Creek flowed between two high, rocky, pine-covered ridges of bad-land formation. These hills average a rifle-shot distance from one parallel range to the other, and the space between was covered with large elms, cottonwood, ash and other trees indigenous to Dakota soil—and fringed, of course, by the usual growth of wild fruit and other bushes. Through this miniature forest along the serpentine stream was a rough, irregular wagon road leading to the river crossing, thence on to the Black Hills and "the great open spaces." The river crossing was a short distance below the government herd camp, where from fifteen hundred to two thousand head of beef cattle were held to supply the semi-monthly issues at the agency beef corral.

Such minute description of this particular section is given at this time because the grassy plats and sheltering hills were always a favorite location for the Indian villages, and later because their concentration camp from which they made their break to the adjacent Bad Lands. This was also the point where about two thousand Indians from Red Cloud's friendly camp at the agency stopped when they went on their wild stampede after being terrorized by sounds of musketry and reports of couriers from Wounded Knee.

In this part of the state, along the streams that are parallel to each other and flow to the Missouri, we find the Bad River, Cheyenne River and Moreau River, with all their tributaries, and always with a vast expanse of rich, rolling prairie between the strange formations which constitute the grand, garish and grotesque variations of the South Dakota bad lands. Along the Big White River, from its Nebraska source some twelve or fourteen miles west of Crawford to its lower reaches, the topography is a succession of valleys of varying dimension. They are encircled by high, grayish hills, while the points of the horseshoe-shaped ridges that near the river bank separate the valleys themselves. Generally there is a valley directly opposite the foot of the hills, but at intervals great stretches of wall approach the banks, and their frowning battlements face each other across a narrow but passable canyon, along the stream.

These hills (especially those fringing the outer edges of the valleys) are often crowned with lofty pinnacles, towers and natural fortresses. Silhouetted against their bases, in the little flats of open space, stand tall, gaunt columns capped with a firmer quality of stone that has stood the erosion of the centuries. Strangely these capstones (about one foot in thickness) conform to the general proportions and rather uniform smoothness of the shaft, projecting an even distance over its top as if placed there by the hand of man. The view of these curios of Nature is enhanced by groups of pines, cedars, junipers, and other mountain shrubbery.

When this scene is viewed beneath a sky where billowy clouds pile high against the deep blue field, or when floating mists are broken by bursts of sunshine, it is a picture to inspire awe, wonder, and joy in the glory of Creation. But to the scientists who delve into the corrugated sides of those rock-ribbed monsters and expose their hidden secrets, they speak a language easily understood and which, when transcribed, tells a story of the ages.

The puzzling, fantastic formations of the Bad Lands constitute but one of its very interesting attractions. Let sightseers who have the time and inclination penetrate their innermost recesses and they will be amply rewarded by a closeup view of Nature's handiwork when in her most whimsical mood. Often when coming through a rugged pass, they will be happily surprised to see a verdant carpet of grasses and native flowers, shaded by giant trees overhanging a gurgling, spring-fed rill.

These beauty-spots of varying size are veritable oases in what seem to be deserts of stone, and are accessible to travelers through the development of the Bad Lands Park of South Dakota, a monument to the determined zeal of the late United States Senator Peter Norbeck.[12] This park lies just north of Interior, South Dakota. The Milwaukee Railroad follows the general course of the White River to this point, then leaves the river to the south and bears westward to Rapid City. It also parallels Highway No. 16, whence a branch highway leads through picturesque Cedar Pass into the beautiful park.

Any description of the peculiar structures and the scattered patches of gray terrain that freckle the face of South Dakota in the west river section must be inadequate. Yet this sketch will suffice to show the topographical surroundings of the northwestern bands of the Sioux—a people then as primitive as their Bad-Land hills were aged. The South Dakota Bad Lands have a small beginning in northwest Nebraska and cross the state line through the Pine Ridge and Rosebud reservations in a zigzag yet northerly course into the Standing Rock country.

At the time of which I write the Indians were emaciated, distressed and bewildered by the manipulation of political machinery which was beyond their ken. Their pitiable condition formed an inviting field for the sowing and the harvest of almost any "ism" that promised succor for mind and body. So it was that the alluring prophecies of the new herald of the Messiah raised high hopes in hearts that had long despaired, and the ritual of the Ghost Dance was followed with all the abandon of passionate devotees until tragic disaster quenched their ardor.

I am not certain that the Sioux originated the "ghost garments," consisting of shirts for the men and gowns for the women; but certainly the first mention made of such apparel, in our section of the country, was by parties from Pine Ridge, and many incidents occurring in the first stages of the dance craze make such origin probable.[13] One of these incidents I will recount.

On December 3, 1890, some scouts brought news from Red Dog's camp on lower Wounded Knee Creek that amply illustrates the fanatical strength of the Indians' belief in the coming of the Messiah. How indeed could they fail to believe in such coming, since it seemed their only earthly hope?

Mrs. Eagle Horn, wife of a prominent leader in the Ghost Dance band, had gained quite a reputation as a powerful Wea-Wakan—which, being translated, means a medicine or mystery woman who performs miracles. To prove her ability along this line she called the band together and told them she could make them impervious to the soldiers' bullets and so be able to go unscathed through battle. Porcupine, a leading brave who had great confidence in her power, volunteered to be the first subject upon whom she should bestow such protection.

It was arranged for him to start from a short distance out in the open and come charging at the camp, where he would be met as an enemy by a small receiving committee. Each was to fire at the same time, so that if the "enemy" should be actually wounded by the volley of shots, no one in particular would be responsible. Porcupine then arrayed himself in his ghost garment and felt secure. After a short ceremony of incantation and mummery he started to mount his pony, but the animal veered suddenly and his gun was caught in the saddle gear and accidentally discharged. The bullet tore through the calf of his left leg and Porcupine dropped to earth amid the derisive yells of both the doubtful and the faithful.[14]

This set-back to the mystery fakers doubtless was not the first of many similar events. One of the stories often told around the campfire when Indian customs were being discussed, was about Spotted Tail. When he was a rising young warrior, ambitious to attain the position of Head Chief of the large Sioux band of Brulé (and which later he did attain), there was also an ambitious young medicine man in his band. Now these medicine men, other than the unpretentious, steady-going herb doctors, claim the ability to perform various wonderful acts. They profess to heal miraculously, and they also profess the power to cause mysterious death (sudden or lingering at will) to their enemies. However, the chief achievement that they claim is ability to turn aside all dangerous missiles from any kind of weapon, even the gun. It seemed the advent of the powder and ball worried the aborigines of this continent as much as it did the Knights of Chivalry in olden days.

As the story goes, this young medicine man was an enemy of the chief, and whenever occasion permitted, he used his influence to prevent the advancement of Spotted Tail to the coveted higher chieftaincy.

He was a boastful young brave, and much given to bragging about his immunity to speeding bullets. One morning Spotted Tail was told that his Nemesis was then entertaining a bevy of friends with his braggadocio. Spotted Tail stepped out of his lodge with a repeating rifle. Seeing that his rival stood apart from the rest, he coolly took aim and fired. The erstwhile bullet-proof one threw up his hands and fell dead.

Instantly the young chief joined the fast-gathering crowd, expressing sorrow and amazement as loudly as any of them. In a conciliatory and contrite spirit, eloquently he harangued the assembly. Overwhelmed by grief, he declared that he believed in the man's power as much as anyone, and had fired his shot merely to prove to the doubters that they were wrong. His personality and logic (or sophistry) prevailed. After days and nights of wailing and expostulating to the Great Spirit, a settlement was reached. The friends of the aggrieved and the aggressor negotiated, agreed as to the number of horses required in compensation, and the incident was closed. The people of the village resumed their normal life and tribal affairs moved on as usual. In the early seventies I often heard this story told, usually with conflicting variations, but never did I hear the truth of it disputed.[15]

While many sorts of superstition were entertained by the tribe in general, there were always persons of independent thought who analyzed such matters and acted accordingly. It was impossible to convince them that any living creature could be made immune to death-dealing missiles. The occasional exposures had but little effect on the mind of the masses, however, for there were always smooth talkers to furnish plausible reasons for the failure of the expected miracle.

CHAPTER 22

The Crush at Pine Ridge

Fine October weather—forerunner of one of those long, balmy fall seasons in South Dakota that often run into the following year, with heavy frosts followed by sunny days, punctuated by an occasional day of bluster and scurries of snow; and such this autumn proved to be.

Enterprising photographers from nearby railroad points along the reservation border had taken the various scenes about the agency during the treaty-making visit of the United States commission previously recorded here. As this break in the humdrum life at the agency was closely followed by the Messiah excitement, they continued their work; and when Pine Ridge had become a prominent headline for the front page of the big dailies they were joined by snapshot artists from all parts of the country.[1]

Thus it was that photographs of all forms of agency activity were easily obtained. The large herds of cowboy-driven cattle, the buildings at the beef camp, the old-time picturesque beef issue, Indian lodges, racing, games and dances, including the new Ghost Dance—all were on sale. And, being augmented by volumes of news, and rumors of news with which the air seemed charged, it was natural that we were anxious to tackle our work for the *New York Herald* at once.

To this end Messrs. Burkholder, Jones and myself had drawn aside from the chattering, milling bunch of idlers on the hotel porch for the purpose of arranging a start. Of course one can pencil a dispatch at any time where there is a book, board or shoe-sole for paper base, but it was not so easy to find room for the initial number we wished to send.

James Asay ("Jim" to all) had a large trading store on the corner where the Catholic Church now stands.[2] His family being absent, he had turned a neatly furnished and roomy residence at the rear of the store over to a congenial bunch of army officers, reporters and visiting friends as a semi-public club room. So we arranged with Jim for the privilege of using his long store counter for desk space, after business was closed for the night. We were joined by two other reporters who had worked for the *Herald* in previous years, and so at ten o'clock that evening, five pencil-pushers were ranged along Mr. Asay's counter, grinding out copy for illustrated pages of the paper.

Before two o'clock we had locked the store and were on our way to bed—I to the agency where the commissary clerk, a friend of mine, had placed a spare room in the living quarters at my disposal; my companions to the hotel, hoping they would find their rooms unoccupied.[3] Business and curiosity had brought so many strangers that the inn-keeper was compelled to run his house on the checkerboard plan—moving one out in order that another may move in.

But there were good points and conveniences also at this little one-story-and-attic country inn. It covered quite an area in a well kept yard in which there were a number of shade trees, and its long, vine-covered porch, well provided with seats, was inviting. Its culinary department was well conducted, its dining room spacious, the service efficient, and none complained of the quality or quantity of the viands served. All the stores kept a well assorted stock of supplies suitable for a cold lunch, so that none hungered.

The lack of sleeping accommodations was soon overcome by the rapid-fire spread of knowledge of this fact, and men were soon providing their own bed rolls. There was always some place where they could be used, and as the weather was warm for the season they got along nicely.

In 1890 Pine Ridge Agency was an obscure Indian business and supply station with a traders' hamlet adjoining; then, Phoenix-like, rose from its ashes to the dignity of a large military encampment. Its tramping columns of uniformed men, maneuvering to the strains of martial music; its pack trains, ambulances, wagons and artillery, all under horse or mule power; its mass of citizens, scouts and Indians, with their mounts and teams—these, from the height of a modern airplane, would suggest a picture of some ancient tented metropolis, all but lost in the haze of illimitable space.

The peak of the "rush and push" period, inevitable when masses of people suddenly converge at any given point and seek strategic positions, continued for a week or ten days. Then order and system began to emerge and the community settled into the habits of an established military camp. Arrivals and departures were still constant, but the excitement had lessened and everything slipped into its proper groove.

Among the daily arrivals there was usually a reporter, perhaps a scout with actual experience in the service, and usually a would-be scout or two who seemed to have let their hair grow for the occasion. Most conspicuous among the genuine scouts, of course, was Buffalo Bill and his retinue. Frequently they rode over from General Colby's headquarters at Rushville to interview his field man, Major John Burke; then, after observing conditions and visiting friends for a few hours, galloped away again.[4]

Major Burke, who for a number of years was Indian manager for the Wild West Show Company, seemed to be partial to exhibits from the

Sioux tribe and from the Oglala band in particular, many of whom had proved to be expert performers during the initial circuit of the show through this country and Europe. It followed that for a number of years afterwards he was an annual visitor at Pine Ridge, selecting his Indians and arranging for their appearance.

The government being the guardian of the Indians in all such transactions, an indemnity bond was required guaranteeing their proper treatment and safe return. Just prior to the Pine Ridge trouble, an organization friendly to the Indians had lodged charges with the Indian Department to effect that the Wild West Show, instead of being education as claimed, was definitely an immoral influence. They asked that the practice of permitting Indians to perform with such shows be stopped.[5]

As a counter move to this action the company placed Major Burke at Pine Ridge and he remained through the entire duration of the trouble, looking after the welfare of former employees of the show. His influence in behalf of peace and loyalty to the government was effective. He organized a score of intelligent, upstanding young braves, under the leadership of Black Heart, who were constantly on the alert among the various factions, counseling not only their fellow showmen but others, and reporting everything to him.

Mention has been made of baseless rumors. These were discouraging to news gatherers, certainly, but it would have been far better in every way had all the rumors been baseless, instead of being sandwiched with distressing and sometimes tragic events. One which occurred near the agency and was known to all is here related.

The precautionary order to bring all government employees and home owners (both Indian and white) into the agency had been complied with. Only here and there were exceptions permitted for good reason.[6]

An experienced prospector and miner by name of William Jones, together with Martin Gibbens, ex-government wagon-master and Jones' son-in-law, each of whom had an Indian family, were among the few who availed themselves of official leniency and remained on lower White Clay Creek. There, in addition to working a placer mine in the Black Hills, they were erecting a group of ranch buildings with a view of engaging in the stock business. They kept a few men busy with construction and had completed a commodious dwelling for use by the two families, also a cook house and a building for men known in the West as a "bunk house." They had employed an old-time camp cook, a friend named Miller, in charge of the kitchen. All was progressing smoothly when brewing trouble called a halt and all the white men withdrew except Jones and Miller, who with the Indian families remained the sole occupants of the new ranch.

This ranch was not isolated, for it lay within sight of the crude road that was the only highway along the canyon-bound stream, and was much used by parties going between the Black Hills and Pine Ridge. Indians often stopped to give their news and views of current events, and were always sure of a cup of coffee and a bite to eat. Military details were not infrequent, and nearly all travelers stopped to exchange rumors and facts, the combination of which comprised our most authentic daily news.

As the war clouds grew denser and of more lurid hue and his partner Martin Gibbens was still at the mine in the Black Hills, the practical Mr. Jones found a secluded spot in the ragged badland formation towering above the ranch buildings on the east edge of the valley, and to which a rapid and safe retreat could be made in an emergency. This he had been cautiously storing with food and other supplies for some time, equipping it for a temporary camp. His family, of course, had their Indian relatives and friends, who apprised them of the intention of the hostiles to make the little timber-sheltered valleys, adjacent to their home, a rendezvous and concentration camp.

When it became necessary to take refuge here, Mr. Jones padlocked each building except the cook-house, a side room of which was used as living quarters by the cook, who at the last moment could not be prevailed upon to leave. The old gentlemen insisted that he knew the Indians and could converse with them understandingly; that he had fed them and otherwise treated them right; that they were his friends and would not harm him.

In vain did Mr. Jones urge Miller to accompany them to shelter, pointing out the fact that he did not know, had not fed nor even seen so much as a sizable fraction of the hostile contingent; that there were wild and vicious characters among them who, with war as an excuse, would ignore any white man's friendship and kill him with delight. Even the women of the family, who liked their old friend, caught hold of his coat collar and tried to drag him to the small foot-bridge spanning the stream beyond which lay comparative safety in the hills and woods, but to no avail. Finally they were forced to leave without him, and remained in hiding until able to trail through the back hills to the agency.

About a week after above scene at the ranch, reporters who were doing a late lobby-lounging act at the hotel, attracted by a commotion, rushed out on the porch and watched a file of Indian police go trotting down the road toward White Clay canyon. Then they learned that a report had just been brought to the agency that Mr. Miller had been killed and a police patrol had been dispatched to investigate and bring in the body. A few hours later the patrol returned, filing behind a team and wagon driven by an old Indian. The box had been removed from the wagon and plank substituted, and on this lay the remains of the faithful but mistaken old camp cook, shot through head and body. That he had been killed by Indians was evident—doubtless by a gang of irresponsible young desperadoes in whose minds, clouded by savage instincts, it was considered an act of loyalty to their tribe.[7]

Later, as the house was being securely closed, a cursory inventory disclosed very little vandalism. Articles had been strewn about the room but were little damaged. Only guns and ammunition, knives, blankets and all edibles were missing. All signs pointed to a hurried killing and get-away; no attempt had been made to burn the buildings. Save for an isolated haystack here and there, arson seems to have been tabooed by the hostiles throughout the struggle. They seemed to reason that, under the Messiah's prophecy, all property would soon be theirs. Hence they took only that which was of immediate use.

The tragic feature of this incident was all that distinguished it from dozens of similar occurrences reported from outlying districts and the adjoining Rosebud Reservation. Each of these furnished topics for excited discussion by the shifting throng at the agency, every man being anxious to secure all possible details.

The reportorial staff by this time had increased to fourteen members. Two or three of those were free-lance space writers, so most of the dailies between St. Paul and St. Louis and from New York to Omaha, if they did not have their own representatives actually on the ground, at least had a look-in on the daily proceedings. A few of these boys who had been there from the first had finally found quarters within the agency enclosure. One of these rooms was large, with a double bed and long table. Furnished with chairs, it was made available to all members of the craft. Those of this devilish, fun-loving bunch who were still at the hotel aptly dubbed the occupants of these new quarters "The Cut-Offs," but did not explain whether this was done to honor Chief Little Wound's band or to razz the reporters.

One moonless evening a number of us were idling at the writing table, chaffing one another, making aimless turkey-tracks or penciling crude sketches, when my friend and landlord entered as was his custom, seated himself beside me and for a moment joined in the fun. Presently he nudged my knee, gave me a meaning look and withdrew. I followed, soon joining him at his quarters. There he informed me that an Indian policeman from a camp on lower White Clay Creek had brought news that Lieutenant Casey, in charge of the Cheyenne Indian Scouts attached to General Carr's command (which was strung along White River between the reservation and the stock ranches to the north), had just been killed at a point near the Jones Ranch on the road leading to the agency, to which he was en route with a patrol of Cheyenne scouts and a Sioux interpreter. The latter spoke English indifferently and Cheyenne not at all, but was very proficient in the sign language, and this is his story:[8]

As the party was riding double-file along the timber-skirted road, the officer and interpreter being in the van, three young Sioux rode out from an intersecting trail. Giving the usual friendly greeting they rode along for a short distance, talking through the interpreter, when suddenly one of them shot the lieutenant, killing him instantly. Then, springing their mounts from the road, they were lost to view, leaving the interpreter and scouts dumbfounded.

As was our custom when within reach, I hastily communicated the meager details to Mr. Burkholder in his room at the hotel. The telegraph company had established an office in the agency and installed one of their crack telegraphers, so the news of this sad affair was soon in the office of the *New York Herald*.

For some time the crew at the herd camp at the confluence of White Clay Creek and White River had been unusually annoyed by the loss of small bunches of cattle that had fed off into some secluded spot where they could be picked up without detection. In such cases the trail always pointed toward the large hostile camp in the Bad Lands, down the river to the east; or to the mixed camp of discontented Indians and friendlies up White Clay Creek to the south. It was decided to abandon the camp and move the remnant of the herd, which the regular semi-monthly beef issues had now reduced to five or six hundred head. For this purpose R. C. Pugh, issue clerk and experienced cow-puncher (and my landlord) was dispatched to oversee the moving of the herd to the range east of the beef corral, near the agency. Knowing the contour of the country well, Pugh took the old road leading west from the agency to where the river bends abruptly to the north before it takes an eastern course leading back toward White Clay Creek. Leaving this road where the hills to the north between it and White River were lower and therefore passible, he followed an old travois trail down the river to the herd camp.

The herd, after trouble threatened, had been as closely confined as was consistent with grazing. The day following Pugh's arrival it was made even more compact. All the stragglers were hunted and brought in, and the whole was then allowed to drift farther up the river as usual. As darkness set in, while the cook and helpers were loading wagons with camp outfit, the saddle crew were moving the herd up the river to where it could be driven southward through the hills to the road that leads into the agency from the west. They made camp on Lime Kiln Creek about noon the next day. Letting the stock graze that afternoon, they were moving quite early the following morning and by ten o'clock crossed White Clay Creek above the cavalry camp and were soon at the appointed range.

This change was followed by another in the system of letting beef contracts. Instead of receiving a supply for six months or a year and having them cared for by government employees, as had been the custom, the contracts now called for delivery of a stated number semi-monthly or as called for, and the contractors cared for their own supply herds.

At this time, having again secured a suitable room at the hotel, I was bunking where I ate for sake of convenience. Like other affairs at Pine Ridge, the coming and going had settled down to more normal basis and sleeping accommodations were obtainable. Among noted arrivals with whom I was able to form or to renew acquaintance, I recall a few. One was a very eager and active young man of about my own age with whom I formed a lasting friendship—Warren K. Moorhead, author and geologist, who remained with us for several weeks.[9] When not engaged in scientific observations he was usually busy with Kodak and pencil in the interest of the *Illustrated American,* long since discontinued. A few years ago copies would have sold at five dollars each if available, but none could be found. Mr. Moorhead was curator of Philip Academy at Andover, Massachusetts, and was the author of several works on geology and ancient Indian arts and customs. For a number of years he was one of the twelve honorary Indian Commissioners comprising the council that directed the affairs of the Indian Rights Association.

Dr. V. T. McGillicuddy, formerly Indian agent at Pine Ridge, came down from his home in Rapid City several times before and after the climax. His observant rambles among the scenes so familiar to him became quite noticeable. At times our course led toward the same objective and we would walk and talk together. Though usually noncommittal, I observed that his keen eyes took in everything worthy of note, and his demeanor recalled to mind the line by Bobby Burns:

"There's a chief amang ye takin' notes, an' faith he'll prent it."

Among the notables were two other men whose continued stay at the hotel and frank, open western ways marked them as old-timers. Coming from different sections of the country to look after their personal affairs, each possessed that indefinable quality that marked him as "to the manor born." The first to arrive was James Cook, riding a splendid blooded bay—a black-marked Hambletonian horse with fine cowboy trappings.[10] His pleasant, affable demeanor and his rich store of western experience against a cultural background soon made him one of our crew of mischief-making pirates about the hotel when off duty. Mr. Cook also made many friends among the Indians, especially with Red Cloud and his immediate followers. While he had been a government scout against the warring tribes of the southwest territories, his present business was to find a desirable ranch location. He finally selected in the valley of the Running Water south of Harrison in Sioux County. There he built a fine ranch and a mercantile establishment, laid out the village of Agate, Nebraska, secured for it a post office and was himself appointed postmaster—then and now a genial host to all comers.

The other distinguished gentleman was Benjamin C. Ash, only son of a pioneer family, and all of whom deserve honorable mention wherever Indians and South Dakota are the subject under discussion. He was born in White County, Indiana, December 19, 1851, the son of Henry C. and Mary Renolds Ash, and with his two sisters came in the covered wagon over the long trail stretching across a vast wilderness toward the setting sun.[11]

CHAPTER 23

Reporters at Pine Ridge

A calm before a storm is usual, but when an unlooked for hush spreads an air of strange quietude over the scenes to which one has been accustomed day after day, and the rattle, bang and bluster that was heard yesterday ceases to be heard today, the change is rather startling. And as all the activities of an old established military post, that during recent weeks had been tremendously accelerated, were now proceeding in orderly manner week after week, a bunch of husky young news-hawks were finding the situation tiresome in the extreme. It seemed to leave them nothing to do except sift a daily batch of rumors—usually without results.[1]

The physical appearance remained the same. The large Indian village and spreading military encampment could be seen immediately to the south, separated only by a narrow stream flowing northward and a broad road leading south. The streets were active with their motley throng of pedestrians and vehicles, but all went quietly about their own affairs. The air of restraint and suppressed excitement, so prevalent of late, was now conspicuously absent.

Short Bull and Kicking Bear were holding their large camp of ghost dancers in the depths of the Bad Lands, while their old rallying point on lower White Clay Creek was occupied by a small cluster of lodges. These were useful as an information and recruiting station and also as a dodge-in refuge for their roving scouts. Up the stream, a mile or two apart, were small camps of Indians that were trying to be neutral, but did not seem to know what to be.

Daily at about ten in the morning Indian riders could be seen going to and fro in the village and smaller camps about the agency. Some of these, no doubt, were out on their own affairs, but most of them were messengers between the small camps remaining on the lower reaches of Grass, Wounded Knee and Porcupine Creeks. These emptied into the White River not far from the hostile camp on the opposite side of the river. Naturally there was daily contact between the camps.

Many of these couriers stopped at the cabins and tepees at the northeast corner of town, presided over by the aged Frenchman Nicolas Janis. He served in the capacity of the commander's private Indian entertainer, and for that purpose was supplied with food by the quartermaster.

Frank Grouard, the noted guide, scout and interpreter, who in his youth had lived for several years with Sitting Bull and accompanied that chief on his sullen retreat into Canada where he shared his hideout, was employed at this time as chief of a dozen scouts of his own choosing to patrol the village and scattered camps outside the agency yards.[2] They constituted a supplementary lookout patrol for the Indian police of the agency proper. During their rest periods they always gathered to smoke and chat on a little grassy knoll in front of the Janis camp, and Grouard himself could usually be found at the cabin in consultation with Mr. Janis; or, with him, questioning some dining guest just in from the camp in the Bad Lands or points near by.

To question these news bearers, with results that could be depended upon, was a task for the initiated; for Indians, especially when their normal hunger has been intensified by a long ride, are quite voluble while partaking of a proffered meal. Being in an appreciative mood, they return the courtesy of their host in the only way they know—by recounting interesting fabrications or garnishing disagreeable facts with a heavy coating of what they think will please. But those familiar with the characteristics of the old-time Indian were adept in sifting the chaff from the wheat and forming reasonable conclusions that often proved dependable. In such cases Grouard soon had his report before the commanding officer, and by the same token (and usually by the same messengers) a like report reached the headquarters of the hostile camp.

The latter fact made little difference, however, as the followers of the Messiah were not rated as real and formidable enemies. They were acting on the defensive while exercising the rites of their new religion, and the military—very wisely or at least humanely—were making no aggressive move. Rather, they seemed to depend upon persuasive consultations that were being held from time to time, and upon the coming of the extremely cold weather normal to that season and long overdue. This, they reasoned, would go far toward inducing the hostiles to return to the comfort of their camps, where fuel and shelter were abundant and food would have been provided. But the mild and invigorating air of a glorious fall season continued far into the new year, as frequently happens in South Dakota. Had our short period of severe storms appeared earlier, it is probable that history would not record the unfortunate affair at Wounded Knee.

So it was that the main body of disaffected Indians remained in their sequestered strongholds in the Bad Lands. There, according to their accustomed standards, they fared sumptuously. The breaks and gorges of the hills still afforded game and quite a number of milk cows and their increase, which the owners had been obliged to turn loose when ordered into the agency, were roaming at large. To these the Indians had access.

Their main supply of fresh meat was secured by forays on the herds of ranchers to the north of them. Whenever a ranch could be found with no one at home it was looted of sugar, coffee, flour, bacon, and other provisions and condiments; and no doubt their relatives among the friendly groups supplied them with whatever edibles could be spared.

But give an Indian beef, or its equivalent in wild game, he will thrive without other foods. Usually they have many varieties of native edibles which to them are both solids and luxuries. One of the most dependable of these is the wild turnip (ti-psin-na), pronounced "timp-sina" or, by the Oglala, "timp-sela."[3] This is a prairie vegetable shaped like a small ruta-baga. Its peel is of brownish color with rough surface and very tough texture. Between this and the stringy, pithy, worthless core there is a mealy, flour-like substance from one-eighth to one-half inch thick—depending on the size of the turnips, which range from one to three inches in diameter.

This vegetable, if obtainable, is always present in the Indian home and constitutes one of their most important staples. It was also relished by the early pioneer for its sweet and really delicious flavor. It seems to contain some of the properties of wheat, and when boiled with fat meat (fresh or dried) is very nourishing.

When the turnip is gathered, its bark-like peel is removed and the vegetable is ready for the pot. If not desired for immediate use, the stems are left on the bulb, braided together in a rope about three feet long, and hung up to dry. If properly cared for the turnip will keep indefinitely, and when cooked resumes its original color and softness.

Whenever Indians are permanently located and have opportunity to raise a garden, they grow corn. This, dried and added to the stew, is a valued addition. Wild turnips grow near the surface of the prairie sod and are dug with a small iron bar with a sharp, flat bit. Before the advent of fur traders bringing implements of metal, a stout burnt and sharp-ened stick was used for this purpose; or a sharp-edged piece of flint bound upon a stick.

But the Indians did not always fare so well. Occasionally there were periods of distress, due to deep snow and long-continued storms, that drove the game to other sections and it was impossible to secure food by hunting; then they had to accommodate themselves to anything obtain-able that would sustain life. This description is introduced in the record to show how they could and did exist in their native wilds, wholly depen-dent upon themselves; also, that their indulgence in an Indian-summer holiday in the Bad Lands was rather a picnic for them so long as the weather remained fine.

From time to time, as occasion required, the writer has undertaken to present crudely drawn pictures from the broad theater of activities of which Pine Ridge Agency held the center of the stage, and where for a time the eyes of the nation were focused. And now liberty is taken to record a few of the impish and ridiculous antics of minor yet necessary actors taking part in the drama: the representatives of the Press.

The calm before mentioned was drifting more and more toward a permanent state, as the opposing forces were offering no offensive move. Even the still-numerous rumors were losing the piquant touch of pomp and pride of impending battle, and the boys of the press, after an evening of ghost-dance chatter and a night of Bad-Lands visions, would rise to the dawn of a new day, soft with sunshine and balmy breezes, only to have their mood of eager expectancy dashed by baseless rumors. Yet, as all these had to be dissected and analyzed, this broke the monotony and furnished reliable material on which to base our brief dispatches—for the majority of editors insist upon facts. They seemed to understand our situation and advised curtailed "wires" to correspond. Mr. Burkholder and I were instructed to confine ourselves to twenty-five words per day unless something of importance arose.

Two of the men among us, Judge Burnes and Professor Bailey, were judged to be space writers, as they continued their work much of the time. Judge Burnes sent copy to the *Chicago Times*, and Professor Bailey mailed his to the old *InterOcean*. There was another very ambitious young man in our group, C. H. Cressey, accredited representative of the old-time *Omaha Bee*. This writer had a penchant for lurid, long-drawn-out stories—they seemed to please his managing editor and were a constant source of amusement to the rest of us. The *World-Herald* man was not much about the hotel and seldom cared to run with the news-hound pack. This fact probably saved Mr. Cressey much critical annoyance in his favorite pastime of grabbing thrilling rumors and converting them into something he considered a "scoop" on his rival, though to the balance of the bunch they more nearly resembled puffballs.

All subjects relating to the situation had been discussed, with queries, guesses, explanations and prognostications of some dire impending catastrophe, until they were worn threadbare. Most of us neglected the customary visits to General Brooke's headquarters, for the reason that all movements, incidents and items of interest occurring on the reservation were easily obtained otherwise. The official look-outs, Janis and Grouard, after their reports to the commander had been made, were free to impart any news they were not specifically instructed to hold. Also, the scouts of Major Burke's Wild West contingent were reporting to him from various camps daily. In addition, "Buckskin Jack" (John Russell), one of General Crook's old reliable Powder River scouts and interpreters, was always a welcome guest among us with his congenial chatter and droll wit and all the reliable information he was able to impart.

In our daily "Bad-Lands Budget" (a legendary publication dedicated to Rumor) there would always be found a slogan to the effect that "They are coming in!" This phrase or its variations was heard so often that it became a byword; in fact, residents at the agency became definitely peeved about it, for naturally they were always under the strain of uncertainty. These conditions continued until long after the tragic climax, which filled the hostiles with terrified awe and uncertainty as to the kind of reception they would get if they did come in. Their fears were gradually allayed by General Miles' messengers of peace, and antagonism yielding to understanding.

But to the reporters, who could find but little to satisfy their urge for news save the repetition of that stale phrase, the time spent in waiting for the "coming in" seemed interminable. To while it away and retain at least a modicum of sanity, they resorted to all the fun and foolishness they could think of.

Having established pleasant relations with the newspaper boys of the nearby towns of the border, and knowing that they were always pleased to get any items relating to Pine Ridge and ghost dances, we decided to send out what purported to be interviews by their own representatives with the metropolitan press—much of course involved ourselves. I quote a few of these fabricated items.

The *Chicago Tribune* (Hawkins): "I wish some one on this agency would tell me a story around which the halo of glorious truth would linger for just fifteen minutes. I am tired of being perforated with quills and blown up with pipe dreams. Were it not for the fact that I have never allowed that 'glourius cheat' to enter the chamber of this 'gifted boy,' and consequently am totally devoid of any desire to enter a star engagement with some future dime museum in the role of fossilized remains from the Bad Lands, I would go over and partake of Crow Dog's highland hospitality myself."

The *Omaha Bee* (Cressey): "I am monarch of all I survey! The *World Herald* isn't in it."

The *Nebraska State Journal* (Kelley): "The *Nebraska State Journal* will prosecute this war according to its own familiar plans."

The *Chicago Herald* (Seymour): "All silent lies the village on the bosom of the vale—So I'll squeeze another pipe dream and grind out another tale."

The *New York Herald* (Burkholder): "The *New York Herald*–she's the stuff!"

St. Paul *Pioneer Press* (Boylan): "Injuns in the Bad Lands on a cattle-killing spree–And fifteen hundred soldiers wait orders from Baby McKee."

The *Chicago Times* (Judge Burnes): "I have saddled and cinched Little Wound's latest nightmare and ridden her into the *Chicago Times*, and with my saber wand I will drive the ghost of Short Bull back into the same tomb."

Professor Bailey: "This war is something like the Black Hills geological formation. There seems to be no well defined fissure vein."

Major Burke: "Cody's Wild West Indians are a credit to the Sioux nation. We invite inspection."

Buckskin Jack: "I have tramped the Bad Lands o'er and o'er and camped on Wounded Knee; but my heart grows faint at the warriors' paint and the lurid hue of the savage Sioux as they charge–in the *Omaha Bee!*"

New York Herald (Allen): "Let's all go down to Company K, 9th Cavalry, and call on Lieutenant Betten and get a drink of clear, cool water from White Clay Creek."[4]

Shortly following this outburst of pencil-pushing nonsense, one beautiful fall morning after we had performed our daily "wire" tasks, someone suggested a game of crack lieu. The motion carried automatically. As the hotel lobby was small we were soon out in front of the porch and had drawn on the ground a groove spaced to accomodate five players, so that their coins would not get mixed. We were standing back about eight feet, as the breeze was too strong for light change we were using silver dollars as quoits.

The game was just nicely under way when Colonel Cooper, special U.S. Indian agent, stepped out of the hotel on his daily rounds and hailed us.

"Say, what are you fellows doing–gambling?"

"Oh no, Colonel,we're just seeing who can come nearest to the mark."

"Oh, all right!" he replied.

Just at that moment there were two very close casts that were difficult to determine, and we asked him to judge. He did so and soon became quite interested in the game. If he noticed that the one who threw nearest the mark always picked up the coins and put them in his own pocket, he did not mention it. The game went merrily on to a short finish, as the players found that some pockets refused to respond longer to the strain.

About the middle of the forenoon Buckskin Jack came in with his customary broad grin, remarking, "The Messiah has come!" Each of us shot him full of question marks at the same instant, then gave him a

chance to unfold his news. He was talking with an Indian in front of one
of the stores when he noticed a stranger eyeing him. Presently the Indian walked away and the stranger approached and enquired the way to
Red Cloud's camp. The instruction was given him; then he told Jack
confidentially that he was the Messiah and had come to council with the
Indians, but wished to consult Red Cloud first. He then went into the
store and Jack came to the hotel.

This amusing recital was but finished when Jack, looking out the window, said,

"There he goes now!"

We all rushed to the porch and saw what we took to be a middle-aged
man, with a slight limp and cane, dressed in ordinary fashion, walking
along the opposite side of the street toward the Wolf Creek bridge. We
watched him descend the hill and emerge, then take the left-hand trail
leading to White Clay Creek and follow it up to Red Cloud's camp. Someone ventured,

"Ah, Cressey shouldn't have gone to the railroad this morning." And
another:

"Oh, he'll be back and writing a column or two out of that guy!"

The next we heard of the would-be Messiah, General Brooke had sent
a patrol to bring him to headquarters. There, after the usual questioning, he gave him a berth in the guard-house. That evening, as we were
taking our after-supper smoke, one of the boys came in with an extraordinary grin spread over his face and was quickly asked what was up. Now
we were aware of Cressey's habit of stuttering when unduly excited, and
it was disclosed that he had just returned and heard of the advent of the
Messiah. Our friend was sitting in the office at headquarters when Cressey
came rushing up to the desk and cried:

"G-G-General, have y-y-you g-g-ot C-C-C-hrist in the g-guard-house?"

About ten o'clock the next morning the agency spring wagon drove
up in front of the guard-house. "The Messiah," who gave his name as
Hopkins, got in with two Indian policemen and was driven across the
state line, placed on the trail that led south, and told to keep going.

All accounts described him as being a pleasant but ordinary person,
aside from being obsessed with the idea that he had a call to fill the role
of Messiah to the Sioux.[5]

CHAPTER 24

Big Foot's Arrival

A quiet routine of affairs was the order of procedure, and it was becoming noticeable that the military tactics of conciliation were gradually having the desired effect. Quite a number of Indian families, either from anticipation of a peaceful settlement or severe storms, were moving from the more or less barren bad-land pinnacles to the timbered and bluff-sheltered bends of their domain on White Clay Creek. But Short Bull and Kicking Bear still retained their principal following at their bad-land camp. This changing of abode, however, ceased suddenly when the news of the escape of Big Foot's band from the command of Colonel Sumner on the Cheyenne River reservation, and his movement toward the south, were heralded throughout the Pine Ridge country.[1] Soon afterward it was reported that the Indians were moving back to the Bad Lands.

A revived spirit of alertness and activity seemed to pervade the military camps as the probability that Big Foot's band would join the malcontents in the Bad Lands was being discussed on all sides.[2] Of the three most noted old-time scouts connected with the war-time maneuvers of the Oglala in the past, Baptiste Pourier, "Big Bat," had retired from such arduous duties because of advancing age and his engagement in the ranching business. John Russell, "Buckskin Jack," was no longer young, but seemed to be operating with Grouard's local patrol. Baptiste Garneau [Garnier], "Little Bat," the youngest of the three, was employed as post guide and interpreter at the near-by Fort Robinson (Nebraska). All these were familiar with the terrain through which Big Foot would have to travel in his approach to the Bad Lands or Pine Ridge Agency. Those of Big Foot's band left behind on the reservation, however, claimed that the chief was headed toward Pine Ridge with the intention of making a peaceful visit to his friend Red Cloud.

But military procedure allows of taking no chances of disaster that can be avoided, so Little Bat had been dispatched to scout through the hills and canyons for the purpose of locating the band, that it might be intercepted.[3] Two or three days after his departure on such mission, several companies of the Seventh Cavalry were en route to a new camp on Wounded Knee Creek on a flat that extends along the creek from the point where the highway bridge now crosses it down to the old road crossing, where at the time a large trader's store stood. From this location they were in position to make a quick dash into the camp of the runaways, when a message from the scout should tell of their having been located.

As all indications pointed to field activities, Mr. Burkholder had arranged with a ranchman for a team and light spring wagon, provided with complete camp outfit and two saddle horses, to be held for his use on short notice. These were now called for, and, after being provisioned at one of the stores, we were on our way to Wounded Knee and soon preparing a camp meal in the commodious yard adjacent to the store, while our driver cared for the stock at the nearby stable and corral.

We were not the only ones on the scene, by any means. Parties from Pine Ridge and across the line from Nebraska were constantly dropping in, some for a few hours' or a day's observation; others came with camp outfits and remained for several days before their curiosity was satisfied. Here, as at the agency, rumors floated in to the effect that Big Foot's band had been located, then faded away without results. But there was a jolly bunch of soldiers, civilians, newshounds and visitors from all points, and we enjoyed the change to an outdoor camp in fine weather. It was four or five days before we became convinced that nothing was likely to happen there that could not be attended to by following out any troops that were sure to be dispatched from the agency the moment anything of importance in the field seemed imminent. Back at the agency, everything had settled down to the former humdrum routine and continued for day after day.

One not familiar with the ways of the wild would naturally wonder why a party of over one hundred and fifty persons, with their horses and camp equipment, could escape detection by an experienced scout for as long a time as did these run-away Indians from the northern reservation.[4] The writer did not witness, nor know anyone who did witness, the escape and subsequent tracking, but any westerners familiar with Indians would agree as to the simple strategy they would use in so bold an undertaking as they succeeded in executing.

In the first place they could not have been under regular military guard, but doubtless were under casual surveillance and had received orders to remain where they were. Having yielded to the call of the war-rumors from the south, and having decided to join their people there, all they had to do was to have it understood that a number of their many wagons (that were daily rolling about on visits from one place to another, loaded with all the family belongings and the family itself) should, instead of returning to the village, meet at some designated, secluded point on the route they intended to take south and remain there until all were congregated. Movements of this kind could be carried on for quite a while without attracting attention from the authorities.

Then, when all was in readiness, they doubtless left their lodges standing and in the care of the old, infirm and crippled, who would have a fire lighted at night and smoke issuing from them in the morning. Nothing but a close inspection would discover the absence of the main body who, mounted and with pack ponies and a few wagons and here and there a travois, would wander through the hills, guided by the occasional flash of a sun-glass, and thus approach the rendezvous from different directions.

Perhaps, in the execution of above plan, a few of the wagons that went out each morning returned at night as a blind. But they worked their getaway effectively in their own fashion and needed no prompter to direct them. This shows how very simple is the explanation of the Indians' escape from the troops at the reservation.

Big Foot knew, from his various scouts, that the hostile camp was being carefully watched by General Carr's troops on the west and north. Therefore the band detoured far to the east through the hills and canyons, no doubt secluding themselves by day and traveling by night. Reaching the White River, they must have followed up the stream, crossing it at a convenient point. Then, keeping their southwesterly course, they were soon in the Pass Creek hills and the rugged Bad Lands whose grotesque formations mostly shielded them from view even while traveling. It was after their emergence from such shelter that Scout Garneau sighted them, saw the course they were keeping to the southwest, and notified headquarters by courier. Later, when they had approached near enough, they were intercepted by the military.

My belief in the probability that the fleeing band had left their better lodges and their aged and infirm behind them, was based upon reasoning from the following facts.

The morning after the soldiers had escorted them in and located them along the north edge of a deep ravine that came directly out from the hills to the west and opened into Wounded Knee Creek a short distance below their camp to the east, I went through their camp with a detail of five soldiers and two interpreters, whose duty took them from lodge to lodge. On this tour I recall seeing but one lodge of standard size. The rest were makeshifts of old canvas stretched over bended willow saplings or over stronger poles.[5] All those seemed to have been improvised on their trip, though there was an occasional pole lodge of small size as well as several old tents. Nor did I see any but active Indians—none who were old or feeble.

Big Foot had been ailing with pneumonia, but on arrival was placed in a warm tent at the southern edge of the soldiers' encampment, facing the camp of his people across a greensward of some hundred yards. Here, directly in front of the chief's tent, all negotiations were held. A middle-aged daughter served as his nurse, and he was under the care of an army physician.[6]

This account of the manner of their trek to the Pine Ridge country, and the route they followed, I believe to be a fair estimate. It is based also on the time spent on the trip—which seemed interminable to those who were anxiously waiting. Mr. Burkholder's order for a wagon and horses had been canceled upon our return from the first trip, as it seemed probable that when those wandering Indians were discovered they would be peacefully escorted to the agency by troops already in the field and the whole affair would be over. This certainly would have been the case had not a severe and cold storm intervened.

Aware also that the young man doing my work in the Chadron office was anxious to be relieved, I wired our paper to that effect. On receipt of a message that Mr. Burkholder would see the job through to the finish, I made my plans accordingly.

At the time all those living out on the reservation were ordered into the agency, the teachers were included, and eight or ten were women. They were fortunate in securing pleasant living quarters from the Presbyterian missionary, Reverend Johnson, whose wife had gone back east for her health and he had been called there suddenly. Accordingly he had turned over to these ladies the large and well furnished parsonage, and there they were always glad to receive visitors who brought the news. Among these was the wide-awake representative of the *St. Paul Pioneer Press*, Mr. Boylan.

Now it chanced that the evening before my intended departure, Mr. Boylan called me to one side and told me confidentially that he had just returned from a visit of several hours with some cavalry officers—friends of his—and had it pretty straight that Big Foot's band had been sighted and that the balance of the Seventh Cavalry would leave camp during the night for Wounded Knee. He was to accompany them and wanted me to go with him. To my statement that I had quit he replied, "That makes a difference in your favor. If anything happens, you can send your stuff to as many papers as you choose, and it will have a value in each office."

The result was that I agreed to join him. This of course stayed my departure for home and made my eventual presence at the affair of Wounded Knee a mere accident.

We at once arranged with the stable man for a couple of mounts and located the position of their stalls, the saddles and a lantern, so that we could get them readily in the dark if needed. The ladies at the parsonage were notified, and shortly after nine o'clock we, with our army bags and light coats, knocked at the door of the living room which opened on a side street. We were admitted by the pleasant elderly woman in charge and shown into a small parlor facing the main street. There in the gray gloom we waited, without light, taking turns lying on the sofa and sitting by the window watching the quiet, deserted street. No fear of falling asleep, for the rattling of accoutrements and the rhythmic beat of hoofs on the hard-worn street would awaken us if they should pass. But they did not pass, and when dawn began to streak the east we faded back to our rooms and went to bed.

Later information showed that the troop might have been very reasonably delayed on the ground that the Indians were advancing to a point where it would be easier to intercept them.

The public soon learned that the Indian advance lay toward the agency, but this proved nothing as regards their intent. If the whole or any part of the band wished to attach themselves to the friendly villages about the agency, they could have done so after arriving well inside the Oglala reservation; and those who had come to join the hostiles could have approached that stronghold in the Bad Lands from the south with greater safety than from any other direction.

From this time on there was an ever-increasing feeling of uneasiness. The air was charged with pending trouble. Uncertainty was noticeable everywhere, yet unexplainable. The long-drawn-out inaction between contending armed forces, each watching every move of the other with suspicion, cast foreboding shadows before that were susceptible of any interpretation. The final scene was imminent. Whether it would be drama, tragedy, or even comedy, no one could tell. For this reason I arranged to linger and see the curtain rise. Affairs were standing thus when another managing editor erred. My friend Boylan was called in to St. Paul, and though bitterly disappointed he had no choice but to go.

While several regiments of soldiers were camped at the agency and another to the north on White River, the scouting was done mostly to the east and north. A company of militia was organized by the citizens of Custer County for protection on the west along the base of the Black Hills. C. E. Denny was captain and Paul McClelland first lieutenant of this company, which patrolled the eastern slopes of the hills country and often made excursions into the Pine Ridge section down White River as far as General Carr's command, for the purpose of recovering stolen stock. On such trips Lieutenant McClelland was in command, he being familiar with the country and acquainted with many of the Indians. This seems to have been a company of efficient men, for a few years later it was mustered into the United States Army and sent to the Philippines almost intact—commissioned officers and all. During this service the first lieutenant of the Indian scouting patrol was promoted, and returned to Custer (South Dakota) as Captain Paul D. McClelland.[7]

Daily, Big Foot and his band were coming nearer, and their objective and intentions none knew but themselves. The younger and more evilly disposed ghost dancers of the Bad Lands, becoming impatient of restraint, were making impudent forays through the hills of White Clay Creek below the Holy Rosary Mission, in an effort to incite the friendly camps of their people to some unlawful action. Add to this picture an occasional sullen and hideously painted warrior entering the agency with a repeating rifle lying across the front of his saddle, moving silently and undisturbed through the streets and byways of the town until his observations were completed, then leisurely disappearing among the hills to the north.

But the picture was suddenly shattered, about four o'clock one afternoon, by an authentic report that Big Foot and his band had been intercepted by Colonel Whitside and his troops of the Seventh Cavalry and were being escorted to their camp on Wounded Knee.[8] Immediately, all was intense but orderly action at the military camp and more or less disorderly confusion in the town. Streets and stores were filled with excited men seeking all available information—which of course was meager.

As travel between the south border of the reservation and the railroad was more or less continuous, the news had reached the nearby towns as soon as at the agency. By the time the remaining troops of the Seventh Cavalry had moved out, a little before dark, the local crowd had been augmented with sight-seers from Rushville, Gordon, and other points in Nebraska, driving a motley collection of wheeling equipages.

A number of newspaper representatives reasoned, as did many others, that the straggling band of runaways would be brought on to the agency. As some of these had made one futile trip to the military camp on Wounded Knee, they now decided not to follow the balance of the Seventh Cavalry, already en route to that point with General Forsyth in command.[9] Their decision to remain at the agency proved justifiable, considering the warlike activities at the agency the following day, when on several occasions dire tragedy was averted only by the watchful commandant General Brooke. His cool, firm commands prevented the horror of bloodshed which would have overshadowed that occurring elsewhere at the time, for friendly Indians would have been the victims.

As I had decided to "follow the flag," I was anxiously seeking a saddle horse on the evening of December 28, 1890, but found that all had been spoken for. Then I began looking for any mode of transportation. Self-disgust provoked me when I considered the months of comparative idleness that I had been putting in, with every convenience at hand; and now, when opportunity seemed to promise exciting action, I was afoot. All ready, yet with no way to go!

Making my way through the crowd at one of the stores, I met an old-time friend and hotel man at Gordon, Nebraska, Mr. Swiggert, who with others had come over the line to satisfy his curiosity.[10] Presently he asked the prevailing question: "Are you going out?" I explained the situation and was told that he had a two-seated rig with only one other occupant, and that I should look no farther. It was agreed that we would start immediately after supper.

When I entered the hotel lobby "the gang" was all there, but only two were booted and spurred for the ride. W. F. Kelley of the *Lincoln State Journal* had been exercising a horse of his own for some time. I was not surprised when he drew me aside and asked if I were going, and seemed glad to know he would not be alone. Mr. Cressey, another reporter who was sitting on the opposite side of the lobby, arose as I was passing, beckoned me into his room near by and asked the same question. He asked how I was going, and remarked, "My, I wish I were getting a ride in a buggy! I'm not used to riding horseback." Until that moment it had entirely passed out of my mind that our Arizona scout friend, Colonel James H. Cook, on his departure a week or so before, had left his fine Hambletonian saddle horse and complete new riding outfit in Mr. Cressey's charge. On the thought I became at once very accommodating and suggested that, if he were not used to the saddle, I would willingly exchange seats with him. He accepted gladly, to our mutual satisfaction, for I had not been happy over the prospect of hunting Indian trouble in a buggy.

Mr. Swiggert was entirely content with the change in passengers; then I sought Mr. Burkholder for a consultation. He echoed the general opinion that in case of serious trouble Pine Ridge and the mission would be the vulnerable points. He regretted that the forthcoming action would not be covered for the *New York Herald*, but did not blame me in any way for having decided to scatter my wires as I chose.

Presently the Swiggert two-seater pulled out with friend Cressey happily ensconced in the rear seat—a position I envied him not, for Mr. Kelley and I were cantering "off to the wars" on horseback. On the road we encountered many groups of vehicles and mounted men, some hurrying and others moving leisurely, as we did. Now and then a friend reined in his mount and joined us. One of the first was R. C. Stirk, one-time scout for General Crook on the Powder River, but now the owner of a horse ranch. As a precaution he had transferred the horses from that ranch on the White River to a temporary camp on Laravie Creek south of the agency. With this gentleman we made arrangements to act as our courier, should one be needed.

As we came through the rolling hills that border the Wounded Knee valley on the west, and reached their crest where the road wound its way down grade to the north about a mile above the tented camp, the rising moon enabled us to see three towering cottonwood trees standing solitary in the midst of small hay meadows. These, we knew, marked the home of Lieutenant Joe Bush of the Indian police, and about a mile to the east was the home of Captain Iron Crow, also of that force. We noticed that the usual cluster of family lodges here had disappeared, and surmised (correctly) that they had moved over to form a part of the fair-sized village encircling the Joe Bush camp.[11]

We moved on down the creek and crossed the gully, where along its north bank to our left were strung the improvised shelters of the captured Indians. Then we crossed an open space and a broad road leading to the west up a short valley that ended in the nearby hills, then on down to the old trading store, passing the large encampment of the Seventh Cavalry on the plateau to our left.[12] Here we learned that the Indian families of this peaceful community, when they saw the tents of the large military camp going up, had vacated their nearby homes and congregated at the village surrounding the cabin of Lieutenant Bush. It was a wise move that later kept them clear of much trouble.

The houses fronting the store across the road to the south belonged to Six Feather and his brother, Plenty Bear. These were steady, well disposed men, leaders in the church and other affairs of their community. Learning that they too had moved, we inspected Plenty Bear's two-room house and found it almost bare of furnishings, though three single iron cots remained. As those were preferable to the floor of the store, we took the blankets proffered by the trader and, with our equipment, were soon in possession of the Plenty Bear cabin.[13]

When we had arranged our blankets for a convenient "flop," no matter at what hour we might return, we went up to the soldier camp for the purpose of getting posted on events up to date. As we came to the road leading west and turned the northeast corner of the main body of the encampment, we had gone but a short distance when we came to a broad opening that extended northward among the tents. Across this opening, before a well lighted tent of fair size, stood a number of men. The tent flaps were drawn back and we could see their movements in and out. A conversation of evident interest was being carried on. We approached and found that the group comprised commissioned officers of various rank, including General Forsyth and Colonel Whitside. The tent was that of Captain Wallace, who had been in immediate charge of the captives on their way into camp.[14]

Most of these officers we had met, and all of them we knew by sight. Soon we were of the group as listeners, but asking occasional questions. Captain Wallace's broad bed was spread on the ground in the middle of the tent, and on a nice new gray army blanket he was building with matches and explaining a diagram showing the position of various parts of the runaway band and the troops at the time of their meeting. Captain Wallace was not only an able officer but also a fine, upstanding specimen of vigorous manhood, and many times in the subsequent years we have been thankful that, while watching his little demonstration that night, Time's kindly veil had obscured the pale, still face we were to gaze upon a few hours later.

We had all drifted from the tent and, as usual when a group of people feel imbued with a desire for conversation, had separated into small knots. Presently I found myself alone with General Forsyth, who began to move slowly forward as he talked. The bright moonlight and balmy breeze caused him to become reminiscent, and as we paced back and forth on the grassy walk I was unforgettably entertained with a graphic account of many incidents in his European tour with General Phil Sheridan while still on his staff after the Civil War.[15] We finally withdrew sometime after midnight and each, wrapping the drapery of his couch about him, lay down to "pleasant dreams."

CHAPTER 25

The Last Fight of North American Indians

On that eventful day of December 29, 1890, we were up shortly after the sun had risen on one of God's glorified, peaceful mornings. In nearby trees the birds were singing their matins. Cooperative quiet prevailed in the military camp, where the last blue fringe of smoke was floating away from company cook-fires. To the initiated, the usual worshipful sunrise singing of Indians from the hilltops near their camp was conspicuous by its absence. Situated as they were, they certainly had little cause to be joyous or thankful, for their hearts must have been filled with sadness and their minds with dark foreboding.

But we who were more fortunate, with no thought of a devil of destruction lurking in a shadowy offing, could feel the tang of life-giving elixir in the soft breeze. This beautiful weather elevated our spirits to a pitch of unusual elation, and yet it was but one of the frequently recurring spells of South Dakota weather which are excelled only in duration (if at all) on any coast in the wide, wide world.

In making our "rough-and-ready" camp toilet that morning we discussed the probabilities of a satisfactory breakfast, and decided that a cup of mooched coffee among the soldier boys would be preferable to a cold meal over the store counter. This accomplished, we sauntered out to find our meal. Noticing a spiral of smoke rising from the roadside near a ravine we had crossed when coming in, we kept on past the main body of tents and soon found ourselves before the tents of the kitchen department, where a kettle-encumbered fire smoldered in the open. Between this fire and the road there lay a mammoth fresh-cut sawlog that, judging from blocks lying at one end of it, served both for fuel and a nice windbreak and dust-break for cooking food. Standing humbly on our side of this log, we accosted a stern-looking cook with the query:

"Mister, have you any coffee that hasn't been used?"

"That's about all I have left," he replied, "except the bacon and hardtack, but you are welcome to that."

Assuring him that the welcome alone furnished all the condiments necessary, he became busy at once, and, using the big log as a table, we soon partook of an enjoyable meal—bacon sandwiches with hardtack and hot coffee and even sugar if desired.

A sort of public square had been reserved as an assembly ground. The plot comprised probably an acre of ground lying in front of the Indian tents. These stretched along the north edge of the famous deep ravine that formed the south base of the encampment. For a time this ravine was the scene of many hand-to-hand conflicts, from which and it was said that no one, either soldier or Indian, ever came out of it alive—though wounded women and children sought refuge in its ragged walls and these were an exception.

From the west end of the main Indian camp, a few of their old tents were strung out in a straggling line to the north, forming a west boundary to the plot of ground reserved for assemblies. From the north end of this line of tents (east along the south side of the east-and-west road to its intersection with the road leading south), about one-third of the distance was open space. Then began a single line of nice white canvas army wall tents that terminated with two or three larger brown wall tents with awning attachments. These seemed to be headquarters and formed the north boundary. The kitchen tents where we had breakfasted formed the only break along the east side.

This crude description may suffice to fix in the minds of those who may be interested a plat of greensward that those in charge most certainly had set aside as a place of conciliatory and peaceful assembly. Instead, it was destined to become an arena of conflict and slaughter that would have brought smiles of satisfaction to the grim-visaged Caesars of ancient Rome.

For a long time after the distressful events at Wounded Knee I would not permit my mind to dwell on the scenes enacted there, but felt inclined to and did sidestep every inducement of my friends to become reminiscent of that conflict. And in this record of my varied experiences in the early West I have felt something akin to ever-mounting dread as my pen drew nearer and nearer to the unavoidable subject. But the record shall be completed.

And in this record I shall neither argue with nor dispute any who have already written on the subject. Common sense requires us to concede that in all sudden and exciting events involving a mass of human beings, no two persons are apt to hold the same position long enough to enable them to view the swiftly-moving action from the same angle and thus to receive like impressions on the whole. Therefore I shall state only what I saw, felt and heard during the melee, hoping for the minimum of error in my statement; and according to all others who were present at the time, a like privilege.

Leaving our friend, the cook, in a jolly humor, we sauntered down to the large brown headquarters tent, in front of which there seemed to be considerable activity. Here we found General Forsyth and Colonel Whitside, their chief interpreter, Philip Wells, and the brothers William and John Shangreau, his assistants. Going and coming were a number of commissioned and non-commissioned officers. The scout, Little Bat (Baptiste Garneau), was also present, and would act as interpreter if needed. Father Craft in his Jesuit robes, with a friend or two, was standing slightly back and to the left of Interpreter Wells.[1] We soon learned that preparations had just been completed to carry out a pacific program, and criers had harangued the village that all men were to assemble on the green where the commander would talk with them.

Now the many interested spectators from the surrounding country had left their buggies parked in the open spaces among the tents of the soldiers' camp across the road to the north, and were standing at a respectful distance to the rear—east of the officers and interpreters.

Presently all the Indian men began coming in bunches of from two to a dozen or more, stringing leisurely along then taking their seats in a circle on the grass before the commander and his staff. This continued until an inner and outer circle had been formed and the usual ceremony of filling and passing the pipe from one to another had begun.

Then General Forsyth addressed in a firm but conciliatory manner, after a friendly greeting and expression of regret for the bad conditions under which they were meeting. The gist of his remarks was about as follows.

First he told them that for the time being they were prisoners, and as such they were to give up their arms peaceably. That a government train was on its way from the agency, and when it arrived all their tents and household goods would be placed therein and they would be taken to a camp of their own, given food, and would be well treated and cared for. There were a few skeptical grunts of "How!" to this statement, but not many. He then told them to go back to their lodges, bring all their firearms, and turn them over to him.

The Indians departed for their camp in a reluctant, obviously sulky mood. Then followed a cessation of official business, a shifting of positions and somewhat subdued babble of conversation, during which I became separated from my companions and we met no more until the lull after the leaden storm.

Later developments justified the belief that during the protracted absence of the Indians, and in order to perfect an absolute control over their followers, some of the shrewder leaders among the Messiah-crazed band had started the rumor (utterly terrifying to them) that the government train was to take them and their possessions to Gordon, Nebraska (the nearest railroad station south of Wounded Knee), and ship them in box cars and stock cars to join the southern tribes—the hot southern climate of which was anathema to Indians of the northern plains.[2]

Now the general had spoken to the Indians in English, of course, and in my presence he made no mention of their destination. Interpreter Wells also said that at no time did the general intimate any such move. Perhaps, if he had known and stated clearly just where they were to be taken, it might have altered the course of events.

After what seemed an unreasonable length of time the Indians came strolling back pretty much as they had come to the first meeting, except that they seemed purposely to adopt a more independent swagger in approaching the council field. Many of them were painted hideously and conspicuously grim of visage. Only a few resumed their seats on the grass but others remained standing in somewhat defiant attitude. Quite a number of their wives had accompanied the braves to this meeting, robed in long blankets reaching almost to the ground, and each took a position immediately behind her husband.

When all were assembled the picture was a weird one. Most of these Indians wore ghost shirts grotesquely painted, fringed leggings, beaded moccasins, and daubs of varicolored paint around their hate-filled eyes. It was an aggregation of semi-maddened fanatics, determined to face any condition, relying with implicit confidence upon their ultimate rescue through the intervention of the mythical Messiah. Yet, in the picture of this grim group, a single stroke had painted one bright gleam of hope for civilization.

At the southeast edge of the group of standing Indians there was a fair-sized plat of grass where, in all the exuberance of early youth, were eight or ten Indian boys dressed in the gray school uniforms of that period. The fun they were having as they played "bucking horse," "leap-frog" and similar games, carried the mind for a fleeting moment back to the days of boyhood.[3]

The scene here pictured was constantly changing, hence it may throw some light into the shadowed places to state here a fact of subsequent discovery. The women who stood close behind their men concealed, under each blanket, a repeating rifle and well filled cartridge belt. Also, a number of the men were found to have had long strips of belting, likewise filled with ammunition, suspended from their waists and extending down the inner side of their leggings.

This was the situation when General Forsyth asked them if they had brought their guns and was answered in the affirmative. He then designated a sergeant and three privates who had been stationed in the open, and instructed the captives to deliver to those men. They then strode forward and handed over their guns, some carrying two or three. As fast as they did so they were escorted to a point west of the main group (and south of where the guns were being piled at the edge of the east-and-west road) and were seated to the ground.

During this proceeding, two of its most important features must have been noticed by all present. First, those bringing the arms seemed to be of the poorer class—lax, spiritless, shabbily dressed. Their ghost shirts were either plain or daubed with inartistic characters; the arms they delivered were of ancient vintage. There were Springfield rifles, muzzle-loading hunting rifles, old-style needle guns, first-model Henry and Winchester rifles, and old Spencer carbines.

When this fake delivery was ended, the general began lecturing them on their duplicity and their faithless disregard of promises. But while he was entertaining them with these mild verbal charges, an aid had detailed five soldiers with two interpreters to search their camp for hidden arms. Chief Big Foot had been escorted from his tent, and urged his followers to maintain peace and comply with the general's orders.

When I saw Little Bat and William Shangreau accompanying the searching detail, I decided to join them.[4] Leaving the general and Interpreter Wells preaching to their sullen audience, we soon reached the east end of the row of dilapidated tepees. One of the soldiers carried a sack and was unarmed, as were the interpreters and myself; the others had their side arms.

After explaining the purpose of the visit to the women and children present, the search began. Not knowing what instructions the men had received, I was surprised to note that every package, small hand-bag, parfleche (Indian valise), and all like receptacles were shaken—and investigated if any metallic sound was heard. All possible weapons such as scissors, long awls, knives of any kind, cartridges and shells were taken. The cooking outfits were deprived of butcher and case knives and axes. Not many large, sharp instruments were found: the most dangerous were small articles. Nothing else was taken away, but the tents were left disarranged.

I watched this proceeding until about half of the tepees had been examined. During this time the loud voices of the speakers could be heard continuously, but only a glimpse of the excited throng in front of headquarters could be had. Leaving the detail for a close-up view of the center of excitement, I saw at once that a cordon of troops had been thrown around the assembled Indians and that the military staff seemed to be quietly awaiting the result of an argument. Stepping up between two troopers, I saw the speaker—a large man of middle age, splendidly proportioned and viciously painted. Even my imperfect knowledge of the language told me that he was a malcontent of extreme type and arguing against General Forsyth's advice. He was an orator of the first water. Every gesture and body-movement flowed rhythmically, adding emphasis to his smoothly enunciated sentences. Suddenly, scooping up a handful of dirt, he tossed it scattering in air, and with eyes turned toward heaven implored the Great Spirit to scatter the soldiers likewise.[5]

Later I learned that this was the medicine man whom those disheartened Indians looked to as their leader, and that he was inciting them to resist the counsel of Big Foot and the general alike. Among other things, he told them that bullets could not harm them, and that the moment the soldiers opened fire the earth could open up and swallow them completely. It must be remembered that these long-suffering people, deceived, betrayed, driven from pillar to post, had lost all hope save that which centered in the coming of their Messiah, and the impressive oratory of their leader found eager response. I remarked to the troopers near by that if that man were an ordained minister of some Christian church he would convert the world. Certainly his impassioned appeal proved to be the lighted fuse that burned slowly to the disastrous end.

Not being able to understand enough of the speaker's words to keep me interested, I started back to rejoin the searching party but paused now and then to note the changes in formation of the groups that had taken place during my absence. Most of the spectators were seated in or standing near their buggies. Mr. Asay, the post trader, was on horseback near his own buggy talking to the men therein. One of those was Captain Kenzie, on leave of absence and a guest of his brother officers of the military camp at the agency.[6] They had all ridden out that morning to see the sights—and they saw them.

I also observed a Hotchkiss gun that had been placed in commanding position on a small knoll at the north edge of camp, not far from the site on which the Catholic church now commemorates the tragedy. In various stories of the affair at Wounded Knee this Hotchkiss gun is referred to in the plural.[7] I saw but the one in the whole field of action, and cannot recall having heard it fired more than three or four times. I had reason to know that it was aimed at distant objects, for I was running like a scared wolf on a line parallel with the gun-fire.

But, presently I joined the searchers at the Indian camp and found that but three of four tepees remained to be inspected. The last of these was a small standard pole lodge, entirely empty but for the form of a woman, her shawl clasped tightly around her, lying just inside on the grass. When accosted by an interpreter she made no move. He shook her gently—no response. Then he turned her over on her face and disclosed a new Winchester rifle that she had covered with her body while simulating the final swoon of an exhausted ghost dancer.

As a soldier seized the gun she jumped up, and with eyes blazing began berating the interpreters in their own language. The boys merely jollied her, and at last, somewhat mollified, she turned to go.

At this moment an extra loud and emphatic utterance floated up from the oratorical medicine man. I had just emptied my pipe and started to place it in the right-hand pocket of my light overcoat when Little Bat, who had stiffened at the last words of the speaker, yelled, "Look out, Charley!" and we all started to run.[8]

Little Bat, who was a noted foot-racer, had but given his warning when a shot was heard from the direction of headquarters. Scarcely had the echo of this lone shot died away when, for a few minutes, volleys were heard that sounded much like the activity of good dry popcorn in a hot pan. He was fleeing up the valley of the ravine to where Captain Taylor with his company of Indian scouts wisely kept them away from the main trouble by maneuvering among the rolling hills southwest of the ravine, just as a company of Gray Horse Cavalry was doing among the hills to the northwest. Their object was to check any possible reinforcement of malcontents who might chance to come from the west. But none came.[9]

I found myself running with three of the soldier searchers who were making directly for their camp across the west side of the assembly ground. There the fighting had started, but had now shifted to smaller groups scattered about nearby.

As we turned to run, the first scene that had met our view showed the spectators, some in their buggies and others clambering in pell-mell, whipping their teams into a stampede down the quarter-stretch to the old traders' store that was now used as citizens' headquarters. Stray bullets were whizzing among them, although no one was shooting at them and none was injured except the visiting Captain Kenzie, who received a slight flesh wound above the ankle and the carriage he was riding in lost a spoke or two, as did a number of the other rigs.

The next glance that registered mentally as we ran along in front of the old tents west of the assembly plat was that the ground at our right, where the fighting started, was covered with dead, and we could hear the firing of scattered groups in various directions. As the three soldiers who were leading in the race passed the last tent, I saw one jerk up his gun and fire at the front of a wagon between the tent and the road. When I reached that point I saw two large, fleshy women, each holding a separate bridle bit, struggling with a harnessed and plunging pony team that they had started to hitch to the wagon, the tongue of which still lay on the ground. The shot must have gone between the ponies and thrown splinters from the wagon tongue. I have never heard any explanation of the episode, and the place was vacant when next I saw it.

The trio kept right on running, nor glanced to see what damage the shot might have caused. But the incident gave me pause and a conclusion: that I would not chance crossing the road, an open space that separated us from their camp, in company with these armed blue-coats. So I whirled around the wagon and into the road and ran west up the valley. Little Bat could be seen raising the dust far ahead, but I surmised his objective and had no idea of following him. I knew that somewhere in the hills, not far north of Captain Taylor and his scouts, was the company of Gray Horse Cavalry which I might hope to contact.

Keeping an eye on the ridge that paralleled the road to the north, I had gone about a quarter of a mile when I saw a saddle-shaped depression in the ridge of hills. Somewhat exhausted after having run my best, my pace slackened as I approached this pass and, stopping at a point opposite, could see a plain path leading through it. At that moment bullets began whizzing up the road at my back. Turning toward the encampment, I saw about a dozen Indians, scattered and with their backs to me, firing at the camp; then it was plain that the bullets I heard were the return shots of the soldiers.

I had decided to pass through the notch in the hills, and here I experienced a peculiar feeling—or lack of feeling. I did not seem to be afraid. I seemed obsessed with a sense of comparative safety, but soon afterward realized that I had no time to entertain fear. I had been frightened into a semi-normal state wherein the only faculties left me were those of acute caution, quick and more or less logical reasoning.

Trying to start again with the same speed as before, at once it became evident that I could not run up grade; then, realizing that those bullets were not being fired at me and that a stray ball could find me as easily running as walking, I walked. A glance toward the Indians showed that, with their usual strategy, they were jumping about at safe distance from each other and still firing at the soldiers.

On reaching the pass between the buttes I could see that the one on the west practically formed a corner of two ridges, one running a short distance west and the other north, along the east base of which lay the path through the pass.[10] To the east of this path a level, grass-covered valley extended for some distance to parallel the ridge running directly west from the encampment. At the north part of this ridge stood a lonely, deserted Indian log cabin. Along the ridge, southward from the cabin, several companies of dismounted cavalry lay behind improvised breastworks with their guns across the freshly thrown up earth.

Running down the incline from the pass to where the valley grass was some eight inches high, I threw myself flat in the path and began crawling like an Indian. Then from the high ridge above and to my left, the Indians began shooting across the valley in front, at the soldiers who were lying on the east. There were not many of them, but they were deployed in such manner as to be impressive. Their fire was returned immediately, but as the Indians were aiming down and the soldiers upward at an acute angle, the bullets were passing high over me.

However, my attempt to imitate an Indian for the purpose of keeping as close to the ground as possible was too well done. The method was first to slide the arm with open palm along the ground, then crook the opposite leg and bring it up just far enough to get a toe-hold, then lurch the body forward as close to the ground as a worm and repeat the action, always with an opposite arm and leg. With this characteristic movement, its effect heightened by my long dark overcoat and yellow leggings, the soldiers mistook me for an Indian.

Demonstrating the extent to which one's mind, under great stress, concentrates so completely on one point as to remain blank to all else, I will state that when I first opened my right hand to move ahead, the empty pipe that I had been grasping until then fell from it. My first flash of thought was—It makes no difference. The second was—If I get out of here I'll want that pipe; if not, nothing matters. So I placed it in my overcoat pocket and proceeded.

I had wormed my way for but a short distance when—Zip! a bullet whizzed about eight inches above my back. This occurred three or four times, but I kept moving with the speed of a turtle. It was at this time that I heard the three or four shots from the Hotchkiss gun.

Later I was told that the Indians who had made the stand between me and the camp had separated a little farther up the road. A few of them took refuge in the ravine to the south where a precipice of hard dirt, that would be a waterfall during freshets, protruded over a small cave which offered some shelter. At the foot of this they began digging in further but were fired upon by the Hotchkiss, on the hill near the site of the trench that now holds their dead.[11]

The other part of the group, who were shooting from the ridge above me, suddenly ceased firing and vanished. Then the soldiers arose. I rose also and walked toward them.

Allen's first draft of his account of the massacre was written in an abandoned cabin behind Louis Mousseau's store on Wounded Knee Creek. The report appeared in the *Chadron Democrat* on Jan. 1, 1891.

At Wounded Knee

A Bloody Fight Between the Seventh Cavalry and Big Foot's Warriors

The Reds Routed after an hour of Hard Fighting

Pine Ridge Agency, S. D. Dec. 30–(Special)–Having passed through the battle at Wounded Knee yesterday and escaped unhurt, I will endeavor to give the readers of *The Democrat* a short description of the fight on the evening [morning] of the 29th:

Four battalions of the Seventh Cavalry, under command of Major Whiteside *[sic]*, went out of the agency to intercept Big Foot and his band who had escaped from Col. Sumner. The battalion went into camp at dark on Wounded Knee creek, seventeen miles east of Pine Ridge. The next day Baptiste Garnier came into camp and reported Big Foot's band on Porcupine creek, about ten miles east. Boots and saddles were sounded at once, and the three companies of the battalion went out and brought them into camp without any resistance. That evening, the 28th, Gen. Forsyth arrived with the remainder of the Seventh Cavalry. The Indians, numbering about two hundred, were surrounded by a cordon of guards and closely watched through the night. The next morning, Dec. 29th, about 8 o'clock, troops began to deploy, and soon a complete chain of cavalrymen surrounded their camp. Lieut. Taylor, with his Indian scouts, was on the south and did excellent service during the engagement that followed. At the movement of the troops the Indians began to evince an uneasiness, and most of the bucks were walking about in front of their tepees. A battery of Hotchkiss guns was placed upon a hill overlooking their camp and all was in readiness. The Indian men were all ordered up in line. They came reluctantly and were told to sit down. This they did, sitting in a semicircle. Major Whitside then proceeded to count them, and at first count it was found that there were only ninety-eight. The major then ordered a search to be made through the lodges and some ten or fifteen more joined the circle. Gen. Forsyth then told them that he wanted their arms. They replied that they had no arms. The general told them that he knew better; that when they were brought in the day before they were armed. Six or seven Indians then volunteered to go and bring arms. They were told to do so, and after some little time spent in rustling through their camp, they returned with three guns, one Winchester, and two old squirrel rifles of the vintage of '49. These they presented to the general, whereupon he proceeded to give them to understand that he knew that they were trying to deceive him, telling them, among other things, that when soldiers surrendered they gave up their arms and that they must do the same. He also told them that they would be well cared for and that a train load of provisions were on the way from the agency for them. They said 'how' to this last but showed no disposition to give up their guns, whereupon Gen. Forsyth ordered a detail of dismounted troops under Capt. Wallace to close in and surround them at a distance of about twenty paces. As soon as this inner cordon was completed several squads of men were detached to search the lodges, which was done, and many guns and considerable ammunition was found. During this procedure, which was very interesting, an Indian ghost dance master, arrayed in full paraphernalia, began to make medicine, holding his hands up to the sun and calling upon the Messiah to visit his wrath upon the soldiers. He would take up handsfull of dirt and scatter it, then hold up his hands as if momentarily expecting the earth to open and swallow up the troops. It was evident that he was getting the Indians worked up and he finally told them to be brave and that bullets would not hit them if the soldiers did shoot at them. The commander was told of what he was saying, and he ordered him to sit down, which order he finally complied with after he had walked clear around the circle as though he owned the earth. After all the guns in the village had been secured the soldiers began to search the Indian men who were held in the circle, upon most of whom they found a belt of cartridges and a gun under their blankets. They had proceeded to disarm but some eight or ten of these, when the brave who had been inciting them jumped up and said something and fired at the soldier who was standing guard over the arms that had been secured. The first gun had no sooner been fired than it was followed by hundreds of others and the battle was on. The fighting continued for about a half hour, and then was continued in skirmish for another hour. When the smoke cleared away from in front of the tent where it began there were forty-five dead Indians with their impregnable ghost shirts on lying dead on a space of ground of about two hundred yards in diameter. Capt. Wallace, of troop K, Ninth Cavalry, was killed with a tomahawk. Lieut. Garlington was wounded in the right arm. Lieut. Hawthorn was wounded through the thigh and twenty-four privates were killed and thirty-three wounded, three of whom have since died. There were about 190 Indians killed, about 100 of whom were bucks, the remainder squaws and children. One Indian scout was killed. All the wounded Indians were brought into the agency and are being cared for. Skirmishing has been going on all day down the creek and the Seventh and Ninth cavalry have just returned. It is reported that about 2,000 Indians are in a body fifteen miles below here. The agency was fired upon yesterday three times but no one was hurt.

C. W. Allen

CHAPTER 26

Back to the Agency

Upon reaching the troops, I was met with hearty handclasps and congratulations in not having been killed by one of them. Several told me of having knocked the gun up, down or sidewise, with the sights on me, just before pulling the trigger. One of them had done this even after I had risen to advance.

While moving among them the order was given to form in line. As I stepped to the rear of the line the marching order came, and the troops moved forward over the valley I had just crossed. Then I saw a wounded man whom they had left under guard—Lieutenant Garlington, who had received a flesh wound just above the elbow.[1] He was lying on blankets on the opposite side of the ditch, the dirt from which had been a protection to them as they lay behind it.

All this time I had felt a lassitude creeping over me, and an intense thirst was developing rapidly. Asking a guard for water, I was told that the doctor had used it all in his first-aid relief; that more had been sent for, but had not arrived. Then I asked for a chew of tobacco and was at once accommodated. It was only in high wind or in handling tinder that this use of tobacco had been resorted to; but, feeling the need of mouth moisture and knowing that smoke would but intensify dryness, the plug was chosen as a saliva producer. Next looking for something to sit on, I found nothing about the old cabin but a battered galvanized water pail. This I turned upside down, and, tying a bandanna handkerchief about my head, sat down and chewed the cud of reflection.

As rest restored normalcy, I concluded that in my flight the chance of having been scared to death was about equal to that of having been struck by bullets. Presently I left the battered bucket, together with my cogitations, and sauntered down to the scene of trouble. During my advance the sound of rifle fire could be heard at intervals and at various places along the south front of the field. Coming to the edge of the ravine valley, I could see that the little defense trench had been extended over the east slope of the ridge and down across the valley to intersect the road, and that a company of troops had been left to guard the west front. Moving on between tents and through lanes, I passed behind the tent where Captain Wallace had given his demonstration the previous evening, and on south to the rear of the line of tents extending north until I reached the corner where the line ran westward. Here, behind the two rows of tents that were spaced sufficiently to permit convenient move-ment, I had a fair view of the main part of the entire surrounding area.

There was a large tent just west of the corner tent that I took to be a munitions storeroom, as two big flat boxes lay between it and an empty ambulance that stood near by. Also, in front of the open space between the two tents there was a guard of four or five soldiers standing with their backs toward me, eagerly watching and commenting on every move along the ravine before them and across the death-strewn space that had been the morning's assembly ground.

I was moving toward a seat on one of the boxes for a little rest and smoke when suddenly the guard changed positions noisily to a point farther west, where the intervening tent obscured them and the space directly before them from my view. But immediately I heard a couple of revolver shots, then loud voices, followed by the report of several rifles. I stepped through between the tents and saw a young Indian, dressed in civilian clothes save for an old army blouse, lying dead and several sol-diers moving about. Approaching one of these, I learned that an Indian had come charging directly toward them across the opening from the ravine. He was shooting and shouting something in his own language, and this led to his death.[2]

Soon afterward it became known that the unfortunate scout was the only son of an aged Indian widow who lived at or near the agency; that he was subject to fits, and the approach of such spells affected him with a mild lunacy and an urge for senseless action before the final stroke. There is no doubt that the unusual excitement had brought on such a spell, and that he rode directly away from Captain Taylor's command when it was nearest the camp and advanced to his death. Of course the soldiers know nothing of his ailment, and his method of approach would inevitably prove fatal. My relation with the Pine Ridge post office later on enabled me to learn that his mother received a pension of $70 per quarter for several years—presumably during the rest of her life.

The train that was to have transported the runaway Indians and their village had arrived and was corralled next to the wagons that had accom-panied the troops the night before. The drivers of most of these teams were civilians, and a number of them were scattered among their soldier friends. Desultory rifle shots could be heard at short intervals.[3]

Once again I stood before the space between the corner tent and the one west of it. At the rear the ambulance waited, and in front of this the guards were constantly shifting position as their interest in the scene seemed to dictate. Gazing upon the ghastly picture before me, I felt an impulse of savagery well up and leap the faint line of demarcation between civilian and savage foes engaged in the fierce combat of a life-and-death struggle. My impulse was not so very vicious, however. I just wished to walk among the bodies and indulge in a little gloating over the fate that had overtaken the more intelligent but fanatical leaders who had brought these poor misguided people to their death.

Taking about three steps forward for this purpose, I was halted abruptly by an old friend that had rarely failed me. His name is Caution, and he whispered:

"Don't do it! Some of them might be alive and welcome you with a shot or knife."

Turning back, I filled my pipe and was about to find a seat on one of the boxes by the road when I saw Big Foot rise to a sitting posture from the ground where he had been lying on his back with his face to the glaring sun, feigning death as long as he could endure such suffering. No sooner had he done so than—"Crack! Crack!" spoke a couple of rifles, and he fell back to earth in actual death. Then his daughter, a woman of middle age, stoutly built and wrapped in a bright red blanket, came running from the tent where she had been nursing him. As she stooped to clasp him in her arms, another shot rang out and she fell dead at his side.[4]

Stunned by the enormity of these two needless deaths, and feeling faint and sick, I fell back behind the ambulance and sat down on a box. After a time, however, I drew out my old pipe—a never-failing friend in such emergencies—and concluded that those boys of the Seventh Cavalry were too excited to think of anything but vengeance.

The noise and hubbub of the field did not disturb me, even though I still heard an occasional shot, and I was beginning to feel fine and very fortunate when presently there was a rush of feet and loud voices. Hurrying out, I saw a sergeant and eight or ten men running toward an old Sibley-model tent on the corner near which I stood. Presently I heard one say,

"I saw him run into Little Bat's tent, but I didn't see him come out."

They surrounded the tent, calling to him to come out, but there was no response. Then the sergeant stepped up to the tent and with his pocket-knife cut a long slit in the old canvas. As he spread it apart to look inside, "bang-bang" came an explosion from within. The sergeant drew back cursing as two comrades grabbed him, but he shook them off saying he was not hurt, and the order was given to fire.

The volleys that then swept the tent were equal to a Gatling gun in effectiveness. Someone suggested that they burn it. Soon a spiral of flame shot skyward, and in a moment the ground beneath was covered with an inch or so of light ash. On a couch improvised from loose hay and two or three army blankets, the Indian lay dead. As the patrol were viewing the body, one stooped and picked up an old bone-handled Derringer. It was a bullet from this that had struck the sergeant, yet fired upward at so acute an angle that it only plowed through the upper breast and shoulder.[5]

These shots at Little Bat's tent were the last ones heard on that momentous day of death and destruction. The patrol had moved on, and I had been sitting on my box but a short time, when the welcome words "Cease firing!" were being echoed throughout the camp. Stepping again into the open I saw General Forsyth, his aides and interpreter, moving among the scattered bodies as I had started to do. Philip Wells, the interpreter, had a bandage about his face. The party paused beside a body and he bent over it with a slight movement of his hands that showed he was speaking. Then an officer, whom I took to be a doctor, laid a hand on the prostrate Indian for a moment. It was evident that they were discussing a badly wounded man. Later Philip Wells told me that the man was mortally wounded, but had moved and made a strange request as they approached him. He had asked for a knife. When Wells inquired what he wanted with a knife, he replied:

"I want to crawl over to that medicine man before I die and stab him through the heart. He caused all this!"[6]

While the officers moved among the bodies, feeling that it might not be in order for a civilian to join them, I walked around east of the grounds viewing the sad spectacle. On reaching the corner of the green where the school boys had been so happy in their sports but a short time before, there was spread before me the saddest picture I had seen or was to see thereafter, for on that spot of their playful choice were scattered the prostrate bodies of all those fine little Indian boys, cold in death.

That they had not been slain purposely was evidenced by their position, which was such that avoidance of the first death-dealing volleys was impossible. The gun-fire blazed across their playground in a way that permitted no escape. They must have fallen like grass before the sickle.

As I walked back to the headquarters tents I notice that the official staff had finished observations and passed from sight. Among the soldiers and citizens who were moving aimlessly about I saw that one of the latter carried a gun easily recognized as belonging to the late disturbance. Asking where he had secured it, he told me that all the guns taken from the Indians had been piled in a haphazard fashion near the breastworks up the valley. He had remarked to one of the guards that he would like to have an old gun as a relic, and as there was no objection he took it. Thereupon I decided to follow suit.

As I stepped out beyond the last tent at the west I saw the stack of guns, also the guards sitting at east along the trench. I saw also General Forsyth and Colonel Whitside walking slowly toward me at my right. They were deep in earnest conversation, realizing the magnitude of the grave responsibility that had suddenly fallen upon them. Waiting for their approach, I advanced, saluted, made my request, and was told to help myself. A well worn but still serviceable Winchester was selected, which now has its place among the curios in the museum of the State Historical Society at Lincoln, Nebraska.

Returning to headquarters, in front of which the parley with the Indians had begun and where the shifting throng of sightseers still lingered, I met Mr. Cressey of the *Omaha Bee*. Neither asked where the other had been during the melee. He told me that orders had been given for the soldiers and teamsters to take all available poles from the vacant tepees and secure others from the creek and begin building stretchers for the dead and wounded. We made our own plans accordingly.

It was still some time before noon, for but little more than an hour had passed while the incidents here chronicled were transpiring with the regularity of the tick of a clock. We had been under a continuous strain during most of this time, and so, feeling more or less fagged, decided to work together—one of us gathering items while the other tabulated them, and taking turns during the process. Before beginning work we went over to the tent where we had breakfasted, in the hope of getting a cup of coffee. Sure enough, the good-natured cook still had a supply but said it was cold. Regardless of its temperature and absence of "trimmin's" we each drank a pint and returned to the task before us, much refreshed.

Here we found a sergeant waiting to direct the transfer of the dead. Just north and slightly to the east, but in line with the headquarters tent, a long strip of heavy canvas had been spread on the grass to receive the bodies of the troopers. Three or four rods to the east, on a small knoll between the intersection of the two roads, several large brown Sibley tents had been raised for the care of the wounded Indian women and children. In order to give them every comfort possible, the walls had been raised to admit the breeze while they were sheltered from direct rays of the very warm December sun.

Presently the stretchers with their gruesome burdens began to pass. After instructing the bearers the sergeant very courteously gave to the representative of the press the name and company of each occupant. Some two yards east of where we stood, there were constantly passing groups of two to five or more wounded Indian women and children, moaning, crying, or weeping silently. Adults who were least wounded supported others who were helpless, while two or more soldiers or team-sters assisted the most seriously wounded as they hobbled along in ex-cruciating pain—often with heartrending cries. Frequently a young girl could be seen hopping on one foot, supported on one side by a woman less disabled and on the other by a trooper. In cases where the shot had passed between the knee and ankle, a protruding bone was disclosed at every step.

No Indians but these who were living and wounded were moved at this time. They proved to be women and children exclusively—no boys. This fact indicates that those slain at the first volley were the only ones home from school on leave of absence at the time the bands stole away from their reservation. The smaller children were carried in arms—some of them wounded, but most of them not. Those whose wounds were all but mortal were brought in on stretchers to the improvised hospital, where doctors coming from the beds of wounded soldiers made hurried visits, furnishing supplies and instructions for first-aid treatment by those who were able to give it and thus relieving much pain.

It soon became evident that this attention, the best that could be given under the circumstances, was lessening the shrieks and groans of the afflicted Indians and making more endurable a pain that must have been hard indeed to endure. These were the remnants of a band of once proud people who for centuries had been monarchs of the plains, but now broken and subdued. Some were weeping for other than physical wounds—wounds that no physician's art could heal.

Practically all of the soldier dead brought in were found near or in the death-trap ravine.[7] This, no doubt, could be accounted for by the fact that the close formation of the cordon about the Indians required, at the first move toward hostility on their part, an immediate and rapid deploying of the troops; hence the only unobstructed opening was toward the ravine.

When our task was completed we checked with the sergeant and found that our list of the twenty-five slain soldiers had been recorded correctly as to name and company, military division &c., we went on down to civil-ian headquarters—the old traders' store. As we walked along I was rumi-nating on how to arrange the high peaks of what I had seen into a con-cise dispatch, and what papers I should wire, when these thoughts flashed into my mind:

"Say, after all the money spent by the *New York Herald* during months of rumor chasing, why not earn it in part at least by sending to that paper, exclusively, what I have gathered?"

And that is exactly what I did.

At the store we enjoyed a leisurely after-lunch smoke and mingled with the mixed throng of citizens, teamsters, troopers and officers, each giving his own interpretation of the events just concluded. And we learned that the windowless cabin behind the store, with its old tables and boxes, where on a former trip some of us had whiled away the time with bits of pasteboard, was still vacant. Soon we were joined by Mr. Kelley of the *Lincoln Journal* and presently repaired to the cabin, Kelley taking the smaller table and Cressey and I the other. With one tab of items between he and I, we began work.

As we wrote we glanced occasionally through the open door, where we could see and hear the commotion incident to the breaking of camp. Ordinarily the dismantling of a large military camp is accomplished as systematically and rapidly as the unrigging of a large circus. But in this instance there were wagon boxes to be arranged as temporary hearses for the slain troopers, and many more to be made into cots (as comfortable as possible) for the wounded Indians on their sixteen-mile ride to the agency. Six-mule teams could be seen moving about throughout the camp, stopping where needed, while soldiers and teamsters were busy everywhere. It was nearly five o'clock when they began moving out on the road.

At the same hour we were just finishing our work, and our courier, R. C. Stirk, appeared according to agreement. As he rode away with our dispatches he told us that he would go straight to Rushville, Nebraska, about thirty miles distant and a little west of south, through the canyons and pine-timbered ridges about the headwaters of Larrabee Creek, stopping only long enough for a quick lunch at his temporary horse ranch while being supplied with a fresh mount. This he evidently did, as he assured us next day at the agency that our dispatches were on the wire a few minutes before eight o'clock the previous evening.

We stowed all our bags in the conveyance standing in the corral, in which Mr. Cressey had ridden on the trip out; but I had the old Winchester snugly fitted to the scabbard under the stirrup leather where Scout Cook, the owner of my mount, on occasion carried his rifle. Then, leaving Mr. Cressey to await the coming of Mr. Swiggert, owner of the team and buggy, Kelley and I secured our mounts and began our trip back to the agency. We rode past what but recently had been the site of a far-flung camp of white and brown army tents and the grimy old canvas of torn tepees; now marked only, here and there, by the bended willow frames and shattered poles of what so lately were shelters for the living. Near by was the debris-strewn grass where lay the lonely dead.

Over this desolation the agency authorities had directed a detail of

Indian police from adjacent villages, to stand guard until further action could be taken. As we crossed the ravine to where Highway No. 18 now passes the thriving station of Brennen, South Dakota, we could see up the creek for two or three miles and there, where at that time the road branched west, close behind an extended column of soldiers moved the long government train with its suffering freight, winding slowly up through the hills toward the agency.

CHAPTER 27
Concluding Incidents

Buggies and men on horseback were overtaking and passing us continually. Most of these were headed for the agency, but some were making their way to homes across the line in Nebraska. A few jogged along beside us for a while, discussing the all-absorbing questions of the day, but all seemed anxious to get forward. We held our mounts to a slow, easy gait and presently were quite a distance behind the cantering bunch, but still the road behind us was thronged.

Knowing the snail-like pace and frequent delays of large overland outfits, we planned to overtake the train about dark when it would be much nearer the agency. This gave us opportunity to reflect on the disaster and con [scan?] the minor incidents comprising the whole picture. I recalled the fact that, notwithstanding the large number of combatants, only two citizens (the Jesuit Father Craft and the interpreter Philip Wells) were slightly wounded; none were killed. The carnage seemed to have been confined to the Indians and soldiers.

As to the two white men, their wounds were so minor as to attract but little interest or inquiry, but the incident was described to me by some of the close observers. It seems that just as the trouble started, a ghost-crazed Indian (actuated by some old personal grudge or the mere fact that the priest was the nearest white man) suddenly leaped at him with a drawn knife, slashing perilously close to Father Craft's throat. Serious tragedy was averted when Mr. Wells seized the wrist of the maddened man, deflecting the stroke so that the knife made only a painful gash in the shoulder. But when the Indian wrenched his hand away, the point of the knife swept across Mr. Wells' face, severely gashing the nose.[1]

When the road left the creek and ascended the ridge to the west, the broad expanse of valleys and low rolling hills lying between it and the agency was disclosed to view. We could see the train (or rather, a part of it) as it crawled over some elevation and vanished again. We had made about half the distance to be traveled when we noted that darkness was falling rapidly and there would be no moon until quite late.

Increasing our speed accordingly, we came up with the train as night closed in, moving slowly along its side up to the cavalry. As we passed I listened intently for sounds of distress, but the wagons gave forth no noises other than their usual rattling and I concluded that the wounded were resting fairly well. On reaching the head of the column Mr. Kelley rode beside the captain of the head company and soon they were deep in conversation. I went on to join the general and an officer or two, with whom the post trader, Mr. Asay, was already riding.

The night became so dark that objects only a short distance away were but dim shadows, yet the caravan crept along. We were troubled with but few short stops. Only once was there a delay of perhaps twenty minutes while a broken wagon tongue was being replaced by mechanics from the wagon load of parts that always accompanied such trains. As we neared Wolf Creek and moved along the south side of its east branch, the skeleton outlines of the tall, young, leafless elms, that for half a mile or more skirted the stream up from the main creek, could just be distinguished. But the numerous tall, white lodges that stood along the edge of this fringe of timber as we passed the evening before were now missing. The entire village of Little Wound seemed to have stampeded.

As we passed over the large flat in front of the beef corral and came to the crest of a gradual incline leading down to the agency on the other side, those of us in the van were surprised to see long ridges of grayish earth, freshly thrown up to a height of about four feet, leading both north and south from the passage before us. The pale light of the rising moon was strong enough for us to note in passing a trench about four feet deep, following the ridge of earth some distance north and south, skipping the Little Wolf Creek bottoms and then soon turning west, extending to White Clay Creek. In short, the agency had been protected by trench and by breastworks all the way from a needful distance to the south, then clear around the east and north sides to above named creek.

The next day, approaching the hastily constructed defense from the inside, it appeared to be a well executed work. There was sufficient room for extra munitions and the action of armed occupants; and while motivating my five-foot-eleven frame through its various sections, I noted that the inside walls came just above my elbows. We learned on our arrival that guards had been posted in the trench, and of course at the first alarm it would have been filled with armed men at once. Therefore it was difficult to understand the fear-inspired commotion prevailing, for to us who had just returned from Wounded Knee everything seemed like an evening in a peaceful parlor.

As the cavalcade had reached the edge of town, Colonel Whitside and the troops in charge of the train followed the main body of troops to the south, going directly on to camp. General Forsyth and his escort continued down the street, halting in front of the row of business houses on the north side. Naturally the whole company was instantly surrounded by a curious throng and deluged with questions. Every man of us had ample opportunity to air his personal opinion and descriptive powers.

Mr. Finley, proprietor of the hotel and of the store where we had halted, gave hearty welcome to the general and his aides, then turned to the rest of us. He seemed unduly excited. We asked what show there was for getting something to eat, referring of course to [illegible word].

"Oh, we'll scare up something for you—crackers and cheese and sardines, anyway!" he replied.

Before we had time to tell him that we had the hotel in mind, the captain invited us to have supper with him in camp. This we declined with sincere thanks, wishing first to relieve our mounts with much needed food and rest. As we turned the opposite corner around the Asay store we saw that the hotel windows were ablaze with lights, and wondered greatly. At the barn we found no one, so we watered, stalled, fed and cared for our horses, then stepped out the rear door of the barn just as Mr. Swiggert stopped to water his team at the pump. Mr. Cressey got out stiffly while we were securing our traps, and the three of us went into the hotel by way of the kitchen, with the spacious dining room open to view through the high broad space left in the partition for that purpose. All we sensed, as we stood up our guns and placed our luggage near the wall, was a wave of warm air dispelling the keen chill of a December evening. But when we turned to look over the room we stood dumbfounded by the sight before us.

All the lights were glowing brightly. At the upper end were two long mess tables, side by side across the room, from one of which freshly placed viands were still steaming. This was the table usually occupied by reporters, clerks and the other employees about town. Its mate, and a square table in a corner at our left, were generally filled by salesmen and other transients. On these there was nothing but tableware. But at our right was a square table with two plates to the side, reserved for army officers. This was the one that fascinated me. All was still. Not a sound was heard save the hissing of a three-gallon coffee pot over a roaring range in the right-hand corner of the kitchen. The aroma from that corner was indescribable.

But that military spread! To the gaze of men just come from fare that seemed delicious at the time—hardtack, bacon sandwiches and cold coffee—the sight and aroma were overwhelming. Upon that table, loaded with tempting viands, the *piece de resistance* was a plump, freshly carved roast pig. Two or three plates had been turned up, one or two cups filled with coffee—this was the only havoc that had been wrought.

We were not long in washing up and seating ourselves at this unexpected feast. As I recall it, only mock conventionalities were observed by addressing each other with any military title, from sergeant to general, that happened on our tongues. It may be added that conversation languished during the course of that memorable meal.

Before we had finished, the excited landlord rushed in, exhorting us to leave at once on the plea that we were in great danger. We gave him the laugh and he soon left, disgusted. Soon afterward Mr. Burkholder, who had been searching for us through the uptown crowds, located us and walked in. We invited him, in the role of brigadier general, to join our party. He declined on the ground that he had just taken on a cargo of crackers and bologna, but would relish a cup of hot coffee. While he sat with us during the meal and long afterward, we learned the day's doings at the agency, as he had witnessed the various events summed up in the story that follows. Of course all the straggling travelers out in that direction, as soon as they heard the first firing at Wounded Knee, hurried in with the alarm; and some were there who claimed to have heard it themselves (at the distance of sixteen miles!), especially after the last boom of the Hotchkiss.

As soon as the news flashed from tongue to tongue, pandemonium broke loose among the friendly Indians. At the large village and all its outlying camps, lodges were falling; and ponies, that are never permitted to wander far in time of stress, were being driven in, saddled, packed, and some hitched to wagons or to travois that were rapidly loaded and moved out. Some were crossing White Clay above the military camp and some below it, but all were heading for a saddle gap about a mile beyond Red Cloud's house which stood directly in the line of their exit. Lodges that stood near by his house were being taken down and their occupants joined the stampede. Little Wound's band could be seen scurrying through the group of hills to the north that separated his abandoned camp from any point on White Clay Creek he chose to make. Some companies of soldiers were held in line, at east; others were excavating the trench we crossed on our way in. Action, commotion and confusion everywhere! Mr. Burkholder (and, later, others) recited this incident:

The artillery boys were at their guns across the street, on the flat that fronted the agent's office. Some of the younger officers, actuated by ambition and the intense excitement of the time, had just gotten a gun or two in position and trained on the retreating throng winding up the long stretch to the pass in the ridge, when General Brooke came on the scene and ordered them to stop instantly. The boys exercised all the persuasion permissible under army discipline, but he replied firmly.

"No! Those people are not fighting us. They are friends scared into a rout, and a shot among them would be murder."

The general of course was right, and no single piece of artillery was fired. Notwithstanding all the turmoil of the day, there were no casualties. In fact, no shots were fired except by the Indian police guards about the ricks of hay just north of the agency on the banks of the creek. Lieutenant John Thunder Bear, patrolling these large ricks with his squad, detected two or three hostiles sneaking up through the brush of the creek, fired on them and they hurried away faster than they had come.[2]

A detachment of troops had been placed in camp near the Mission, and the annoyance from trouble-making hostiles who could shoot from concealed positions behind trees and rocks of the nearby bluffs had been growing worse day by day. Mr. Burkholder had been covering that point for observation and camp items regularly until the morning of the climax.

But what caused the last disturbance in the evening just as things seemed to be quieting down, and also caused the hotel to be vacated at the moment when he and others were about to dine, was the presence of grim, armed, hostile spies who were privileged to ride through the agency and adjacent camps, carefully watched but unmolested. One of them, waxing bold and defiant over the happenings of the day, went through the town chanting a war song and threatening to burn it that night. While many of the roofs were tinned or sodded, there were quite a number of dry shingled roofs and among these the hotel was the most tempting mark.

And sure enough, soon after it became perfectly dark several Indian riders came over the ridge and, keeping well back from the trench, released a few flaming arrows and were gone. The missiles fell short, but resulted in a hurried exit from all the houses in that part of town, a good meal for three of us, and a night of undisturbed slumber for four of us.

Early on the morning of the 30th the hotel force returned and meals were served as usual. Quite early also we heard the beat of horses' hoofs coming down the hard-surfaced road toward the hotel. All of us were on the porch at once and watched a troop of the Ninth Cavalry (Colored) passing in double-quick time until it had crossed the trench beyond the bridge. Here it whirled to the northeast onto the road leading over the ridge to Cheyenne Creek and was soon lost to sight. Though all were speaking at once, we could distinguish gun-shots in that direction.

Shortly after breakfast the troop came slowly back, followed by six army wagons. Recognizing J. J. Boesl, who seemed to be in charge, I followed the short distance to their camp and learned these facts: The teams were coming from a detached camp of General Carr's command on the White River, where they had delivered some military supplies and then camped at Manderson Station on Wounded Knee Creek. They had broken camp quite early and were well through the most dangerous places for an attack in White Horse canyon by daylight, had come through the hills to the long incline leading down to Cheyenne Creek, and then were fired upon from the scrub pines to their right.[3]

Immediately bunching the wagons in a protective formation, the teamsters returned the fire. At intervals the Indians sent over a few shots, which were always returned. Each side seemed to be sparring for a shot at an exposed target. This continued for some little time while the Indians, shifting from cover to cover, seemed to be getting closer. But when they saw the soldiers they slipped away, all was over, and no one hurt.

My partner and I now found time for a private chat before he started for what seemed to have become a permanent cauldron of trouble in the vicinity of the mission. When I told of the disposition made of my dispatch he was much pleased. As we concluded our visit and he was starting for his mount he very kindly offered to secure another horse if I cared to accompany him. I declined with thanks, saying that I was inclined to take it easy for awhile and believed I had found all the shooting Indians that I had ever lost.

About one o'clock that afternoon a part of volunteer sextons (mostly men who had been called into the agency from outlying districts when the trouble began) started for Wounded Knee. They had grown weary of idling away the time and were anxious for any kind of action. They were provided with transportation, tools and an adequate military escort—some of whom were to help with the work also. These were they who excavated the long sepulchre at the north edge of the flat where the tented camp had stood, and extending on up the slope of the hill to its crest. In such long-approved and accepted "battle-field tomb" were all the bodies interred. The services of the Episcopal church were performed by the Reverend Charles Cook and Reverend Amos Ross.[4]

Notwithstanding the advent of cold blustery weather the evening before and all day of the 31st, the workers returned in time for New Year's dinner. Later a tall cross was placed at the head of the tomb and an imposing Catholic church was built near by.[5] A good view of this historic scene can be had in passing through Brennan, South Dakota, on Highway No. 18.

That the hostiles had chosen the Holy Rosary Mission as their principal field of operations seemed paradoxical, for Father Jutz, the Superior, and all the personnel of the institution were held in high regard by the Indians generally, regardless of creed. But there was a reason. It was a question of strategy. The topographical structure was ideal for their purpose. A well covered approach, with an exit at the east, west and north sides gave them shelter. The location was at just the right distance from the agency to enable them to harass the authorities with continual annoyances. With the stampeded friendlies down the creek behind them, the high point in their strategy was to involve them in an outbreak of old-time Indian warfare.

All the settlers in the adjacent section across the state line to the south were keeping themselves posted on the daily occurrences here, and some rode past the hotel daily to the high ground this side of the mission, where they could view the whole field. On this particular day quite a number had passed in such fashion. It was often amusing to observe their nonchalant attitude as they rode slowly along, engaging in jovial neighborly chatter. Occasionally one might see a mount with no gear other than an old quilt folded and a blind bridle, suggesting that it had just been unhitched from wagon or plow.

We were on the hotel porch one day, having an afternoon smoke and listening to the desultory firing with an occasional crash from a volley of musketry near the mission, and someone remarked that it sounded as though our farmer friends were being entertained all right. Presently the sunshine became less frequent through the rifts of gathering clouds, the air grew chilly, and despite our interest in the firing down the creek that seemed to increase in volume and frequency, we went inside.

Scarcely had we seated ourselves when, startled by the thundering hoofs of rushing horses, we were out on the porch again watching several companies of colored troops galloping by, with heads bent low to split the keen wind. They were equipped for any emergency, even to their heavy buffalo overcoats. We saw them disappear over the ridge toward the mission and realized that it was not the usual annoying skirmish going on down there, but something of more import; and were all agog for the first reports to come in. Then our farmer friends, who must have stood aside to let the cavalry pass, came hurriedly over the ridge. As they approached we were at the gate, expectant, but they never paused nor even looked our way. The only reply we got to our shouted queries as they cantered on was succinct and expressive:

"They're fighting like hell down there!"

Mr. Burkholder's oral report that evening was as clear and concise as interruptions would permit, and in substance as follows.

Firing opened and continued for some time, as usual, from a safe distance back in the pines and rocks on the hillside. The attack was answered by deployed skirmishers, but the Indians' force seemed to be augmented from time to time and it was soon that they were venturing nearer and nearer. Presently troops were thrown into proper formation and the fight was on. It grew hotter as the attacks grew bolder, and for a time it looked as though there might be a repetition of the Wounded Knee tragedy in reverse. The hillsides had become covered with Indians, and indications were that a charge was being arranged, when they saw the "Black Buffalo"—as they termed the Ninth Cavalry—come tearing over the hill to our relief. Immediately they resorted to the Fabian tactics and vanished.

As Mr. Burkholder finished his story he was handed a telegram, and as he read it I saw him smile. He passed it across to me, and a glance showed that it was addressed, as usual, to both of us. It brought a generous compliment to the effect that we were doing well, and told us to keep it up and work together for the *Herald*. Incidentally it meant that I was still on the pay-roll and would not be considered as ever having been off of it. But the greater satisfaction to us was the fact that we had proved worthy of our hire and were still together.

The check given the hostiles at the mission seemed to cool their ardor for revenge, and the cold blustery weather cooled it still farther. Those who had left the bleak gray walls of their summer retreat, but had hurriedly returned during the conflict at Wounded Knee, soon began moving back to the sheltered hills and timbered bends of White Clay Creek where fuel was abundant, and even those who had been most obdurate were following them. Soon the little stream had all its grassy plats occupied, from a point just below the mission and for ten or twelve miles down stream, by both hostile and friendly villages. Naturally, they were all one people in distress.

From these camps, comprising practically all the Indians of the Pine Ridge reservation, increasing numbers visited the agency daily. Business was good at the stores, for these people had become accustomed to little commodities that had been missing for some time, and they were buying again. A spirit of cheerful quietude now seemed to pervade an atmosphere that had long been burdened with dread uncertainties. Of course many dejected hostiles were sulking in their lodges, forced to realize that their day was over. Their people's faith in the Messiah and his disciples was fading fast away. They had seen the impervious ghost shirt shot to pieces, but had not seen the earth open and swallow the soldiers.

One day I saw Peter Richard, Red Cloud's son-in-law, with his wife and her mother among the incoming visitors.[6] Knowing them quite well I went out to meet them. Using Pete as an interpreter I told the woman to ask Red Cloud to come back to his home: that his going was a mistake, and all his friends were anxious for him to return. I was a little surprised when they replied,

"That is what he wants to do, but they won't let him. He and a friend or two have tried to slip away but were stopped, and our lodge is watched all the time."

Some strategy, eh? If the hostiles, while holding him as a friendly hostage, could have worked up a general revolt, their old-time plains general would have come in handy by aiding them in planning forays, negotiating terms of peace, and in other ways. However, conditions changed so that he was soon back home, and the surrounding lodges of his personal followers formed the old familiar picture.

Toward the end of the first week of the New Year General Nelson E. Miles, division commander, moved his headquarters from Rapid City to Pine Ridge. He soon had native emissaries expounding his conciliatory messages in all the villages. Sulking leaders came to life at once and began holding frequent councils at military headquarters, with the result that an agreement of surrender was reached. This was planned to be quite a spectacular affair. All of the Indian bands on the reservation assembled on the broad flat near headquarters.

It was my intention and desire to witness this event, but the day before it occurred I had an opportunity to ride directly across country to Chadron and decided to accept. After wiring the *Herald* to that effect I departed from the historic scene, thus undramatically ending the most exciting chapter of my life.

Notes

Introduction

[1] Allen's report on the massacre appeared in the *Chadron Democrat* on Jan. 1, 1890. The story by another eyewitness, William F. Kelley of the *Nebraska State Journal*, was taken by Richard C. Stirk to the telegraph office in Rushville and was the first account to be published. William Fitch Kelley, *Pine Ridge 1890*, eds. Alexander Kelley and Pierre Bovis (San Francisco: Pierre Bovis, 1971); Donald F. Danker, "The Wounded Knee Interviews of Eli S. Ricker," *Nebraska History* 62 (1981):219.

[2] Biographical data about Allen is from *In The West That Was*; the Charles W. Allen Collection, MS 2635, Nebraska State Historical Society, Lincoln (hereafter cited as Allen Collection); the *Lincoln Journal and Star*, Feb. 20, 1938; the *Martin* (South Dakota) *Messenger*, Nov. 19, 1942; and personal communication from Randy and Sheila Reese to Richard E. Jensen, Mar. 6, 1995 (hereafter cited as Reese letters). Mr. Reese is a great-great-grandson of Charles Allen and the Reeses have provided invaluable information on Allen.

[3] Bayard H. Paine, *Pioneers, Indians and Buffaloes* (Curtis, Nebr.: Curtis Enterprise, 1935), 136.

Company B was under the command of Capt. W. A. Winsell. Settlers had been driven from their homes and lived for a time in a stockade they built east of present Beloit, Kansas. A. T. Andreas, *History of the State of Kansas* (Marceline, Mo.: Walsworth Co., 1976 reprint of 1883 edition), 1:211; 2:1022.

[4] Charles Allen to Addison E. Sheldon, Dec. 17, 1934, Allen Collection.

[5] Paul L. Hedren, *Fort Laramie in 1876* (Lincoln: University of Nebraska Press, 1988), 45–46; L. G. Flannery, ed., *John Hunton's Diary 1873–'75* (Lingle, Wyo.: Guide Review, 1956), 2:160.

[6] Henry Hawkins, Emma's father, had anglicized his name from the variously spelled Hockenstriser. Joseph Bissonette Biographical File, South Dakota State Historical Society, Pierre.

Emma Hawkins Allen was born at Fort Laramie on March 24, 1855. The Allen children were Nellie (b. 1875), who married Eugene C. Means; Joseph Perry Allen (b. 1876), who married Rosanna Rooks; Alma (b. 1878), who married Louis Provost; Sophia (b. 1879), who married Andrew Russell; Charles Sumner (b. 1881), who married Elsie Cummings; Samuel Emmitt (b. 1883), who married Nellie Carlow; Jessie (b. 1884), who married Rodney Veirling; Lizzie (b. 1886), who married Robert Carlow; Robert C. (b. 1888), who married Lillie Salway; and Julia A. (b. 1889), who married Clarence Vert. Two children died in infancy. Albert W. Allen died on Aug. 27, 1891, age two months and twenty-nine days and Edgar P. Allen died on May 8, 1894, age ten months and twenty-six days. *The Martin Messenger*, Apr. 3, 1925; Arthur Otis Allen, "Chapter 6—Family Histories," *Seventy Years of Pioneer Life in Bennett County* (Martin, S. Dak.: Bennett County Historical Society, 1981), 152; and Bissonette File.

[7] Robert E. Strahorn, *The Hand-Book of Wyoming* (Cheyenne, Wyo., 1877), 159 and 35. There was no usury law in Wyoming at the time. Ibid., 162.

In Cheyenne in 1876 a two-horse team could be purchased for between $100 and $350. Edwin A. Curley, *Guide to the Black Hills* (Chicago, 1877), 17.

[8] J. E. Smith to assistant adjutant general, Feb. 12, 1874, National Archives, Record Group 75, Letters Received by the Office of Indian Affairs, Red Cloud Agency, Microcopy 234, Roll 715 (hereafter cited as Red Cloud Agency letters). William Garnett,

who was at Fort Laramie at the time, recalled that whites were stealing the Indians' horses on a regular basis. Donald F. Danker, "The Violent Deaths of Yellow Bear and John Richard Jr.," *Nebraska History* 63 (1982):144.

Shortly after this incident a Charles W. Allen was arrested for vagrancy in Omaha, Nebraska. He left town before being brought to trial. *Omaha Daily Herald*, Mar. 4, 1874.

⁹ The town of Pine Ridge, South Dakota, grew up around the Pine Ridge Reservation administrative offices. Pine Ridge also refers to a geographical feature in the area.

¹⁰ The Fremont, Elkhorn, and Missouri Valley Railroad reached the Chadron townsite on July 31, 1885. *Chadron Democrat*, Apr. 15, 1886. By the end of the year track was laid to the Wyoming border and the following summer a branch went north from Chadron to Rapid City, South Dakota. *Chadron Centennial History* (Chadron: Chadron Narrative History Project Committee, 1985), 21.

¹¹ U.S. General Land Office Tract Books, Record Group 509, 16:82, Nebraska State Historical Society; Reese letter, Apr. 13, 1995.

¹² Lucas was the first to go to Chadron and was followed by Hill. Allen did not leave Valentine until late July. *Democratic Blade*, Sept. 18, 1885.

During Allen's editorship the subscription price of the *Democrat* was two dollars per year. The first page was devoted to local news items, while inside pages carried Nebraska, national, and some international news. Beginning early in 1890 one or two columns of donated space carried news and editorials by the Nebraska Woman Suffrage Association. About one-third of the paper was advertising, ranging from sales at the local grocery store to mail order patent medicines.

¹³ *Democratic Blade*, Sept. 18, 1885, and *Chadron Citizen*, Mar. 19, 1891. *Chadron Democrat*, Sept. 9, 1886. No issues of the *Gordon Advocate* have survived so, perhaps, Robert Lucas's venture was unsuccessful. During his absence he retained his affiliation with the *Chadron Democrat*, but by February 1887 he had "severed connections" with Allen and Hill. Ibid., Feb. 10, 1887. Lucas left in February 1887 to begin a law practice in Iowa. Allen Shepherd, et. al., eds., *Man of Many Frontiers: The Diaries of "Billy The Bear" Iaeger* (Omaha: Making History, 1994), 131.

Hill stayed with the paper after Allen left. The paper was renamed the *Chadron Citizen*. *Chadron Citizen*, Mar. 19, 1891.

¹⁴ *Dawes County Journal*, Nov. 6, 1885.

¹⁵ *Northwestern Temperance Advocate*, Dec. 8, 1887.

¹⁶ *Chadron Advocate*, Aug. 9, 1889.

Allen and Sheldon remained friends throughout their long lifetimes, but there was a reversal in fortunes. When Sheldon arrived in Chadron he was a bookish, Doane College, Nebraska, graduate with few if any connections in western Nebraska or much knowledge of it. On the other hand Allen was the outgoing old timer who knew everyone. As the years passed Sheldon would be elected to the state legislature, receive his doctorate at Columbia University, and become superintendent of the Nebraska State Historical Society, where he became acquainted with many influential leaders of business and politics. By this time it was Allen who had to beg favors and help from Sheldon.

Sheldon died in Lincoln on November 26, 1943. *Lincoln Star*, Nov. 26, 1943.

¹⁷ *Northwestern Temperance Advocate*, Nov. 1, 1888. In one issue Sheldon noted in his paper: "The *Advocate* believes in cold water but thinks it must be a strange sight in the *Democrat*." Ibid., June 21, 1888.

¹⁸ *Chadron Democrat*, June 6, 1889.

¹⁹ Ibid., Nov. 27, 1890.

[20] Henry C. Clifford married a Lakota woman about 1865. He made several trips to Chicago to exhibit and sell fossils. Eli S. Ricker Collection, MS8, Interviews, tablet 8, 79, Nebraska State Historical Society. His interest in fossils was acquired when he served as a guide to paleontologist O. C. Marsh of Yale University. James H. Cook, *Fifty Years on the Old Frontier* (Norman: University of Oklahoma Press, 1957), 277.

While the Gold Bar was advertised as an opera house, it was primarily a saloon and at times a house of prostitution. Shepherd, *Man of Many Frontiers*, 138–39. The Chadron exhibit was at least modestly successful. *Chadron Democrat*, Aug. 15, 1889, and June 20, 1889.

Allen left for Chicago in early August 1889. *Chadron Democrat*, Aug. 1, 1889. During his absence Charles M. Conger took over and promised to "battle for the democratic cause" until Allen returned. Ibid., Aug. 8, 1889.

[21] *Chadron Advocate*, Oct. 11, 1889.

Allen returned to Chadron on October 27, 1889. Shepherd, *Man of Many Frontiers*, 483.

[22] *Chadron Democrat*, Oct. 15, 1885, and Nov. 12, 1885. Allen served briefly in 1886 as a justice of the peace. George D. Watson, Jr., *Prairie Justice, 1885–1985* (Chadron: B and B Printing, n.d.), 17.

In 1913 Allen was living in Bennett County, South Dakota, where he was elected to the state house of representatives. When the election was held, the county was not yet legally organized, and Allen was denied the right to vote in the legislature. As a gesture of goodwill members of the house appointed him doorkeeper. South Dakota Legislative Research Council, comp., *Biographical Dictionary of the South Dakota Legislature*, 1929, 1:23.

[23] *Chadron Democrat*, Nov. 6, 1890.

[24] Ibid., Mar. 24, 1887.

[25] "Short Bull—Brigand of the Badlands" was published in the *Chadron Democrat*, Jan. 22, 1891. A reporter would write a few paragraphs, then give it to a colleague who would add a few more paragraphs, continuing the story as he saw fit. The opening lines of the narrative, written by C. C. Seymour, the *Chicago Herald* correspondent, provides an adequate sample. "It was a hot night in the dead of winter. A red man who had lost his right arm shaking dice sat in his tent in the Bad Lands sucking the only thumb he had. He was mad, and his clothing showed it."

Many years later Allen sent a copy to his friend Elmo Scott Watson, who published it in the *Publishers' Auxiliary*, Jan. 31, 1942, and Feb. 7, 1942.

[26] Allen's first article on the Ghost Dance appeared in the *Chadron Democrat*, May 8, 1890. On May 15, 1890, he published the more detailed report.

[27] Richard E. Jensen, "Big Foot's Followers at Wounded Knee," *Nebraska History* 71 (1990):194–212.

For much of the material relating to the Ghost Dance troubles the editor has relied heavily upon Richard E. Jensen, R. Eli Paul, and John E. Carter, *Eyewitness at Wounded Knee* (Lincoln: University of Nebraska Press, 1991).

[28] *Chadron Citizen*, Mar. 26, 1891.

In 1889 Allen had reported a circulation of 500, while the *Chadron Advocate* reported 250 and the *Dawes County Journal* 500. *American Newspaper Directory* (New York: George W. Powsell and Co., 1889), 419.

Allen's fortunes were directly related to those of farmers and ranchers in the Chadron vicinity, who made up the majority of his subscribers. They enjoyed adequate rainfall until 1890, when precipitation was twenty percent below normal, a drastic drop in an area that could be described as semiarid in normal times. This was followed by two average years and then three years of severe drought, when rainfall was more than thirty percent below normal. *Climate and Man: Yearbook of Agriculture.* (Washington, D.C.: U.S. Department of Agriculture, GPO, 1941), 971, 1112.

Charles and Emma's son, Samuel, recalled these years when "the crops were burning up, and the farmers did not raise anything. . . . The dust would whirl in the air and form big dust clouds. It would get dark and you couldn't see the sun. Everyone had hard times during the drought." Reese letter, Apr. 13, 1995.

[29] *Chadron Democrat*, Mar. 12, 1891.

[30] *Chadron Citizen.*, Mar. 19, 1891.

[31] G. L. Brown to commissioner of Indian affairs, Feb. 8, 1893, National Archives, Record Group 75, Letters Sent to the Office of Indian Affairs from Pine Ridge Agency, Microcopy 1282, Roll 19 (hereafter cited as Pine Ridge Agency letters).

In September 1892 the Pine Ridge agent wanted Allen to serve as an informal inspector at the proposed school near the mouth of Porcupine Creek. G. L. Brown to commissioner, Sept. 10, 1892, Pine Ridge Agency letters, Roll 16. Charles's daughter Nellie was appointed substitute teacher at the school. G. L. Brown to commissioner, Feb. 8, 1893, Pine Ridge Agency letters, Roll 19.

A census of Pine Ridge Reservation residents places the Allens on the reservation about this time. Although the census is not dated, internal evidence shows it was taken in either 1892 or 1893. Residents of Pine Ridge Agency, National Archives, Central Plains Region, Record Group 75, Pine Ridge Agency, #3 Miscellaneous Correspondence Received.

In a sworn deposition on October 8, 1892, concerning some stolen mules, Allen gave his occupation as stock raiser and his residence as "Pine Ridge Agency, Shannon County, South Dakota." National Archives, Record Group 123, Court of Claims, Indian Depredation no. 4803. Proceedings of Meeting of Delegates, Apr. 10, 1893, Pine Ridge Agency letters, Roll 20.

About this same time the honorary rank of major was bestowed upon Allen by the local press. *Chadron Citizen*, Jan. 19, 1893.

[32] Allen's appointment was dated April 6, 1893. National Archives, Record Group 28, Record of Appointment of Postmasters, Microcopy 841, Roll 117 (hereafter cited as Record of Appointment of Postmasters). His wish to become a postmaster was reported in the *Chadron Citizen* on Jan. 19, 1893.

Agent William Clapp mentioned a general exodus from Porcupine Creek beginning in 1893, but he did not offer any reason for this migration. W. Clapp to commissioner, Aug. 13, 1897, Pine Ridge Agency letters, Roll 27.

Daughter Nellie Allen resigned her teaching position at the Porcupine Creek school on April 13, 1893, which would also suggest a move at about this time. Memo dated Apr. 13, 1893, Pine Ridge Agency letters, Roll 20.

The Allens sold their homestead to E. A. Pratt on December 7, 1893, as recorded in Deed Book 15:33. Personal communication from Florence Mikesell, Dawes County Clerk, to Richard E. Jensen, May 1995.

[33] G. L. Brown to commissioner, Mar. 19 and 22, 1893, Pine Ridge Agency letters, Roll 19.

[34] Allen obtained a trader's license as required by law. C. Allen to commissioner, Aug. 6, 1895 and G. L. Brown to commissioner, Jan. 3, 1893, Pine Ridge Agency letters, Roll 19.

[35] *Chadron Citizen*, Dec. 21, 1893.

C. W. Allen, "Red Cloud, Chief of the Sioux," *The Hesperian* 1 (1895):144–47 and 173–87; (1896):211–16. Years later, Allen gave a draft to Addison E. Sheldon, who retitled it *Life of Red Cloud* and placed it in the archives of the Nebraska State Historical Society. Allen used some material from the article when he wrote *In The West That Was*. Since only a portion of the *Hesperian* version of "Red Cloud, Chief of the Sioux" has survived, Sheldon's *Life of Red Cloud* is cited in this work. The tangled history of Allen's Red Cloud manuscript has been unraveled by R. Eli Paul, "Recovering Red Cloud's Autobiography," *Montana: The Magazine of Western History* 44 (1994):2–17.

[36] Allen must have stayed in Pine Ridge until late October 1895 when his successor in the post office was appointed. October 29, 1895, Record of Appointment of Postmasters, Roll 117.

C. Allen to commissioner, Aug. 6, 1895, Pine Ridge Agency letters, Roll 25.

The store was sold to Clarence Three Stars in the fall of 1896. W. Clapp to commissioner, Apr. 24 and Oct. 27, 1897, Pine Ridge Agency letters, Roll 27.

[37] Albert A. Lamb became the first postmaster at Allen, South Dakota, on September 21, 1897. Carol Livermont, "Chapter 24 – Post Offices," *Seventy Years of Pioneer Life in Bennett County, South Dakota* (Martin, S. Dak.: Bennett County Historical Society, 1981:83.

The issue station on Pass Creek was moved to present-day Allen in 1900. A day school was also established at Allen about this time. James J. Duncan, "Report of the Day-School Inspector, Pine Ridge Reservation," *Annual Report of the Department of the Interior, Indian Affairs* (Washington, D.C.: GPO, 1902), 369 (hereafter refered to as *Annual Report, Indian Affairs*).

The first mention of an issue at Allen, South Dakota, was in the fall of 1900, but the move could have occurred a little earlier. J. Jenkins to commissioner, Oct. 18, 1900, Pine Ridge Agency letters, Roll 31.

An Indian camp in the immediate vicinity of Allen, South Dakota, was probably much older. An Episcopal mission had been founded on Corn Creek only about three miles to the west by February 1892. G. L. Brown to commissioner, Feb. 15, 1892, Pine Ridge Agency letters, Roll 13.

A sketch map shows "Alens Ranch" about twelve miles above the mouth of Eagle Nest Creek. C. A. Craven to J. Brennen, Dec. 13, 1901, National Archives, Central Plains Region, Record Group 75, Pine Ridge Agency, #3 Miscellaneous Correspondence Received.

[38] Arthur Otis Allen, "Chapter 6–Family Histories," 153.

John R. Brennan, "Report of Agent for Pine Ridge Agency," *Annual Report, Indian Affairs*, 1906:338.

Emma and her children received approximately 2,800 contiguous acres in the allotment. Married daughters and members of the Hawkins family, probably related to Emma, received about 2,400 acres adjacent to the Allen property. Personal communication from Roseana L. Blount to Richard E. Jensen, Aug. 22, 1995.

[39] Addison E. Sheldon diary, Dec. 1, 1908, Addison E. Sheldon Collection, MS 2039, Nebraska State Historical Society (hereafter cited as Sheldon diary).

[40] W. Moorehead to C. Allen, Mar. 9, 1909 and C. Allen to W. Moorehead, Mar. 23, 1909. Warren K. Moorehead Papers, Collection 106, Ohio Historical Society, Columbus, Ohio.

[41] Settlement by whites began almost immediately after the issuance of the proclamation opening Bennett County. Charles Lowell Green, "The Administration of the Public Domain in South Dakota," *South Dakota Historical Collections* 20, (1940):176.

Since the early issues of the *Martin Messenger* have not survived, the founding date is unknown, but based upon Allen's comments publication probably began about this same time.

[42] A. E. Sheldon to F. H. Abbott, Apr. 28, 1913, Superintendent's Correspondence, RG 14, Box 85, Nebraska State Historical Society.

[43] The exact nature of the experiments was not mentioned. E. S. Ricker to Leslie Ricker, Mar. 4, 1917, Ricker Collection, Correspondence. According to the family tradition Emma died of influenza. Reese letter, Mar. 6, 1995, and *Martin Messenger*, Apr. 3, 1925, and Nov. 19, 1942.

[44] Sheldon diary, Feb. 25, 1910.

[45] In 1889 Sheldon and Allen went to the Pine Ridge Reservation to invite Red Cloud's Lakota to Chadron. It was not uncommon for towns bordering reservations to invite Native Americans to attend certain celebrations and perform some of their social dances. Sheldon's speech was first published in the *Chadron Democrat*, June 27, 1889.

Occasionally Sheldon would get revenge by composing a bit of doggerel and publishing it in his paper, crediting Allen as the author. See "Ode to a Mule," *Chadron Advocate*, July 12, 1889; Sheldon, "Major Charles W. Allen," *Nebraska History* 21 (1940):292.

[46] C. Allen to A. E. Sheldon, Dec. 15, 1936 and A. E. Sheldon to C. Allen, Dec. 17, 1936, Allen Collection.

[47] C. Allen to A. E. Sheldon, May 29, 1936, Ibid..

[48] Sheldon diary, Feb. 7, 10, 12, 21, Apr. 25, 26, and July 6, 1938. Sheldon wrote that Loraine Ferris "gave the manuscript its final critical expert revision and form." Sheldon Collection.

The manuscript was submitted to at least six publishers. C. Allen to E. S. Watson, April 16, 1941, and C. Allen to A. E. Sheldon, Nov. 21, 1938, Allen Collection.

[49] Charles Allen, "Red Cloud and the U.S. Flag," *Nebraska History* 21, (1940):293–304.

[50] E. S. Watson to C. Allen, Apr. 4, 1941, and C. Allen to E. S. Watson, Apr. 16, 1941, Allen Collection.

[51] "Short Bull—Brigand of the Badlands" survives in the Allen Collection.

[52] C. Allen to E. S. Watson, Apr. 16, 1941, Allen Collection.

[53] *Publishers' Auxiliary*, Sept. 12, 1942.

[54] *Martin Messenger*, Nov. 19, 1942.

[55] *Publishers' Auxiliary*, Nov. 28, 1942, and Dec. 5, 1942. This was republished in a 1990 article by John D. McDermott, "Wounded Knee: Centennial Voices," *South Dakota History* 20 (1990):245–92.

[56] Note in the Allen Collection dated Aug. 6, 1982, by Leigh G. DeLay, historian of the Nebraska State Historical Society.

1. A Pioneer in Embryo

[1] Allen's sketches span a twenty-year period from 1871 to 1891, rather than a fifty-year interval.

[2] The first Texas longhorns came up the Chisholm Trail and were loaded on eastbound trains at Abilene, Kansas, just four years before Allen was hired as a herder. While most of the cattle were destined for slaughterhouses, others were driven into Wyoming to establish new ranches. Wayne Gard, *The Chisholm Trail* (Norman: University of Oklahoma Press, 1954), 67.

In 1880 Goodwin purchased a road ranche twenty-eight miles north of Cheyenne. Agnes Wright Spring, *The Cheyenne and Black Hills Stage and Express Routes* (Glendale: Arthur H. Clark Company, 1948), 102.

[3] Elias W. Whitcomb came to Wyoming in 1861 and opened a trading post about forty miles above Fort Laramie on Horseshoe Creek. Flannery, *John Hunton's Diary*, 1:77; Virginia Cole Trenholm, *Footprints on the Frontier* (Douglas, Wyo.: Douglas Enterprise Co., 1945), 71. About 1870 Whitcomb began ranching on Box Elder Creek west of Fort Collins, Colorado. I. S. Bartlett, ed., *History of Wyoming* (Chicago: S. J. Clarke Publishing Co., 1918), 1:145.

[4] Hiram B. Kelly came to Fort Laramie in 1858 and in the 1870s had a ranch near present Chugwater, Wyoming. He is credited with shipping the first carload of live cattle out of Wyoming. When Allen went to work for him there was only one other cattle ranch in the area. It was owned by B. B. Mills and W. G. Bullock. Trenholm, *Footprints on the Frontier*, 219, 247, and 249. By 1875 there were eight ranches and more than 4,000 cattle along the Chugwater. J. H. Triggs, *History of Cheyenne and Northern Wyoming* (Omaha: Herald Steam Book and Job Printing Service, 1876), 53.

Chugwater Stage Station, owned by Kelley, was near present Chugwater, Wyoming. The Point of Rocks Allen mentioned was about two miles north of the station. Spring, *The Cheyenne and Black Hills Stage and Express Route*, 35.

[5] Allen is referring to the Red Cloud Agency of 1871-73. Located on the north side of the North Platte River about thirty miles below Fort Laramie, it was the distribution point for annuities promised the Oglala in the treaty of 1868. At times there may have been as many as 10,000 Indians camped in the vicinity. James C. Olson, *Red Cloud and the Sioux Problem* (Lincoln: University of Nebraska Press Bison Book, 1975).

[6] At the end of this chapter Allen concludes his story of Levi Powell. In 1871 Powell was bound for Montana with 1,200 Texas cattle, but as it was late in the season he decided to winter near the mouth of the Chugwater. J. E. Smith to adjutant general, Mar. 1, 1872, and E. Ord to J. B. Fry, Apr. 14, 1872, Red Cloud Agency letters, Roll 715.

In 1926 John Hunton began writing about his experiences in the Fort Laramie area in the 1870s. He recalled that Powell wintered at the mouth of Fish Creek on the North Laramie and sold his herd of 2,200 Texas cattle to F. M. Phillips who lived at the mouth of the Chugwater. Unfortunately Hunton's recollections do not always agree with eyewitness accounts. John Hunton, "Reminiscences by John Hunton," *Annals of Wyoming* 6 (1930):263.

[7] Fort Fetterman was established in July 1867 near present Douglas, Wyoming. It was designed to quarter 300 troops who were to protect emigrants on the Overland and Bozeman trails. The fort was abandoned in 1882. Robert W. Frazer, *Forts of the West* (Norman: University of Oklahoma Press, 1965), 181. J. W. Barlow, *Outline Descriptions of the Posts in the Military Division of the Missouri* (Chicago, 1876), 97-98.

[8] Adolph Cuny and Jules Ecoffey were old timers in the area when Allen arrived. They were the biggest operators at the time with a large cattle ranch and a road ranche. Hedren, *Fort Laramie in 1876*, 45-46.

Ecoffey was a Swiss who had been educated at the University of Freiburg. He began trading with the Lakota about 1854 and was a good friend of Red Cloud. George Hyde, *Red Cloud's Folk, A History of the Oglala Sioux Indians* (Norman: University of Oklahoma Press, 1937), 196.

Ecoffey was paid $3,800 for building storehouses at the Red Cloud Agency on the Platte. He was also the licensed trader there. Voucher dated Aug. 18, 1871, Red Cloud Agency letters, Roll 715. Ecoffey died on November 26, 1876, as a result of an attack by a man named Stonewall. Spring, *The Cheyenne and Black Hills Stage and Express Routes*, 113. Cuny was killed on July 22, 1877, while assisting in the arrest of two bandits at Three Mile Ranch. Ibid., 219.

[9] Three Mile Ranch was on the north side of the Laramie River just west of the Fort Laramie military reservation. Merrill J. Mattes, *Fort Laramie Park History* (Rocky Mountain Regional Office: National Park Service, 1980), 39.

[10] The stock ranch on Sibylle Creek would have been about five miles southwest of present Wheatland, Wyoming.

[11] In 1862 Jim Bridger was employed by the army as a guide for the party bound for Salt Lake City. Stanley Vestal, *Jim Bridger, Mountain Man* (Lincoln: University of Nebraska Press Bison Book, 1970), 209.

Fort Halleck was named in honor of Maj. Gen. Henry W. Halleck. It was built in 1862 under the command of Maj. John O'Ferrall. The fort was located at the north base of Elk Mountain about forty miles east of Rawlins, Wyoming. It was established to protect the Denver-Salt Lake stage route and was abandoned in 1866. Francis Paul Prucha, *A Guide to the Military Posts of the United States* (Madison: State Historical Society of Wisconsin, 1964), 77; Frazer, *Forts of the West*, 181.

[12] Laramie, Wyoming, was founded in 1868 and by 1876 it had a population of 3,500. Strahorn, *The Hand-Book of Wyoming*, 146.

[13] John "Buckskin Jack" Russell was described by one of the reporters covering the Ghost Dance incident in 1890 as "a small Irishman who had grown up among the Sioux." Christer Lindberg, "Foreigners in Action at Wounded Knee," *Nebraska History* 71 (1990):172. Frank Grouard concurred, saying he "might be called the 'Midget of the Plains.'" Russell served as a scout for the army in the 1870s and later traveled with William F. Cody's Wild West Show. Joe DeBarthe, *Life and Adventures of Frank Grouard* (Norman: University of Oklahoma Press, 1958).

[14] F. M. Phillips started one of the first ranches in the Fort Laramie region. The *H* outfit would become one of the largest in the area with headquarters at the confluence of the Chugwater and Laramie rivers. Trenholm, *Footprints on the Frontier*, 128, 236.

[15] Levi Powell's body was found on a tributary of the North Laramie River. He had been shot three times and scalped. The Oglalas were blamed for his murder and when the Office of Indian Affairs began pressuring the tribe to move their agency to the White River the tribal leaders agreed to do so if the demands for Powell's killers were dropped. Although the office did not formally adopt this arrangement, the agency was moved and the identity of Powell's murderer was never determined. J. E. Smith to adjutant general, Mar. 1, 1872, and E. Ord to J. B. Fry, Apr. 14, 1872, Red Cloud Agency letters, Roll 716.

2. Mystery and Mules

[1] Allen's blasé attitude is likely to be the result of recalling events after the passage of more than fifty years. During the first part of 1872 there had been a series of bloody incidents keeping everyone on edge and giving rise to rumors of an outbreak. Levi Powell was killed about February 10. J. E. Smith to adjutant general, Mar. 1, 1872, Red Cloud Agency letters, Roll 716. Two Cheyenne Indians were killed by whites when they tried to steal some cattle, and an army sergeant and two white civilians were killed in separate incidents by Native Americans. Some Oglalas were implicated in one of these killings. J. W. Daniels to T. A. Walker, Mar. 21, 1872, and May 6, 1872, Red Cloud Agency letters, Roll 716.

In mid-May John Richard killed Yellow Bear as the result of a long-standing feud. Richard was then killed by Yellow Bear's supporters. The Indian agent feared there might be more violence directed towards mixed bloods and whites. D. R. Risley to commissioner of Indian affairs, May 18, 1872, Red Cloud Agency letters, Roll 716. Danker, "The Violent Deaths of Yellow Bear and John Richard Jr.," 137–49.

Hila Gilbert's biography of Big Bat Pourier, which relies heavily upon family history and secondary sources, claimed Richard was killed by an unknown assailant in 1875 on the Niobrara River. Hila Gilbert, *Big Bat Pourier* (Sheridan, Wyo.: Mills Publishing Co., 1958), 44.

As unsettling as these incidents were, they were overshadowed by the government's insistence on moving the Indian agency. It was on the north side of the North Platte, where there were many opportunities for clashes with whites traveling along the trail. The Office of Indian Affairs wanted to move the agency to the White River about seventy miles to the northeast. The strong opposition to such a move by many Oglalas and Brulés kept both sides in a constant state of near hysteria. In spite of the opposition the move took place in mid-August 1873. J. W. Daniels to E. P. Smith, Aug. 23, 1873, Red Cloud Agency letters, Roll 717.

2 Drivers either rode in the wagon or on   a saddle on the animal closest to the left front wheel. William E. Lass, *From the Missouri to the Great Salt Lake: An Account of Overland Freighting* (Lincoln: Nebraska State Historical Society, 1972), 10.

3 The initials U.S.I.C. signified government property that had been inspected and condemned.

4 Nicholas Janis was born in 1827. In 1845 he and his brother, Antoine, began trading with the Lakota and spending much of their time in the vicinity of Fort Laramie. Nicholas married a niece of Red Cloud. In the 1870s he owned a ranche east of the fort, which he sold in 1880. He moved to Pine Ridge to be with his wife's people, where he died in 1902. Janet Lecompte, "Antoine Janis," *The Mountain Men and the Fur Trade of the Far West* (Glendale: Arthur H. Clark Co., 1971), 8:196–201. The ranche was about thirty miles east of Fort Laramie. Spring, *The Cheyenne and Black Hills Stage and Express Routes*, 57. When Allen met him, Janis also served as an interpreter. Second auditor to commissioner of Indian affairs, Oct. 7, 1872, Red Cloud Agency letters, Roll 716. Allen published a biography of Nicholas Janis in the *Chadron Democrat*, Oct. 1, 1885.

5 The prairie turnip was one of the most widely distributed wild food crops on the plains. Waldo W. Wedel, "Notes on the Prairie Turnip," *Nebraska History* 59 (1978):154–79.

6 Later, George Colhoff was a clerk for the Yates Trading Company near Fort Robinson. Roger T. Grange, Jr., "Fort Robinson, Outpost on the Plains," *Nebraska History* 39 (1958):207.

7 Andrew Tabor was listed in the 1870 census as a twenty-eight-year-old laborer born in Canada. Personal communication from Ann Nelson, senior historian, Wyoming State Museum to Richard E. Jensen, Sept. 20, 1994 (hereafter cited as Nelson letter).

Sixty-five dollars a month for Allen and his two horses was a very generous salary. At this time a driver alone could earn only about $25 a month. Strahorn, *The Hand-Book of Wyoming*, 159.

8 With only four horses Allen's freight wagon would have been relatively small. On his first trip to the Black Hills the leader of the caravan used six-mule teams. They were able to pull a wagon with a twelve-foot bed three and one-half feet wide and eighteen inches deep with a carrying capacity of up to 3,500 pounds. This was a common size for a freight wagon. Henry Pickering Walker, *The Wagonmasters* (Norman: University of Oklahoma Press, 1966), 98.

9 The move of about seventy miles from the North Platte to the White River began on August 14, 1873. J. W. Daniels to E. P. Smith, Aug. 23, 1873, Red Cloud Agency let-

ters, Roll 717. Problems did not diminish at the new site. Within a few months two agency employees were killed by the Lakota. Grange, "Fort Robinson, Outpost on the Plains," 195. It was here that Allen witnessed the confrontation over the flag described in Chapters 3 and 4.

In 1877–78 the agency was on the Missouri River at the mouth of Medicine Creek. It was moved again to White Clay Creek and renamed Pine Ridge Agency, where it continues to the present. Olson, *Red Cloud and the Sioux Problem*, 254–63.

[10] On March 5, 1874, a temporary military post was set up to protect agency employees from further violence. At first it was called Camp at Red Cloud Agency, but on March 29 it was officially christened Camp Robinson in honor of Lt. Levi H. Robinson, who had been killed by a party of Miniconjous and Hunkpapas the previous month. In May the camp was moved about one and one-half miles up the river to a site that is today's Fort Robinson. Thomas R. Buecker, *A History of Camp Robinson, Nebraska* (Masters thesis, Chadron State College, 1992).

3. Red Cloud Cuts the Flag-Pole (Part One)

[1] This chapter and the following one were slightly condensed and published in *Nebraska History*. Allen, "Red Cloud and the U.S. Flag," 293–304.

Baptiste "Big Bat" Pourier came to the Fort Laramie area in 1857 as a ranch hand in the employ of John Richard. Later he worked as a prospector, trader, and government scout. Pourier finally settled on a ranch on Wounded Knee Creek and was a witness to the 1890 massacre. Gilbert, *Big Bat Pourier*.

[2] Lt. Peter Dumont Vroom was the regimental adjutant of the Third Cavalry. Francis B. Heitman, *Historical Register and Dictionary of the United States Army* (Washington, D.C.: GPO, 1903), 990. In 1880 Vroom was stationed at Fort Robinson. William T. Corbusier, "Camp Sheridan, Nebraska," *Nebraska History* 42 (1961):52.

The trail they were taking had thirteen fords. Grange, "Fort Robinson, Outpost on the Plains," 198.

[3] The incidents Allen describes can not be precisely matched to contemporary accounts. He may have been referring to a stagecoach driver who was ambushed about this same time on the trail to Sidney, Nebraska, south of the Red Cloud Agency. Remi Nadeau, *Fort Laramie and the Sioux Indians* (Englewood Cliffs, N.J.: Prentice-Hall Co., 1967), 272. Another possibility is an incident in May 1876, when the driver of a mail wagon was killed near the head of White Clay Creek. John G. Bourke, *On The Border With Crook* (Glorieta, N. Mex: Rio Grande Press, Inc., 1968), 288.

[4] In 1832 George Catlin visited the Mandans and noted that about one person in twelve had "hair of a bright silvery grey" regardless of sex or age. George Catlin, *Letters and Notes on the Manners, Customs, and Condition of the North American Indians* (New York: Wiley and Putnam, 1841), 1:94.

[5] The commander of Fort Robinson in October 1874 was Capt. William H. Jordan. Grange, "Fort Robinson, Outpost on the Plains," 204.

[6] Rocky Bear was the head of a small Oglala band of about eighty-five people. Olson, *Red Cloud and the Sioux Problem*, 131. He was employed by the agent, Dr. J. J. Saville, as a guard at Red Cloud Agency. J. J. Saville to E. P. Smith, Mar. 1, 1874, Red Cloud Agency letters, Roll 718.

Manuel Romero was hired at the Red Cloud Agency as a laborer on July 1, 1874. J. J. Saville's List of Employees, Sept. 21, 1874, Red Cloud Agency letters, Roll 718.

[7] William Garnett was employed as a Lakota interpreter at Red Cloud when Allen visited with him. List of Employees, Sept. 21, 1874, Red Cloud Agency letters, Roll 718.

Garnett was the son of Richard Brooke Garnett, who was commander of Fort Laramie from 1852 to 1854. William's mother was Looks at Him, a Lakota. William went to work for Jules Ecoffey about the same time as Allen. Danker, "The Violent Deaths of Yellow Bear and John Richard Jr.," 139.

8 Dr. J. J. Saville took over as agent from J. W. Howard on August 8, 1873. J. J. Saville, "Red Cloud Agency," *Annual Report, Indian Affairs,* 1874:251. Throughout Saville's tenure he and Red Cloud were engaged in a constant battle of wits and words concerning the administration of the agency. Olson, *Red Cloud and the Sioux Problem,* 159.

9 Jules Ecoffey had been the licensed trader when the agency was on the North Platte River. Voucher dated Aug. 18, 1871, Red Cloud Agency letters, Roll 715. After the agency was moved to the White River the new agent, J. J. Saville, removed Ecoffey and issued trading licenses to John W. Dear and to B. F. Walter. J. W. Dear to J. J. Saville and B. F. Walter to J. J. Saville, June 30, 1874, Red Cloud Agency letters, Roll 718.

Dear went along when the agency was moved to the Pine Ridge, but he soon ran afoul of the agent. He quit the trade in about 1878. Thomas R. Buecker, "Red Cloud Agency Traders, 1873–1877," *The Museum of the Fur Trade Quarterly* 30 (1994):6.

Early in 1876 Dear established five road ranches between Fort Laramie and the Black Hills anticipating the gold rush in the spring. Allen would use this route on his first trip to the Hills (see Chapter 5). Smith, *The Cheyenne and Black Hills Stage and Express Routes,* 80.

Frank D. Yates was the justice of the peace at Fort Laramie in 1871. Two years later he helped move the Spotted Tail Agency to the White River and was the Brulés' trader. He bought out B. F. Walters and received his license to trade at the Red Cloud Agency on April 16, 1875. Buecker, "Red Cloud Agency Traders."

8 Yates, also operated a stage line between Cheyenne and Custer City in 1876. Spring, *The Cheyenne and Black Hills Stage and Express Routes,* 81. Allen said he was the brother of Capt. George W. Yates who died with Custer in the Little Big Horn battle. C. Allen to A. E. Sheldon, Dec. 17, 1934, Allen Collection.

4. Red Cloud Cuts the Flag-Pole (Part Two)

1 The flagpole incident occurred on October 24, 1874. J. J. Saville to E. P. Smith, Oct. 24, 1874, and W. Jordan to G. D. Ruggles, Oct. 29, 1874, Red Cloud Agency letters, Roll 718.

2 John Farnham was an interpreter. Hedren, *Fort Laramie in 1876,* 44. Louis Richard and Nicholas Janis were the Lakota interpreters at the agency when Allen was there. J. J. Saville to E. P. Smith, Oct. 29, 1874, Red Cloud Agency letters, Roll 718.

Interpreter Joseph Bissonette had been discharged due to illness on August 3, 1874. List of Employees, Sept. 21, 1874, Red Cloud Agency letters, Roll 718.

Louis Shangreau was a mixed blood Oglala, but his name does not appear on agency records as an interpreter. A few years later he would be evicted from the Pine Ridge Reservation by Agent McGillycuddy for some unspecified misdeeds. Olson, *Red Cloud and the Sioux Problem,* 227.

William Garnett was employed as a Lakota interpreter at Red Cloud Agency. List of Employees, Sept. 21, 1874, Red Cloud Agency letters, Roll 718.

3 In 1874 the Spotted Tail Agency was established for the Brulé on Beaver Creek in present northwestern Sheridan County, Nebraska. It was about thirty-five miles northeast of the Red Cloud Agency. George Hyde, *Spotted Tail's Folk: A History of the Brulé Sioux* (Norman: University of Oklahoma Press, 1961).

Louis Bordeau was Agent Howard's interpreter. E. A. Howard to commissioner of Indian affairs, June 2, 1875, National Archives, Record Group 75, Letters Received by the Office of Indian Affairs, Spotted Tail Agency, Microcopy 234, Roll 840 (hereafter cited as Spotted Tail Agency letters). Bordeau, John Bruguier, and Louis Robideaux were included on a list of white men and mixed bloods living at Spotted Tail Agency dated Jan. 1, 1875. Ibid.

[4] Michael Dunn was a teamster at Red Cloud and at the old agency on the Platte. List of Employees, Aug. 8, 1873, and Sept. 21, 1874, Red Cloud Agency letters, Roll 718. By the end of the century Dunn would be a successful cattle rancher on the Bad River. Wayne C. Lee, *Scotty Philip, The Man Who Saved The Buffalo* (Caldwell, Idaho: Caxton Printers, 1975), 139–40, 256.

[5] Lt. Emmet Crawford and twenty-two men of the Third Cavalry rode to the rescue. W. H. Jordan to G. D. Ruggles, Oct. 29, 1874, Red Cloud Agency letters, Roll 715.

[6] Allen was unable to see all of the action and missed an even more "ominous incident." As the soldiers neared the agency they were rushed by an overwhelming number of Lakotas. Crawford gave the order to dismount, load weapons, and prepare to fire. It was a brave performance in the face of ten to one odds and Crawford's men probably would have been killed had it not been for the intervention of Sitting Bull. This Oglala chief pushed his way in front of the soldiers and managed to convince the Indians to let them go. The soldiers quickly slipped into the comparative safety of the agency. After about three hours the rioters calmed down and the soldiers went back to Camp Robinson.

Allen gave much credit to the mixed blood interpreters for keeping the peace but in his report of the incident, Lieutenant Crawford candidly admitted it was Sitting Bull who saved them. In addition, the army recognized the support of Red Dog, Red Leaf, Old Man Afraid of His Horses, Young Man Afraid of His Horses, and several others. W. H. Jordan to assistant adjutant general, Oct. 23, 1874, and W. H. Jordan to G. D. Ruggles, Oct. 29, 1874, Red Cloud Agency letters, Roll 715; Harry H. Anderson, "The War Club of Sitting Bull the Oglala," *Nebraska History* 42 (1961):56–57.

[7] Lt. Emmet Crawford died in the line of duty on January 11, 1886, while in pursuit of Indians near Nacori, Mexico. Heitman, *Historical Register*, 336.

[8] The army's reports of the incident agreed with Allen on Red Cloud's passivity and placed the blame entirely upon the Miniconjous. Captain Jordan recommended they "exterminate the wretches." W. H. Jordan to G. D. Ruggles, Oct. 29, 1874, Red Cloud Agency letters, Roll 715.

5. Freighting to the Black Hills

[1] The Bettelyouns were a prominent family in the Fort Laramie area for many years. Hedren, *Fort Laramie in 1876*, 197.

Austin Means was listed in the 1880 census as a forty-year-old teamster born in Pennsylvania. Nelson letter, Sept. 20, 1994.

[2] When Allen arrived Cheyenne was a thriving frontier town. It was founded in 1867 only a few months before the Union Pacific Railroad reached it on November 13. Two miles west of the town was Camp Carlan, where military supplies and the Indians' annuity goods were stored while awaiting shipment by wagon to the north on the Cheyenne-Fort Laramie Road. Triggs, *History of Cheyenne and Northern Wyoming*, 17 and 116.

Ithmer C. Whipple was a Cheyenne pioneer and a leading retail grocer and a banker. Cheyenne *Wyoming Tribune*, Jan. 31, 1912.

Erasmus Nagle came to Cheyenne in 1868 and by the time of Allen's visit ran the largest retail and wholesale grocery businesses in Wyoming. Later he was an incorporator of the Cheyenne and Northern Railroad Company. E. O. Fuller, "Cheyenne Looking North," *Annals of Wyoming* 23 (1951):29. Nelson letter, Sept. 20, 1994.

[3] There are several Charles Millers in the census and cemetery records, but it is not possible to determine to whom Allen is referring. Nelson letter, Sept. 20, 1994.

[4] Hartwell S. Tracy was listed as a thirty-four-year-old stable keeper from Vermont. An 1868 Cheyenne city directory listed him as owning corrals on Eddy Street. Ibid.

[5] James McDaniels came to Cheyenne in 1867 and opened an art museum of stereoscopic views, which was free to anyone patronizing his bar. Later he had a variety of other entertainments. Campton Bell, "The Early Theaters of Cheyenne, Wyoming," *Annals of Wyoming* 25 (1953):8–13.

[6] Edwin A. Curley took the stage coach to the Black Hills at about this same time (May 1876) and confirmed that freighters had to wait at Fort Laramie until there was a large enough number to go safely. Curley, *Guide to the Black Hills*, 33.

[7] Charles Metz, his wife, and several traveling companions were returning from Custer in the Black Hills. They reached Red Canyon on April 16, 1876, where they were ambushed by white outlaws. Only one man from the Metz party escaped. Hedren, *Fort Laramie in 1876*, 76–77.

Annie D. Tallent's slightly different version of the event seems less reliable. Annie D. Tallent, *The Black Hills: or, The Last Hunting Ground of the Dakotas* (Sioux Falls, S. Dak.: Brevet Press, 1974), 121, 218–19.

[8] The steel bridge across the Laramie River at Fort Laramie was completed in the spring of 1876. Mattes, *Fort Laramie Park History*, 37. The government farm was on Rawhide Creek about fourteen miles northwest of the fort. It was abandoned by 1872. Spring, *The Cheyenne and Black Hills Stage and Express Routes*, 118.

[9] Jack Bowman and his partner, Joe Walters, were developing a major commercial center to include a hotel, bakery, butcher shop, brewery, and blacksmith shop with the post office and later a telegraph station. Hedren, *Fort Laramie in 1876*, 191.

An outpost of Fort Laramie was established in 1875 on Old Woman's Creek to prevent prospectors from entering the Black Hills. Capt. Samuel Munson, Ninth Infantry, was then in command. When prospectors were allowed to enter the hills a stage station and post office were added and used for several years. Isabel M. Willson, "Hat Creek Station," *Annals of Wyoming* 10 (1938):12–13. Despite its location the outpost was called Camp Hat Creek. Spring, *The Cheyenne and Black Hills Stage and Express Routes*, 122. This may explain Allen's confusion about the name of the stream. Maps of the era show Hat Creek about forty miles to the east.

Lt. George McMannis Taylor, Twenty-third Infantry, was in charge of the military post. Hedren, *Fort Laramie in 1876*, 191.

Infantry detachments were stationed at intervals along the trail while cavalry units patrolled between these temporary camps. Bourke, *On The Border With Crook*, 284.

[10] William F. "Buffalo Bill" Cody rejoined the Fifth Cavalry as a scout in June 1876. The unit left Fort Laramie with orders to contain any Indians who had fled, or were about to flee, from the Red Cloud and Spotted Tail agencies in noncompliance with the Treaty of 1868. On July 17 Cody located a camp of about 1,000 Cheyennes. A war party from this camp was preparing to attack the cavalry's supply wagons, but Cody and some of the soldiers charged the Indians. Cody killed and scalped the Cheyenne subchief Yellow Hair. Don Russell, *The Lives and Legends of Buffalo Bill* (Norman: University of Oklahoma Press, 1960), 222–26. Paul L. Hedren, *First Scalp for Custer: The Skirmish at Warbonnet Creek, Nebraska, July 17, 1876* (Glendale: Arthur H. Clark Co., 1980), 67–68.

[11] According to Annie D. Tallent Colonel Brown was an agent of the Cheyenne and Black Hills Stage Company. On April 22, 1876, he and two companions were attacked in Red Canyon either by Indians or white bandits. They were rescued, but not before all three were wounded. Brown and his friends were taken to the stage station on the Cheyenne River, where Brown and one companion died. Tallent, *The Black Hills*, 120, 217–18.

Agnes Wright Spring gives almost the same account. Spring *The Cheyenne and Black Hills Stage and Express Routes*, 136–39.

Paul L. Hedren concluded that H. E. Brown was employed by the Cheyenne-Black Hills stage line when he was killed in an Indian raid on a coach on April 21 in Red Canyon. Hedren, *Fort Laramie in 1876*, 77–78.

[12] The Cheyenne-Black Hills Stage Line began running early in April 1876, when a six-horse coach left Cheyenne with eighteen passengers. Little more than a decade would pass before the railroads made the line obsolete. Inez Babb Taylor, "Career of Cheyenne-Black Hills Stage Line Owner, Colorful Story of the 'Old West,'" *Annals of Wyoming* 11 (1939):224–25.

The company had twenty-five stations between Cheyenne and Deadwood and had invested about $300,000. Curley, *Guide to the Black Hills*, 133.

Mr. Madden must have been an employee of J. W. Dear, who owned the ranche on the Cheyenne River at the time. Dear also had a ranche on the Niobrara early in the spring, but it burned. Somewhat later Jack Madden built another Niobrara River ranche. Spring, *The Cheyenne and Black Hills Stage and Express Routes*, 121, 124.

[13] In the summer of 1875 when Custer City was founded it was merely a stockade built by prospectors. Because the gold seekers were trespassing on Indian land the army forced them to leave. By the following year thousands of gold seekers flooded the Black Hills and the army was simply unable to halt the trespassers. The city boomed to more than 2,000 inhabitants, but there was an exodus after the discovery of gold near Deadwood. When Allen went through Custer City it had a population of only about 500. Strahorn, *The Hand-Book of Wyoming*, 234–37.

[14] Miners' rubies are garnets. Watson Parker, *Deadwood, The Golden Years* (Lincoln, University of Nebraska Press, 1981), 23.

6. On to Deadwood

[1] In May 1876 Hill City had about 150 houses with "an extremely neat and pleasing appearance," but without a single inhabitant. Failure to find gold in paying quantities led to the town's abandonment. Curley, *Guide to the Black Hills*, 54.

[2] Allen is referring to the Cheyenne-Black Hills Stage Line.

[3] A few squatters camped in Deadwood Gulch in 1875. The boom commenced the following spring and by the time of Allen's visit it had a population of several thousand. Strahorn, *The Hand-Book of Wyoming*, 231.

[4] Apparently Berry did not remain long in Deadwood for he was gone by 1878. Charles Collins, *Collins' Black Hills History and Directory for 1878–9* (Charles Collins, publisher, 1879).

[5] The earliest reference to a Green Front in Deadwood is an 1891 insurance map, which described it as a "female boarding house." Personal communication from Mark Wolfe, historic preservation officer, Deadwood, S. Dak. to Richard E. Jensen, Sept. 22, 1994. Allen may have confused the Deadwood establishment with Tim Higgens's saloon in Valentine, which was also called the Green Front. *Democratic Blade*, Sept. 25, 1885.

⁶ Annie D. Tallent was in Deadwood at about the same time as Allen and wrote about her experiences thirty years later. She begins with a very decorous history of the town and then turns to "Deadwood by Lamplight." Her descriptions of saloons, gambling houses, and "gaudily-attired, paint-bedaubed creatures—whom for grammatical accuracy we will call women" are similar to Allen's description, but more graphic. Tallent, *The Black Hills*, 262.

⁷ John W. "Captain Jack" Crawford had left the hills before Allen's arrival. His poetry was mediocre and his assignments as a scout were few, but he was an exceptional showman and became extremely popular, first appearing in Buffalo Bill Cody's show and then in his own. Darlis A Miller, *Captain Jack Crawford: Buckskin Poet, Scout, and Showman* (Albuquerque: University of New Mexico Press, 1993).

Martha "Calamity Jane" Cannary had been a frequent visitor to the Cuny and Ecoffey ranch when Allen worked for them in the early 1870s. Hedren, *Fort Laramie in 1876*, 115. According to L. G. Flannery she was one of the prostitutes there. Flannery, ed., *John Hunton's Diary*, 2:31.

Tallent recounted her conversation with James Butler Hickok and portrayed him as a very refined and chivalrous gentleman. She said, "Wild Bill was by no means all bad. It is hard to tell what environments may have conspired to mould his life into the desperate character he is said to have been." Tallent, *The Black Hills*, 73.

⁸ Contemporary accounts of other incidents described by Allen make it clear the date was February 1879. In Chapter 10 Allen tells of spending a winter building schools at Pine Ridge, but these were completed by February 1881. Certification signed by John Robinson and F. E. McGillycuddy, Feb. 22, 1881, Pine Ridge Agency letters, Roll 2; Valentine McGillycuddy, "Red Cloud Agency, 1881," *Annual Report, Indian Affairs*, 1881:49. Elsewhere Allen tells of meeting Agent James Irwin at Pine Ridge. Irwin left the agency on May 21, 1879. J. Irwin to E. A. Hayt, June 9, 1879, Red Cloud Agency letters, Roll 724. Allen says he moved to Pine Ridge "immediately after" the Cheyennes' attempted escape from Fort Robinson. This occurred in January 1879.

7. Old Fort Laramie

¹ Jacques LaRamie is frequently mentioned in western history, but remains a shadowy figure. Most writers suggest he was killed by Indians near the river bearing his name. LeRoy R. Hafen and Francis Marion Young, *Fort Laramie and the Pageant of the West* (Glendale: Arthur H. Clark Co., 1938), 20.

² William L. Sublette and Robert Campbell formed a partnership in 1832 and tried to compete with the giant American Fur Company on the upper Missouri. In 1834 Sublette and Campbell built Fort William near the mouth of the Laramie River. Most of the pelts and buffalo robes were purchased from Indians who regularly visited the fort.

In 1834 Pratte and Chouteau and Company bought part of the American Fur Company. Allen cannot be faulted for continuing to call it the American Company, because the name remained in the vernacular of the West despite the legal change. Pratte and Chouteau bought Fort William in 1836 and changed the name to Fort John. In 1841 the log structure was replaced with an adobe fort. Ibid, 4–13.

³ In 1932 Allen wrote to the Wyoming Department of History in Cheyenne requesting information on the history of Fort Laramie. Mrs. Cyrus Beard to C. Allen, Feb. 1, 1932, Allen Collection.

⁴ The young daughter of the Brulé Chief Spotted Tail became enamored with the life at Fort Laramie during a visit there in 1864. After her death two years later, Spotted Tail brought her body to the fort and placed it in a burial scaffold according to Brulé

custom, while an army honor guard performed their ceremony according to Christian military custom. Wilson O. Clough, "Mini-Aku, Daughter of Spotted Tail," *Annals of Wyoming* 39 (1967):187–216; Robert B. David, *Malcolm Campbell, Sheriff* (Casper, Wyo.: Wyomingiana, Inc., 1932), 37–42.

[5] Sgt. Leodegar Schnyder served at Fort Laramie from 1849 to 1886. It was alleged the sergeant kept loaded cannons about the fort and even positioned stovepipes to simulate more cannons. Hedren, *Fort Laramie in 1876*, 264, n. 59. Hedren felt the cannon story was fanciful and Allen's account of Schnyder seems equally implausible, although there may be a germ of truth somewhere in both.

[6] James Bordeaux came to Fort John in 1840 and was soon the defacto superintendent. When the army purchased the post, Bordeaux moved to a site about nine miles down the Platte River. Later, Allen correctly calls the site the Nine Mile Ranche, but does not locate Bordeaux there.

Bordeaux was married to a Brulé and the tribe was camped near the post in 1854 when Lt. J. L. Grattan's command was slaughtered. In 1868 Bordeaux abandoned the post to follow the Brulés to their new agency on the Missouri River. John Dishon McDermott, "James Bordeaux," *Mountain Men and the Fur Trade of the Far West* (Glendale: Arthur H. Clark Co., 1968), 5:65–80; Lloyd E. McCann, "The Grattan Massacre," *Nebraska History* 37 (1956):5.

[7] John Hunton recalled that Cy Williams and a man named Swalley were stationed at James Bordeaux's ranch on Chugwater Creek. In March 1868 Baptiste LaDeau, an employee, was killed there by Williams and Swalley. That summer Williams was murdered by LeDeau's friends, but not before he killed one of his attackers, Charley Richard, and wounded two others. There was no mention of the ranch being burned or that the Janis brothers were involved. Hunton, "Reminiscences by John Hunton," 268–69.

L. G. Flannery, the editor of John Hunton's diary, agrees that Williams was killed at Cuny and Ecoffey's ranch, but does not mention that it was burned. Flannery, ed., *John Hunton's Diary*, 1:39.

Allen may be combining two stories. Antoine Janis's sons, William and Peter, were killed in 1872 in a fight with the Richard brothers. LeCompte, "Antoine Janis," 200.

In the summer of 1865 Cuny & Ecoffey bought Geminien Beauvais' Five Mile Ranche below Fort Laramie. Charles E. Hanson, Jr., "Geminien P. Beauvais," *Mountain Men and the Fur Trade of the Far West* (Glendale: Arthur H. Clark Co., 1969), 7:35–43. Prior to this the post trader was J. P. B. Gratiot. McCann, "The Grattan Massacre," 5.

[8] Antoine DuBray was probably at Fort John in 1843 and then spent many years with the Arapahos and Apaches. In his later years he lived on the Rosebud Reservation. Harvey L. Carter, "Chat Dubray," *Mountain Men and the Fur Trade of the Far West* (Glendale: Arthur H. Clark Co., 1968), 6:143–46.

[9] The slaughter of the Mormons' cow and the events it precipitated was one of the major incidents in Fort Laramie history. Except for some details, Allen's hearsay version is an acceptable composite. It is somewhat more likely the Mormons abandoned the cow because it was so lame and nearly worthless.

The Mormons reported the loss of the animal to Lt. H. R. Fleming, commander of Fort Laramie. When the Brulé chief Conquering Bear (or Brave Bear) was apprised of the incident he hurried to the fort and offered to pay for the animal, but no action was taken on the proposal. The Oglala chief, Man Afraid of His Horses, also tried to mollify the post commander and the Mormons as well, but without success. McCann, "The Grattan Massacre," 6–7.

[10] The incident occurred on August 18, 1854. After pleading with the commanding officer for the assignment, Lt. John L. Grattan was ordered to arrest the culprit. He was

cautioned to use great care in arresting the guilty party, who had been identified as High Forehead, a Miniconjou staying in a very large camp of Brulés. On August 19 Grattan left the fort with twenty-nine soldiers. McCann, "The Grattan Massacre," 1–25; Hyde, *Spotted Tail's Folk*, 48–53.

[11] Auguste Lucien was the interpreter, but his role in the affair is uncertain. It has been suggested he was intoxicated and translated the Indian's words in such a way as to anger Grattan. Coincidentally, one of Lucien's daughters lived in Martin, South Dakota, in the 1920s when Allen was there. Hyde, *Spotted Tail's Folk*, 51.

[12] Conquering Bear again offered to pay for the cow, but Grattan stubbornly refused. High Forehead would not surrender and negotiations for him began to break down when the Indians started to threaten the soldiers. There is no other evidence to suggest Grattan had imposed a time limit as Allen claims, but at some point Grattan foolishly issued a command to fire on the Indians. Conquering Bear was killed in this volley. Several hundred Brulés, Oglalas, and Miniconjous immediately counterattacked and in a short time the entire command was killed. McCann, "The Grattan Massacre," 1–25; Hyde, *Spotted Tail's Folk*, 48–53.

[13] When the fighting started the outnumbered soldiers began to retreat. The interpreter and one soldier galloped through the Brulé camp and past Bordeaux's post. They were overtaken and the Lakotas first crippled their horses and finally killed the two men. McCann, "The Grattan Massacre," 19.

[14] Grattan was buried at Fort Laramie and the soldiers were interred in a mass grave at the scene of the fight. McCann, "The Grattan Massacre," 23–24. Later, the soldiers were reinterred at Fort McPherson National Cemetery.

[15] Fort Laramie was abandoned by the army in 1890 and the buildings and land sold at auction. Less than twenty years later Wyoming preservationists began working for public acquisition of the site. In 1937 the Wyoming legislature appropriated funds to purchase the site and it was turned over to the National Park Service. Mattes, *Fort Laramie Park History*, 54, 108.

8. The Founding of Pine Ridge

[1] In September 1878 three-hundred Cheyennes under Dull Knife and Little Wolf deserted their reservation in present Oklahoma in a daring attempt to return to their old homeland in Montana. In northeastern Colorado they separated. Little Wolf's people disappeared for a time in the Nebraska Sand Hills, but were eventually captured. Dull Knife's group of about 150 was captured on October 24 and taken to Fort Robinson, where they were imprisoned while the government tried to decide what to do with them. On January 9, 1879, the group made a desperate dash for freedom across the frozen parade ground of the fort. Some were shot within a few steps of their prison, but others did reach the rugged bluffs west of the fort. Their situation was hopeless and they were soon overwhelmed by the army and seventy-nine were recaptured. The rest died in the so-called Cheyenne Outbreak. Corbusier, "Camp Sheridan, Nebraska," 41–42.

[2] The Red Cloud and Spotted Tail agencies were established in northwestern Nebraska in 1874. Since these locations were outside the Lakota reservation and since it was very costly to transport annuities so far overland, Congress authorized moving them on August 15, 1876. The new Red Cloud Agency was on the west side of the Missouri River northwest of present Lower Brulé, South Dakota, and just below Medicine Creek. Allen calls it Yellow Medicine Creek. The abandoned Ponca Agency on the west side of the river due east of present Verdel, Nebraska, became the new Spotted Tail agency. Both locations could be easily and cheaply supplied by steamboat, but the Oglalas and the Brulés complained bitterly about these locations be-

cause they did not want to leave the more familiar home in western South Dakota. The move to the Missouri began in October 1877, but only after the Lakota were promised that the agencies on the river would be temporary. James Irwin, "Red Cloud Agency," *Annual Report, Indian Affairs,* 1878:36–38. Ray H. Mattison, "Report on the Historic Sites in the Big Bend Reservoir Area, Missouri River, South Dakota," *South Dakota Historical Collections and Reports* 31 (1962):255–57; Ray H. Mattison, "Report on the Historic Sites Adjacent to the Missouri River Between the Big Sioux River and Fort Randall Dam," *South Dakota Historical Collections and Reports* 28 (1956):88–89.

In the spring and summer of 1878, not 1879 as Allen claimed, they moved back to their old homeland. The Brulés went to the present day Rosebud Agency, while the Oglalas went to present Pine Ridge Agency. Irwin, "Red Cloud Agency," (1878), 37.

[3] Dr. James Irwin began his duties on June 27, 1877. Irwin, "Red Cloud Agency,"(1877), 62. On January 1, 1879, he submitted his letter of resignation in which he severely criticized the commissioner of Indian affairs for incompetency. J. Irwin to E. A. Hayt, Jan. 1, 1879, Red Cloud Agency letters, Roll 724. Irwin left the agency on May 21, 1879. J. Irwin to E. A. Hayt, June 9, 1879, Red Cloud Agency letters, roll 724.

On March 10, 1879, Valentine T. McGillycuddy arrived on the reservation to replace Irwin. V. McGillycuddy to E. A. Hayt, Mar. 17, 1879, Red Cloud Agency letters, Roll 724.

[4] James Rowen O'Beirne enlisted in the New York volunteers during the Civil War and reached the rank of brigadier general. Heitman, *Historical Register,* 755. In 1878 he was a special agent of the Office of Indian Affairs sent from Washington, D.C., to supervise moving the Lakotas from the Missouri River agency to Pine Ridge. He was also responsible for the construction of the new agency. His appointment was from September 21, 1878, to June 20, 1879. C. Schurz to E. A. Hayt, July 9, 1879, Red Cloud Agency letters, Roll 724.

[5] Capt. William H. Jordan, Ninth Infantry, assumed command of Camp Robinson in June 1874. Grange, "Fort Robinson, Outpost on the Plains," 203.

Charles Philander Jordan's career is summarized in William Red Cloud Jordan's, "Eighty Years on the Rosebud," South Dakota Historical Society, *Report and Historical Collections* 35, (1970):323–83. He also had a ranch on the Rosebud Reservation and in the late 1890s staged wild west shows. He was a trader at Rosebud from 1883 to 1901. Charles P. Jordan Papers, H74.42, South Dakota Historical Society, Pierre.

During the time Allen worked at Pine Ridge, Jordan was in serious trouble with Agent McGillycuddy. The agent accused him of "dissipated habits" and requested his permanent removal from the reservation. V. McGillycuddy to C. Schurz, Jan. 19, 1880, Red Cloud Agency letters, Roll 726.

Jordan was the chief clerk while Irwin was agent, but he was replaced by J. W. Alder when McGillycuddy became the agent. V. McGillycuddy to E. A. Hayt, Mar. 17, 1879, Red Cloud Agency letters, Roll 724. There is no evidence in the records of the Office of Indian Affairs to suggest that Jordan was transferred to Rosebud Landing. The landing was due west of present Academy, South Dakota, on the west side of the Missouri River just above Dry Creek. Mattison, "Report on Historic Sites," 28.

[6] This was probably Louis Benjamin Lessert, a mixed blood Osage and legal resident of the reservation. He was a licensed trader at the agency. G. L. Brown to commissioner, June 30, 1892, Jan. 18 and Feb. 7, 1893, Pine Ridge Agency letters, Roll 19.

[7] George F. Blanchard was a licensed trader who built a frame store twenty-five by fifty feet in 1879. Two log additions served as storerooms. V. McGillycuddy to E. A. Hayt, Dec. 12, 1879, Pine Ridge Agency letters, Roll 2.

[8] Near the end of 1879 licensed trader Thomas Cowgill was building a store of squared logs. Agent McGillycuddy estimated he had between $12,000 and $15,000 worth of goods on hand. V. McGillycuddy to E. A. Hayt, Dec. 12, 1879, Pine Ridge Agency letters, Roll 2.

Cowgill had been at Pine Ridge only a few months before he was accused of selling whiskey and running a "gambling hell." P. R. Johnson to secretary of the interior, Jan. 20, 1880, Red Cloud Agency letters, Roll 726. In May he was charged with taking grain from the agency warehouse and selling it to Indians. John Heister testimony, May 6, 1880, Ibid. Cowgill was never found guilty of any wrongdoing.

[9] In the latter part of 1880 David Cockrell contracted to build three schoolhouses on the reservation for which he was paid $1,500. Certification signed by John Robinson and F. E. McGillycuddy, Feb. 22, 1881, Pine Ridge Agency letters, Roll 1. Allen worked for him on this job. In 1893 Cockrell was operating an ice business in Chadron. *Chadron Advocate*, Mar. 20, 1891.

[10] Henry Janis was killed on September 2, 1891. Since it was considered to be an accident, no special effort was made to learn the identity of the one who fired the fatal shot. The agent considered slaughtering cattle in a mock buffalo hunt to be "barbarous" and recommended the practice be discontinued immediately. C. Penney to commissioner, Sept. 17, 1891, Pine Ridge Agency letters, Roll 12. The event was also recalled by Jordan, "Eighty Years on the Rosebud," 332.

In March 1892 orders were issued directing agency policemen to shoot the cattle in a holding pen and then drag the carcasses out to be issued to families. G. L. Brown to I. J. Stowitts, Mar. 22, 1892, Pine Ridge Agency letters, Roll 14. The Indians complained about this practice, but the agent did not give their protests serious consideration. G. L. Brown to commissioner, Mar. 28, 1892, Ibid. Four years later the Indians living in the White Clay District northwest of the agency were still staging the mock hunts on issue day. According to the agent "nearly all of the malcontents and former hostiles" of the Ghost Dance era lived there and were the most unwilling to change. W. Clapp to commissioner, Aug. 22, 1896, Pine Ridge Agency letters, Roll 26.

[11] In 1881 the Pine Ridge Reservation had a population of 7,202. Rosebud had 7,688 people. These were among the largest, but dwarfed by Union Agency of Choctaw, Cherokee, and Creek with over 50,000. H. Price, "Report of the Commissioner of Indian Affairs," *Annual Report, Indian Affairs*, 1881:276, 280.

Reservation politics frequently shifted alliances, but generally Red Dog did support Red Cloud. Red Dog was a member of the Loafer band and, unlike Red Cloud, was in favor of an agency on the White River. J. E. Smith to assistant adjutant general, Sept. 27, 1872, Red Cloud Agency letters, Roll 715. After months of arguing, it was Red Dog with a few others who selected the site for the agency on Little White Clay Creek. Olson, *Red Cloud and the Sioux Problem*, 150, 273.

[12] Names of the divisions of the Oglala found in historic sources were examined by William K. Powers, who abundantly demonstrated that they were not static and that the ideal seven council fires was the exception. William K. Powers, *Oglala Religion* (Lincoln: University of Nebraska Press, 1975), 28–31.

Allen's Names		Powers's names	
Eta Secha	Bad Face	Itesica	Bad face
Keyoksa	Cut Off	Kiyaksa	To divide by speaking
O yu Ghe Pe	Pulls Down	Oyuhpe	To throw down, away
Wa Ga Ku Ka	Loafers	Wagluhe	Gather up scraps
Wa Za Za	Osage	Wajaje	Osage
Chee Hu Hu Tum	Legs on a Pot*	Payabya	Head of the circle*
Eya Secha	Bad Talkers	Tapisleca	Split liver

Wo Gha Yuta Sne	Don't Eat Fish
Wan Na Wa Ge	Broken Arrow

* Allen and Powers agree that Young Man Afraid of His Horses was the leader of this band.

[13] Allen was told that Bull Bear was killed by Red Cloud when the former tried to rescue a woman from his band who had been stolen by a man from Red Cloud's band. Sheldon, *Life of Red Cloud*, 33–34.

George Hyde offered a different story. In a fit of anger, Bull Bear, chief of the Oglalas, killed a horse belonging to Smoke, who was the white traders' choice for head chief. In November 1841 Smoke and his friends, including Red Cloud, saw a chance to get revenge when Bull Bear and some of his men wandered into Smoke's camp. Smoke gave the Bull Bear people liquor and then started an argument. When Bull Bear rushed forward to prevent a fight he was shot and killed, perhaps by Red Cloud. The incident divided the Oglalas, but it was many years before Red Cloud became a recognized leader. Hyde, *Red Cloud's Folk*, 53–55.

[14] The following typed footnote was at the bottom of the page in Allen's manuscript. "My understanding is that the Cut-Offs or Kayas were so named somewhere long before the killing of Bull Bear by Red Cloud—probably before the coming of white men in any number. —Mari Sandoz." Allen was told the name literally meant "bitten in two." Sheldon, *Life of Red Cloud*, 34–35.

[15] By the early 1870s Little Wound was the leader of the Cutoffs, who numbered about 300. At the time he was not overly concerned about obeying the rules laid down by the Office of Indian Affairs. E. D. Townsend to secretary of interior, Nov. 9, 1872, Red Cloud Agency letters, Roll 716.

Allen somewhat overestimates the friendship between Little Wound and Red Cloud. There were several incidents when they opposed one another. Olson, *Red Cloud and the Sioux Problem*, 273–82.

9. Changing Conditions

[1] Dr. McGillycuddy served as the Sioux agent from March 10, 1879, until May 8, 1886. Like all agents of his time, he attempted to remake the Indians in the image of the whites. Julia Blanchard McGillycuddy, *McGillycuddy-Agent, A Biography of Dr. Valentine T. McGillycuddy* (Stanford: Stanford University Press, 1941).

Allen avoids judging the people about whom he writes. However it is evident from his letters that he did not like McGillycuddy. He accused the agent of "unjust and unreasonable bitterness" towards white men married to Native American women. C. Allen to A. E. Sheldon, May 29, 1936, Allen Collection. In 1941 Allen was asked to review *McGillycuddy-Agent* for *Nebraska History*, the Nebraska State Historical Society's quarterly magazine. In his letter of refusal to Superintendent Addison Sheldon Allen wrote, "But now, having read it from cover to cover, I regret that you should have gone to the trouble of sending it to me." Allen described the book as going "thru some exceptionally misty clouds of egoism, [and I] find myself unable to distinguish glorified personal actions and movements of trivial nature from real historic incidents." C. Allen to A. E. Sheldon, May 1941, Allen Collection.

In early May 1879 Special Agent O'Beirne reported that the Oglalas had begun plowing for the first time. J. R. O'Beirne to E. A. Hayt, May 7, 1879, Red Cloud Agency letters, Roll 725.

[2] McGillycuddy wanted the chief to live in a frame house in the hope it would encourage others to do the same. The four-room house with a kitchen lean-to was completed late in 1879. Olson, *Red Cloud and the Sioux Problem*, 267, n.6.

[3] The old Red Cloud Agency near the confluence of Medicine Creek with the Missouri River was approximately 190 miles from Pine Ridge. V. T. McGillycuddy to E. A. Hayt, Feb. 11, 1880, Pine Ridge Agency letters, Roll 2.

[4] In October 1878 the Oglalas received one hundred wagons and harnesses for hauling freight, but the agent thought there were fewer than a dozen men who could drive a team. Within a year the Oglala were regularly using a four-horse hitch to haul 2,400 pounds of freight from Rosebud Landing to the Pine Ridge Agency. McGillycuddy, "Red Cloud Agency, 1879," *Annual Report, Indian Affairs,* 39.

Allen may have witnessed the second issue of wagons in April 1879, when Agent McGillycuddy led a caravan of 120 to Rosebud Landing. V. McGillycuddy to E. A. Hayt, Apr. 25, 1879, Red Cloud Agency letters, Roll 724. No doubt there was a "rodeo exhibition" while the Lakotas broke their riding ponies to the harnesses.

In September 1879 Secretary of the Interior Carl Schurz visited the reservation and pronounced the "freighting experiment" a success. C. Schurz to E. A. Hayt, Sept. 4, 1879, Red Cloud Agency letters, Roll 724. By February 1881 the freight for the agency was being carried by Lakota teamsters. McGillycuddy, "Red Cloud Agency, 1879," *Annual Report, Indian Affairs,* 39.

[5] George F. Blanchard and Thomas Cowgill were the licensed traders. Together they may have had $30,000 in stock. V. McGillycuddy to E. A. Hayt, Dec. 12, 1879, Pine Ridge Agency letters, Roll 2.

[6] It was necessary to import lime. C. Schurz to E. A. Hayt, Nov. 13, 1879, Red Cloud Agency letters, Roll 724.

Allen's decision "to take a vacation from the freight line" may have been forced upon him. While searching for lime, he was also looking for work. He submitted a bid to Agent McGillicuddy to cut 250 cords of wood for $2.75 per cord, but nothing was found suggesting he received the contract. C. Allen to V. McGillycuddy, Aug. 9, 1879, National Archives, Central Plains Region, Record Group 75, Pine Ridge Agency, #3 Miscellaneous Correspondence Received.

[7] The school Allen helped build measured twenty by thirty feet. An addition measuring fifteen by thirty-six feet was divided into three rooms for the teacher's quarters. Certification signed by John Robinson and F. E. McGillycuddy, Feb. 22, 1881, Pine Ridge Agency letters, Roll 2. McGillycuddy, "Red Cloud Agency, 1881," *Annual Report, Indian Affairs,* 49. The roof was covered with tarpaper and then capped with a layer of sod. V. McGillycuddy to K. E. Trowbridge, Apr. 13, 1880, Pine Ridge Agency letters, Roll 2.

[8] George Catlin tells of the suicidal rampage of the Lakota leader, One Horn, after the death of his son. One Horn swore to kill the first thing to stand in his way and it proved to be a large rutting buffalo bull. Both died in the exchange. Catlin, *Letters and Notes,* 1:221.

[9] Rev. Amos Ross, an Episcopal missionary from the Santee Reservation in northeastern Nebraska, came to Pine Ridge in December 1880 and taught school at Two Lance's camp about two miles north of the Wounded Knee massacre site. Ricker Collection, Interviews, Tablets 26 and 75.

10. Building for Schools

[1] Henry C. Clifford traveled with Little Wound and other Lakota bands in the early 1870s. E. O. C. Ord to assistant adjutant general, Nov. 1, 1872, Red Cloud Agency letters, Roll 716.

By the end of the decade Clifford ran the Niobrara Crossing station on the road from Fort Laramie to Fort Robinson. Clarence Schnurr, "Edgar Beecher Bronson," *Sioux*

County, Memoirs of its Pioneers, ed. Ruth Van Ackeren (Harrison, Nebr.: Harrison Ladies' Community Club, 1967).

Clifford completed construction of two schools on Porcupine Creek and one near the agency by the end of 1881. Certification signed by John Robinson and F. E. McGillycuddy, Dec. 20, 1881, Pine Ridge Agency letters, Roll 1.

Allen may have worked on a building at the agency, but it could not have been the school. Compared to the small, sod-roofed country schools, the schoolhouse at the agency was palatial. It was a heavy frame structure, thirty-five by one hundred feet, with a gabled roof and bell tower. Construction began under the direction of Special Agent O'Beirne at least a month before the arrival of either Allen or McGillycuddy. J. R. O'Beirne to E. A. Hayt, Feb. 12, 1879, Red Cloud Agency letters, Roll 725.

[2] John Y. Nelson, a West Virginia native, joined the Lakotas in 1853. He married the daughter of Lone Horn, an Oglala. *Omaha Weekly Bee*, July 4, 1883. In the 1880s he joined William F. Cody's Wild West Show. Russell, *The Lives and Legends of Buffalo Bill*, 308.

Around 1880 Nelson joined with Henry Clifford and his brother in a venture to trade whiskey to the Lakotas for horses the Indians had stolen. The partners then sold the horses back to the whites. Harrington O'Reilly, *Fifty Years on the Trail; Remarkable Story of the Life of John Y. Nelson*, (Norman: University of Oklahoma Press, 1963), 244–45.

[3] Allen is probably referring to John W. Wham who was appointed late in 1870 to be the Indian agent for the Lakota. He served for just one year. Olson, *Red Cloud and the Sioux Problem*, 132, 143.

High Wolf was a recognized Oglala leader, who participated in most of the major tribal decisions in the 1870s and 1880s. Olson, *Red Cloud and the Sioux Problem*, 163, 192.

[4] William H. Hare was the Protestant Episcopal bishop for South Dakota. M. A. DeWolfe Howe, *The Life and Labors of Bishop Hare* (New York: Sturgis and Walton Co., 1913). In August 1879 he brought two missionaries to Pine Ridge, who began teaching school at the agency. W. Hare to J. W. Alder, Aug. 26, 1879, Red Cloud Agency letters, Roll 725.

A school on Wounded Knee Creek eighteen miles northeast of the agency was being taught by Julia McCloskey Kocer. She was listed as the "principal teacher" and her husband, Joseph, was the "industrial teacher." They had forty-eight students. Another day school was at the Little Wound camp on Medicine Root Creek thirty-five miles northeast of the agency. It was taught by Joseph Marshell. Monthly School Report for July 1880, Red Cloud Agency letters, Roll 726.

Classes were being taught by the Kocers in the spring of 1880 and possibly earlier. V. McGillycuddy to R. E. Train, Sept. 8, 1880, ibid. Apparently the classes were held in temporary structures for the Indian bureau did not begin building day schools until the fall of 1880.

St. Mary's School for Girls was at the Santee Reservation. K. Brent Woodruff, "The Episcopal Missions to the Dakotas," *South Dakota Historical Collections* 17 (1934):580.

[5] Later Allen identifies James McCloskey as being from Marysville, Kansas. Although a lengthy list of founders and early businessmen of Marysville has been compiled, McCloskey's name was not included. Frank W. Blackman, ed., *Kansas, a Cyclopedia of State History* (Chicago: Standard Publishing Co., 1912), 2:245–46. McCloskey was the interpreter who went to Washington with Red Cloud and other leaders in 1870. Olson, *Red Cloud and the Sioux Problem*, 97.

John R. Dowty of Falls City, Richardson County, was elected for the 1881 term to the Nebraska House of Representatives by a sixty-five vote margin. Falls City, Nebr. *Globe-Journal*, Nov. 6, 1880.

[6] The Iowa tribe lived on the Great Nemaha Reservation located in the extreme northeast corner of Kansas. A boarding school was opened in the spring of 1881. Augustus Brosius, "Great Nemaha Reservation," *Annual Report, Indian Affairs*, 1881:123–24.

[7] Later William A. Coffield was employed as a farmer and his wife was the teacher at Porcupine Creek. W. A. Coffield to V. McGillycuddy, Nov. 18, 1885, National Archives, Central Plains Region, Record Group 75, Pine Ridge Agency, #3 Miscellaneous Correspondence Received.

The telegraph to Pine Ridge was installed in the latter part of 1880. V. McGillycuddy to R. E. Train, Sept. 10, 1880, Red Cloud Agency letters, Roll 726.

[8] Mr. Palmer was not mentioned in the Pine Ridge records.

[9] Robert O. Pugh, a native of Great Britain, had been in the West for about twenty years and had held a variety of jobs at the agency for the past ten years. He was married to a Lakota woman. Danker, "Wounded Knee Interviews of Eli S. Ricker," 224; *Chadron Democrat*, June 17, 1886, and Feb. 12, 1891. Pine Ridge Agent Royer called him the head herder. D. F. Royer to T. J. Morgan, Jan. 3, 1891, National Archives, Record Group 94, Records of the Adjutant General's Office, Reports and Correspondence Relating to the Army Investigations of the Battle of Wounded Knee and to the Sioux Campaign of 1890–1891, Microcopy 983 (hereafter cited as Reports, Campaign of 1890–91).

Jenney's Stockade was a short distance west of Custer City. The army's Camp Jenney was established on June 3, 1875, by Lt. Col. Richard Irving Dodge, who was in command of a military escort for a scientific party exploring the Black Hills. Walter P. Janney was the geologist with the party. Lesta V. Turchen and James D. McLaird, *The Black Hills Expedition of 1875* (Mitchell, S. Dak.: Dakota Wesleyan University Press, 1975).

11. Trails and Trials of a Primitve People

[1] This chapter replaces one titled "Short Bull—Brigand of the Badlands" in an earlier draft. "Short Bull" was published in the *Chadron Democrat*, Jan. 22, 1891. Allen sent a copy to his friend Elmo Scott Watson, who published it in the *Publishers' Auxiliary*, Jan. 31, 1942, and Jan. 7, 1942.

[2] Sam Deon began trading with the Lakota in the early 1850s and married one of the women of the tribe. Deon was a good friend of Red Cloud and in 1893 Deon persuaded the old chief to tell his life story. Deon repeated the stories to Allen, who wrote them down in note form. R. Eli Paul, "Recovering Red Cloud's Autobiography," 8–9.

[3] This story was also in Sheldon, *Life of Red Cloud*, 104–12. The white trader's name was Leghan, probably a corruption of a French name. The event occurred in 1861.

[4] The part of the story Allen enclosed in quotation marks was copied almost word for word from Sheldon, *Life of Red Cloud*, 113–22.

Casper Collins recorded the same story when he was in the army stationed in the Fort Laramie vicinity. Collins was there from 1862 until his death in 1865. The two versions are strikingly similar, but there are differences. For example, Allen tells us that the fight between the Sioux and the Cheyenne started when a Cheyenne stole the wife of a Sioux, but Collins had a Sioux abducting a Cheyenne woman. Agnes Wright Spring, *Casper Collins: The Life and Exploits of an Indian Fighter* (Lincoln: University of Nebraska Press, 1969), 174–77.

12. The First White Men among the Indians

[1] The rumor can not be supported by the historical record.

² Joseph Vlandry was ordered to leave the Pine Ridge Reservation in 1891 for selling whiskey. He moved just over the border into Nebraska, where he continued his trade. In 1893 he was awaiting trial for this illegal activity. C. G. Penney to commissioner, Sept. 26, 1893, Pine Ridge Agency letters, Roll 21.

John Y. Nelson was hired by a Vlandry to interpret while on a trading expedition to the Wajajas north of Rawhide Butte about 1850. O'Reilly, *Fifty Years on the Trail*, 97.

³ Frank Salway was born in 1828 of French and Indian parents. He held a variety of government jobs in South Dakota beginning as an assistant farmer in 1868. He was at Fort Robinson when Crazy Horse was killed. In 1906 he was living eight miles northeast of Allen, South Dakota. Ricker Collection, Interviews, Tablet 26, 71, and Tablet 27, 1–2.

Fort Pierre was a fur trading post founded in 1832. In 1855 it was purchased by the government for use as a military post. Harold H. Schuler, *Fort Pierre Chouteau* (Vermillion: University of South Dakota Press, 1990).

⁴ Neither "The Strong Man" or Frank Salway were listed in the index of the Historical Society's publications.

⁵ The Treaty of 1868 defined a reservation for the Sioux, but since there was not yet any demand for the land by whites this reservation included nearly all the territory claimed by the Indians. It extended west from the Missouri River to the Big Horn Mountains and north from the forty-sixth parallel to Canada. Hunting was allowed south of the southern boundary. In addition, the Sioux would receive annuities for thirty years. Charles J. Kappler, *Indian Affairs, Laws and Treaties* (Washington: GPO, 1903), 770–75.

13. The Advent of the Railroad

¹ The Fremont, Elkhorn, and Missouri Valley Railroad reached Thatcher, Nebraska, about six miles southeast of Valentine, in 1882. This was the end of the line for nearly a year while the precipitous rocky cliffs along the Niobrara River were graded and a bridge was built across the river. The first business buildings at Valentine were erected in the spring of 1882. Albert Watkins, *History of Nebraska* (Lincoln: Western Publishing Co., 1913), 3:448–49 and *Valentine Reporter*, Aug. 9, 1883.

Charles H. Cornell was among the pioneer developers of Valentine. According to the *Valentine Reporter* (Jan. 17, 1884) he homesteaded the land where Valentine was later founded, but land records show David Y. Mears as the original owner. Cornell bought many lots after the town was platted in April 1883. Marianne Brinda Beel, ed., *A Sandhill Century: Book 1 The Land* (Henderson, Nebr.: Service Press, 1986), 1:264.

When Allen met Cornell the firm of Thatcher and Cornell had a large general merchandise store in Valentine. By the early 1900s Cornell was the president of the Nebraska Stock Growers Association and lobbied in Washington for legislation to allow cattle ranchers to lease large sections of government land thus excluding the small homesteader. Bartlett Richards, Jr., *Bartlett Richards, Nebraska Sandhills Cattleman* (Lincoln: Nebraska State Historical Society, 1980), 131–34.

Cornell worked at the sutler's store at Fort Niobrara in 1880 and then opened a store in Valentine and later a bank. *Compendium of History, Reminiscence and Biography of Western Nebraska* (Chicago: Alden Publishing Co., 1909), 124.

Fort Niobrara was one of the ten new military posts built in 1880. The principal purpose of the forts was to contain the Indians on the Sioux Reservation in case of a threatened uprising. About 300 men of the Fifth Cavalry, Fourth Infantry, and Ninth Infantry were stationed at the fort when Allen began working at the warehouse in Valentine in April 1883. Thomas R. Buecker, "Fort Niobrara, 1880–1906: Guardian of the Rosebud Sioux," *Nebraska History* 65 (1984):300–25: Frazier, *Forts of the West*, 89.

[2] J. M. Thatcher served for many years as the sutler at Fort Niobrara. Buecker, "Fort Niobrara, 1880–1906," 304.

His brother, Albert, also worked at the fort and later had a general store in Valentine. Olive Van Metre, *The Old Town, 1880–1889* (Norfolk, Nebr.: Norfolk Printing Co., 1977), 42.

In the postal records the name of the town is rendered Thacher. The post office was established in February 1884 and discontinued in August 1889. Record of Appointment of Postmasters, Roll 77.

[3] The army built the telegraph line from Fort Robinson to Camp Sheridan. In the latter part of 1880 an extension was strung to Pine Ridge using Indian laborers. McGillycuddy, "Red Cloud Agency, 1880," *Annual Report, Indian Affairs*, 1880:41 and V. McGillycuddy to R. E. Train, Sept. 10, 1880, Red Cloud Agency letters, Roll 726.

[4] Richard C. Stirk came from Indiana in 1870. He trailed cattle from Texas, hauled freight between Sidney and the Black Hills, and campaigned with Gen. George Crook. He carried the first news stories of the Wounded Knee massacre to the telegraph office at Rushville. Danker, "Wounded Knee Interviews of Eli S. Ricker," 217–19. He died in 1942 at age 87 at Rushville, Nebraska. *Publishers' Auxiliary*, Jan. 17, 1942.

While Allen may have hauled "moveable property" from the landing on Medicine Creek, it would have been prior to the coming of the railroad to the Niobrara River in 1882. The Indian bureau was ready to remove building lumber from the landing in the summer of 1879. V. McGillycuddy to E. A. Hayt, June 19, 1879, Red Cloud Agency letters, Roll 724.

[5] Butter was preserved by boiling it, removing any foam or scum, and then sealing it in an airtight container. Lass, *From the Missouri to the Great Salt Lake*, 14.

[6] James "Scotty" Philip came from Scotland and settled in Kansas in 1874. A year later he moved to Cheyenne, Wyoming, and then to the Black Hills, where he was an unsuccessful gold prospector before becoming a freighter. In 1879 he married a Lakota and began ranching north of White Clay Creek on the Pine Ridge Reservation. In 1881 they moved to the Bad River, where Philip built up a highly successful ranch including a herd of buffalo. He died unexpectedly in 1911. Lee, *Scotty Philip, The Man Who Saved The Buffalo*.

Fort Pierre was a trading post purchased by the army in 1855 but because of insufficient grass and timber in the area it was abandoned just two years later. Frazer, *Forts of the West*, 136.

14. Meeting Civilization

[1] The distinguished visitors were members of the 1883 Sioux Commission, who were traveling throughout the reservations in an attempt to convince the Lakota to surrender more of their land. The commission had been appointed by Secretary of the Interior Henry M. Teller and consisted of his brother, James H. Teller, Peter Shannon, an elderly South Dakota lawyer, and Newton Edmonds, who had negotiated treaties a decade earlier. Missionary Samuel D. Hinman served as the interpreter and was probably with them. Mr. Butterfield, the Indian inspector, was not mentioned as a member of the commission. Olson, *Red Cloud and the Sioux Problem*, 287.

[2] Stephen F. Estes was the receiving clerk for annuity goods unloaded at Valentine and Allen was one of his many employees. For a year the government warehouse had been at Thatcher, but in mid-May it was being dismantled for the move to Valentine. *Valentine Reporter*, May 17, 1883. The Valentine warehouse measured forty by two-hundred feet. It was south of the railroad tracks. Ibid., Jan. 17, 1884.

[3] Frank Dorr opened the blacksmith shop in the summer of 1883. *Valentine Reporter*, July 12, 1883. Allen purchased a half interest in it in March 1884. Ibid., Mar. 6,

1884. A month later the newspaper reported that David S. Cockrell bought Dorr's interest in the shop, but Allen was not mentioned. Dorr stayed on to do the blacksmithing. Ibid., Apr. 3, 1884.

The 1885 census for the village of Valentine lists six blacksmiths, F. Dorr, D.S. Cockeral [sic], C. Allen, Julius Dorr, J. Paxton, and J. Lumis. National Archives, *Schedules of the Nebraska State Census of 1885*, RG 29, Microcopy 352, Village of Valentine, 3–13. Those not affiliated with Allen must have worked for the railroad. Allen's wife and children were not listed in this census.

[4] Gambling by "the boys" was frequently mentioned in the *Valentine Reporter*. An article on May 10, 1883, explained they ran a mobile card room and had just spent a week near Fort Niobrara "picking up loose change from the soldiers."

[5] In August 1884 the Chicago and Northwestern took over the Fremont, Elkhorn, and Missouri Valley Railroad, but the name was not changed until 1903. *Chadron Centennial History*, 22.

While Allen correctly recalled many Valentine businesses, the relative locations are frequently at odds with land records dating from the 1880s.

Joseph A. "Al" Sparks worked at Fort Niobrara before coming to Valentine, where he opened the Tracy and Sparks general store. The partnership was dissolved during the summer of 1883, but the general merchandise business was continued under the name Sparks Brothers and Company. *Valentine Reporter*, July 26, 1883. In the summer of 1883 brother Eldon Sparks arrived and they opened the Cherry County Bank. Van Meter, *The Old Town*, 59. The business was located on the west side of Main Street a short distance north of Railroad Street.

There was also the OK Barber Shop owned by John Thomas. *Valentine Reporter*, Aug. 2, 1883. Dr. Alfred Lewis not only practiced medicine but sold a variety of drugs, perfume, paint, and glass. *Valentine Reporter*, May 3, 1883. Joe Hall owned the Phoenix saloon. It offered wine, liquor, Milwaukee beer, and a fifteen-ball pool table and was praised as "the nobbiest building in town." Ibid., May 24, 1883. F. H. Warren operated the Chrystal Palace advertising only wine, liquor, and cigars. Ibid., May 3, 1883. In 1883 Warren was elected county judge. Ibid., Nov. 15, 1883.

[6] Perry Lawson's barber shop was on the next lot north of the *Valentine Reporter*. Lawson had been an orderly at Fort Niobrara. Beel, ed., *A Sandhill Century*, 1:265.

Robert Fink and Peter Donoher opened the Valentine House, the only hotel in town. *Valentine Reporter*, June 28, 1883. In the fall Donoher bought out his partner. Ibid, Oct. 25, 1883. He later opened the OK Saloon, but sold both in 1887. Van Metre, *The Old Town*, 57.

In October 1883 the *Valentine Reporter* moved into new quarters north of the Valentine House. *Valentine Reporter*, Nov. 1, 1883. David Y. Mears resigned as postmaster and Burley C. Hill took his place on October 9, 1883. Record of Appointment of Postmasters, Roll 77. The *Valentine Reporter* discontinued publication in the summer of 1883. *Valentine Reporter*, May 3, 1883 and *Democratic Blade*, Sept. 18, 1885.

[7] Edward McDonald came from Leadville, Colorado, where he had a store. Van Metre, *The Old Town*, 64. He sold hardware, tinware, furniture, and paint in his store in Valentine. *Valentine Reporter*, May 3, 1883. The store was on the south side of Catharine near Cherry Street. Beel, ed., *A Sandhill Century*, 1:269.

William H. Carter's Stock Exchange Saloon was on the west side of Main Street four buildings from Catharine Street. Ibid., 1:267. It was one of the first businesses to open in Valentine. Van Metre, *The Old Town*, 84.

Henry and John Stetter's butcher shop was the second building north of the northeast corner of Main and Catharine street. Beel, ed., *A Sandhill Century*, 1:265. They had been cattle ranchers in the Sidney, Nebraska, area in the early 1870s and came to the Niobrara valley with the opening of the fort. Van Metre, *The Old Town*, 8–9. In 1884 John opened a saloon in Valentine and shortly thereafter ran a meat market in Chadron until 1890 when he returned to Valentine. *Compendium of History, Reminiscence and Biography of Western Nebraska*, 646–47.

Tim Higgins's saloon may have been north of Warren's saloon. Beel, ed., *A Sandhill Century*, 1:265. It was called the Green Front. *Democratic Blade*, Sept. 25, 1885.

[8] The courthouse was on the northwest corner of Virginia and Main streets. Hiram Cornell purchased the hewn timber structure at Green Bay, Wisconsin, disassembled it, and moved it to Valentine in 1884. Beel, ed., *A Sandhill Century*, 1:268.

[9] When Allen arrived David Y. Mears was a county commissioner of the newly formed Cherry County. *Valentine Reporter*, June 7, 1883. Mears returned to his home in the east in the fall. Ibid., Oct. 4, 1883. In the late 1880s he lived in Chadron. Shepherd, *Man of Many Frontiers*, 411.

[10] This may have been Rev. J. Herbert, a Congregational minister from Neligh, who began preaching in Valentine on alternate Sundays in May 1883. *Valentine Reporter*, May 31, 1883.

[11] Kirkley's "Hog Ranch" was southwest of the depot. Beel, ed., *A Sandhill Century*, 1:256.

[12] There are missing issues of the Valentine newspapers, which may account for the absence of reports about all of these incidents. It is also possible Allen was recalling events of a later date. In the fall of 1883 the sheriff did shoot and kill a Wyoming cowboy who was creating a disturbance at the Hog Ranch. *Valentine Reporter*, Oct. 18, 1883.

[13] J. J. Hamlin, not Hammond, and John Smith married the McDonald sisters from O'Neill. Smith was outraged when Mrs. Hamlin told him she was being beaten by her husband and appealed to Smith for protection. Smith talked to Hamlin and perhaps threatened him. Then on the train between O'Neill and Valentine Hamlin attacked Smith with a knife, but the train personnel intervened. The next morning on December 3, 1883, near Valentine, Smith and three friends chased Hamlin out on the prairie at gunpoint. All were on horseback and after a short race Hamlin was shot and killed. A coroner's jury decided Smith and his friends acted in self defense.

Mrs. Hamlin then denied she was ever beaten. She claimed Smith had attacked her husband on the train and said he was unarmed when Smith and his friends killed him. If Mrs. Hamlin offered a motive for the killing it was not recorded. *Valentine Reporter*, Jan. 3, 1884, and O'Neill, Nebr. *Frontier*, Dec. 6, 1883. Except for one oversight Allen crossed out Smith's name in the final draft and referred to him as the wiry Texan or Hamlin's brother-in-law.

[14] The next page of the manuscript beginning at this point did not photocopy properly and approximately the first ten lines of the page are missing. The remainder of this sentence and the following two paragraphs were taken from Allen's first manuscript.

Warren's practice of hearing court cases in the gambling room was noted by Van Metre, *The Old Town*, 89.

15. At Valentine

[1] Unfortunately there is not a complete run of Valentine newspapers during the time Allen lived there. The story of Patrick Corney, the cheated homesteader, was not recorded elsewhere.

[2] Frances Miria Brainard O'Linn moved from Blair, Nebraska, in 1884 after the death of her husband. A small community grew up around O'Linn post office on her homestead, but the people left when the railroad was built about six miles away. Grant L.

Shumway, *History of Western Nebraska and Its People* (Lincoln: Western Publishing Company, 1921), 2:554–55.

Mrs. O'Linn began studying law after moving to Chadron and was admitted to the bar in 1887. *Compendium of History, Reminiscence and Biography of Western Nebraska,* 151.

[3] Democrat Grover Cleveland won the 1884 election. His party's endorsement of free silver and low tariffs was especially appealing to middle and lower income westerners. Allen Johnson, ed., "Grover Cleveland," *Dictionary of American Biography* (New York: Charles Scribner's Sons, 1943), 3:205–12.

[4] Each spring there were brief stories in the Valentine papers about the influx of homeseekers, but there was no hint of fraud.

[5] Robert H. Lucas, a young lawyer, came to Valentine in the summer of 1882. *Valentine Reporter,* Oct. 25, 1883. His paternal grandfather was Robert Lucas, who was appointed the first governor of Iowa Territory in 1838. In 1841 he began farming near Iowa City. Benjamin F. Gue, *History of Iowa* (New York: Century History Company, 1893), 172.

16. At Chadron

[1] The *Chadron Democrat,* Sept. 3, 1885, provided a description of Chadron when it was being built:

So many tales are told of this truly termed magic city that one very naturally expects to see a city of sidewalks, graded streets, lampposts and uniformed police. But, with all his preperation it strikes him "all in a heap" when he catches a first glimpse of it. Apparently it is a huge conglomeration of one and two story buildings in all stages of erection, tents, "bullwhackers" and mechanics; but, on closer inspection, order comes out of the apparent chaos, and we find handsome two story buildings on the principal corners, well on towards completion and good buildings in the various stages of construction on nearly every other business lot. The town which four weeks ago was naked prairie is fast assuming the style and pretension of a western city of the plains.

The first building lots in Chadron were sold on August 1, 1885, by the Western Town Lot Company for the railroad. *Chadron Journal,* Dec. 17, 1909.

[2] The opening of the Clarke Bridge across the North Platte River on May 10, 1876, gave Sidney, Nebraska, a great boost as a jumping off place for the Black Hills. The bridge was on the Sidney-Black Hills Trail just west of present Bridgeport, Nebraska. Hedren, *Fort Laramie in 1876,* 118.

[3] Allen's recollection of the building locations is confirmed by the 1887 fire insurance maps of Chadron on file at the Nebraska State Historical Society. Sanborn Map and Publishing Company, New York, Map of Chadron, Nebraska, July 1887.

Furman B. Carly was a Dawes County pioneer and served as the clerk of the county commissioners. On May 7, 1889, he became the Chadron postmaster. Record of Appointment of Postmasters, Roll 77.

The Richards brothers, DeForest and Bartlett, opened the Chadron Banking Company in 1885 and would become prominent bankers and ranchers. Walter C. Brown was the cashier. Richards, *Bartlett Richards, Nebraska Sandhills Cattleman,* 50. Brown was also president of the Chadron Hotel Company. *The Great Northwest* (Omaha: Herald Job Printing, 1899), 6.

The Lake and Halley bank was among the earliest businesses in Chadron. In January 1888 it was moved to a new brick building on the corner of Main and Second street. Shepherd, *Man of Many Frontiers,* 231, 280.

[4] Eli S. Ricker was admitted to the Iowa bar in 1884 and came to Chadron the following year. He was elected to three terms as the county judge on the Populist ticket. From about 1905 until his death in 1926 he spent much of his time interviewing participants in the Indian wars. Danker, "The Wounded Knee Interviews of Eli S. Ricker," 152.

Peter B. Nelson homesteaded on Bordeaux Creek about two miles east of Chadron in 1878. He later moved to Chadron and built an opera house there. *The Great Northwest*, 6; *Hay Springs News*, Dec. 31, 1937.

[5] Ben Loewenthal was the mayor of Chadron in 1914–15. He ran a clothing store in Chadron from 1885 until his death in 1935. His brother, Max, was in the business from 1886 until 1916. Gertrude Lutz, *Sketches of Some Pioneers* (Chadron: Chadron Printing Co., 1953), 8.

[6] Mary E. Smith was born in Pennsylvania in 1842. In 1885 she set out for Seattle, Washington, but decided instead to investigate the business opportunities at Chadron. She arrived there in April and in September opened a millinery and dry goods store. She operated the business until her retirement in 1929. She married William Hayward, but he died shortly thereafter. C. Raymond Woodward, Jr., "A Frontier Leader of Men and Women," *Nebraska History* 18 (1938):200–02. Mrs. Hayward died at Chadron on February 7, 1938. *Chadron Journal*, Feb. 11, 1938.

[7] It was probably the Chadron Building and Loan Company that built the Blaine Hotel. The firm went bankrupt. Lutz, *Sketches of Some Pioneers*, 30.

[8] In 1862 Milton Montgomery was named colonel of the Twenty-fifth Wisconsin Infantry. In early 1865 he was promoted to brevet brigadier general for his service in Georgia and the Carolinas. Heitman, *Historical Register*, 720.

Albert W. Crites practiced law in Columbus, Nebraska. In June 1887 he was appointed the first receiver of public funds at the land office at Chadron. He held the position for just over two years. Later, he was appointed Fifteenth District judge to fill a vacancy, but served only a short time. He also served a term as mayor of Chadron and as the Dawes County Attorney. *Chadron Journal*, Aug. 27, 1915.

John W. Cutright was born in Illinois in 1855. He went to the Black Hills in 1876 and later worked for a newspaper in Plattsmouth, Nebraska. While there Albert Crites invited him to come to Chadron to work in the land office. Cutright stayed only one year. He worked for various newspapers and spent many years in Lincoln prior to his retirement in 1912. *Lincoln Star*, Sept. 28, 1921.

John G. Mahr or Maher, the son of a Nebraska homesteader, opened the government land office in Chadron in 1887. He studied law under C. H. Bane and after passing his bar examinations entered the insurance business in Lincoln in 1913. Addison E. Sheldon, *Nebraska the Land and the People* (Chicago: Lewis Publishing Company, 1931), 2:198. Mahr has been credited for inaugurating a one-thousand-mile horse race from Chadron to Chicago in the summer of 1893. William E. Deahl, Jr., "The Chadron-Chicago 1,000 Mile Cowboy Race," *Nebraska History* 53 (1973):191.

C. H. Lutz came to Chadron in 1888. He and several partners built the first flour mill in the town. *Northwestern Temperance Advocate*, Oct. 11, 1888.

[9] The Congregational school was Chadron Congregational Academy opened December 3, 1890. J. Sterling Morton, *Illustrated History of Nebraska* (Lincoln: Jacob North and Co., 1906), 2:504. In 1911 it was purchased by the state and became Chadron State Teachers College. R. McLaran Sawyer, "No Teacher for the School: The Nebraska Junior Normal School Movement," *Nebraska History* 52 (1971):201.

[10] Alfred Bartow came to Chadron in August 1885 and was admitted to the bar the following year. He served as the judge of the Fifteenth Judicial District in 1892–96. In 1898 he moved to Colorado. Watson, *Prairie Justice*, 13.

T. F. Powers was the fourth judge to serve in Dawes County. He resigned in September 1889. Ibid., 16.

Allen G. Fisher received a law degree from Washington University (St. Louis) in 1884 and moved to Chadron in 1886. During the Spanish-American War he served in the Second Nebraska Infantry. Sheldon, *Nebraska the Land and the People,* 3:458. Fisher was commissioned a captain when the Nebraska National Guard was called to service in 1891 near the end of the Ghost Dance troubles. *Compendium of History, Reminiscence and Biography of Western Nebraska,* 286.

[11] James D. Pattison was a county commissioner in 1886. Shepherd, *Man of Many Frontiers,* 91.

[12] James C. Dahlman was elected county sheriff in November 1887 after an unsuccessful bid for the office of mayor. *Chadron Democrat,* Oct. 6, 1887, and Feb. 2, 1888. He was sheriff of Dawes County until 1894. Sheldon, *Nebraska the Land and the People,* 324. The firm of Simmons and Dahlman supplied beef to the construction firm building the railroad spur to the Black Hills in 1885. *Chadron Democrat,* Oct. 15, 1885. In January 1886 the Dahlman and Simmons Meat Market opened in Chadron. Ibid., Jan. 14, 1886. Dahlman moved to Omaha, where he was elected mayor for eight terms from 1906 through 1920. Sheldon, *Nebraska the Land and the People,* 324.

Peter G. Cooper and C. Von Harris were from Whitney, Nebraska. Shepherd, *Man of Many Frontiers,* 124.

Louis John Frederick "Billy the Bear" Iaeger was a world traveler who made and lost fortunes. He came to western Nebraska to start a giant cattle ranch, but settled in Chadron after his feet and most of his fingers were frozen in a blizzard and had to be amputated. On numerous occasions Iaeger helped Allen get the *Chadron Democrat* ready for publication. Shepherd, *Man of Many Frontiers.*
In a letter to Addison Sheldon, Allen wrote, "you and I could write a volume on Billy's adventures . . . but a paragraph will have to suffice" in *In The West That Was.* C. Allen to A. E. Sheldon, May 29, 1936, Allen Collection.

[13] On February 27, 1887, a fire started in Waller's drug store and spread through part of the business district on Main Street south of Second Street. Of the fourteen affected businesses, six had damages exceeding $1,000. Allen's office at the time was just west of Main on Second Street at the edge of the burned area. His losses totaled only $60 and he was able to publish a paper the following week. *Chadron Democrat,* Mar. 3, 1887; *Dawes County Journal,* Mar. 4, 1887.

17. The Early Far West Weekly Newspapers

[1] Isaac M. Rice was the editor of the *Valentine Democrat.* Beel, ed., *A Sandhill Century,* 1:309.

[2] Frank Broome was born in Augusta, Georgia, in 1864. In 1879 he went to Ida County, Iowa, and then to Valentine in 1884. A year later he went to Chadron, where he worked for Allen learning the newspaper business. After a failed attempt to publish a paper in Nonpareil he went to Alliance and published a paper for many years. *Nebraska Cattleman,* 9 (1953):69–70.

[3] Charles H. Pollard was born in London, England, in 1877. His family came to Valentine in 1882. He worked for the *Valentine Republican* and then came to Chadron in 1907 and worked for the *Chadron Journal* for ten years, when he became editor and publisher of the *Chadron Chronicle* until his retirement in 1943. *Chadron Record,* Apr. 1, 1954.

[4] Jim Owens opened his saloon on May 4, 1889. Shepherd, *Man of Many Frontiers,* 427.

18. A "Good Neighbor" Act–A Burlesque Speech

[1] Chadron's mayor, Herbert A. Cox, was a partner in the American Land and Security Company. This Chadron investment firm dealt in real estate, purchasing land and holding it until it could be resold at a higher price. *The Great Northwest*, 1889, 10.

[2] C. C. Hughes, railroad superintendent, was elected mayor of Chadron in 1887. Some of his employees were on the city council and some townspeople complained he wielded excessive control over the community's business. Shepherd, *Man of Many Frontiers*, 189, 196.

[3] Gifts to the Johnstown, Pennsylvania, flood victims had a value of about $5,000. *Chadron Democrat*, June 20, 1889. The *Democrat* reported there were five train car loads of corn and two of potatoes including donations from other nearby communities. Ibid., June 13, 1889. Allen was a member of the committee appointed by the townspeople to manage the collection of the produce. Shepherd, *Man of Many Frontiers*, 441.

[4] A rumor of an Indian "outbreak" was reported in the summer of 1889 in the Valentine area. Stories spread that the Brulés from the Rosebud Reservation were preparing for a massive cattle- stealing raid. Allen published the story, but scoffed at it as unfounded gossip. *Chadron Democrat*, May 30, 1889. The rumor may have resulted from action taken by the Brulés to evict white squatters from their reservation. The Indians' land was not open to settlement by whites, but a "little colony" had taken up residence there. After a time they were forced to abandon their farms out of "fear of the Indians who had threatened to exterminate them if they did not clear out." *Valentine Republican*, May 31, 1889.

During the summer of 1890, more rumors of outbreaks were reported than in previous years. One story originated at a farming community near Chadron (*Chadron Democrat*, June 12, 1890) and another was heard in the vicinity of Oelrich, South Dakota, (Ibid., June 26, 1890), but neither of them had any basis in fact. About the same time there were similar unfounded rumors concerning the Cheyennes in Montana (Ibid., June 19, 1890) and the Nez Perces in Idaho, who were thought to be preparing for war (Ibid., September 18, 1890). One of the more outrageous stories circulated in the vicinity of Mandan, North Dakota. It was claimed some Indians had discovered a cache of weapons lost by the army during the Custer fight on the Little Bighorn. As a result "every Indian on the reservation will shortly go on the warpath," presumably armed with military weapons that were obsolete at the time of Custer's defeat. Ibid., May 23, 1890. Allen chided newspaper editors who repeated the stories without questioning their validity or noting they were merely rumors.

[5] The purpose of the 1889 Sioux Commission was to negotiate for the sale of approximately one-half of the Sioux Reservation so it could be opened to white settlement. The year before, Congress had passed a law calling for the sale of this land, but the Lakotas resoundingly rejected the 1888 proposal. In 1889 a similar bill was passed offering more generous payments. In spite of the increased compensation, there was overwhelming opposition for a time, but the 1889 commissioners were able to convince the required three-fourths majority to approve the sale. It seems likely the necessary votes were gained by a variety of tactics including many that were unethical if not illegal. Jerome A. Greene, "The Sioux Land Commission of 1889: Prelude to Wounded Knee," *South Dakota History* 1 (1970):41–72.

This commission consisted of Charles Foster, former governor of Ohio, Maj. Gen. George Crook, who was well known to the Sioux having fought them in the 1870s, and William Warner, former senator from Missouri. Herbert T. Hoover, "The Sioux Agreement of 1889 and Its Aftermath," *South Dakota History* 19 (1989):56–94.

Allen's newspaper carried lengthy reports of the councils on the Rosebud Reservation (*Chadron Democrat*, June 13, 1889) and then at Pine Ridge (Ibid., June 20, 1889). After the first Pine Ridge meeting Allen felt "all the white men and mixed bloods on the reservation are in favor of the bill," while those who opposed "are simply holding out for bluff and beef." Allen thought "the bill on the whole is a fair one," but was quick to point out that the Indians had no part in formulating the agreement that would deprive them of much of their remaining land. Nevertheless, he was of the opinion the Indians should and would sign the agreement. There is a noticeable tone of resignation in the conclusion to his article when he wrote, "The land described will be taken from them [the Indians] whether they sign it or no." Ibid., June 20, 1889.

⁶ Hugh D. Gallagher arrived at Pine Ridge in October 1887 to begin his duties as agent. Hugh D. Gallagher, "Pine Ridge Agency," *Annual Report, Indian Affairs,* 1887:40. After leaving the agency in 1890 he then made his residence in Chadron. *Chadron Democrat,* Oct. 23, 1890.

⁷ Indians from Pine Ridge had been invited to participate in Fourth of July celebrations since 1886, only a few months after the town was founded. *Chadron Democrat,* July 8, 1886. In 1891, after the Ghost Dance troubles were over, the Indians hoped to receive an invitation, but in an editorial Addison E. Sheldon made it quite clear they were not wanted. *Chadron Advocate,* June 26, 1891.

⁸ Little Wound was a conservative Oglala. He was described by Carl Smith, a reporter for the *Omaha World-Herald,* as "an investigator and wants to look into the coming of the Messiah before expressing himself on that point." *Omaha World-Herald,* Nov. 27, 1890.

Blue Horse was head of the Oglala Loafer band and opposed the Ghost Dance. D. F. Royer to R. V. Belt, October 30, 1890, Reports, Campaign of 1890–91. A decade later Blue Horse was interviewed about Lakota religion by James R. Walker. Raymond J. DeMallie and Elaine A. DeMallie, eds., *Lakota Belief and Ritual* (Lincoln: University of Nebraska Press, 1980), 208.

No Water was an early Ghost Dance leader. R. N. Getty to assistant adjutant general, Apr. 13, 1891, Reports, Campaign of 1890–91. Elsewhere in his manuscript Allen lists No Water as chief of the Don't Eat The Fish band.

Fire Thunder was a member of Red Cloud's Oglalas and was educated at Carlisle. He was born about 1860. Merrill J. Mattes, Memo for the Files, October 30, 1942, Fort Laramie National Historic Site. Allen called him a Wa-za-za band member.

⁹ The "imaginary narrative" appeared in the *Chadron Democrat,* June 27, 1889. A few minor changes were made in the manuscript so Sheldon did not appear quite so foolish. Sheldon published only a brief notice of the trip and Red Cloud's promise to attend the Independence Day celebrations. *Chadron Advocate,* June 28, 1889.

¹⁰ James Asay operated a trading post at the Pine Ridge Agency and witnessed the Wounded Knee massacre. *Chadron Democrat,* July 4, 1889. A month later his trader's license was revoked for selling whiskey on the reservation and he moved to Rushville. C. G. Penney to commissioner, Sept. 19, 1893; T. J. Morgan to F. E. Pierce, Jan. 31, 1891, Pine Ridge Agency letters, Roll 21.

¹¹ This was the "imaginary bombastic agency speech" for which Allen apologized profusely when his autobiography was being edited by Sheldon. Sheldon said he had no objection to the speech and felt it served to "enliven the literary landscape if nothing more." C. Allen to A. E. Sheldon, Dec. 15, 1936, and Sheldon to Allen, Dec. 17, 1936, Allen Collection.

19. The Celebration

[1] A great many of the Chadron area residents had come from the East within the last four years and not knowing their Indian neighbors were undoubtedly apprehensive about their actions. The members of the white community who served as the Indians' formal hosts did include several experienced westerners.

Louis Iaeger attended a celebration in 1887 and estimated there were 1,500 Indians camped near Chadron. At that time the townspeople donated $64 to buy beef to feed their guests. Shepherd, *Man of Many Frontiers*, 217-19. Indians were also hired to perform traditional dances during the county fair. Ibid., 349-50.

[2] F. M. Dorrington helped organize Dawes County. Shumway, *History of Western Nebraska and Its People*, 2:550. In 1886 he was admitted to the bar and in addition to his law practice was active in real estate. *Chadron Democrat*, Nov. 12, 1885, Feb. 18, 1886, Mar. 28, 1888, and Apr. 5, 1888.

Thomas A. Coffey opened a saloon in Chadron in March 1888. He seems to have been one of the town's leading gamblers, betting heavily on Chadron's baseball team. Shepherd, *Man of Many Frontiers*, 311, 454. He also ran high stakes faro games. *Chadron Advocate*, Aug. 22, 1890.

Warren L. Cassady attended college in Des Moines, Iowa, and came to Chadron in March 1885. *Omaha Daily Herald*, June 9, 1886. He was a surveyor in the Chadron real estate firm of Ballou and Cassady. *Chadron Democrat*, Oct. 15, 1885. Although apparently a successful businessman, he lost elections for county surveyor and for Chadron city treasurer. In 1890 he was loan agent for the Michigan Loan and Trust Company. Ibid., Nov. 12, 1885, Mar. 17. 1887.

George W. Clark, a Republican, was elected sheriff of Dawes County in November 1885, but was defeated in the election two years later. *Chadron Democrat*, Nov. 12, 1885, Oct. 6, 1887, and Feb. 2, 1888. He was the Chadron chief of police in 1886-87. Watson, *Prairie Justice*, 175. He owned a ranch about fifteen miles south of Chadron. *Compendium of History, Reminiscence and Biography*, 561.

[3] Thomas H. Glover and his partner, L. A. Bower, owned the OK Store dealing in general merchandise. They placed advertisements in the first issue of the *Chadron Democrat*. Branches of the OK Store were opened in Gordon and Hay Springs. *Chadron Democrat*, Jan. 14, 1886. Glover was also the president of the Dawes County Bank, the first bank in Chadron. Ibid., Oct. 8, 1885. Shumway, *History of Western Nebraska and Its People*, 575.

James F. Tucker moved to Chadron from Valentine, where he sold insurance. In August 1883 he was appointed Cherry County judge. *Valentine Reporter*, Aug. 9, 1883.

Allen belonged to Damascus Lodge Number 53, Knights of Pythias. *Chadron Democrat*, Dec. 2, 1886. He was "QM" of local Lennington GAR Post Number 227. Ibid., Dec. 9, 1886.

[4] Mrs. Putnam's husband was Arthur C. Putnam, president of the Chadron Banking Company and treasurer of the Black Hills Marble Company. *The Great Northwest*, 10-11.

Mrs. Waller was the wife of Dr. George P. Waller, who was co-proprietor of the Waller and Lyman Drug Store. *Chadron Democrat*, Oct. 8, 1885, June 13, 1889.

Miss Blanchard was the daughter of O. R. Blanchard, Methodist Church choirmaster. Ibid., Aug. 8, 1889 and Feb. 6, 1890.

Professor Joseph S. Denton was the principal of the Chadron schools. Shumway, *History of Western Nebraska and Its People*, 560 and *Chadron Democrat*, July 12, 1888. He moved to California in the summer of 1890. *Chadron Advocate*, July 11, 1890.

Judge C. H. Bane had formerly been an attorney in Ainsworth, Nebraska, before taking up practice in Chadron. Valentine *Democratic Blade*, Sept. 18, 1885. He was originally from Boston. Sheldon, *Nebraska the Land and the People*, 198.

[5] Allen is referring to his move to Bennett County, South Dakota.

[6] In April 1898 President William McKinley sent troops to Cuba to begin the Spanish-American War.

Lafayette A. Dorrington became the superintendent of prisons in the Philippine Islands after the Spanish-American War. Shumway, *History of Western Nebraska and Its People*, 566.

Edward L. Godsall was also the deputy sheriff of Dawes County. *Chadron Democrat*, Aug. 15, 1889, and Feb. 6, 1890.

[7] Red Cloud's Fourth of July 1889 speech appeared in the *Chadron Democrat*, July 4, 1889.

[8] The Omaha Dance was once a ritual of the Omaha Society and the Lakotas adopted it from them. Members of the society who performed the proper rituals would not be injured in battle. In time the ceremony was considered misused, the power was lost, and when Allen witnessed the dance it was merely a social function. Since the dance could include a reenactment of a participant's successes in battle, it was sometimes referred to as a war dance. Clark Wissler, "Societies and Ceremonial Associations in the Oglala Division of the Teton-Dakota," *Anthropological Papers* 11, American Museum of Natural History, 1912:49.

[9] The Sun Dance was at the very heart of the old religion and did include self-torture. It was banned in the 1880s, but was revived in the 1960s. James Owen Dorsey, *A Study of Siouan Cults*, Eleventh Annual Report of the Bureau of American Ethnology (Washington, D.C.: GPO, 1894) and James R. Walker, "The Sun Dance and Other Ceremonies of the Oglala Division of the Teton Dakota," *Anthropological Papers* 16, American Museum of Natural History, 1917.

[10] John Henry also served as a paralegal for the small black community in the Chadron area. *Chadron Democrat*, July 17, 1890. He was described in the *Chadron Advocate* (June 20, 1890) as an "irresponsible colored comedian" who "would rather be hanged in Chadron than live anywhere else."

[11] Photographs of this or another Black Horse are in the archives of the Nebraska State Historical Society (photos W-938-75 and I-392-290).

[12] In the manuscript Allen identified the assistant as George Stover, but carefully lined out the name. Stover operated the cattle ranch owned by Dahlman and Simmons. *Chadron Democrat*, Sept. 11, 1890. He was on the Pine Ridge Reservation at least by 1879. V. McGillycuddy to E. A. Hayt, Apr. 9, 1879, Red Cloud Agency letters, Roll 724.

20. Gathering War Clouds

[1] Republican Benjamin Harrison defeated Grover Cleveland for the presidency. There were no significant changes in the new administration's Indian policy. With the spoils system still in effect, many new Indian agents were appointed almost immediately, but Gallagher did complete his term.

[2] Agent Gallagher did attempt to break up the Ghost Dances, but without success. H. D. Gallagher, "Report of Pine Ridge Agency," *Annual Report, Indian Affairs*, 1890:49.

Father John Jutz, S.J., was in charge of the Drexel or Holy Rosary Catholic mission about four miles north of the agency. Father Jutz was first assigned to the Rosebud

Reservation in 1886 and then to Holy Rosary in 1889. Sister Mary Clement Fitzgerald, "Bishop Marty and His Sioux Missions," *South Dakota Historical Collections* 20 (1940):540, 548.

Charles Smith Cook, son of a Yankton mother and white father, was adopted by Rev. Joseph W. Cook. He attended Episcopal theological schools in Connecticut and Minnesota. In 1883 he began his missionary service on the Yankton Reservation near present Wagner, South Dakota, and shortly thereafter was transferred to Pine Ridge. He died there in 1894. Will G. Robinson, "Charles Smith Cook," *South Dakota Historical Collections and Reports* 22 (1946):32–33. His Holy Cross Episcopal Church at Pine Ridge was used for a hospital for the Indian wounded brought back from Wounded Knee. Although it has been moved, this church still stands (1996) on the Pine Ridge Reservation.

Rev. and Mrs. A. T. Johnson served as Presbyterian missionaries at Pine Ridge for over a decade, but did not arrive until 1892 to replace Rev. John P. Williamson, who was leaving due to ill health. Williamson replaced Reverend C. G. Sterling, who founded the mission in 1886. Sterling retired in 1890, but was still at the agency during the early part of 1891. *Chicago Inter Ocean*, Jan. 12, 1891; C. G. Stirling, "Report of the Missionary, Pine Ridge Agency," *Annual Report, Indian Affairs*, 1888:53 and Ricker Collection, Interviews, Tablet 13, 97–99. It is possible both Sterling and Williamson were at Pine Ridge during the winter of 1890–91, but Allen is probably mistaken in placing Johnson there at the time.

[3] Daniel F. Royer, an Alpena, South Dakota, dentist, was appointed agent for the Pine Ridge Reservation and arrived there in late September 1890. His paramount concern was the suppression of the Ghost Dance, but it was soon apparent he did not have the temperament for such an undertaking. In a letter to Thomas J. Morgan, commissioner of Indian affairs, he wrote: "I have been carefully investigating the matter [of the Ghost Dance] and I find I have an elephant on my hands." U.S. Senate, *Executive Documents of the Senate of the United States*, 51st Congress, 2d Session, 1891–92, Document 9:5, D. F. Royer to T. J. Morgan, Oct. 12, 1890. By the end of the month he was insisting that military intervention was necessary not only to suppress the new religion, but to protect whites from an outbreak. He believed a war was inevitable and his actions proved to be a self-fulfilling prophecy.

This paragraph was one of the few major changes between Allen's final draft and the 1938 typescript. In the final draft this page was retyped and Allen deleted the parenthetical phrase and the mention of Woonsocket.

[4] Allen decided to treat Royer more gently so he added this almost complimentary paragraph to the final draft. Allen did not hold Royer in high regard and judged his administration to be "notoriously weak and incompetent." *Chadron Democrat*, Nov. 27, 1890.

[5] This paragraph was in the 1938 draft, but deleted in the final version. The paragraph more clearly expresses Allen's attitude toward Royer than the former one.

[6] In August 1884 the Chicago and Northwestern took over the Fremont, Elkhorn, and Missouri Valley Railroad, but the name was not changed until 1903. *Chadron Centennial History*, 22.

[7] James Gordon Bennett was the flamboyant owner of the *New York Herald*. *Chadron Advocate*, Nov. 21, 1890.

[8] After less than two months at Pine Ridge Agency, Royer and some of his employees moved to Rushville fearing an attack by the Indians. *Chadron Advocate*, Nov. 21, 1890.

[9] Short Bull and Kicking Bear were two of the more prominent leaders of the Ghost Dance. They had visited with its founder in Nevada and returned in March of 1890 as

confirmed disciples. Kicking Bear first went to the Cheyenne River Reservation and then to the Standing Rock Reservation near present Mobridge, South Dakota, to preach the new religion while Short Bull went to Rosebud. U.S. Senate, *Executive Documents*, 9:35–36, W. T. Selwyn to E. W. Foster, Nov. 25, 1890.

Allen overemphasizes these early movements. There had been confrontations between believers and agents and as a result the ceremonies were moved to more remote areas prior to the arrival of the army, however, there were no mass movements of Indians. When the army occupation began, the Indians in outlying districts were ordered to move to the agency. The nonbelievers obeyed, but most of the Ghost Dancers retreated to a rugged section of the Badlands, called the Stronghold, where they were relatively safe. This camp of "hostiles" could be easily defended and any attempt to take it by frontal attack would have proved very costly to the army. The believers correctly assumed an assault would not be attempted.

[10] As a result of Royer's telegrams, the regular army began arriving on the Pine Ridge and Rosebud reservations on November 20, 1890. The initial force at Pine Ridge included four companies of the Second Infantry, one company of the Eighth Infantry, and three troops of the Ninth Cavalry. The infantry guarded the agency, while the cavalry scouted the surrounding area.

Brig. Gen. Leonard W. Colby and the Nebraska National Guard did not arrive until January 5, 1891. This unit took positions between the reservations and the Nebraska towns immediately to the south. It was an unnecessary precaution, but it did calm the fears of the settlers. The guardsmen returned to their homes less than two weeks later after the Ghost Dancers surrendered to General Miles. L. W. Colby, "The Sioux Indian War of 1890–91," Nebraska State Historical Society, *Transactions and Reports* 3, (1892):161.

[11] Alfred Burkholder, an editor of his own paper in Chamberlain, South Dakota, represented the *New York Herald*. He must have arrived shortly after the regular army because his reports first appear on November 24. George R. Kolbenschlag, *A Whirlwind Passes* (Pierre: University of South Dakota Press, 1990), 15–19.

[12] Henry Clark Corbin served on the staff of Gen. Nelson A. Miles, who was in overall charge of the occupation. Corbin may have been the ranking officer at Pine Ridge at the time Allen mentioned, but only if Miles and General Brooke were absent.

Corbin had served in the Civil War attaining the rank of brevet brigadier general of the Ohio volunteers. He was a lieutenant colonel and assistant adjutant general during the Ghost Dance era. Heitman, *Historical Register*, 327.

John R. Brooke was a career soldier in the infantry and was promoted to brigadier general on April 6, 1888. Ibid., 248. He was commander of the Department of the Platte and accompanied the troops to the Pine Ridge Reservation.

Nelson A. Miles was a thirty-year infantryman who had campaigned against Plains tribes, including the Lakota, on numerous occasions. He was promoted to major general in the spring of 1890. As commander of the Division of the Missouri, he was in charge of the overall operations against the Sioux during the Ghost Dance. On December 31, 1890, he moved to the Pine Ridge Agency. Robert M. Utley, "Nelson A. Miles," *Soldiers West* (New Haven: Yale University Press, 1963), 213–27.

[13] Allen seems to have relied largely upon memory for his discussion of agents at Pine Ridge, because his listing is not entirely accurate. Capt. Jason M. Bell, Seventh Cavalry, took over from Valentine T. McGillycuddy in 1886 and served briefly. Then Hugh D. Gallagher served until 1890, when Daniel F. Royer was appointed. Royer served for only about three months until the army took over administrative responsibility of the reservation on January 12, 1891, when Capt. Francis E. Pierce, Eighth Infantry, was named agent. Because of an illness he was replaced a month later by

Capt. Charles Penney, Sixth Infantry. Near the end of the year Penney was replaced by Capt. George LeRoy Brown, Eleventh Infantry. Penney was reinstated in 1893 and served until early in 1896. Capt. William Henry Clapp, Sixteenth Infantry, then served until early 1900. Special Agent J. E. Jenkins served briefly until the duties were passed on to John R. Brennan, the first civilian in over a decade. He was appointed agent for Pine Ridge on November 1, 1900, and resigned on July 1, 1917. *Annual Report, Indian Affairs*, 1885 through 1901; *Chadron Advocate*, Nov. 20, 1891, Ricker Collection, Interviews, Tablet 26, 5–12. After leaving the agency Brennan went to Rapid City, a town he had helped found in 1876, to look after his many business interests. He died two years later. John C. Borst, "Dakota Resources: The John R. Brennan Family Papers at the South Dakota Historical Resource Center," *South Dakota History* 14 (1984):68–72.

[14] Estimates vary as to the number of troops on the reservations, but about 9,000 or one third of the U.S. Army would not be an exaggeration.

[15] Henry A. Dawson's store appears in two photographs of Pine Ridge street scenes in 1890. Jensen, Paul, and Carter, *Eyewitness at Wounded Knee*, plates 47 and 48. In 1893 Dawson sold his store to William McGaa. L. Brown to commissioner, Mar. 22, 1893, Pine Ridge Agency letters, Roll 20.

[16] John J. "Zither Dick" Boesl had been a teamster at Fort Robinson before coming to the Pine Ridge in 1893 as "boss farmer." Will G. Robinson, "Daughters of Dakota," *South Dakota Department of History Report and Historical Collections* 33 (1966):65–66.

The order to tax cattle was received on the reservation on October 6, 1900. A rancher could own one hundred cattle, but anything in excess of that was taxed at one dollar a head. During the next five months $2,241 was collected in spite of much opposition. J. R. Brennan to commissioner, Dec. 6, 1900, and Feb. 23, 1901, Pine Ridge Agency letters, Roll 32. The agent estimated "a little over" 3,000 cattle were sold from the reservation to avoid the tax by the end of 1904. Ibid., Jan. 4, 1905.

21. The Ghost Dance at Pine Ridge

[1] Wovoka, or Jack Wilson, was a Paiute shaman who lived near the Walker Lake Reservation in western Nevada. In January 1889 he had a vision that was the genesis of a religious movement commonly known as the Ghost Dance. James Mooney, *The Ghost-Dance Religion and the Sioux Outbreak of 1890*, Fourteenth Annual Report of the Bureau of American Ethnology (Washington, D.C.: GPO, 1896), 764; Paul Bailey, *Wovoka, The Indian Messiah* (Los Angeles: Westernlore Press, 1957).

[2] Doane Robinson, a historian with the South Dakota Historical Society, collected data for a history of the Lakota not long after the Wounded Knee massacre. As a result of his interviews, some of his work classifies as a primary source. Although the book contains some highly questionable conclusions, the outline of Wovoka is accurate. Doane Robinson, "A History of the Dakota or Sioux Indians," *South Dakota Historical Collections and Reports* 2 (1904), 461–62.

At the bottom of page 211 of the Allen manuscript is a typed note, "South Dakota Historical Collections, Doane Robinson; vol. ii" referring to the above article.

[3] The Ghost Dance as revealed by Wovoka was modified by his disciples from other tribes. In October 1890 Kicking Bear went to the Standing Rock Reservation, where he told the Hunkpapa his interpretation of the religion:

My brothers, I bring to you the promise of a day in which there will be no white man to lay his hand on the bridle of the Indian's horse; when the red men of the prairie will rule the world. . . . I bring you word from your fathers the ghosts, that they are now marching to join you, led by the Messiah who came once to live on earth with the white

man, but was cast out and killed by them. He then quoted Wovoka as saying "The earth is getting old, and I will make it new for my chosen people, the Indians, who are to inhabit it, and among them will be all those of their ancestors who have died . . . I will cover the earth with new soil to a depth of five times the height of a man, and under this new soil will be buried the whites. . . . The new lands will be covered with sweet-grass and running water and trees, and herds of buffalo and ponies will stray over it, that my red children may eat and drink, hunt and rejoice."
James McLaughlin, *My Friend the Indian* (Boston: Houghton-Mifflin Co., 1916), 185–87.

When the agency police attempted to break up the ceremonies, believers drove them away at gunpoint. This refusal to obey orders convinced some whites an uprising was imminent. Allen may have been too close to the events to realize that the only time the believers acted aggressively was when someone tried to disrupt their ceremonies.

[4] For many years it was popular to cite the food shortage as the cause of the Ghost Dance. It did have the advantage of being an easily understood and seemingly logical reason. There can be no doubt the food supply was less than in previous years since the government- supplied rations had been reduced after a new census was taken showing a decrease in population. The drought had injured the Indians' gardens, but these tiny plots had never produced any appreciable quantity of food in the best of years. The government still provided over a pound of usable meat per person per day in addition to a variety of other foodstuffs, which did not include the substantial numbers of cattle raised by the Indians. Richard E. Jensen, "Notes on the Lakota Ghost Dance." Paper read before the Thirty-third Annual Missouri Valley History Conference, Omaha, Mar. 8, 1990.

Red Cloud carried the food shortage theme to extremes when he claimed that 217 people on the Pine Ridge Reservation died of starvation in one year. T. A. Bland, *A Brief History of the Late Military Invasion of the Home of the Sioux* (Washington, D.C.: 1891), 20.

[5] Allen was satisfied with translating "Wakan" as sacred, but there are many subtleties of the word. Powers, *Oglala Religion*, 45–47.

[6] The exact number of converts to the Ghost Dance was never accurately ascertained, but about one-third of the Lakota seems likely, while many others gave their tacit support.

[7] The dance was based upon a Paiute round dance in which men and women formed a circle, held hands, and sidestepped to the left. Warren K. Moorehead, "Ghost-Dances in the West," *Illustrated American*, Jan. 17, 1891, 327. Daniel Dorchester, "Report of the Superintendent of Indian Schools," *Annual Report, Indian Affairs*, 1891:529. This was a completely foreign dance form for the Lakota and they added familiar elements from their own religious rituals. In the center of the circle of dancers, the Lakota placed a sacred tree or pole. A tree such as this had been part of the Sun Dance, the most sacred ceremony of the old Lakota religion, which had been banned by the Indian Bureau in the 1880s. Dancers also looked toward the sun, another feature of the Sun Dance.

Mary Collins, a missionary with long experience among the Lakota, watched a dance and "came to the conclusion that the 'ghost dance' is nothing more than the old sun dance revived." With her experience, she may have understood that both dances were a means of obtaining supernatural aid and not a prelude to war as many whites suspected. Mary Collins, "Mary Clementine Collins, Dacotah Missionary," *North Dakota History* 19 (1952):77.

Other features of the Lakota version of the Ghost Dance had deep roots in their old traditions. Before the ceremony participants underwent a sweat lodge purification ritual. This had been part of many of their old religious ceremonies. Vision quests were also part of the Sioux experience and during the dance the believers might have a vision in which they saw the promised new world and talked to the ghosts of dead friends and relatives.

Elaine Goodale witnessed a Ghost Dance in late November, which she described: It was held in the open, with neither fire nor light, after the participants had fasted for a day or two and passed through the purifying ordeal of the sweat-lodge. . . . perhaps a hundred men, women, and children, with clasped hands and fingers interlocked, swung in a great circle about their "sacred tree," chanting together the monotonous Ghost Dance songs. The hypnotic repetition of the words: "Once more we shall hunt the buffalo—Our father has said it!" alternated with short invocations by prophet or priest and occasional intervals of wailing by the women—that musical heart-piercing sound which, once heard, is never forgotten. No one with imagination could fail to see in the rite a genuine religious ceremony, a faith which, illusory as it was, deserved to be treated with respect.

Kay Graber, *Sister to the Sioux: The Memoirs of Elaine Goodale Eastman* (Lincoln: University of Nebraska Press, 1978), 148.

[8] At first the Ghost Dancers made no attempt to hide their ceremonies. In his newspaper Allen noted, "The new dance among the Indians is said to be worth going many miles to see." *Chadron Democrat*, Sept. 25, 1890. Elaine Goodale agreed saying, "There was no secrecy about the dance which had caused such frantic alarm." Graber, *Sister to the Sioux*, 148. When pressure was put upon the believers to desist, they retreated to more inaccessible areas where whites were not welcome.

[9] The dispatch was published in the *Chadron Democrat* on Dec. 4, 1890.

White officials were attempting to persuade the Ghost Dancers to abandon the Badlands and camp instead in the vicinity of the agency. In the latter part of December Little Wound did come in, but fled again on December 29.

In the *Omaha World-Herald*, Nov. 27, 1890, Carl Smith wrote:

I succeeded in getting a chance at Little Wound, who . . . expressed himself in this wise: "There has been a great deal of talk about me being a bad man, this talk comes from the Indian scouts, who not only misrepresent me to the people here, but in turn say things which they assert come from the agent and which I have found untrue. As an instance of this, I was told by a scout who came out to my camp that I was to be imprisoned and that my arms were to be taken from me and all my men. The fact is, my children are growing up around me and my desire is to do nothing which would result disastrously for them. I do not wish, nor have I wished, to defy the agent, and when all this is sifted you will find a deal of responsibility with the over zealousness or the ignorance of the messengers who have gone between us. . . ." Yellow Hair or Bad Yellow Hair, Yellow Bear, and Broken Arm were Little Wound's lieutenants. *Omaha World-Herald*, Nov. 27, 1890.

James A. Cooper, a Bureau of Indian Affairs employee, went to Pine Ridge with the army. He was sent by the commissioner of Indian affairs to aid and advise Agent Royer.

[10] Sitting Bull, a Hunkpapa, gained renown as a leader in the Custer Battle in 1876. Continued pressure by the U.S. Army forced him and his followers into Canada, where Sitting Bull lived for five years. Upon his return to the United States, he spent two years in confinement at Fort Randall before being allowed to return to his people, who were then settled at the Standing Rock Agency. After a visit from Kicking Bear in October of 1890, Sitting Bull's people embraced the Ghost Dance. On December 15 agency police were sent to arrest Sitting Bull and a fight broke out in which fourteen Indians were killed, including the Hunkpapa leader. Frank Bennett Fiske, *Life and Death of Sitting Bull* (Fort Yates, N. Dak.: Pioneer Arrow Print, 1933), 48–51. McLaughlin, *My Friend the Indian*, 218–21.

[11] Holy Rosary or Drexel Mission was a Jesuit mission opened in 1889. It was primarily a boarding school and could accommodate over one hundred children. Katherine Drexel donated $6,000 towards the education of Lakota children. Fitzgerald, "Bishop Marty and His Sioux Missions," 541.

[12] Peter Norbeck was governor of South Dakota from 1917 to 1921, when he became a U.S. Senator. Doane Robinson, "Peter Norbeck," *South Dakota Historical Collections and Reports* 22 (1946): 296–305.

[13] The Lakota did originate the Ghost Dance garments. These cotton shirts and dresses were sanctified and made bulletproof. Many whites took this as additional evidence of the warlike nature of the Ghost Dance, choosing to ignore the primarily defensive character of a bulletproof garment. The Indians had no need for aggressive weapons or for warfare because the whites would disappear through supernatural means.

[14] The story of Porcupine's experiment was taken from the *Chadron Democrat*, Dec. 4, 1890, with only minor changes. For example, in the newspaper Allen described Mrs. Eagle Horn as a member of "the Messiah crazed band," but in the manuscript it is reduced to "the Ghost Dance band."

Allen probably had better informants than did Leonard W. Colby, who claimed "the bullet proof medicine was tested upon Chief Porcupine, at a war dance on Wolf Creek, a few miles out from Pine Ridge Agency, and as a result he was seriously wounded at the first volley, by two bullets passing through his limbs." Colby, "The Sioux Indian War of 1890–91," 149.

[15] Allen's story is a myth. When Spotted Tail was old enough to consider the possibility of becoming a chief, Brave Bear and then Little Thunder were the recognized leaders of the Brulés. About 1866 Little Thunder retired and Spotted Tail became the chief. The change was peaceful with not the slightest hint of an assassination. Hyde, *Spotted Tail's Folk*, 110–12.

Although there are only a few similarities, Allen's tale may have had its origin in Spotted Tail's killing of Big Mouth in 1869. Ibid., 149–50.

22. The Crush at Pine Ridge

[1] Photographers who were at Pine Ridge at the time of the Ghost Dance included George Trager and possibly his partner, Frederick Kuhn, of Chadron, George Meddaugh of Rushville, Clarence Grant Moreledge, possibly in the employ of the *Omaha World-Herald*, and after the trouble subsided, Solomon D. Butcher of West Union, Nebraska. Many of their photographs have been published in Jensen, Paul, and Carter, *Eyewitness at Wounded Knee*.

[2] The Catholic Church has since been relocated.

[3] The commissary clerk was Robert O. Pugh.

[4] William F. "Buffalo Bill" Cody got his start as a scout, but by 1890 was the star of his own Wild West Show. He had just returned from a tour of Europe with a number of Pine Ridge Indians, who were also in the show. John R. Burke was the show's press agent and general manager and was well known to the Oglalas. Russell, *The Lives and Legends of Buffalo Bill*.

Brig. Gen. Leonard W. Colby and the Nebraska National Guard arrived on January 5, 1891. The troops took positions between the reservations and the Nebraska towns immediately to the south for about two weeks. Colby, "The Sioux Indian War of 1890–91," 161.

[5] The friendly organization was the Indian Rights Association, composed primarily of influential whites. It was founded in 1882 and was a firm advocate of programs it be-

lieved would lead to the assimilation of Indians into white society. William T. Hagen, *The Indian Rights Association* (Tucson: University of Arizona Press, 1958), 121.

[6] The government employees at the outlying Indian settlements were ordered to Pine Ridge agency in mid-December.

[7] The tragic events Allen described occurred after the Wounded Knee massacre and were a part of the sporadic fighting initiated by the Lakotas in a futile attempt to retaliate for the killings on December 29.

William Jones also operated the stage line from Chadron to the Pine Ridge agency. Jensen, Paul, and Carter, *Eyewitness at Wounded Knee*, 48.

The slain man was identified by Agent Royer as "Isaac Miller, a white man, and former irregular employee on the beef herd [who] was killed by hostile Indians yesterday ten miles north of the agency." D. F. Royer to T. J. Morgan, Jan. 2, 1891, Reports, Campaign of 1890–91. On February 8, 1891, Lt. S. A. Cloman arrested Miller's alleged killer near the mouth of White Clay Creek. S. A. Cloman to camp adjutant, Feb. 19, 1991, and J. N. Brooke to adjutant general, Feb. 19, 1991, Ibid. Cloman did not name the accused, but called him No Water's son. He was later identified as Leaves His Woman when he was indicted by a grand jury in Deadwood. Despite the indictment, the U.S. attorney, William B. Sterling, believed he was innocent. W. B. Sterling to U.S. attorney general, Mar. 16, 1891, Ibid.

Martin Gibbens from Missouri worked at the Red Cloud Agency in 1871. List of Employees, Nov. 10, 1871, Red Cloud Agency letters, Roll 715.

[8] Since the killing of Casey received more attention in the press than any other story except the massacre, Allen's brief and incomplete account is surprising. Lt. Edward W. Casey, Twenty-second U.S. Infantry, recruited about forty Cheyenne scouts at the Tongue River Reservation in Montana. On December 30 they joined Col. B. G. Sanford's Ninth Cavalry and began patrolling the southern perimeter of the Stronghold to prevent the escape of the Ghost Dancers. On January 7, 1891, Lieutenant Casey, accompanied by two scouts, White Moon and Rock Road, were going toward No Water's "hostile" camp about eight miles up White Clay Creek. Casey hoped to talk to the leaders and convince them to move to the agency. Pete Richards, who spoke English, was sent by Red Cloud from the No Water camp to talk to the lieutenant. Richards was to tell Casey that Red Cloud was going to the agency in the morning. While the men were talking, Plenty Horses, a Carlisle-educated Ghost Dancer, rode up behind Casey and listened to the conversation for a time. Without any warning, he drew his rifle and shot Casey in the back of the head and then calmly rode away. None of the witnesses was willing to detain him although he was arrested later. R. N. Getty to assistant adjutant general, Apr. 13, 1891, and S. A. Cloman to camp adjutant, Feb. 21, 1891, Reports, Campaign of 1890–91. Also *Report of the Secretary of War: Being Part of the Message and Documents Communicated to the Two Houses of Congress at the beginning of the First Session of the Fifty-second Congress* 1 (Washington D.C.: GPO, 1892), 250–51; and Katherine M. West, "Ned Casey and His Cheyenne Scouts: A Noble Experiment in an Atmosphere of Tension," *Montana, The Magazine of Western History* 27 (1977):26–39.

Eugene A. Carr was awarded a Medal of Honor in the Civil War for action in the Battle of Pea Ridge and was promoted to brigadier general of volunteers. During the occupation of the Sioux reservations he was a colonel in command of the Sixth Cavalry. Heitman, *Historical Register*, 285. Early in the occupation his troops took up positions along the Cheyenne River east of the Black Hills. When he received word of the capture of Big Foot's band, he moved south along the White River and established his headquarters at the mouth of Wounded Knee Creek. James T. King, *War Eagle, A Life of General Eugene A. Carr* (Lincoln: University of Nebraska Press, 1963), 240–44.

[9] Warren K. Moorehead had been working on his archeological investigations of Fort Ancient and Hopewell sites in Ohio when the Ghost Dance spread to the Sioux. In the fall of 1890 he went to Pine Ridge and witnessed one of the dances. Moorehead, "Ghost-Dances in the West," 327.

[10] In his memoirs, Cook recalled their meeting at the agency. Cook, *Fifty Years on the Old Frontier*, 236.

[11] Allen devoted well over four pages of his manuscript to a laudatory biography of Ben Ash. The sketch has been deleted because it was an unrelated intrusion into the Wounded Knee story.

Allen met Benjamin C. Ash in Chadron in 1886 (*Chadron Democrat*, May 13, 1886) and it is apparent they remained close friends throughout their lives. The 1938 draft concluded with the following accolade of Mr. Ash. "This young pioneer of eighty years certainly developed into a citizen of whom South Dakota may well be proud, and the humble log cabin where he grew to manhood proved to be the beginning of the historic old city of Yankton, South Dakota."

When Ash was eight years old his parents homesteaded in the vicinity of present Lake Andes, South Dakota. When he was a young man he was a scout for Lt. Col. George A. Custer. Ash was sheriff of Hughes County from 1882 to 1886 and the Lower Brulé Indian Agent from 1890 to 1896. His ranch in Perkins County, South Dakota, was renowned for its buffalo herd. Doane Robinson, ed., *Encyclopedia of South Dakota* (Pierre, 1925), 47. Don Patton, "The Legend of Ben Ash," *South Dakota Historical Collections and Reports* 23 (1947):185–211. Ben Ash papers, H75.182, South Dakota Historical Society, Pierre.

23. Reporters at Pine Ridge

[1] A few reporters arrived at Pine Ridge with the first companies of soldiers, while others arrived days or even weeks later. By mid-December there were at least seventeen reporters at the agency. They included: C. W. Allen and Alfred Burkholder, *New York Herald*; Gilbert F. Bailey, *Chicago Inter-Ocean*; R. J. Boylan, *St. Paul Pioneer Press*; Judge Burnes, *Chicago Times*; Guy Butler, *Duluth Tribune*; Edward B. Clark and Irving Hawkins, *Chicago Tribune*; Charles H. Cressey, *Omaha Bee*; "Mr. Jones," *Olerich Advocate*; William Finch Kelley, *Nebraska State Journal*; John A. McDonough, *New York World*; Warren K. Moorehead, *Illustrated American*; Ed A. O'Brien, Associated Press; Dent H. Roberts, *St. Louis Post Dispatch*; Charles C. Seymour and Teresa Dean, *Chicago Herald*; Carl Smith, Thomas Tibbles, and Mrs. Thomas Tibbles or Bright Eyes, *Omaha World-Herald*; R. Zilliacus, Chicago *Svenska Tribunen*. Kolbenschlag, *A Whirlwind Passes*.

In addition to Allen, two other reporters, Charles H. Cressey and William Kelley witnessed the massacre. Kelley, *Pine Ridge 1890*.

Charles B. Ewing was an army assistant surgeon and an 1886 Military Academy graduate. Heitman, *Historical Register*, 411. He also joined the reporters in writing comic articles not intended for publication. He went to Wounded Knee with Colonel Forsyth only as a spectator. Robert M. Utley, *Last Days of the Sioux Nation* (New Haven: Yale University Press, 1963), 202.

[2] Frank Grouard was about nineteen years of age when he was captured by Sitting Bull's band in 1869, but he left before the band fled to Canada. In 1875 he became a scout for Brig. Gen. George Crook. DeBarthe, *Life and Adventures of Frank Grouard*. The scouts who patrolled in the vicinity of the agency were "headquarters scouts" to distinguish them from Indians who enlisted in the regular army. Danker, "Wounded Knee Interviews of Eli S. Ricker," 204.

[3] See Wedel, "Notes on the Prairie Turnip," 154–79.

[4] Heitman, *Historical Register*, 215, lists only a Lt. Philip Augustus Bettens, but he was in the Ninth Cavalry at the time and this unit did not arrive until after the massacre.

[5] Albert C. Hopkins appeared in Two Strikes' camp on December 21, 1890, claiming to be the Messiah. He was arrested and ordered to leave the reservation. *Omaha World-Herald*, Dec. 23 and 25, 1890. Hopkins was a Civil War veteran and for years thereafter had sold crockery in northeastern Iowa for the firm of Burley and Tyrrell. *Norfolk* (Nebraska) *Daily News*, Dec. 30. 1890.

24. Big Foot's Arrival

[1] Big Foot was the leader of a Minniconjou band who came to the Cheyenne River reservation in 1876. Generally, these people refused to adopt white ways and were viewed with suspicion by their agents. Herman J. Viola, *Diplomats in Buckskins* (Washington, D.C.: Smithsonian Institution Press, 1981), 185. Big Foot was born about 1830. He was also called Si-Tanka or Spotted Elk. He may be the same Spotted Elk who signed the 1868 Treaty at Fort Laramie. Kappler, *Indian Affairs, Laws and Treaties*, 1055.

Troops of the Eighth Cavalry had been scouting the general area of Big Foot's village on the Cheyenne River for most of the summer of 1890. Although the Indians were not thought to be an immediate threat, their reactionary attitude made the army commanders suspicious of them. T. H. Ruger to adjutant general, Oct. 19, 1890, *Report of the Secretary of War*, 1890, 180. Army patrols in the field were apparently on friendly terms with Big Foot's people. In August 1890 J. C. H. Grabill photographed an Omaha Dance where some of the soldiers were spectators. Jensen, Paul, and Carter, *Eyewitness at Wounded Knee*, plates 7–10. About this time the band embraced the Ghost Dance.

Lt. Col. Edwin V. Sumner of the Eighth Cavalry was placed in charge of the patrols and, at first, viewed Big Foot with suspicion, but after the two men talked, Sumner's opinion softened. He accepted Big Foot's promise to go to Fort Bennett near their agency and surrender to the military. E. V. Sumner to N. A. Miles, Dec. 22 and 23, 1890, *Report of the Secretary of War*, 1890, 233–34.

[2] The band probably would have surrendered had it not been for the intervention of John Dunn, a white squatter married to a Minneconjou woman. When Colonel Sumner became impatient with Big Foot for not immediately leaving the village for Fort Bennett, he sent Dunn to urge them to hurry. Dunn's story, as recalled by the Indians, was that the men were going to be sent to an island prison in the Atlantic Ocean while the women would be left behind at some undisclosed point. Dunn urged them to go to Pine Ridge "right away if you want to save your lives." Danker, "Wounded Knee Interviews of Eli S. Ricker," 165, 181. Dunn later denied telling such a tale, but an army interpreter, Felix Benoit, supported the Indians' interpretation. Statements by John Dunn and Felix Benoit, *Report of the Secretary of War*, 1890, 235–38. The Indians accepted Dunn's warning as a distinct possibility. Big Foot argued they should stay in their village, but a majority favored the move and on the night of December 23 they slipped out of the village. Danker, "Wounded Knee Interviews of Eli S. Ricker," 168, 185. Later, Sumner complained bitterly that Dunn "got into their camp and told them I was on the road to attack and kill them all . . . so they just stampeded . . . traveling so fast I could not overtake them." E. V. Sumner to Col. H. C. Merriman, Dec. 27, 1890, *Report of the Secretary of War*, 1890, 211. Big Foot's decision to go to Pine Ridge was undoubtedly influenced by other factors. For example, Red Cloud and several other Oglala leaders invited Big Foot to come to their agency. Danker, "Wounded Knee Interviews of Eli S. Ricker," 180.

[3] It was Baptiste "Little Bat" Garnier, not Baptiste Garneau, who first discovered Big Foot's band. Jensen, Paul, and Carter, *Eyewitness at Wounded Knee*, 35.

[4] The evidence suggests Allen underestimated the population of the fleeing Miniconjou at least by half. Jensen, "Big Foot's Followers at Wounded Knee," 194–212.

[5] Photographs of the massacre site taken on January 3 and 4, 1891, show the tipi frames and support Allen's observation that they were "makeshifts." Jensen, Paul, and Carter, *Eyewitness at Wounded Knee*, plates 63–78.

[6] Big Foot contracted pneumonia after his band left their village on the Cheyenne River. His daughter was Brings White or White Horse Woman, about twenty years of age. James McLaughlin Papers, Microfilm Roll 17, Notebook 40, Assumption College, Richardson, North Dakota.

[7] Charles S. Denny was a captain in Company I of the First Infantry, South Dakota Volunteers, during the Spanish-American War. Paul D. McClelland was a lieutenant in the same unit. Wright Tarbell, "History of the South Dakota National Guard," *South Dakota Historical Collections* 6 (1912):455–56.

The company served in the Philippines during the war, where McClelland was wounded. Fred W. Whitley, "A History of Custer City, South Dakota," *South Dakota Historical Collections* 37 (1975):311–12.

[8] Maj. Samuel M. Whitside of the Seventh Cavalry had served for over thirty years in the military. Heitman, *Historical Register*, 1031. He was in command of Troops A, B, I, and K of the Seventh Cavalry with a platoon of the First Artillery and on December 26 made camp on the site of the Wounded Knee massacre. J. W. Forsyth to assistant adjutant general, Dec. 31, 1890, Reports, Campaign of 1890–91.

[9] Col. James W. Forsyth graduated from the Military Academy in 1851 and served in the Civil War. He took command of the Seventh Cavalry in 1886. Heitman, *Historical Register*, 430. Forsyth left the agency with Troops C, D, E, and G on the afternoon of December 28, 1890, and arrived at the Wounded Knee camp in the evening. A platoon of the First Artillery and a troop of Indian scouts made up the remainder of the column. J. W. Forsyth to assistant adjutant general, Dec. 31, 1890, Reports, Campaign of 1890–91. Also testimony of W. J. Nicholson, Ibid.

[10] Mr. Swiggert of Gordon apparently went to Wounded Knee as a spectator. Danker, "Wounded Knee Interviews of Eli S. Ricker," 233.

[11] Joe Bush was among those in favor of allowing Ghost Dancers from other reservations to remain at Pine Ridge. He lived on Wounded Knee Creek. U. S. Senate, *Executive Documents of the Senate of the United States*, 52d Congress, 1st Session, 1891–92, Document 58:94, "Letter . . . in relation to . . . South Dakota." The "fair sized village" was a tent camp. There were a few log houses scattered about in the Wounded Knee vicinity.

[12] Louis Mousseau operated the store at Wounded Knee and was there on December 29. Danker, "Wounded Knee Interviews of Eli S. Ricker," 228.

[13] Six Feather and Plenty Bear lived at Wounded Knee. A Plenty Bear was also a scout for Agent Royer. *Nebraska State Journal*, Nov. 29, 1890. The trader Allen refers to was probably Louis Mousseau, but could have been James Asay, an agency storekeeper, who was also at Wounded Knee.

[14] George Daniel Wallace graduated from the Military Academy in 1868. Heitman, *Historical Register*, 998. He was the commanding officer of Troop K of the Seventh Cavalry when he was killed at Wounded Knee. Utley, *Last Days of the Sioux Nation*, 201.

[15] Forsyth undoubtedly held Gen. Philip H. Sheridan in high regard. He had served on Sheridan's staff during the Civil War and the general's patronage helped Forsyth win an appointment as a colonel in the regular army after the war. Sheridan had died

only two years prior to Allen's meeting with Forsyth. The European tour was during the winter of 1867–68. Paul Andrew Hutton, *Phil Sheridan and His Army* (Lincoln: University of Nebraska Press, 1985).

25. The Last Fight of North American Indians

[1] Philip Wells was one of the handful of eyewitnesses at Wounded Knee who was fluent in both Dakota and English. Philip R. Wells, "Ninety-six Years among the Indians of the Northwest," *North Dakota History* 15 (1948):85-312.

Louis or Louie Shangreau and his brother, John, served as civilian scouts and interpreters for the army for many years and were Wounded Knee survivors. John brought the news back to Colonel Whitside on December 28 that Big Foot had been sighted from Porcupine Butte northeast of the army camp on Wounded Knee Creek. Ricker Collection, Interviews, Tablet 27, 82–96. Also statements by John Shangrau and Louie Shangrau, Jan. 24, 1891, Reports, Campaign of 1890–91.

Father Francis M. J. Craft, S.J., was a longtime missionary to the Sioux. He accompanied Forsyth's command to Wounded Knee on the evening of December 28. He said he went there "to see if I could be of any service . . . by going among the Indians and reassuring them." Statement of Rev. Francis M. J. Craft, Reports, Campaign of 1890–91.

[2] Early in December General Miles decided it would be best to take the band either to Fort Meade or Fort Omaha until the trouble on the reservations had passed. On December 23 Colonel Sumner was authorized to arrest Big Foot and his people and take them to Fort Meade or Fort Bennett. Maus to E. V. Sumner, Dec. 23, 1890, *Report of the Secretary of War*, 1892, 231-32.

[3] Later, Allen mentioned the death of the boys, which was confirmed by George Sword. George Sword, "Account Given by Indians of the Fight at Wounded Knee Creek," *Annual Report, Indian Affairs*, 1891:180.

[4] John Shangreau (not William) and Little Bat Garnier were ordered to search the Indian camp for weapons. Shangreau recalled that while the search was going on he saw Allen wandering about in the camp. A short time later the first shot was fired. Ricker Collection, Interviews, Tablet 27, 82–96. Also statements by John Shangrau and Louie Shangrau, Jan. 24, 1891, Reports, Campaign of 1890–91.

[5] Allen is undoubtedly describing Good Thunder, also called Sits Straight, whose harangue was noted by many eyewitnesses. Nearly all of the accounts mention him throwing some dirt in the air as part of his incantations. Allen described the incident in a signed article in the *Chadron Democrat*, Jan. 1, 1891. Some of the military insisted it was the signal for the Indians to open fire on the soldiers. The Ghost Dancer who threw the dirt has been frequently misidentified as Yellow Bird. Jensen, Paul, and Carter, *Eyewitness at Wounded Knee*, 20-21.

[6] Lt. John Kinzie, Second Infantry, went to Wounded Knee as a spectator with Colonel Forsyth's column. Utley, *Last Days of the Sioux Nation*, 202.

[7] The Hotchkiss gun is a breechloading cannon of 3.2 inch caliber. Four of these cannons were placed on the small hill overlooking the camps. The dead Indians were later buried atop this hill. A Catholic church was built there in 1913 and then destroyed by fire during the 1973 takeover of Wounded Knee by the American Indian Movement.

[8] Eyewitness accounts differ concerning the moment when the fighting started, but the consensus opinion is that there was a single accidental shot followed by a very brief pause and then everyone started shooting. Black Coyote, sometimes called

Black Fox, had refused to surrender his rifle to the soldiers and a struggle ensued, which resulted in the first accidental gunshot. Danker, "Wounded Knee Interviews of Eli S. Ricker," 173 and 192.

[9] Charles W. Taylor was a Military Academy graduate from New York. Heitman, *Historical Register*, 946. He commanded the troop of Oglala scouts at Wounded Knee. These were regular army troops as opposed to the civilian scouts. The Gray Horse Cavalry was Troop G of the Seventh Cavalry commanded by Capt. Winfield S. Edgerly.

[10] Three illegible notes by Allen are interlined in this sentence and in the margin is "to be rewritten."

[11] Many Indians tried to escape up the ravine. Those who dug in were at a location often referred to as the pocket. Cpl. Paul H. Weinert rolled one Hotchkiss cannon down the hill and into the ravine, where he kept firing until "pretty soon everything was quiet at the other end of the line." W. F. Beyer and O. F. Keydel, eds., *Deeds of Valor* 2 (Detroit, 1907), 316.

26. Back to the Agency

[1] Allen is probably referring to Lt. Ernest A. Darlington, who was wounded in the elbow. Utley, *Last Days of the Sioux Nation*, 213.

[2] Allen refers to High Back Bone or High Back, one of the Oglala scouts commanded by Lt. Charles W. Taylor. The army's scout, Philip Wells, said High Back Bone "stripped off his uniform and with nothing but his breechcloth on, rushed forward to help the soldiers. His appearance was that of any hostile and as soon as the soldiers saw him they . . . promptly filled him full of lead. This is the only scout killed so far as known." J. B. Peterson, *The Battle of Wounded Knee* (Gordon, Nebr.: News Publishing Co., 1941), 22.

[3] Allen softens this sentence considerably. The 1938 version read "Desultory rifle shots could be heard at short intervals, aimed wherever a blanket was seen to move regardless of what or who might be under it."

[4] Big Foot and his daughter, Brings White or White Horse Woman, were killed, but Allen was the only eyewitness to describe the manner of their deaths. Big Foot's wife was Small Tail or Sinte-chigela. James McLaughlin Papers. McChesney, "Census of Cheyenne River Agency S. Dak. Indians, June 30, 1890." Perain P. Palmer, "Census of the Sioux of different Bands of Indians of Cheyenne River Agency . . . June 30, 1891," National Archives, RG 75, Microcopy 595, Roll 33.

[5] John Shangreau tells a very similar story. Ricker Collection, Interviews, Tablet 27, 82–96.

[6] Wells also told this story, but in much greater detail. Wells, "Ninety-six Years Among the Indians," 287.

[7] Allen's belief that "practically all" of the army's fatalities were in or near the ravine is incorrect. The majority died in the initial shooting around the council circle. The troops formed a U around the Indians attending the council and some of the soldiers were certainly killed by friendly fire.

27. Concluding Incidents

[1] The report Allen received combined two separate events. According to Wells an Indian "approached to within three or four feet of me with a long cheese knife, ground to a sharp point, and raised to stab me. The fight between us prevented my seeing

anything else at the time. He stabbed me during the melee and nearly cut off my nose. I held him off until I could swing my rifle to hit him, which I did. I shot and killed him in self-defence and as an act of war as soon as I could gain room to aim my rifle and fire." Wells, "Ninety-six Years Among the Indians," 287. In the 1938 manuscript Allen wrote that Wells's nose was "completely severed."

There is no evidence that Wells assisted Father Craft when the latter received his wound. The wound was a severe knife wound in his right lung. Despite this Craft ministered to the wounded soldiers until he collapsed. Testimony of Reverend Francis M. J. Craft, Reports, Campaign of 1890–91.

[2] Lieutenant Thunder Bear of the Pine Ridge police force had also attempted to arrest an Oglala named Little, but was prevented from doing so by Ghost Dancers. This was one of the events that convinced Agent Royer the army was needed to prevent an uprising. Jensen, Paul, and Carter, *Eyewitness at Wounded Knee*, 75.

[3] Allen has again combined two separate but related incidents. The detached camp of Colonel Carr's command was Maj. Guy V. Henry's squadron. They received the news of the Wounded Knee massacre and were ordered to return to the agency to help defend it if necessary. They left their camp on the evening of December 29 for an all night march. Since their supply wagons traveled so slowly, Henry and most of his men rushed ahead, arriving exhausted at the agency the following morning. Shortly after reaching the agency a messenger arrived to report that the wagons were under attack. Lt. Guy H. Preston and his Oglala Scouts, followed shortly by the Seventh Cavalry under Colonel Forsyth, raced to their rescue.

On December 30 "hostiles" set fire to two day schools and a shed in the vicinity of the Holy Rosary Mission. Colonel Forsyth's command went to investigate and were soon pinned down by the "hostiles." Casualties included one killed and six wounded, one of whom died later. Four troops of the Ninth Cavalry under Major Henry were sent from the agency to the relief of the Seventh. Although the Indian force, estimated at about fifty, had been outnumbered from the beginning, they withdrew only after the arrival of still more troops. These attacks, born of anger and frustration over the Wounded Knee massacre, were the only attempts to retaliate against the army. Statements taken on Jan. 24, 1891, from Major Henry, Lieutenant Preston, and Colonel Forsyth to J. N. Brooke, Dec. 30, 1890, Reports, Campaign of 1980–91.

[4] Allen again condenses and combines events. A blizzard and fear of an attack on the agency delayed the departure of a burial detail, however, a hastily organized rescue party of Indians went to Wounded Knee on January 1 and found several survivors. The rescuers were forced to abandon their mission when they were fired upon by other Indians, who misunderstood their intentions. *Omaha Bee*, Jan. 2, 1891, and Jan. 14, 1891.

A burial party of paid civilian workers was recruited by the army and the dead were interred on January 3 and 4. F. D. Baldwin to assistant adjutant general, Feb. 5, 1891, Reports, Campaign of 1890–91.

[5] A granite monument was dedicated on May 28, 1903. *Rushville* (Nebraska) *Standard*, May 22, 1903, and *Omaha World-Herald*, June 7, 1903.

[6] Peter Richard was a mixed-blood relative of Red Cloud, who witnessed the murder of Lieutenant Casey. S. A. Cloman to camp adjutant, Feb. 20, 1891, Reports, Campaign of 1890–91.

Bibliography

Books, Articles, Reports, and Manuscripts

Allen, Charles W. Collection. MS 2635. Nebraska State Historical Society, Lincoln.

———. "Red Cloud and the U.S. Flag." *Nebraska History* 21 (1940):293–304.

———. "Red Cloud, Chief of the Sioux." *The Hesperian* 1 (1895):144–47 and 173–87, (1896):211–16.

Allen, Arthur Otis. "Chapter 6–Family Histories." *Seventy Years of Pioneer Life in Bennett County, South Dakota.* Martin, S. Dak.: The Society, 1981, 152–53.

American Newspaper Directory. New York: George W. Powsell and Co., 1889.

Anderson, Harry H. "The War Club of Sitting Bull the Oglala." *Nebraska History* 42 (1961):55–62.

Andreas, A. T. *History of the State of Kansas.* 2 vols., 1883. Reprint, Marceline, Mo.: Walsworth Co., 1976.

Ash, Ben. Papers. H 75.182. South Dakota Historical Society, Pierre.

Athearn, Robert G. *Forts of the Upper Missouri.* Englewood Cliffs, N. J.: Prentice-Hall Inc., 1967.

Bailey, Paul. *Wovoka, The Indian Messiah.* Los Angeles: Westernlore Press, 1957.

Barlow, J. W. *Outline Descriptions of the Posts in the Military Division of the Missouri.* Chicago: n. p., 1876.

Bartlett, I. S., ed. *History of Wyoming.* 3 vols. Chicago: S. J. Clarke Publishing Co., 1918.

Beel, Marianne Brinda, ed. *A Sandhill Century: Book 1 The Land.* Henderson, Nebr.: Service Press, 1986.

Bell, Campton. "The Early Theater of Cheyenne, Wyoming. *Annals of Wyoming* 25 (1953):3–21.

Beyer, W. F. and O. F. Keydel, eds. *Deeds of Valor.* 2 vols. Detroit: n. p., 1907.

Bissonette, Joseph. Biographical file. South Dakota Historical Society, Pierre.

Blackman, Frank W. ed. *Kansas, a Cyclopedia of State History.* 3 vols. Chicago: Standard Publishing Co., 1912.

Bland, T. A. *A Brief History of the Late Military Invasion of the Home of the Sioux.* Washington, D.C.: n. p., 1891.

Borst, John C. "Dakota Resources: The John R. Brennan Family Papers at the South Dakota Historical Resource Center." *South Dakota History* 14 (1984):68–72.

Bourke, John G. *On The Border With Crook.* 1891. Reprint, Glorieta, N. Mex.: Rio Grande Press, Inc., 1968.

Brennan, John R. "Report of Agent for Pine Ridge Agency." *Annual Report of the Department of the Interior, Indian Affairs, 1905.* Washington, D.C.: GPO, 1906, 337–39.

Brosius, Augustus. "Great Nemaha Agency." *Annual Report of the Commissioner of Indian Affairs.* Washington, D.C.: GPO, 1881, 123–24.

Buecker, Thomas R. "Red Cloud Agency Traders, 1873–1877." *The Museum of the Fur Trade Quarterly* 30 (1994):4–14.

Bibliography

————. *A History of Camp Robinson, Nebraska*. Masters Thesis, Chadron State College, 1992.

————. "Fort Niobrara, 1880–1906: Guardian of the Rosebud Sioux." *Nebraska History* 65 (1984):300–25.

Catlin, George. *Letters and Notes on the Manners, Customs, and Condition of the North American Indians*. 2 vols. New York: Wiley and Putnam, 1841.

Carter, Harvey L. "Chat Dubray." *Mountain Men and the Fur Trade of the Far West* 6. Glendale, Calif.: Arthur H. Clark Co. (1968):143–46.

Chadron Centennial History. Chadron, Nebraska: Chadron Narrative History Project Committee, 1985.

Climate and Man: Yearbook of Agriculture. Washington, D.C.: U.S. Department of Agriculture, GPO, 1941.

Clough, Wilson O. "Mini-Aku, Daughter of Spotted Tail." *Annals of Wyoming* 39 (1967):187–216.

Colby, L. W. "The Sioux Indian War of 1890–91." Nebraska State Historical Society. *Transactions and Reports* 3 (1892):144-90.

Collins, Charles. *Collins' Black Hills History and Directory for 1878–9*. Charles Collins, publisher, 1879.

Collins, Mary. "Mary Clementine Collins, Dacotah Missionary." *North Dakota History* 19 (1952):59–81.

Compendium of History, Reminescence, and Biography of Western Nebraska. Chicago: Alden Publishing Co., 1909.

Cook, James H. *Fifty Years on the Old Frontier*. Norman: University of Oklahoma Press, 1957.

Corbusier, William T. "Camp Sheridan, Nebraska." *Nebraska History* 42 (1961):29–53.

Curley, Edwin A. *Guide to the Black Hills*. Chicago: n. p., 1877.

Danker, Donald F. "The Violent Deaths of Yellow Bear and John Richard Jr." *Nebraska History* 63 (1982):136–49.

————. "The Wounded Knee Interviews of Eli S. Ricker." *Nebraska History* 62 (1981):151–243.

David, Robert B. *Malcolm Campbell Sheriff*. Casper, Wy.: Wyomingiana, Inc., 1932.

Deahl, William E. Jr. "The Chadron-Chicago 1,000 Mile Cowboy Race." *Nebraska History* 53 (1973):167–93.

DeBarthe, Joe. *Life and Adventures of Frank Grouard*. Norman: University of Oklahoma Press, 1958.

DeMallie, Raymond J. and Elaine A. DeMallie, eds. *Lakota Belief and Ritual*. Lincoln: University of Nebraska Press, 1980.

Dorchester, Daniel. "Report of the Superintendent of Indian Schools." *Sixtieth Annual Report of the Commissioner of Indian Affairs*. Washington, D.C.: GPO, 1891, 528-38.

Dorsey, James Owen. *A Study of Siouan Cults*. Eleventh Annual Report of the Bureau of American Ethnology, Smithsonian Institution. Washington, D.C.: GPO, 1894.

Duncan, James J. "Report of the Day-School Inspector, Pine Ridge Reservation." *Annual Report of the Department of the Interior, Indian Affairs, 1901*. Washington, D.C.: GPO, 1902, 368–70.

Bibliography

Fiske, Frank Bennett. *Life and Death of Sitting Bull.* Fort Yates, N.Dak.: Pioneer Arrow Print, 1933.

Fitzgerald, Sister Mary Clement. "Bishop Marty and His Sioux Missions." *South Dakota Historical Collections* 20 (1940):522–88.

Flannery, L. G., ed. *John Hunton's Diary 1873–'75.* 5 vols. Lingle, Wyo.: Guide Review, 1956.

Frazier, Robert W. *Forts of the West.* Norman: University of Oklahoma Press, 1965.

Fuller, E. O. "Cheyenne Looking North." *Annals of Wyoming* 23 (1951):3–51.

Gallagher, H. D. "Report of Pine Ridge Agency." *Fifty-ninth Annual Report of the Commissioner of Indian Affairs.* Washington, D.C.: GPO, 1890, 48–55.

————. "Pine Ridge Agency." *Annual Report of the Commissioner of Indian Affairs.* Washington, D.C.: GPO, 1887, 40–42.

Gard, Wayne. *The Chisholm Trail.* Norman: University of Oklahoma Press, 1954.

Gilbert, Hila. *Big Bat Pourier.* Sheridan, Wyo.: Mills Publishing Company, 1968.

Graber, Kay. *Sister to the Sioux: The Memoirs of Elaine Goodale Eastman.* Lincoln: University of Nebraska Press, 1978.

Grange, Roger T., Jr. "Fort Robinson, Outpost on the Plains." *Nebraska History* 39 (1958):191–240.

Great Northwest, The. Omaha: Herald Job Printing, 1889.

Green, Charles Lowell. "The Administration of the Public Domain in South Dakota." *South Dakota Historical Collections* 20 (1940):7–279.

Greene, Jerome A. "The Sioux Land Commission of 1889: Prelude to Wounded Knee." *South Dakota History* 1 (1970):41–72.

Gue, Benjamin F. *History of Iowa.* 4 vols. New York: Century History Co., 1893.

Hafen, LeRoy R. and Francis Marion Young. *Fort Laramie and the Pageant of the West.* Glendale, Calif.: Arthur H. Clark Co., 1938.

Hagen, William T. *The Indian Rights Association.* Tucson: University of Arizona Press, 1958.

Hanson, Charles E. Jr. "Geminien P. Beauvais." *Mountain Men and the Fur Trade of the Far West* 7. Glendale, Calif.: Arthur H. Clark Co. (1969): 35–43.

Hedren, Paul L. *Fort Laramie in 1876.* Lincoln: University of Nebraska Press, 1988.

————. *First Scalp for Custer: The Skirmish at Warbonnet Creek, Nebraska, July 17, 1876.* Glendale, Calif.: Arthur H. Clark Co., 1980.

Heitman, Francis B. *Historical Register and Dictionary of the United States Army.* Washington, D.C.: GPO, 1903.

Hoover, Herbert T. "The Sioux Agreement of 1889 and Its Aftermath." *South Dakota History* 19 (1989):56–94.

Howe, M. A. DeWolfe. *The Life and Labors of Bishop Hare.* New York: Sturgis and Walton Co., 1913.

Hutton, Paul Andrew. *Phil Sheridan and His Army.* Lincoln: University of Nebraska Press, 1985.

Hunton, John. "Reminiscences by John Hunton." *Annals of Wyoming* 6 (1930):262–70.

Hyde, George. *Spotted Tail's Folk: A History of the Brulé Sioux.* Norman: University of Oklahoma Press, 1961.

Bibliography

————. *Red Cloud's Folk, A History of the Oglala Sioux Indians*. Norman: University of Oklahoma Press, 1937.

Irwin, James. "Red Cloud Agency." *Annual Report of the Commissioner of Indian Affairs*. Washington, D.C.: GPO, 1877, 62–63.

————. "Red Cloud Agency." *Annual Report of the Commissioner of Indian Affairs*. Washington, D.C.: GPO, 1878, 36–38.

Jensen, Richard E. "Notes on the Lakota Ghost Dance." Paper read before the Thirty-third Annual Missouri Valley History Conference, Omaha, Nebr., March 8, 1990.

————. "Big Foot's Followers at Wounded Knee." *Nebraska History* 71 (1990):194–212.

Jensen, Richard E., R. Eli Paul, and John E. Carter. *Eyewitness at Wounded Knee*. Lincoln: University of Nebraska Press, 1993.

Johnson, Allen, ed. "Grover Cleveland." *Dictionary of American Biography* 8. New York: Charles Scribner's Sons (1943):205–12.

Jordan, Charles P. Papers. H74.42. South Dakota Historical Society, Pierre.

Jordan, William Red Cloud. "Eighty Years on the Rosebud." South Dakota Historical Society. *Report and Historical Collections* 35 (1970):323–83.

Kappler, Charles J. *Indian Affairs, Laws and Treaties*. Washington, D.C.: GPO, 1903.

Kelley, William Fitch. *Pine Ridge 1890*. Edited by Alexander Kelley and Pierre Bovis. San Francisco: Pierre Bovis, 1971.

King, James T. *War Eagle, A Life of General Eugene A. Carr*. Lincoln: University of Nebraska Press, 1963.

Kolbenschlag, George R. *A Whirlwind Passes*. Pierre: University of South Dakota Press, 1990.

Lass, William E. *From the Missouri to the Great Salt Lake: An Account of Overland Freighting*. Lincoln: Nebraska State Historical Society, 1972.

LeCompte, Janet. "Antoine Janis." *Mountain Men and the Fur Trade of the Far West* 8. Glendale, Calif.: Arthur H. Clark Co. (1971): 196–201.

Lee, Wayne C. *Scotty Philip, The Man Who Saved The Buffalo*. Caldwell, Idaho: Caxton Printers, 1975.

Livermont, Carol. "Chapter 24—Post Offices." *Seventy Years of Pioneer Life in Bennett County, South Dakota*. Martin, S. Dak.: The Society, 1981, 83.

Lindberg, Christer. "Foreigners in Action at Wounded Knee." *Nebraska History* 71 (1990):170–81.

Lutz, Gertrude. *Sketches of Some Pioneers*. Chadron, Nebr.: Chadron Printing Company, 1953.

Mattes, Merrill J. *Fort Laramie Park History*. Rocky Mountain Regional Office: National Park Service, 1980.

————. Memo for the files, October 30, 1942, Fort Laramie National Historic Site.

Mattison, Ray H. "Report on the Historic Sites in the Big Bend Reservoir Area, Missouri River, South Dakota." *South Dakota Historical Collections and Reports* 31 (1962):243–86.

————. "Report on the Historic Sites Adjacent to the Missouri River Between the Big Sioux River and Fort Randall Dam." *South Dakota Historical Collections and Reports* 28 (1956):22–98.

McCann, Lloyd E. "The Grattan Massacre." *Nebraska History* 37 (1956):1–25.

McChesney, C. E. "Census of Cheyenne River Agency S. Dak. Indians, June 30, 1890." National Archives. Record Group 75, Microcopy 595, Roll 33.

McDermott, John D. "Wounded Knee: Centennial Voices." *South Dakota History* 20 (1990):245–92.

———. "James Bordeaux." *Mountain Men and the Fur Trade of the Far West* 5. Glendale, Calif.: Arthur H. Clark Co. (1968): 65–80.

McGillycuddy, Julia Blanchard. *McGillycuddy Agent, A Biography of Dr. Valentine T. McGillycuddy.* Stanford, Calif.: Stanford University Press, 1941.

McGillycuddy, V. T. "Red Cloud Agency." *Annual Report of the Commissioner of Indian Affairs.* Washington, D.C.: GPO, 1881, 47–49.

———. "Red Cloud Agency." *Annual Report of the Commissioner of Indian Affairs.* Washington, D.C.: GPO, 1880, 39–42.

———. "Red Cloud Agency." *Annual Report of the Commissioner of Indian Affairs.* Washington, D.C.: GPO, 1879, 37–40.

McLaughlin, James. *My Friend the Indian.* Boston: Houghton-Mifflin Co., 1916.

———. Papers. Microfilm Roll 17, Notebook 40. Assumption College, Richardson, N. Dak.

Miller, Darlis A. *Captain Jack Crawford: Buckskin Poet, Scout, and Showman.* Albuquerque: University of New Mexico Press, 1993.

Mooney, James. *The Ghost-Dance Religion and the Sioux Outbreak of 1890.* Fourteenth Annual Report of the Bureau of Ethnology, Smithsonian Institution. Washington, D.C.: GPO, 1896.

Moorehead, Warren K. "Ghost-Dances in the West." *The Illustrated American,* January 17, 1891, 327.

———. Papers. Collection 106. Ohio Historical Society, Columbus, Ohio.

Morton, J. Sterling. *Illustrated History of Nebraska.* 3 vols. Lincoln: Jacob North & Co., 1906.

Nadeau, Remi. *Fort Laramie and the Sioux Indians.* Englewood Cliffs, N.J.: Prentice-Hall Co., 1967.

National Archives. Record Group 28. Record of Appointment of Postmasters. Microcopy 841, Rolls 77 and 117.

———. Record Group 29. Schedules of the Nebraska State Census of 1885. Cherry County. Microcopy 352, Roll 8.

———. Record Group 75. Letters Received by the Office of Indian Affairs. Red Cloud Agency. Microcopy 234, Rolls 715–18 and 724–26.

———. Record Group 75. Letters Received by the Office of Indian Affairs. Spotted Tail Agency. Microcopy 234, Roll 840.

———. Record Group 75. Letters Sent to the Office of Indian Affairs from Pine Ridge. Microcopy 1282, Rolls 1–2 and 12–34.

———. Record Group 75. Central Plains Region. Pine Ridge Agency, #3 Miscellaneous Correspondence Received.

———. Record Group 94. Records of the Adjutant General's Office. Reports and Correspondence Relating to the Army Investigations of the Battle of Wounded Knee and to the Sioux Campaign of 1890–1891. Microcopy 983.

———. Record Group 123. Court of Claims. Indian Depredation No. 4803.

Nebraska State Historical Society. RG 14. Superintendent's Correspondence.

Nelson, Ann. Senior Historian, Wyoming State Museum. Personal communication to Richard E. Jensen, 1994.

O'Reilly, Harrington. *Fifty Years on the Trail; Remarkable Story of the Life of John Y. Nelson.* Norman: University of Oklahoma Press, 1963.

Olson, James C. *Red Cloud and the Sioux Problem.* Lincoln: University of Nebraska Press Bison Book, 1975.

Paine, Bayard H. *Pioneers, Indians and Buffaloes.* Curtis, Nebr.: Curtis Enterprise, 1935.

Palmer, Perain P. "Census of the Sioux of different Bands of Indians of Cheyenne River Agency . . . , June 30, 1891." National Archives. RG 75. Microcopy 595, Roll 33.

Parker, Watson. *Deadwood, The Golden Years.* Lincoln, University of Nebraska Press, 1981.

Patton, Don. "The Legend of Ben Ash." *South Dakota Historical Collection and Reports* 23 (1947):185–211.

Paul, R. Eli. "Recovering Red Cloud's Autobiography." *Montana: The Magazine of Western History* 44 (1994):2–17.

Peterson, B. J. *The Battle of Wounded Knee.* Gordon, Nebr.: News Publishing Co., 1941.

Powers, William K. *Oglala Religion.* Lincoln: University of Nebraska Press, 1975.

Price, H. "Report of the Commissioner of Indian Affairs." *Annual Report of the Commissioner of Indian Affairs.* Washington, D.C.: GPO, 1881, 1–70.

Prucha, Francis Paul. *A Guide to the Military Posts of the United States.* Madison: State Historical Society of Wisconsin, 1964.

Reese, Randy and Sheila Reese. Personal communications to Richard E. Jensen, 1995–96.

Report of the Secretary of War: Being Part of the Message and Documents Communicated to the Two Houses of Congress at the Beginning of the First Session of the Fifty-Second Congress. Vol. 1. Washington, D.C.: GPO, 1892.

Richards, Bartlett, Jr. *Bartlett Richards, Nebraska Sandhills Cattleman.* Lincoln: Nebraska State Historical Society, 1980.

Ricker, Eli. Collection. MS8. Nebraska State Historical Society, Lincoln.

Robinson, Doane. "Peter Norbeck." *South Dakota Historical Collections and Reports* 22 (1946):296–305.

———., ed. *Encyclopedia of South Dakota.* Pierre, S. Dak., 1925.

———. "A History of the Dakota or Sioux Indians." *South Dakota Historical Collections and Reports* 2 (1904):1–523.

Robinson, Will G. "Daughters of Dakota." *South Dakota Department of History Report and Historical Collections* 33 (1966):65–66.

———. "Charles Smith Cook." *South Dakota Historical Collections and Reports* 22 (1946):32–33.

Russell, Don. *The Lives and Legends of Buffalo Bill.* Norman: University of Oklahoma Press, 1960.

Sanborn Map and Publishing Company, New York. Map of Chadron, Nebraska, July 1887.

Bibliography

Saville, J. J. "Red Cloud Agency." *Annual Report of the Commissioner of Indian Affairs.* Washington, D.C.: GPO, 1874, 251–52.

Sawyer, R. McLaran. "No Teacher for the School: The Nebraska Junior Normal School Movement." *Nebraska History* 52 (1971):191–203.

Schnurr, Clarence. "Edgar Beecher Bronson." *Sioux County, Memoirs of Its Pioneers.* Edited by Ruth Van Ackeren. Harrison, Nebr.: Harrison Ladies' Community Club, 1967.

Schuler, Harold H. *Fort Pierre Chouteau.* Vermillion: University of South Dakota Press, 1990.

Sheldon, Addison E. Collection. MS 2039, diary. Nebraska State Historical Society, Lincoln.

——. "Major Charles W. Allen." *Nebraska History* 21 (1940):292.

——. *Life of Red Cloud.* Manuscript. Nebraska State Historical Society, 1932.

——. *Nebraska the Land and the People.* 2 vols. Chicago: Lewis Publishing Company, 1931.

Shepherd, Allen, Belvadine R. Lecher, Lloy Chamberlin, and Marguerite Radcliffe, eds. *Man of Many Frontiers: The Diaries of 'Billy The Bear' Iaeger.* Omaha: Making History, 1994.

Shumway, Grant L. *History of Western Nebraska and Its People.* 2 vols. Lincoln: Western Publishing Company, 1921.

South Dakota Research Council, comp. *Biographical Directory of the South Dakota Legislature.* Vol. 1., 1929.

Spring, Agnes Wright. *Casper Collins: The Life and Exploits of an Indian Fighter.* Lincoln: University of Nebraska Press, 1969.

——. *The Cheyenne and Black Hills Stage and Express Routes.* Glendale, Calif.: Arthur H. Clark Company, 1948.

Stirling, C. G. "Report of the Missionary, Pine Ridge Agency." *Fifty-seventh Annual Report of the Commissioner of Indian Affairs.* Washington, D.C.: GPO, 1888, 53.

Strahorn, Robert E. *The Hand-Book of Wyoming.* Cheyenne, Wyo., 1877.

Sword, George. "Account Given by Indians of the Fight at Wounded Knee Creek." *Sixtieth Annual Report of the Commissioner of Indian Affairs.* Washington, D.C.: GPO, 1891.

Tallent, Annie D. *The Black Hills: or, The Last Hunting Ground of the Dakotas.* Sioux Falls, S. Dak.: Brevet Press, 1974.

Tarbell, Wright. "History of the South Dakota National Guard." *South Dakota Historical Collections* 6 (1912):363–490.

Taylor, Inez Babb."Career of Cheyenne - Black Hills Stage Line Owner, Colorful Story of the 'Old West'." *Annals of Wyoming* 11 (1939):222–27.

Trenholm, Virginia Cole. *Footprints on the Frontier.* Douglas, Wyo.: Douglas Enterprise Co., 1945.

Trigg, J. H. *History of Cheyenne and Northern Wyoming.* Omaha: Herald Steam Book and Job Printing Service, 1876.

Turchen, Lesta V. and James D. McLaird. *The Black Hills Expedition of 1875.* Mitchell, S. Dak.: Dakota Wesleyan University Press, 1975.

U.S. General Land Office, RG 508, Land Tract Books, vol. 16. Nebraska State Historical Society, Lincoln.

U.S. Senate. *Executive Documents of the Senate of the United States.* 51st Congress,

Bibliography

2d Session, 1891–1892. Document 9. "Letter . . . relative to . . . Indians in certain states."

―――. *Executive Documents of the Senate of the United States.* 52d Congress, 1st Session, 1891–92. Document 58, 1892. "Letter . . . in relation to . . . South Dakota."

Utley, Robert M. "Nelson A. Miles." *Soldiers West.* Lincoln: University of Nebraska Press, 1987:213–27.

―――. *Last Days of the Sioux Nation.* New Haven: Yale University Press, 1963.

Van Metre, Olive. *The Old Town, 1880–1889.* Norfolk, Nebr.: Norfolk Printing Co., 1977.

Vestal, Stanley. *Jim Bridger, Mountain Man.* Lincoln: University of Nebraska Press Bison Book, 1970.

Viola, Herman J. *Diplomats in Buckskins.* Washington: Smithsonian Institution Press, 1981.

Walker, Henry Pickering. *The Wagonmasters.* Norman: University of Oklahoma Press, 1966.

Walker, James R. "The Sun Dance and Other Ceremonies of the Oglala Division of the Teton Dakota." *Anthropological Papers* 16. American Museum of Natural History, 1917.

Watkins, Albert. *History of Nebraska.* 3 vols. Lincoln: Western Publishing Co., 1913.

Watson, George D., Jr. *Prairie Justice, 1885–1985.* Chadron: B and B Printing Company, n.d.

Wedel, Waldo R. "Notes on the Prairie Turnip." *Nebraska History* 59 (1978):154–79.

Wells, Philip F. "Ninety-six Years among the Indians of the Northwest: Adventures and Reminiscences of an Indian Scout and Interpreter in the Dakotas." Edited by Thomas E. Odell. *North Dakota History* 15 (1948)85:312.

West, Katherine M. "Ned Casey and His Cheyenne Scouts: A Noble Experiment in an Atmosphere of Tension." *Montana, The Magazine of Western History* 27 (1977):26–39.

Whitley, Fred W. "A History of Custer City, South Dakota." *South Dakota Historical Collections* 37 (1975):234–343.

Willson, Isabel M. "Hat Creek Station." *Annals of Wyoming* 10 (1938):12–13.

Wissler, Clark. "Societies and Ceremonial Associations in the Oglala Division of the Teton-Dakota." *Anthropological Papers* 11. American Museum of Natural History, 1912.

Woodruff, K. Brent. "The Episcopal Missions to the Dakotas." *South Dakota Historical Collections* 17 (1934):553–603.

Woodward, C. Raymond, Jr. "A Frontier Leader of Men and Women." *Nebraska History* 18 (1938):200–02.

Newspapers

Chadron Advocate, Chadron, Nebr.
Chadron Citizen
Chadron Democrat
Chadron Journal
Chadron Record
Chicago Herald

Bibliography

Chicago Inter-Ocean

Dawes County Journal, Chadron, Nebr.

Democratic Blade, Valentine, Nebr.

Frontier, O'Neill, Nebr.

Globe-Journal, Falls City, Nebr.

Hay Springs News, Hay Springs, Nebr.

Lincoln Journal and Star, Lincoln, Nebr.

Martin Messenger, Martin S. Dak.

Nebraska Cattleman, Omaha, Nebr.

Nebraska State Journal, Lincoln, Nebr.

Northwestern Temperance Advocate, Chadron, Nebr.

Norfolk Daily News, Norfolk, Nebr.

Omaha Bee

Omaha Daily Herald

Omaha Weekly Herald

Omaha World-Herald

Publisher's Auxiliary, Chicago, Ill.

Rushville Standard, Rushville, Nebr.

Valentine Reporter, Valentine, Nebr.

Valentine Republican

Wyoming Tribune, Cheyenne, Wy.

Index

Abilene, Kan., 1
Abner, James, 96–101
Agate, Nebr., 174
Ah-ho-appa, 40
Ainsworth, Nebr., 102
Alcohol. *See* Liquor
Allen, Emma, xix, xx, 13
Allen, Peter, xxii
Allen, Saphronia Meeker, x
Allen, S. Dak., xix
Allen, William Maynard, x
Alliance, Nebr., 128
Allotment, xix
Alum Springs, 29
American Fur Co., 40, 84
American Horse, 54
Andover, Mass., 173
Annuities, xii, 92, 150
Antelope, 100–101
Arapaho Indians, 16, 20, 23–24, 30
Arkansas R., 1
Armstrong, George, 19
Artillery. *See under* U.S. Army
Asay, James, 137, 167, 196, 212
Ash, Benjamin C., 174
Ash, Henry C., 174
Ash, Mary Renolds, 174
Atlantic Monthly, xxi

Bad Face Band, 54–55
Bad Lands, 50, 152, 163–64, 172, 175, 176–77, 179, 182, 184
Bad Lands Park, S. Dak., 164
Bad R., 163
Bad Talker Band, 54
Bad Yellow Hair, 162
Bailey, Gilbert F., 178, 180
Bailey, W. L., xviii
Band of Hope, 128

Bane, Judge C. H., 141
Banquets. *See* Feasts
Barber shops, 27, 30
Bartow, Alfred, 122–23
Baxter, Alex, 68–70
Bear In The Lodge Cr., xix
Beaver, 40
Beef Camp. *See* Herd Camp
Beef issue, 51–53
Bell, Capt. Jason M., 153
Belle Fourche R., 73
Bennett, James Gordon, 151
Bennett County Booster, 127
Bennett County, S. Dak., xix, 127–28
Berry's Store, 35
Bettelyoun, Amos, 26
Bettens, Lt. Philip A., 180
Big Foot, xvii, 61, 182, 184; band, 183–85, 187, 195–96; daughter, 205; warriors, 200
Big Road, 54
Bissonette, Joseph Jr., 21
Black Buffalo, 218
Black Hills, xi, 26, 32, 41, 49, 73, 105, 119–20, 134, 169–70, 180, 186
Black Hills freight line, 97
Black Horse, 146–47
Blacksmith, xii, xv, xxv, 51, 61, 102, 108
Blaine Hotel, 121
Blanchard, George F., 51
Blanchard, Misses, 141
Bloody Pocket. *See* Ravine
Blue Horse, 54, 135
Blue R., 71, 89
Boarding school, 72
Boats, 8
Boesle, John J., 154, 215
Boone, Daniel, 127
Bordeaux, James, 42

Index

Bordeaux, Louis, 21–22

Bordeaux Cr., 140

Bowman, Jack, 28

Box Butte County, Nebr., 128

Boxelder Cr., 1

Box Springs, 16

Boylan, R. J., 180, 185

Breastworks, 212

Brennan, John R., 153–54

Brennen, S. Dak., 210, 216

Brickyard, 120

Bridger, Jim, 5

Bridges, 28, 34, 119, 153, 181, 215

British Army, 113

Broken Arm, 162

Brooke, Brig. Gen. John R., 153, 178, 181, 187, 214–15

Broome, Frank, 128

Bross, Ernest, 126

Brown, H. E. "Stuttering," 29

Brown, Capt. LeRoy, 153–54

Brown, Walter C., 120

Bruguier, John, 21

Brulé Indians, xii, 49, 91, 165

Buchanan, Pres. James, 116

Buffalo, 134, 158

Buffalo Bill. See Cody, William F.

Buffalo ranch, 98

Bull Bear, 55

Bureau of Indian Affairs. See U.S. Indian Service

Burke, John R., 168–69, 178–80

Burkholder, Alfred, 152–53, 167, 172, 178, 180, 183, 185, 188, 214–15, 217–18

Burnes, Judge, 178, 180

Bush, Lt. Joe, 189

Butler, Mo., 71

Butterfield, Mr., 102

Byron, George G., 157

Cache La Poudre R., 1

Calamity Jane. See Cannary, Martha

Campbell, Malcolm, 41

Canada, 176

Cannary, Martha "Calamity Jane," 38

Carly, F. B., 123, 140

Carly, F. S., 120

Carr, Col. Eugene A., 171, 184, 186, 215

Carter's (William H.) Saloon, 104

Casey, Lt. Edward W., 171

Cassady, Warren L., 140

Catholic Church, 85, 167, 196, 216

Cattle, and cattle drives, x, xviii, 1, 2, 3–4, 6, 11, 23, 51–2, 98, 105–06, 109, 154–55, 163, 167, 172

Cattle ranches, 103

Cavalry. See under U.S. Army

Cawker City, Kan., x

Cedar Pass, 164

Cedar Rapids, Iowa, xx

Ceremonies, 161, 165. See also Dance

Chadron, Nebr., xii–xvi, xx, xxiii, 108, 114, 116–19, 121, 124, 126, 128–29, 131, 133, 135, 138–39, 141–42, 144–45, 149, 152, 185

Chadron Advocate, xiii–xiv, 135, 128–29, 137

Chadron Banking Company, 120, 122

Chadron Building and Loan Company, 121

Chadron Chronicle, 129

Chadron Citizen, xviii

Chadron Cr., 114

Chadron Democrat, xiii, xiv, xvi, xviii, 117–19, 123–24, 135, 185, 20

Chadron Journal, 114

Chadron Silver Cornet Band, 141

Chamberlain, S. Dak., 152

Cherry County, Nebr., 107, 128

Cheyenne and Ft. Laramie mail road, 1

Cheyenne Cr., 67, 215–16

Cheyenne Indians, x, 12, 16, 20, 23–24, 29, 49, 78–79

Cheyenne R., 29, 32, 73, 163

Cheyenne R., North Fork. See Belle Fourche R.

Cheyenne River Res., 182
Cheyenne Scouts, 171–72
Cheyenne Stage Co., 29
Cheyenne uprising, 49
Cheyenne, Wy., x–xi, 8, 27–29, 48, 80–81, 106, 119
Chicago, Ill., xiv
Chicago and Northwestern RR., 103, 132, 142, 151
Chicago Herald, 179
Chicago Inter-Ocean, 178
Chicago Times, 178, 180
Chicago Tribune
Chisholm Trail, 1
Christ, xvi–xvii, 158–59
Christianity, 85
Chugwater R., 2, 54
Chugwater Station, Wy., 1
Chugwater Valley, 2, 6
Civil War, 115, 121, 149, 190
Clapp, Capt. William H., 153
Clark, George W., 140
Clarke Bridge, 119
Cleveland, Pres. Grover, 115
Clifford, Henry C., xiv, 67–68
Coal veins, 60
Cockrell, David, 51, 61–62, 102, 117
Cody, William F., 29, 168
Coffey, Thomas A., 140
Coffield, William, 71
Coffield, Mrs. William, 72
Colby, Gen. Leonard W., 152, 168
Cold Springs, 12
Colhoff, George, 12
Concord Coaches, 119
Conger, Charles, 123
Congregational Church, 121
Conners, "Curly" Jim, xi–xii
Conquering Bear, 46–47
Cook, Rev. Charles S., 150, 216
Cook, James, 173–74, 188, 209
Cooper, James A., 162, 180

Cooper, Peter, 123
Corbin, Lt. Col. Henry Clark, 153
Corn, 177
Cornell, Charles H., 196, 203
Corney, Patrick, 113–15
Correspondents. See Reporters
Cottier, David, 17
Councils, 55–56, 79–80, 133, 162, 193–96, 201
County Judge, xiv
Coup, 145
Cowgill, Thomas, 51
Cox, Herbert A., 131–32, 141
Craft, Francis M. J., 193, 211
Craven Cr., 49
Crawford, Lt. Emmet, 23–24
Crawford, John W. "Captain Jack," 38
Crawford, Nebr., xxi, 13, 18, 24, 163
Cressey, Charles H., 178–79, 181, 188, 207, 209, 213
Crete, Nebr., 128
Crites, Albert W., 121–122, 125
Crockett, Davy, 127
Crook, Gen. George, 133–34, 179, 189
Crow Dog, 179
Cuny, Adolph, 13
Cuny and Ecoffey Freight and Contracting Co., x–xi, 4, 42
Custer, George A., 50
Custer Battle, 28, 30
Custer City, S. Dak., 30, 33–34, 71, 187
Custer County, 186
Cut Fingers. See Cheyenne Indians
Cut Off Band, 54–55
Cutright, John W., 121
Dahlman, J. C., 123, 140–41
Dahlman, Mrs., 146–47
Dakota Indians, 56
Dance, Omaha, 143, 146; dancers, 63, 93, 141, 144; war, 157
David, Robert, 40
Davidson, John, 17

Index

Dawes County, Nebr., 132; officers, 123; courthouse, 120-121

Dawes County Journal, xiii, 114, 119-20, 122-24, 126, 129

Dawson, Henry A., xviii, 153

Deadwood, S. Dak., xi, 26-27, 34-39, 119

Deere, J. W., 18

DeLay, Leigh G., xxii

Democratic Blade (Valentine, Nebr.), xiii, 127

Democratic Party, xiv-xv, 116, 123, 129

Democrat Publishing Company, xiii, 116

Denny, C. E., 186

Denton, Joseph S., 141

Deon, Sam, 74-75

Derringer pistols, 206

Disease, 90

Doane College, 128

Dog Soldiers, 56, 77-78, 146

Donaher, Peter, 104

Donehue, William, 121

Don't Eat Fish Band, 54

Dorrington, F. M., 140-41

Dorrington, L.A., 142

Dorrington Railway Hose Teams, 141

Doty, John, 71

Drought of 1890, xviii

Dubray, Chat, 44-45

Dull Knife, 49, 67

Dunn, Michael, 23, 25, 96

Eagle Horn, Mrs., 165

Eagle Nest Cr., xix

Eclipse, 156

Edgemont, S. Dak., 32

Egan, Ed E., xiii, 114, 119, 123-124, 126, 129

Egan, Lucien, 123, 126

Elections, xiv-xv, 115, 123, 125, 127, 129

Elk Mountain, 5

Ellsworth, Kan., 108

English language, 22, 44

Episcopal Church, 50, 70, 150, 216

Episcopal missionary, 66

Episcopal Mission School, 70

Estes, Stephen F., 102

Fall, F. H., xv

Falls City, Nebr., 71

Farnham, John, 21-22, 24

Fay, Ralph, 32

Feasts, 11, 23, 75, 79, 93

Federal Court, 94

Finley, Mr., 213

Fire, 120

Fire Thunder, 54, 135

Fisher, Allen G., 122-23, 142

Flag dispute, 17, 20-24

Forsyth, Col. James W., 187, 190, 193, 194-96, 200-01, 206-07, 212-13

Ft. Fetterman, xi, 2, 4, 8, 41, 85

Ft. Halleck, 5

Ft. John, 40

Ft. Laramie, x-xi, 4-5, 8-9, 13-15, 17, 27-28, 30, 39-40, 43, 45-46 49-50, 68, 85-86, 88, 115

Ft. Niobrara, 96

Ft. Pierre, 88, 98

Ft. Robinson, 13-16, 49-51, 67, 96, 149, 182

Ft. William, 40

Fossils, xiv

Foster, Charles, 133-34

Fourth of July, xx, 126, 135-36, 144

Framing, 155

Fraternal orders, 94

Freeman, Mr., 62

Freighters, Indian, 59, 96

Freighters and Freighting, x-xii, xxv, 6, 8; teams, 11; 13-14, 26-27, 39, 42; outfits, 43; 51, 58-60, 68, 91, 96-97, 101, 119

Fremont, Elkhorn and Missouri Valley RR., xii, 96, 103-04, 107, 113, 132

French Cr., 30-31

French language, 44

French settlers, 93

Index

Fur Traders, 42, 177

Gallagher, Hugh D., 133, 149–151

Gambling and gamblers, 37–38, 103, 105, 109–10, 180

Garlington, Lt. Ernest A., 202–03

Garnett, William, 17, 21

Garnier, Baptiste "Little Bat," 182, 184, 193, 195, 197–98, 200, 206

Gatling guns, 205

Ghost Dance and dancers, xiv, xvii, 149–51, 157, 160; described, 161; 162, 164–65, 162 167, 175, 179, 187, 197, 201

Ghost Dance religion, xvi, 158

Ghost garments, 164, 194, 202; bullet-proof, 165–66

Gibbens, Martin, 169–70

Glover, Thomas H., 141

God, 156–59

Godsell, Edward L., 142, 146–47

Gold Bar Opera House, xiv

Good Templars, 128

Goodwin, O. P., 1

Gordon, Nebr., xiii, 117, 187–88, 194

Gordon Advocate, xiii

Government Farm, 28

Grand R., 162

Grass Cr., 175

Grattan, Lt. John L., 46–48

Great Spirit, 55, 57, 63, 138, 156, 166, 196

Great White Father, 133, 142

Green Front Dance Hall, 37

Green R., 9

Greensborough, Ind., 149

Greenwood Cemetery Association, 122

Grey Hairs, 16

Grouard, Frank, 175–76, 178, 182

Hall, Joe, 103

Halleck, Gen. Henry W., 5

Halleck's Canyon, 5

Hambletonian horses, 173, 188

Hamlin, J. J., 106–07

Hare, Rev. William H., 70

Harris, Von, 123

Harrison, Pres. Benjamin, 149, 157

Harrison, Nebr., 114, 121, 174

Hat Cr., 28–29

Hawkins, Emma, x, 13

Hawkins, Henry, x

Hawkins, Irving, 179

Hawks, Mr., 126

Healy, William, 127

Heath, E. L., xv

Henry, John, 145–47

Henry rifles, 195

Herd Camp, 51, 163, 172–73

Hickok, James B. "Wild Bill," 38

Higgins, Tom, 104

High Wolf, 54, 68

Higman, Mr., 120

Hill, Burley C., xii–xiii, xviii, 104, 112, 116–17, 119, 123

Hill City, S. Dak., 34

History of the Sioux, 156

Hitchcock, Olive, 127

Holy Rosary Mission, 150, 162, 187–88, 215–218

Homesteads, xiii, 14, 52, 108, 112, 115, 128, 134, 151

Hood, Robert, 121

Hopkins, Albert C., 181

Hotchkiss gun, 196, 199, 200, 214

Hotels, 27, 51, 104, 121, 137, 139, 168, 170–71, 173, 180, 188, 213, 215, 217

Hot Springs, S. Dak., xx, xxii, 32

Hoyt, Mr., 121

Hudson Bay Co., 84

Hughes, C. C., 131

Hunter, Billy. *See* Garnett, William

Hunting, 4, 9–10

Iager, L. J. F., 123

Illustrated American, 173

Independent Order of Odd Fellows (I.O.O.F), 141

280

India, 113
Indian Cr., 29
Indian Department. *See* U.S. Indian
  Service
Indian Rights Association, 173
Indian Territory, xvii
Infantry. *See under* U.S. Army
Influenza, xx
Interior, S. Dak., 164
Iowa City, Iowa, 116
Iowa City Law School, 116
Iowa Indian Res., 71
Iron Crow, Capt., 189
Irrigation, 28
Irwin, Dr. James, 50–51
Issue station, xix

Janis, Antoine, 42
Janis, Henry, 52
Janis, Nicholas, 11–12, 42, 175–76, 178
Jasper County, Iowa, x
Jenney's Stockade, 71
Jesuits, 193
Johnson, Rev. A. T., 150, 185
Johnson, Joe, 32
Johnson, Mrs., 185
Johnstown flood, 131–32
Jones, Mr., 152
Jones, William, 167, 169–70
Jones Ranch, 172
Jordan, Charles P., 50–51, 102
Jordan, Maj. William H., 50
Jury duty, 109–10
Jutz, John, 150, 216

Kansas State Agricultural College, x
Kelley, Hiram, 1, 2, 4
Kelley, William F., 179, 188, 209, 211
Kicking Bear, 152, 157, 160, 175, 182
Kinzie, Lt. John., 196–97
Knights of Pythias, 141
Knights of the Blackstonian Circle, 122
Kocer, Joseph, 70

Kocer, Mrs., 71

Lake & Halley Bank, 120
Land office, 113
LaRamie, Jacques, 40
Laramie City, Wy., xii, 6, 29–30
Laramie Peak, 5, 42
Laramie Plains, 5, 41
Laramie R., xii, 2, 5–6, 13–14, 17, 28,
  39–42, 48
Laravie Cr., 189
Larive Cr., 49–50
Larrabee Cr., 209
Lawson, Perry, 104
Legs On A Pot Band, 53–54
Lessert, Louis Benjamin, 51
Lewis, Dr. Alfred, 103
Lice (greybacks), 27, 30–31
Lime, 60
Lime kiln, xii, 60
Lime Kiln Cr., 61, 173
Limestone, 60, 121
Lincoln, Pres. Abraham, 127
Lincoln, Nebr., xix, xxi, 207
Liquor, xi–xiv, 42, 49, 54, 75, 77, 130, 147
Liquor peddlers, 73, 146
Little Bordeaux Cr., 118
Little Laramie R., 2
Little White R., xix, 101
Little Wolf, 55
Little Wolf Creek, 212
Little Wound, 54–55, 135, 162, 171, 180,
  212, 214
Loafer Band, 53–54
Loewenthal, Ben, 120
Loewenthal, Max, 120
Lomond, Bab, 98
Long Bow, 79
Lucas, Robert, xiii, 116–17, 119, 123–24
Lunan, Susan, x
Lutz, C. H., 121

Madden, Jack, 29

Index

Maher, John G., 121, 140
Manderson, S. Dak., 70
Manderson Station, 215
Manhattan, Kan., x
Marshall County, Kan., 71, 89
Martin, S. Dak., xix–xx, 13, 127–28
Martin Messenger (S. Dak.), xix, 127
Marysville, Kan., 89
McClelland, Paul, 186–87
McCloskey, James, 71, 89–90
McCloskey, Julia, 70–71
McDaniels Theater, 27
McDonald's (Edwin) Hardware Store, 104
McGaa, William, xviii
McGillicuddy, Valentine, 58, 62, 67, 70, 72, 97, 99, 143, 149, 154, 173
McKinley, Pres. William, 142
Mears, Austin W., 26
Mears, David Y., 104
Medicine men, 55, 57, 55, 158–59, 160, 162, 165, 196, 206
Melvin, Luella E., 71
Merriman, Nebr., 127
Messiah, 156–58, 164–65, 167, 176, 181, 194–94, 196, 201, 218
Messiah craze. *See* Ghost Dance
Metz, Charles, 28–29, 32
Midland, S. Dak., 127
Miles, Gen. Nelson A., 153, 179, 219
Militia, Kan., x
Militia, Nebr., 152, 186
Miller, Charles, 26
Miller, Isaac, 169–71
Milwaukee RR., 164
Miniconjou Indians, xvii
Mink, 40
Minnikadusa Cr., 96
Missionaries, 84, 86, 185–86
Montgomery, Gen. Milton, 121
Moorehead, Warren K., xix, 173
Moreau R., 163
Mormon cow incident, 45–49

Mormons, 9, 42, 45
Mormon Trail, 9
Mourning, 63–66
Mousseau, Louis, 200
Murders, 80, 87, 105, 170, 172
Muzzle-loading rifles, 195
Nagle General Merchandise Co., 26
Native Americans: friendly, 153, 161, 187; hostile, xvii, 153, 161–62, 172, 175–76; hostile camp, 184; students, 144
Navajo blankets, 54, 85
Nebraska Legislative Reference Bureau, 129
Nebraska Legislature, 71
Nebraska settlers, 91
Nebraska State Historical Society, xx–xxii, 88, 129, 207
Nebraska State Journal, 179, 188, 209
Nebraska State Teachers' College, 121
Needle rifles, 195
Nelson, John Y., 68
Nelson, P. B., 120
New York Herald, xvi, 152, 162, 167, 172, 180, 188, 208, 218–19
Nine Mile Ranch, 42–43, 45–46
Niobrara R., 28, 96, 103–04, 106–07, 109
Noble County, Ind., x
Nonparle Cr., 4
Norbeck, Peter, 164
North Platte R., 2–3, 4–6, 9–10, 13–14, 28, 40, 42–43, 47, 68, 119
Northwestern Temperance Advocate (Chadron, Nebr.), xiii, 128
No Water, 54, 135
O'Beirne, James Rowen, 50
Oglala Indians, xii, xix, xxi, xxv, 17–18, 21, 49, 53, 55–56, 58, 67–68, 71, 91, 133, 135, 150, 169, 182
Oglala Stock Association, xviii
Olerich Advocate, 152
O'Linn, Frances, 114
Omaha, Nebr., 171

Index

Omaha Bee, 178–80, 207
Omaha World-Herald, 178–79
O'Neill, Nebr., 106
Onions, xi, 35
Oregon Trail, 9, 40, 42–43, 46, 48
Osage Band, 54
Otter, 40
Owens, Jim, 130

Paiute Indians, xvi, 156
Paiute round dance, xvii
Palmer, Mr., 71
Parrot, Jerome, 28
Parry. *See* Lawson, Perry
Pass Cr., xix, 184
Pass Creek District, 154
Pattison, J. D., 123–25
Payton, James, 2
Penny, Capt. Charles, 153–54
Philip, James "Scotty," 96, 98–101
Philip Academy, 173
Phillips, F. M., 6
Photographers, 167
Physicians, army, 185
Pickler, Congressman, 151
Pierce, Capt. Francis E., 152
Pierre, S. Dak., 97
Pine Ridge Agency, xii–xiv, xvi, xxv, 39,
   49–53, 56–61, 67–68, 70–72, 91, 96,
   102, 126, 133–34, 136, 149–54, 158,
   160, 162–63, 167–70, 172, 178–79,
   182, 188
Pine Ridge Res., xvii–xix, xx, 49, 68,
   117, 154–55, 158, 164, 159, 182, 218
Pioneer Press (St. Paul), 180, 185
Plattsmouth, Nebr., 121
Plenty Bear, 189
Pneumonia, 13
Point of Rocks, 1
Police, 56, 60, 72, 142, 170–71, 176,
   181, 189, 210, 215
Pollard, Charles H., 129
Populist Party, 129

Porcupine (animal), 99–100
Porcupine (Lakota), 165
Porcupine Cr., xviii, 61, 67–68, 175, 200
Porcupine school, 72
Porcupine station, 68
Postmaster, xviii, xxv, 104, 116, 174
Post offices, xv, xviii–xix, 45, 71, 104,
   119, 149, 174, 204
Pourier, Baptiste "Big Bat," 14–17, 21,
   25, 182
Powder R., 179, 189
Powell, Mr., 2–4, 6
Powers, T. F., 122–23
Prairie dogs, 99
Prairie Turnip, 12, 177
Presbyterian Church, 50–51
Presbyterian Mission, 150
Pretty Fork. *See* Belle Fourche R.
Prohibition, xiii, 128, 136
Prohibition Party, xiv, 129
Prostitution, x, xv, 105
Publishers' Auxiliary, xxi–xxii
Pugh, R. O., 71–72, 96
Pulls Down Band, 54
Putman, Mr., 120
Putnam, Mrs. Arthur C., 141
.Pyramid Lake, 156

Railroad Townsite Co., 114
Ranching and ranches, x–xi, xviii, xx, 1,
   4–6, 8–9, 13, 27, 29, 71, 105, 109,
   127, 155, 169–72, 177, 209
Rapid City, S. Dak., 120, 153, 164, 219
Rations. *See* Annuities
Ravine, 192, 199, 208
Rawhide Butte, 14, 16
Rawhide Cr., 14
Rawhide Hills, 28
Red Canyon, 28–29, 32
Red Cloud, xix, 21–22, 24, 53–56, 58,
   89, 133, 135–37, 140–43, 150, 152–
   53, 163, 174, 181–82, 214, 218

Red Cloud Agency, xxi, 2, 5, 8–10, 13–14, 17–25, 68
Red Dog, 53, 70–71, 165
Red Dog School, 71–72
Reporters, xvi, 135, 167, 170–71, 175, 178–80, 187
Republican Party, xiv, xviii, 116, 123–24, 129
Rice, Isaac M., 127
Richard, Peter, 218
Richards, Bartlett, 120
Richards, DeForest, 120
Richards, Louis, 21
Richards Brothers and Brown Co., 120
Richardson County, Nebr., 71
Ricker & Houghton Law Firm, 120
Rienzi, 138
Road Ranches, x, 42, 49
Robideaux, Louis, 22
Robinson, Doane, 156–57
Robinson, Lt. Levi H., 13
Rocky Bear, 17, 20–21, 25
Romero, Manuel, 17
Rosebud Agency, xii, 51, 96, 102, 135
Rosebud Cr., 49
Rosebud Landing, 51, 58
Rosebud Res., 102, 164, 171
Ross, Rev. Amos, 66, 150, 216
Royer, Daniel F., xvii, 151, 153, 162
Rubies, 31
Rumors, xi, xvi, 9, 18, 20, 34, 106, 133, 158, 169, 193–94
Running Water R., 14–16, 28, 174
Rushville, Nebr., 132, 152, 154, 168, 187, 209
Russell, John "Buckskin Jack," 6, 179–81

Sadler, Mr., 126
St. Louis, Mo., 74, 85, 171
St. Mary's Young Ladies Academy, 70
St. Paul, Minn., 171, 186
Saloons, 30, 37, 104–05, 110, 129, 145–6
Salt Lake, Utah, 42

Salway, Frank, 88
Sandoz, Mari, xxi
Satterlee, Ed, 121
Saville, Dr. J. J., 17
Schnyder, Sgt. Leodegar, 41
Schools, xix, 38, 58, 61–62, 66–68, 70–72, 84, 92, 108, 121–22, 153, 206, 208
Schoolhouses, xii, 62, 64, 102
School uniforms, 194
Seymour, Charles C., 179
Shangreau, John, 193
Shangreau, Louis, 21, 193, 195
Shannon, Peter, 102
Shannon County, S. Dak., 49
Sheldon, Addison E., xiii–xiv, xix–xxii, 88, 128–30, 135
Sheridan, Gen. Philip H., 190
Sheridan County, Nebr., 132
Short Bull, 152, 157, 160, 175, 182
Sibley tents, 205, 207
Sibylle Cr., 5
Sidney, Nebr., 119
Sioux City, Iowa
Sioux Commission of 1889, 133–35
Sioux County, Nebr., 174
Sioux Falls, S. Dak., 102
Sioux Fund, 134
Sioux Indians (See also band names), xiv, xxv, 1, 12, 21, 29, 43, 49, 53, 61, 70–71, 73, 78–79, 80, 82, 83, 86, 91–92, 94, 133–34, 143–44, 152, 160, 164–65, 169, 180
Sioux language, 22, 44, 65, 68, 74, 139
Sioux tribal bands, 54
Sitting Bull, 162, 175
Six Feather, 189
Smallpox, 44
Smith, John, 107
Smith, Col. John E., xi–xii
Smith, M. E., Ladies' Furnishing Establishment, 121
Smith-Hayward, Mary E., 121
Soldier Cr., 16

Index

Solomon R., x

Spangler, J. L., 133

Spargur & Fisher Law Firm, 122

Sparks, Eldon, 103

Sparks, Joseph A. "Al," 103

Speeder, 25

Spencer rifles, 99, 195

Spotted Tail, 21, 40, 133, 165–66

Spotted Tail Agency, 22

Springfield rifles, 9, 195

Squirrel rifles, 201

Stagecoaches, 29

Stage lines, 119

Standing Rock Res., 162, 164

State Soldier's Home (S. Dak), xx, xxii

Steamboat landing, 96

Steam engines, xx

Stetter, Henry, 104

Stetter, John, 104

Stirk, R. C., 96, 188, 209

Stores, xix, xviii, 5, 8, 189

Stronghold, 176, 186

Sublette and Campbell, 40

Sumner, Lt. Col. Edwin V., 182, 200

Sun Dance, 144

Swiggert, Mr., 188, 209, 213

Tabor, Andrew "French Andy," 12

Taylor, Capt. Charles W., 197–98, 200, 204

Taylor, Lt. George McMannis, 28

Teachers, 66, 70–72, 121, 185

Telegraph, 96, 172

Teller, James H., 102

Thatcher, Albert, 96

They're Afraid Of His Horse, 54

Three Mile Ranch, 5–6

Thunder Bear, John, 215

Tobacco, 203

Todd County, S. Dak., 49

Torch Publishing Co., xx

Tracy, Hartwell S., 26

Traders, Mexican, 54

Traders and trading posts, x, xxi, xix, 4, 9–10, 11, 18, 40, 42, 45–46, 48, 51, 71, 73–74, 78, 84–86, 89, 96, 137, 197, 167, 208

Trappers, 4, 10, 84, 86

Treaties, 43, 57

Treaty of 1868, 92

Trials, 110

Tucker, James F., 141

Two Lance, 61

Two Lance Camp, 66

Union Pacific RR, 1, 6, 8, 48, 108

University of Nebr., 128, 129

U.S. Army, xiv, xvii, 15, 142, 187, 152–53, 175; artillery, 153, 214–15; cavalry, 8, 23, 25, 45, 149, 153–54, 173, 199, 211; fifth cavalry, 29; gray horse company, 197–98; ninth cavalry, 180, 202, 215, 217–18; seventh cavalry, xvii, 61, 182, 185, 187, 189, 200, 202, 205; infantry, 28, 153

U.S. Constitution, 128

U.S. Indian Service, xix. 49, 51, 72, 94–96, 149, 169

U.S. Land Office, 112, 121, 125

U.S. Quartermaster Department, 51

Valentine, Nebr., xii–xiii, 96, 102–03, 106–09, 112, 114–15, 116–17, 127, 152

Valentine Reporter, xii, 104, 112

Verne, Jules, 159

Visions, 156

Vlandry, Joseph, 87–88

Vroom, Lt. Peter Dumont, 15

Wagon Hound Cr., 3

Wallace, Capt. George D., 190, 201–03

Waller, Mrs. George P., 141

Walters Brothers, 18

Wamego, Kan., x

Warner, William, 133–34

Warren, F. H. "Fritz," 103–04

Index

Warren's saloon, 108–09
Washington, D.C., xvii, 43, 94, 133–34, 149
Watson, Elmo Scott, xxi–xxii
Wa Za Za Band, 54
Wells, Philip, 193–95, 206, 211
Western Stage Co., 35
West Point Military Academy, 46
Wham, Major, 68
Wheatland, Wy., 6
Whipple, I. W., 26
Whiskey. *See* Liquor
Whitcomb, E. W., 1
White Clay Canyon, 170
White Clay Cr., 49–51, 57, 71, 135, 153, 162, 169, 171–73, 175, 180–82, 187, 212, 214, 218
White Cloud, Kan., 71
White County, Ind., 174
White Horse canyon, 216
White R., 9, 13–16, 18, 50, 57, 108, 114, 118, 152, 162, 164, 171, 175, 184, 186, 189, 215
Whitside, Maj. Samuel M., 187, 190, 193, 200, 207, 212
Wichita, Kan., x, 1, 131
Wild West Show, 68, 168–69, 179, 180
Williams, Cy, 42

Wilson, E. P., 122
Wilson, David, 156–57
Wilson, Jack, 156–57
Winchester rifles, 2, 195, 201, 207, 209
Wind River Mts., 158–59
Wolf Cr., 49–51, 57, 67, 212
Wolf Creek Bridge, 181
Woodruff, John, 67–70
Woonsocket, S. Dak., 151
Wounded Bear, 162
Wounded Knee Creek, xii, xvii, 61, 70, 175, 163, 165, 182–85, 187, 194, 212, 215–16
Wounded Knee Massacre, xii, xvi, xviii–xix, xxii, xxv, 160, 176, 189, 192, 196, 200, 214, 218
Wovoka, xvi, xvii, 156
Wright, James "Jack Nasty Jim," xi–xii
Wyoming Territory, 54

Yankton, S. Dak., 99
Yates, Frank, 18
Yellow Bear, 162
Yellow Horse, 78–83
Yellow Medicine Cr., 58
Yellow Medicine Landing, 96
Yellowstone Park, 124
Yellowstone R., 99

286